SOLUTIONS MANUAL
to accompany

CALCULUS AND
ANALYTIC GEOMETRY
Second Edition

by Al Shenk

Prepared by
Victoria Inness-Brown
Jim Rapp
Al Shenk

Goodyear Publishing Company
Santa Monica, California

INTRODUCTION

This optional manual for student use contains detailed solutions of 743 exercises selected from the Second Edition of *Calculus and Analytic Geometry* by Al Shenk. The answers or answers and outlines of solutions of all exercises included here are given in the back of the textbook and all exercises in this manual are taken from the exercises sets at the ends of the chapter sections; none are from the sets of Miscellaneous Exercises.

Exercises included

Chapter 1, p. 1 (35 exercises)
Section 1.1   4, 11, 13
Section 1.2   7, 13, 14
Section 1.3   7, 9, 15, 17, 18
Section 1.4   5, 9, 11, 13, 15
Section 1.5   5, 9, 14, 16
Section 1.6   11, 13, 15, 18a, 21
Section 1.7   2, 5, 7
Appendix   1a, 3a, 4, 7, 11g

Chapter 2, p. 10 (29 exercises)
Section 2.1   5a, 5b, 10, 13, 16, 22
Section 2.2   3, 9, 13
Section 2.3   7, 11a, 11b, 13f
Section 2.4   5, 9, 12, 15
Section 2.5   1, 7
Section 2.6   6, 10, 13
Section 2.7   5, 12, 14
Section 2.8   3, 8
Section 2.9   8, 33

Chapter 3, p. 19 (33 exercises)
Section 3.1   3, 6, 16, 23, 25g
Section 3.2   3, 9, 11
Section 3.3   8, 11, 15, 17, 21
Section 3.4   5, 11, 14
Section 3.5   7, 8
Section 3.6   3a, 10
Section 3.7   2, 7, 16, 20
Section 3.8   1b, 2b, 7, 11, 24, 30
Section 3.9   6, 9, 16

Chapter 4, p. 29 (52 exercises)
Section 4.1   1, 9, 15
Section 4.2   4, 8, 12, 19, 22
Section 4.3   2, 10
Section 4.4   4, 7, 12
Section 4.5   2, 8, 15, 22, 24
Section 4.6   5, 16, 18
Section 4.7   5, 8, 15, 19
Section 4.8   10, 17, 22, 24, 26
Section 4.9   3, 9, 16, 18, 26, 29
Section 4.10 2, 5, 12, 17, 20
Section 4.11 4, 7
Section 4.12 1, 5, 9
Section 4.13 3

Chapter 5, p. 49 (31 exercises)
Section 5.1   3, 7, 13
Section 5.2   4, 8, 11, 13, 17, 21, 38
Section 5.3   3, 6, 10
Section 5.4   7, 10, 15
Section 5.5   5, 13, 15, 17, 22, 27, 31, 36
Section 5.6   4, 11, 15, 18

Chapter 6, p. 60 (35 exercises)
Section 6.1   8, 11, 19, 21, 25
Section 6.2   5, 7
Section 6.3   2, 9, 13, 20
Section 6.4   6, 9
Section 6.5   1, 7
Section 6.6   3, 6
Section 6.7   6, 8, 11, 15, 16, 20, 24
Section 6.8   4, 8, 9
Section 6.9   1, 5, 10
Section 6.10 3a, 6a, 12a
Section 6.11 1c, 2a

Chapter 7, p. 83 (96 exercises)
Section 7.1   1a, 2c, 2e, 2j, 3e, 5d, 5f, 5h, 15, 16, 17, 27, 32, 38, 40
Section 7.2   3c, 5b, 6, 7, 11, 15, 17, 19, 26, 29, 32, 39
Section 7.3   4, 7, 9, 14, 17a, 20
Section 7.4   3, 5
Section 7.5   1b, 2b, 5, 9, 13, 17, 22, 26, 28, 30, 32, 38, 44
Section 7.6   7, 8, 11, 13, 19
Section 7.7   5, 7, 11
Section 7.8   1a, 1c, 1d, 2a, 2d, 3a, 3g, 4b, 4d, 7, 10, 12, 18, 20, 22, 26, 34, 36, 39, 43, 65
Section 7.9   1b, 1e, 1g, 3, 9, 14, 17, 19, 24, 32
Section 7.10 4, 6, 8, 14, 20, 22c, 37

Chapter 8, p. 106 (50 exercises)
Section 8.1   1, 5, 7, 9, 13, 15, 19, 23, 29, 31, 45, 51, 58, 61
Section 8.2   1, 5, 7
Section 8.3   5, 7, 11, 21, 31, 33
Section 8.4   1, 5, 7, 15, 17, 28
Section 8.5   5, 9, 13, 21
Section 8.6   5, 7, 13, 21, 23, 33, 41
Section 8.7   5
Section 8.8   2, 6, 16, 28, 38, 42, 45, 50
Section 8.9   3

SECTION 1.1

(4) Because of the "or", any t which satisfies one or both of the inequalities is a solution. We sketch the individual solution sets (Figs. 1.1.4a and 1.1.4b) and combine them to obtain the desired solution set in Fig. 1.1.4.

(11) The inequality requires that the distance between the points -5 and t be greater than 3. Find the number -5 on a t-axis and measure 3 units in each direction to the points -8 and -2. The solutions are described by the condition "x < -8 or x > -2". (An alternate procedure: Rewrite the inequality as the condition "-5 - t > 3   or   -5 - t < -3" and solve the resulting inequalities.) Fig. 1.1.11.

(13) Because x is greater than -4, the distance between x and -4 is x - (-4) = x + 4.

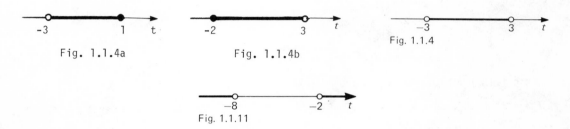

Fig. 1.1.4a   Fig. 1.1.4b   Fig. 1.1.4

Fig. 1.1.11

SECTION 1.2

(7) Subtract 6x from both sides of the inequality to obtain -5x + 3 < 10. Subtract 3 from both sides to obtain -5x < 7. Divide by -5 and reverse the inequality to obtain the solution $x > -\frac{7}{5}$.   Fig. 1.2.7.

(13) Write the given inequalities as "0 < 3x + 1 and 3x + 1 ≤ 4x - 6". Subtract 3x from both to obtain "-3x < 1 and   1 ≤ x - 6. Divide the first inequality by -3 and reverse it and add 6 to the second to obtain "x > $-\frac{1}{3}$ and   x ≥ 7". These are satisfied by those x's with x ≥ 7.   Fig. 1.2.13.

$-\frac{7}{5}$ x

Fig. 1.2.7

7   x

Fig. 1.2.13

(14) Subtracting 6t from the first inequality and 2t from the second gives the equivalent condition "-5t < -10   or -t ≥ 5". Dividing the first inequality by -5 and the second by -1 and reversing their directions yields the condition "t ≤ -5 or t > 2", in which the inequalities are solved for t. Fig. 1.2.14.

Fig. 1.2.14

SECTION 1.3

(7) Since the x-axis is perpendicular to PQ, the point Q is on the line x = 3. Since the x-axis bisects PQ, the y-coordinate of Q is -4. Thus Q = (3,-4).

(9) Let P(x,y) be such a point. Since the distance from P to the origin is 5, we have $x^2 + y^2 = 25$. Since x = 4, we have $16 + y^2 = 25$, which implies $y^2 = 9$ and y = ± 3. P = (4,3) or P = (4,-3).

(15) $\overline{AB}^2 = (-3 - 1)^2 + (0 - (-2))^2 = 20;$ $\overline{BC}^2 = (1 - 5)^2 + (-2 - 0)^2 = 20;$

$\overline{CD}^2 = (5 - 1)^2 + (0 - k)^2 = 16 + k^2;$ $\overline{AD}^2 = (-3 - 1)^2 + (0 - k)^2 = 16 + k^2.$

To be a parallelogram, the opposite sides must be equal. Hence we must have $20 = 16 + k^2$, which occurs for k = ± 2. The case of k = -2 does not give a parallelogram since in this case the points B and D coincide. For the case of k = 2, we have a rhombus because the four sides are equal. We do not have a square (or a rectangle) because $\overline{AB}^2 + \overline{BC}^2 = 40$ is not equal to $\overline{AC}^2 = (-3 - 5)^2 + (0 - 0)^2 = 64.$

(17) The points are on a line provided the largest of $\overline{AB}$, $\overline{BC}$, and $\overline{AC}$ is the sum of the other two. We have $\overline{AB}^2 = (1 - 2)^2 + (1 - 3)^2 = 5$, $\overline{BC}^2 = (2 - 4)^2 + (3 - 7)^2 = 20$, and $\overline{AC}^2 = (1 - 4)^2 + (1 - 7)^2 = 45.$ Hence, $\overline{AB} + \overline{BC} = \sqrt{5} + 2\sqrt{5} = 3\sqrt{5}$, which equals $\overline{AC}$, and the points are on a line.

(18) Let D and E be the feet of the perpendicular lines from B and C to the horizontal line through A (Fig. 1.3.18). The right triangles ABD and ACE are similar because $\overline{AE}/\overline{AD} = 3/1 = 3$ and $\overline{CE}/\overline{BD} = 6/2 = 3$ are equal. Hence the angles ABD and ACE are equal and A, B and C lie on a straight line.

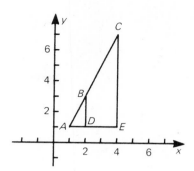

Fig. 1.3 18

SECTION 1.4

(5) The formula $x = -\sqrt{16 - y^2}$ gives the nonpositive solution of the equation $x^2 + y^2 = 16$, so the curve is the left half of the circle of radius 4 with its center at the origin. Fig. 1.4.5.

(9) Plot a number of points, such as those whose coordinates are given below, to see that the graph is the line in Fig. 1.4.9.

u	0	1	-1	2	-2	3	-3
v = 1 - u	1	0	2	-1	3	-2	4

(11) Plot a number of points, such as those whose coordinates are given below, to see that the graph is the pair of intersecting lines in Fig. 1.4.11.

x	0	1	-1	2	-2	3	-3
y = ±x	0	±1	±1	±2	±2	±3	±3

(13) There are no solutions with $x = 0$ or with $y = 0$ so the graph has no intercepts. Replacing x by $-x$ in the equation $yx^2 = 4$ yields $y(-x)^2 = 4$, which is equivalent to the original equation because $(-x)^2 = x^2$. Hence the graph is symmetric about the y-axis. Replacing y by $-y$ yields $-yx^2 = 4$, which is not equivalent to the original equation; the graph is not symmetric about the x-axis. Replacing x by $-x$ and y by $-y$ gives $-y(-x)^2 = 4$, which is not equivalent to the original equation; the graph is not symmetric about the origin. Plot a number of points with positive x, such as those

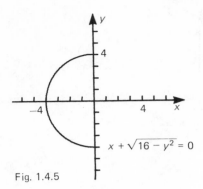

Fig. 1.4.5

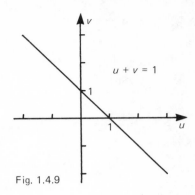

Fig. 1.4.9

whose coordinates are given below, and the points symmetric about the y-axis to obtain the curve in Figure 1.4.13.

x	1	2	3
$y = \dfrac{4}{x^2}$	4	1	$\dfrac{4}{9}$

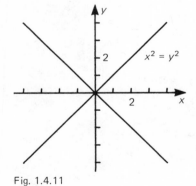

Fig. 1.4.11

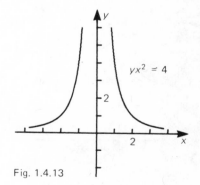

Fig. 1.4.13

(15) Setting x = 0 yields y = 0 and setting y = 0 yields x = 0, so the x- and y-intercepts are 0 (the graph passes through the origin). Replacing x by -x and y by -y yields the equation 2(-x) + 3(-y) = 0, which is equivalent to the original equation, so the graph is **symmetric** about the origin. Replacing only x by -x or

only y by -y does not give an equivalent equation, so the graph is not symmetric about either axis. Plot a number of points, such as those in the table below, to obtain the line through the origin in Fig. 1.4.15.

x	0	1	-1	2	-2	3	-3
$y = -\dfrac{3}{2}x$	0	$-\dfrac{3}{2}$	$\dfrac{3}{2}$	-3	3	$-\dfrac{9}{2}$	$\dfrac{9}{2}$

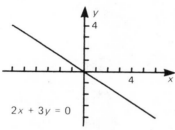

$2x + 3y = 0$

Fig. 1.4.15

SECTION 1.5

(5) The points P, Q, and R lie on a line because slope $(PQ) = \dfrac{2 - 6}{3 - (-3)} = -\dfrac{2}{3}$ and slope$(QR) = \dfrac{0 - 2}{6 - 3} = -\dfrac{2}{3}$ are equal.

(9) We have slope$(PQ) = \dfrac{6 - (-1)}{-6 - (-1)} = -\dfrac{7}{5}$, slope $(QR) = \dfrac{5 - 6}{0 - (-6)} = -\dfrac{1}{6}$, and

slope$(PR) = \dfrac{5 - (-1)}{0 - (-1)} = 6$. The sides QR and PR are perpendicular and the triangle has a right angle at R because slope(QR) and slope (PR) are negative reciprocals.

The area of the triangle is $\dfrac{1}{2}$ bh (one-half the length of its base times its height), with b = $\overline{PR}$ = $\sqrt{(-1 - 0)^2 + (-1 - 5)^2}$ = $\sqrt{37}$ and h = $\overline{QR}$ = $\sqrt{(-6 - 0)^2 + (6 - 5)^2}$ = $\sqrt{37}$. Area = $\dfrac{1}{2}(\sqrt{37})(\sqrt{37})$ = $\dfrac{37}{2}$.

(14)   Slope AB $= \frac{0-1}{0-2} = \frac{1}{2}$; Slope CD $= \frac{6-5}{(k+2)-k} = \frac{1}{2}$; Slope AD $= \frac{0-5}{0-k} = \frac{5}{k}$; Slope BC $= \frac{1-6}{2-(k+2)} = \frac{5}{k}$. Since Slope AB = Slope CD, the sides AB and CD are parallel. Since Slope AD = Slope BC, the sides AD and BC are parallel. Hence the figure is a parallelogram. To have a rectangle, we must have (Slope AB)(Slope CD) = -1. This gives the equation $(\frac{1}{2})(\frac{5}{k}) = -1$, which implies that $k = -\frac{5}{2}$.

(16)   The radius connects the origin with the point (-2 , -4) hence its slope is $\frac{-4-0}{-2-0} = 2$. Since the tangent line is perpendicular to the radius its slope must be $-\frac{1}{2}$.

SECTION 1.6

(11) Solve $6x - 4y = 7$ for y to put it in the slope-intercept form: $y = \frac{3}{2}x - \frac{7}{4}$. Here $m = \frac{3}{2}$ so the given line has slope $\frac{3}{2}$ and the lines parallel to it have equations $y = \frac{3}{2}x + b$. Set $x = 1$ and $y = -1$ to find the constant b: $-1 = \frac{3}{2}(1) + b$ $\Rightarrow b = -\frac{5}{2}$. The line has the equation $y = \frac{3}{2}x - \frac{5}{2}$. (Alternate procedure: The lines parallel to $6x - 4y = 7$ have equations $6x - 4y = C$. Set $x = 1$ and $y = -1$ to compute $C = 10$. The line has the equation $6x - 4y = 10$ or $3x - 2y = 5$.)

(13)   The two-intercept equation for the line is $\frac{x}{5} + \frac{y}{-6} = 1$ or $\frac{x}{5} - \frac{y}{6} = 1$. We could solve for y to find the slope. Instead we use the fact that the points (5,0) and (0,-6) are on the line: Slope $= \frac{-6-0}{0-5} = \frac{6}{5}$.

(15a)   All points on the horizontal line through (-4,7) have the same y-coordinate, so the line has the equation $y = 7$.

(15b)   All points on the vertical line through (-4,7) have the same x-coordinate, so the line has the equation $x = -4$.

(18a)   We find the intersection of the lines $y = -2x$ and $y = -\frac{1}{3}x + 5$ by

solving the simultaneous equations $y = -2x$, $y = -\frac{1}{3}x + 5$ for x and y. Equating

the expressions for y gives the equation $-2x = -\frac{1}{3}x + 5$, which we solve for the

x-coordinate $x = -3$ of the intersection. Setting $x = -3$ in $y = -2x$ or in

$y = -\frac{1}{3}x + 5$ gives the y-coordinate $y = 6$ of the vertex $(-3,6)$ of the triangle.

Similarly, solving the equations $y = \frac{1}{2}x$ and $y = -2x$ gives the vertex $(0,0)$, and

solving the equations $y = \frac{1}{2}x$ and $y = -\frac{1}{3}x + 5$ gives the vertex $(6,3)$.

(21)   Since the pressure increases 62.4 pounds per square foot for

every additional 1 foot of depth, the graph is a straight line with

slope 62.4: $P = 62.4h + C$ for some choice of the constant C.   Since

the pressure at the surface of the ocean is 0 we have $0 = 62.4(0) + C$

$\Rightarrow C = 0$.   Thus $P = 62.4h$.   Fig. 1.6.21

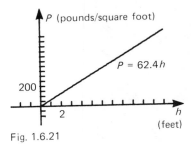

Fig. 1.6.21

SECTION 1.7

(2) The cubic $y = 3 - \frac{1}{4}x^3$ is of the type shown in Figure 1.58 with $a = -\frac{1}{4}$

and $b = 3$. The horizontal line $y = 3$ separates the upper and lower halves of the

curve. We compute the coordinates of a few points on the curve, such as $(0,3)$,

$(2,1)$, and $(-2,5)$, and draw the curve through those points. Fig. 1.7.2.

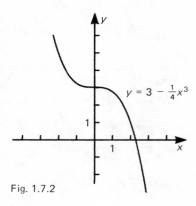

Fig. 1.7.2

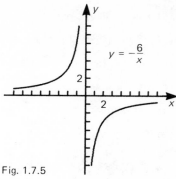

Fig. 1.7.5

(5)   The hyperbola $y = -\dfrac{6}{x}$ is of the type shown in Figure 1.60 with $a = -6$ and $b = 0$. The x-axis $(y = 0)$ lies between the two halves of the curve and the points $(1,-6)$, $(-1,6)$, $(6,-1)$, and $(-6,1)$ lie on it. Fig. 1.7.5.

(7)   The equation $R = 3 + t^{-2}$ may be written $R = \dfrac{1}{t^2} + 3$, so the curve (in a tR-plane) is of the type shown in Figure 1.61 with $a = 1$ and $b = 3$. The horizontal line $R = 3$ lies beneath the curve and the points $(1,4)$, $(-1,4)$, $(2,3\tfrac{1}{4})$, and $(-2,3\tfrac{1}{4})$ lie on it. Fig. 1.7.7.

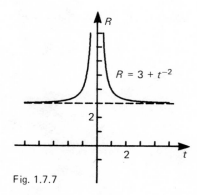

Fig. 1.7.7

APPENDIX TO CHAPTER 1

(1a)   Recall that -3^n means $-(3^n)$; $-3^0 = -(3^0) = -1$; $-3^{-2} = -(3^{-2}) = -\frac{1}{3^2} = -\frac{1}{9}$;
$-3^3 = -(3^3) = -27$.

(3a)   We use the rules for exponents to reduce this to an exercise in fractions.
We work from the inside of the expression toward the outside. First, we have
$\sqrt[5]{x^3} = (x^3)^{1/5} = x^{3/5}$. Then the expression inside the square brackets is
$\frac{x^2}{x^{3/5}} = x^{(2 - 3/5)} = x^{7/5}$. Hence the whole expression is $[x^{7/5}]^3 = x^{(7/5)(3)} = x^{21/5}$.

(4)   We simplify the expressions in parts (a) through (h) and
compare: $\frac{1 + (5/x)}{1 + (3/x)} = \frac{x + 5}{x + 3} \neq \frac{5x + 1}{3x + 1}$; $\frac{5 + (1/x)}{3 + (1/x)} = \frac{5x + 1}{3x + 1}$;

$(5/3)x + 1 = \frac{5}{3}x + 1 \neq \frac{5x + 1}{3x + 1}$; $\frac{1}{1 + (2x/(3x + 1))} = \frac{(3x + 1)}{(3x + 1) + 2x} =$

$\frac{3x + 1}{5x + 1} \neq \frac{5x + 1}{3x + 1}$; $1 - \frac{8x}{3x - 1} = \frac{(3x - 1) - 8x}{3x - 1} = \frac{-5x - 1}{3x - 1} \neq \frac{5x + 1}{3x + 1}$;

$\frac{8x}{3x + 1} - 1 = \frac{8x - (3x + 1)}{3x + 1} = \frac{5x - 1}{3x + 1} \neq \frac{5x + 1}{3x + 1}$; $5x + \frac{1}{3x + 1} =$

$\frac{(5x)(3x + 1) + 1}{3x + 1} = \frac{15x^2 + 5x + 1}{3x + 1} \neq \frac{5x + 1}{3x + 1}$; $5x + \frac{1 - 15x^2}{3x + 1} =$

$\frac{(5x)(3x + 1) + (1 - 15x^2)}{3x + 1} = \frac{15x^2 + 5x + 1 - 15x^2}{3x + 1} = \frac{5x + 1}{3x + 1}$.

(7a) 0^{-5} is undefined since it represents $\frac{1}{0^5}$.

(7b) $(-5)^0 = 1$ is defined since $a^0 = 1$ for any $a \neq 0$.

(7c) $(-7)^{643/645}$ is defined because it involves an odd root.

(7d) $7^{643/644}$ is defined since it involves an even root of a positive number.
$7^{-643/644}$ is defined because it is the reciprocal of the nonzero number $7^{643/644}$.

(7e) $(-7)^{643/644}$ is not defined because it is an even root of a negative number.

(7f) $\dfrac{(-2)^{-1/3}}{(-3)^{-1/2}}$ is not defined because it involves the square root of the negative

number -3.

(7g) $(1 - 1)^{1+1} = 0^2$ is defined.

(7h) $(1 + 1)^{1-1} = 2^0 = 1$ is defined.

(11g) First, compute the product of $2x + 1$ and $3x - 1$; then multiply the result

by $4x + 5$:

$$
\begin{array}{r}
2x + 1 \\
3x - 1 \\
\hline
6x^2 + 3x \\
- 2x - 1 \\
\hline
6x^2 + x - 1
\end{array}
\qquad\qquad
\begin{array}{r}
6x^2 + x - 1 \\
4x + 5 \\
\hline
24x^3 + 4x^2 - 4x \\
30x^2 + 5x - 5 \\
\hline
24x^3 + 34x^2 + x - 5
\end{array}
$$

SECTION 2.1

(5a)   The function is not defined for values x which make the denominator zero. These

are $x = -2, 1, -5$.

(5b)   Replace x by -3 in the equation: $\dfrac{(-3 - 3)(-3 + 4)}{(-3 + 2)(-3 - 1)(-3 + 5)} = -\dfrac{3}{4}$.

(10) Let L be the length and w the width of the rectangle. The diagonal of the

rectangle has length $\sqrt{L^2 + w^2}$ and is the diameter of the circle so

$L^2 + w^2 = 20^2$. Solve for L to obtain the formula $L = \sqrt{400 - w^2}$. The area of

the rectangle is $A = wL = w\sqrt{400 - w^2} = 2w\sqrt{100 - \tfrac{1}{4}w^2}$.

(13) The point on the curve with x-coordinate x has y-coordinate $y = 3x^2 - 4$.

Its distance to the point $(-2,3)$ is $\sqrt{(x - (-2))^2 + (y - 3)^2}$

$= \sqrt{(x - (-2))^2 + ((3x^2 - 4) - 3)^2} = \sqrt{(x + 2)^2 + (3x^2 - 7)^2}$.

(16) When the water is h feet deep and the radius of the surface of the water

is r feet, the water has volume $V = \tfrac{1}{3}\pi r^2 h$ (Fig. 2.1.16a). By similar

triangles (Fig. 2.1.16b), r and h are related by the equation $\dfrac{r}{h} = \dfrac{30}{90}$. Hence,

$r = \tfrac{1}{3} h$ and $V = \tfrac{1}{3}\pi(\tfrac{1}{3} h)^2 h = \tfrac{1}{27}\pi h^3$.

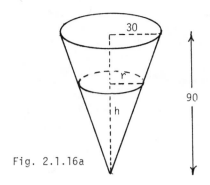

Fig. 2.1.16a

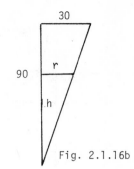

Fig. 2.1.16b

(22a) The profit is the revenue from sales minus the manufacturing cost. The revenue from selling x dolls is [x dolls][5 dollars/doll] = 5x dollars,and the cost of manufacturing x dolls is $1000 + 20x^{2/3}$ dollars. Hence, the profit on x dolls is $P(x) = 5x - (1000 + 20x^{2/3}) = 5x - 1000 - 20x^{2/3}$ dollars.

(22b) The average profit is the profit divided by the number of dolls. The average profit on x dolls is $A(x) = \dfrac{P(x)}{x} = \dfrac{5x - 1000 - 20x^{2/3}}{x} = 5 - \dfrac{1000}{x} - 20x^{-1/3}$ dollars/doll.

(22c) Since x denotes the number of dolls, the profit function is defined for nonnegative integers x. Since average profit is not meaningful for zero dolls, the domain of the average profit function is the set of positive integers.

SECTION 2.2

(3) The graph of the function $\dfrac{6}{x} - 3$ is the hyperbola $y = \dfrac{6}{x} - 3$, which is of the type shown in Figure 1.59 with a = 6 and b = -3. The horizontal line y = -3 separates the two halves of the graph, which passes through the points (1,3), (2,0), (3,-1), (-1,-9), (-2,-6), and (-3,-5). Fig. 2.2.3.

(9) The graph is in three pieces: the portion of the hyperbola $v = -1 + \dfrac{2}{u}$ for $-4 \le u < 0$, the point (0,0), and the portion of the hyperbola $v = 1 + \dfrac{2}{u}$ for $0 < u \le 4$. The first part passes through the points $(-4,-\tfrac{3}{2})$, (-2,-2), and (-1,-3). The third part passes through (1,3), (2,2), and $(4,\tfrac{3}{2})$. Fig. 2.2.9.

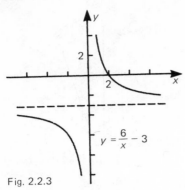

Fig. 2.2.3

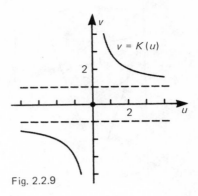

Fig. 2.2.9

(13) The graph is in two parts: the portion of the line $s = 96 + 32t$ for

$-3 \leq t \leq -1$ and the portion of the parabola $s = 80 - 16t^2$ for $-1 < t \leq \sqrt{5}$. The

first part is the line segment between the points $(-3,0)$ and $(-1,64)$. The

parabola passes through the points $(-1,64)$, $(0,80)$, and $(\sqrt{5},0)$. The two parts

join at $(-1,64)$. The rocket goes to a height of $s = 80$ feet, represented by the

highest point on the graph. Fig. 2.2.13.

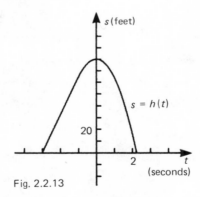

Fig. 2.2.13

SECTION 2.3

(7a) The graph of f consists of the portion of the line $y = -x$ for $x < -1$,

the point $(-1,-2)$, and the portion of the parabola $y = x^2$ for $x > -1$ (Fig. 2.3.7).

As x approaches -1 from the left or from the right the point $(x,f(x))$ on the graph approaches the circle at $(-1,1)$. Hence $f(x) \longrightarrow 1$ as $x \longrightarrow -1$.

(7b) For x just to the left of or just to the right of 0, the point $(x,f(x))$ is on the parabola $y = x^2$ and $f(x) = x^2$. Hence $\lim\limits_{x \to 0} f(x) = \lim\limits_{x \to 0} x^2 = 0$.

(11a) The graph of G consists of the portion of the line $y = x + 4$ for $x < 0$ and the portion of the parabola $y = x^2 + 1$ for $x > 0$ (Fig. 2.3.11). As $x \to 0^-$, the point $(x,G(x))$ is on the line and approaches the circle at $(0,4)$. Therefore, $G(x) \longrightarrow 4$ as $x \longrightarrow 0^-$.

(11b) As $x \to 0^+$, the point $(x,G(x))$ is on the parabola and approaches the circle at $(0,1)$. Therefore, $\lim\limits_{x \to 0^+} G(x) = 1$.

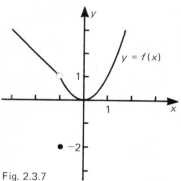

Fig. 2.3.7

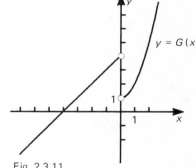

Fig. 2.3.11

(13f) From the table of values given below we guess that the limit is -1.

x	0.9	1.1	0.99	1.01	0.999
$\sqrt[3]{\dfrac{2 - 2x}{x^2 - 1}}$	-1.017244...	-0.983868...	-1.001672...	-0.998338...	-1.000166...

1.001	0.9999	1.0001
-0.999833...	-1.000016...	-0.999983...

SECTION 2.4

(5) Since the denominator $F(x) - 100$ tends to the nonzero number $350-100 = 250$

as x tends to 100, we may apply Theorem 2.1 to obtain

$$\lim \left\{ \frac{F(x) - 5G(x)^2}{F(x) - 100} \right\} = \frac{[\lim F(x)] - 5[\lim G(x)]^2}{[\lim F(x)] - 100} = \frac{350 - 5(-4)^2}{350 - 100} = \frac{27}{25}$$

where "lim" means   " $\lim\limits_{x \to 100}$ ".

(9) Because the denominator $x^2 - 9x$ tends to 0 as x tends to 9, we cannot apply

Theorem 2.1 directly. We rationalize the numerator and factor the denominator and then

cancel the x - 9 that appears in both:

$$\frac{\sqrt{x} - 3}{x^2 - 9x} = \frac{(\sqrt{x} - 3)(\sqrt{x} + 3)}{x(x - 9)(\sqrt{x} + 3)} = \frac{x - 9}{x(x - 9)(\sqrt{x} + 3)} = \frac{1}{x(\sqrt{x} + 3)}$$

Now, we can apply Theorem 2.1. The expression on the right tends to $\dfrac{1}{9(\sqrt{9} + 3)} = \dfrac{1}{54}$

as $x \to 9$.

(12) We cannot apply Theorem 2.1 directly because the denominator $1 - (25/x^2)$ tends

to 0 as x tends to 5. We first simplify the fraction. Then we factor the resulting

numerator and denominator and cancel the factor of x - 5 that appears in both:

$$\frac{25 - 5x}{1 - \dfrac{25}{x^2}} = \frac{25 - 5x}{\dfrac{x^2 - 25}{x^2}} = \frac{x^2(25 - 5x)}{x^2 - 25} = \frac{-5x^2(x - 5)}{(x - 5)(x + 5)} = \frac{- 5x^2}{x + 5}$$

As $x \to 5$, the expression on the right tends to $\dfrac{-5(5)^2}{5 + 5} = -\dfrac{125}{10} = -\dfrac{25}{2}$.

(15)   We rationalize the numerator and then cancel the factor y that appears

in the numerator and in the denominator:

$$\frac{[1 - \sqrt{1 + y}][1 + \sqrt{1 + y}]}{7y(1 + \sqrt{1 + y})} = \frac{1 - (1 + y)}{7y(1 + \sqrt{1 + y})} = \frac{-y}{7y(1 + \sqrt{1 + y})}$$

$$= \frac{-1}{7(1 + \sqrt{1 + y})} \longrightarrow \frac{-1}{7(1 + \sqrt{1})} = -\frac{1}{14} \quad \text{as } y \to 0.$$

SECTION 2.5

(1a,e) $\frac{1}{x^2}$ is small for large (positive or negative) x and tends to 0 as $x \to -\infty$

and as $x \to \infty$. Hence $\lim\limits_{x \to -\infty} [2 + (1/x^2)] = 2$ and $\lim\limits_{x \to \infty} [2 + (1/x^2)] = 2$.

(1b,c) $\frac{1}{x^2}$ is a large positive number for small (positive or negative) x and tends

to ∞ as $x \to 0^-$ and as $x \to 0^+$. Therefore, $\lim\limits_{x \to 0^-} [2 + (1/x^2)] = \infty$ and

$\lim\limits_{x \to 0^+} [2 + (1/x^2)] = \infty$.

(1d)   Since the one-sided limits determined in parts (b) and (c) are both ∞ , we have

$\lim\limits_{x \to 0} [2 + (1/x^2)] = \infty$.

(7a) For negative x, $V(x) = \frac{3}{x} + 3$, which tends to 3 as $x \to -\infty$. Therefore,

$\lim\limits_{x \to -\infty} V(x) = 3$.

(7b) Because $V(x) = \frac{3}{x} + 3$ for negative x, $\lim\limits_{x \to 0^-} V(x) = \lim\limits_{x \to 0^-} [\frac{3}{x} + 3] = -\infty$.

(7c) Because $V(x) = \frac{3}{x} - 3$ for positive x, $\lim\limits_{x \to 0^+} V(x) = \lim\limits_{x \to 0^+} [\frac{3}{x} - 3] = \infty$.

(7d) Because the limits of V(x) as $x \to 0^-$ and as $x \to 0^+$ are different, the

limit as $x \to 0$ does not exist.

(7e) For positive x, $V(x) = \frac{3}{x} - 3$, which tends to -3 as $x \to \infty$. Therefore,

$\lim\limits_{x \to \infty} V(x) = -3$.

SECTION 2.6

(6a,b) We find the highest power of x in the numerator by taking the highest power

of x in each of the factors: $\dfrac{(x^2 + 1)(3x - 4)}{1 + 2x + 3x^2}$ has the same limits as x

as does the function $\dfrac{(x^2)(3x)}{3x^2} = x$; the limit as $x \to \infty$ is ∞ and the

limit as $x \to -\infty$ is $-\infty$.

(6c) We factor out the highest power of x from each of the factors in the numerator

and from the denominator: $x^2 + 1 = x^2(1 + \frac{1}{x^2})$; $3x - 4 = x(3 - \frac{4}{x})$; and

$1 + 2x + 3x^2 = x^2(\frac{1}{x^2} + \frac{2}{x} + 3)$. Thus, for $x \neq 0$

$$\frac{(x^2 + 1)(3x - 4)}{1 + 2x + 3x^2} = \frac{x^2(1 + \frac{1}{x^2})x(3 - \frac{4}{x})}{x^2(\frac{1}{x^2} + \frac{2}{x} + 3)} = x\left[\frac{(1 + \frac{1}{x^2})(3 - \frac{4}{x})}{(\frac{1}{x^2} + \frac{2}{x} + 3)}\right]$$

The expression in square brackets on the right tends to $\frac{(1)(3)}{3} = 1$, **a nonzero** positive

number, as $x \longrightarrow \pm\infty$, so the original expression as the same limits as $x \longrightarrow \pm\infty$ as

does the function x.

(10) The given expression has the same limits as $x \longrightarrow \pm\infty$ as does the function

$\frac{x^2(-6x)}{5x^3} = -\frac{6}{5}$, so those limits are both $-\frac{6}{5}$.

(13) To apply Rule 2.2 we have to first express the given function as a ratio of

polynomials: $x + \frac{2x^2 - 1}{3 - 2x} = \frac{x(3 - 2x) + (2x^2 - 1)}{3 - 2x} = \frac{3x - 2x^2 + 2x^2 - 1}{3 - 2x} = \frac{3x - 1}{3 - 2x}$

By Rule 2.2 the limits as $x \longrightarrow \infty$ and as $x \longrightarrow$ $-\infty$ are the same as those

of $\frac{3x}{-2x} = -\frac{3}{2}$. Both limits are $-\frac{3}{2}$.

SECTION 2.7

(5) This rational function is continuous except where its denominators are zero.

The denominator in $\frac{2}{x}$ is zero at $x = 0$ and the denominator $1 - \frac{2}{x}$ is zero at

$x = 2$. The function is continuous except at $x = 0$ and $x = 2$.

(12) The function H is continuous for $0 \leq x < 1$ because it equals $\frac{1 - \sqrt{x}}{x - 1}$ there.

To have it be continuous in the closed interval $0 \leq x \leq 1$, we must also have

$H(1) = \lim\limits_{x \to 1^-} H(x)$. $H(1) = k$ and for $0 \leq x < 1$ rationalization gives

$$H(x) = \frac{1 - \sqrt{x}}{x - 1} = \frac{(1 - \sqrt{x})(1 + \sqrt{x})}{(x - 1)(1 + \sqrt{x})} = \frac{1 - x}{(x - 1)(1 + \sqrt{x})} \quad \frac{-1}{1 + \sqrt{x}}$$

so $\lim\limits_{x \to 1^-} H(x) = \lim\limits_{x \to 1^-} \frac{-1}{1 + \sqrt{x}} = -\frac{1}{2}$. We must take $k = -\frac{1}{2}$.

(14) The function g is equal to a polynomial in an open interval containing

each $x \neq \pm 1$, so it is continuous at all $x \neq \pm 1$. To have g continuous at -1,

we must have $\lim\limits_{x \to -1^-} g(x) = \lim\limits_{x \to -1^+} g(x) = g(-1)$. To have it continuous at 1,

we must have $\lim\limits_{x \to 1^-} g(x) = \lim\limits_{x \to 1^+} g(x) = g(1)$. Because $\lim\limits_{x \to -1^-} g(x) = \lim\limits_{x \to -1^-} x^3$

$= -1$, $\lim\limits_{x \to -1^+} g(x) = \lim\limits_{x \to -1^+} (ax + b) = -a + b$, and $g(-1) = [ax + b]_{x=-1} = -a + b$,

we must have (*) $-ax + b = -1$. Because $\lim\limits_{x \to 1^-} g(x) = \lim\limits_{x \to 1^-} (ax + b) = a + b$,

$\lim\limits_{x \to 1^+} g(x) = \lim\limits_{x \to 1^+} (x^2 + 2) = 3$, and $g(1) = [x^2 + 2]_{x=1} = 3$, we must also have

(**) $a + b = 3$. (*) and (**) give the simultaneous equations $\begin{cases} -a + b = -1 \\ a + b = 3 \end{cases}$.

Adding them gives $2b = 2$ to show that $b = 1$. Then either equation yields $a = 2$.

SECTION 2.8

(3) Suppose that the runner's speed after he has run x feet is v(x) feet per second

and that the circumference of the track is 2a feet. Because he starts from rest and

stops after one lap, we have $v(0) = v(2a) = 0$. We assume that $v(x)$ is continuous for

$0 \leq x \leq 2a$. Then the function $f(x) = v(x + a) - v(x)$, which gives the difference between

his speeds at diametrically opposite points, is continuous for $0 \leq x \leq a$. We have

$f(0) = v(a) - v(0) = v(a)$ and $f(a) = v(2a) - v(a) = -v(a)$. If $v(a) = 0$, then

the runner has the same speed (zero) at $x = 0$ and at the opposite point, $x = a$.

If $v(a)$ is not zero, then $f(0)$ and $f(a)$ are of opposite signs and by the Intermediate

Value Theorem there is some x with $0 < x < a$ such that $f(x) = 0$. With this x

we have $v(x + a) = v(x)$, so the runner has the same speed at x and at the opposite

point, $x + a$.

(8) The graph of S is shown in Fig. 2.8.8. The maximum value of the function is 5 and

occurs at the highest point on the graph. The function has no minimum value because the

graph does not include the points at $(-4,-3)$ and $(4,-3)$. The hypotheses of the Extreme

Value Theorem are not satisfied because the interval $-4 < x < 4$ is not closed.

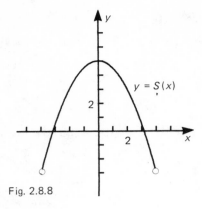

Fig. 2.8.8

SECTION 2.9

(8) Because we want to show we can make $\left|\frac{10}{x} - 2\right|$ small by making $|x - 5|$ small,

we write $(*)$ $\frac{10}{x} - 2 = \frac{2}{x}(5 - x)$. Our choice of δ cannot depend on x, so we

restrict our attention to x in the interval $|x - 5| < 1$. For such x we have $x > 4$

and $\left|\frac{2}{x}\right| < \frac{1}{2}$, so that by $(*)$ we have $(**)\left|\frac{10}{x} - 2\right| < \frac{1}{2}|5 - x|$. To use this estimate

we define δ by the following rule: for any $\epsilon > 0$ let δ be the smaller of the

numbers 1 and 2ϵ. Then $0 < |x - 5| < \delta$ implies that $|x - 5| < 1$ so that

$(**)$ is valid and we have $\left|\frac{10}{x} - 2\right| < \frac{1}{2}|5 - x| < \frac{1}{2}(2\epsilon) = \epsilon$.

(33) δ is the distance between 2 and the nearest solution x of the equation

$|(x^2 - 1) - 3| = \frac{1}{2}$. The equation may be written $x^2 - 4 = \pm\frac{1}{2}$ and has the solutions

$x = \sqrt{\frac{9}{2}}$ and $x = \sqrt{\frac{7}{2}}$. Of these two numbers it is $\sqrt{\frac{9}{2}}$ that is closer to 2. Hence

$\delta = \sqrt{\frac{9}{2}} - 2 = -2 + 3/\sqrt{2} = 0.1213\ldots$

SECTION 3.1

(3) Definition (2) of the derivative with $x_0 = 2$ gives $g'(2) = \lim\limits_{x \to 2} \dfrac{g(x) - g(2)}{x - 2}$.

For any $x \ne 2$ we have $\dfrac{g(x) - g(2)}{x - 2} = \dfrac{4 - 4}{x - 2} = 0$, so $g'(2) = \lim\limits_{x \to 2} (0) = 0$.

(6) Definition (2) with x replaced by u and x_0 replaced by 4 gives

$G'(4) = \lim\limits_{u \to 4} \dfrac{G(u) - G(4)}{u - 4}$. Since $G(u) = \dfrac{1}{5 - 2u}$ and $G(4) = \dfrac{1}{5 - 2(4)} = -\dfrac{1}{3}$, we have

$G'(4) = \lim\limits_{u \to 4} \dfrac{\dfrac{1}{5 - 2u} + \dfrac{1}{3}}{u - 4}$. To find the limit we simplify the fraction and then cancel

the factor of $u - 4$ that occurs in the numerator and denominator:

$$\dfrac{\dfrac{1}{5 - 2u} + \dfrac{1}{3}}{u - 4} = \dfrac{1}{u - 4} \left[\dfrac{1}{5 - 2u} + \dfrac{1}{3} \right] = \dfrac{1}{u - 4} \left[\dfrac{3 + (5 - 2u)}{(5 - 2u)(3)} \right] = \dfrac{1}{u - 4} \left[\dfrac{8 - 2u}{15 - 6u} \right]$$

$$= \dfrac{-2(u - 4)}{(u - 4)(15 - 6u)} = \dfrac{-2}{15 - 6u} \longrightarrow \dfrac{-2}{15 - 6(4)} = \dfrac{2}{9} \quad \text{as} \quad x \to 4. \; G'(4) = \dfrac{2}{9} .$$

(16) The equation of the tangent line is $y - y_0 = m(x - x_0)$ where (x_0, y_0) is the

point of tangency on the curve and m is the slope of the tangent line. The point at

$x = 0$ on the curve $y = -\dfrac{1}{4} x^3 - 2$ has y-coordinate $y = -\dfrac{1}{4}(0)^3 - 2 = -2$, so we

have $(x_0, y_0) = (0, -2)$. Set $f(x) = -\dfrac{1}{4} x^3 - 2$. Then

$$m = f'(0) = \lim\limits_{x \to 0} \dfrac{f(x) - f(0)}{x - 0} = \lim\limits_{x \to 0} \dfrac{-\dfrac{1}{4} x^3 - 2 - (-2)}{x - 0} = \lim\limits_{x \to 0} \dfrac{-\dfrac{1}{4} x^3}{x}$$

$$= \lim\limits_{x \to 0} (-\dfrac{1}{4} x^2) = 0, \text{ so the tangent line has the equation}$$

$y - (-2) = 0(x - 0)$ or $y = -2$.

(23) The equation of the normal line is $y - y_0 = m(x - x_0)$ where (x_0, y_0) is the

point on the graph and m is the slope of the normal line. The point at $x = 4$ on the

graph of $\sqrt{x + 5}$ has y-coordinate $y = \sqrt{4 + 5} = 3$, so $(x_0, y_0) = (4, 3)$. Set

$f(x) = \sqrt{x + 5}$. Then the slope of the tangent line at $x = 4$ has slope $f'(4)$ and

the slope of the normal line is $m = -1/f'(4)$. We compute $f'(4)$ by rationalization:

$$f'(4) = \lim_{x \to 4} \frac{f(x) - f(4)}{x - 4} = \lim_{x \to 4} \frac{\sqrt{x + 5} - 3}{x - 4} = \lim_{x \to 4} \frac{(\sqrt{x + 5} - 3)(\sqrt{x + 5} + 3)}{(x - 4)(\sqrt{x + 5} + 3)}$$

$$= \lim_{x \to 4} \frac{(x + 5) - 9}{(x - 4)(\sqrt{x + 5} + 3)} = \lim_{x \to 4} \frac{1}{\sqrt{x + 5} + 3} = \frac{1}{\sqrt{4 + 5} + 3} = \frac{1}{6}.$$

Hence $m = -6$ and the normal line has the equation $y - 3 = -6(x - 4)$ or $y = -6x + 27$.

(25g) The slope $\frac{f(x) - f(3)}{x - 3}$ of the secant line with $f(x) = (x^2 - 1)^{-1/3}$ and with the prescribed values of $x - 3$ are computed in Table 3.1.25. From these values we guess the value $f'(3) = -\frac{1}{8} = -0.125$ for the derivative.

TABLE 3.1.25

$x - 3$	x	$f(x)$	$f(x) - f(3)$	$\frac{f(x) - f(3)}{x - 3}$
0.1	3.1	0.48790164..	-0.01209835..	-0.1209835...
-0.1	2.9	0.51293294..	0.01293294..	-0.1293294...
0.001	3.001	0.49987504..	-0.0001249583..	-0.1249583...
-0.001	2.999	0.50012504..	0.0001250417..	-0.1250417...
0.0001	3.0001	0.49998750..	-0.0000124995..	-0.1249950...
-0.0001	2.9999	0.50001250..	0.0000125005..	-0.1250050...

SECTION 3.2

(3) $\quad \frac{dh}{dt}(4) = \lim_{\Delta t \to 0} \frac{h(4 + \Delta t) - h(4)}{\Delta t} = \lim_{\Delta t \to 0} \frac{\sqrt{(4 + \Delta t) + 5} - \sqrt{4 + 5}}{\Delta t}.$

$\quad\quad = \lim_{\Delta t \to 0} \frac{\sqrt{9 + \Delta t} - 3}{\Delta t}$. We rationalize the numerator and then cancel the factors of Δt:

$$\frac{\sqrt{9 + \Delta t} - 3}{\Delta t} = \frac{(\sqrt{9 + \Delta t} - 3)(\sqrt{9 + \Delta t} + 3)}{\Delta t(\sqrt{9 + \Delta t} + 3)} = \frac{9 + \Delta t - 9}{\Delta t(\sqrt{9 + \Delta t} + 3)} = \frac{\Delta t}{\Delta t(\sqrt{9 + \Delta t} + 3)}$$

$$= \frac{1}{\sqrt{9 + \Delta t} + 3} \longrightarrow \frac{1}{\sqrt{9 + 0} + 3} = \frac{1}{6} \text{ as } \Delta t \to 0. \quad \frac{dh}{dt}(4) = \frac{1}{6}.$$

(9) $(a + b)^3 = a^3 + 3a^2b + 3ab^2 + b^3$, so for $f(x) = \frac{1}{8} x^3$, we have

$$\frac{df}{dx}(x) = \lim_{\Delta x \to 0} \frac{f(x + \Delta x) - f(x)}{\Delta x} = \lim_{\Delta x \to 0} \frac{\frac{1}{8}(x + \Delta x)^3 - \frac{1}{8} x^3}{\Delta x} = \lim_{\Delta x \to 0} \frac{1}{8\Delta x}[(x + \Delta x)^3 - x^3]$$

$$= \lim_{\Delta x \to 0} \frac{1}{8\Delta x}[x^3 + 3x^2 \Delta x + 3x(\Delta x)^2 + (\Delta x)^3 - x^3]$$

$$= \lim_{\Delta x \to 0} \frac{1}{8\Delta x}[3x^2 \Delta x + 3x(\Delta x)^2 + (\Delta x)^3] = \lim_{\Delta x \to 0} \frac{1}{8}[3x^2 + 3x \Delta x + (\Delta x)^2] = \frac{3}{8} x^2.$$

The graph of $\frac{1}{8} x^3$ is the cubic $y = \frac{1}{8} x^3$ in Fig. 3.2.9a. The graph of the derivative
$\frac{3}{8} x^2$ is the parabola $y = \frac{3}{8} x^2$ in Fig. 3.2.9b.

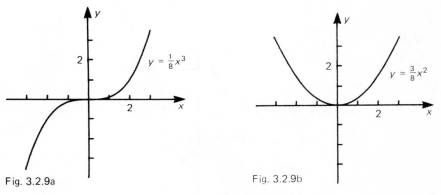

Fig. 3.2.9a   Fig. 3.2.9b

(11) Set $f(x) = 2x^2 + 3x - 4$. Then $f(x + \Delta x) = 2(x + \Delta x)^2 + 3(x + \Delta x) - 4$ and

$$\frac{f(x + \Delta x) - f(x)}{\Delta x} = \frac{[2(x + \Delta x)^2 + 3(x + \Delta x) - 4] - [2x^2 + 3x - 4]}{\Delta x}$$

$$= \frac{2[x^2 + 2x \Delta x + (\Delta x)^2] + 3x + 3 \Delta x - 4 - 2x^2 - 3x + 4}{\Delta x}$$

$$= \frac{2x^2 + 4x \Delta x + 2(\Delta x)^2 + 3x + 3 \Delta x - 4 - 2x^2 - 3x + 4}{\Delta x}$$

$$= \frac{4x \Delta x + 2(\Delta x)^2 + 3 \Delta x}{\Delta x} = 4x + 2 \Delta x + 3 \longrightarrow 4x + 3 \quad \text{as} \quad \Delta x \longrightarrow 0.$$

$$\frac{df}{dx}(x) = 4x + 3.$$

SECTION 3.3

(8) We write $\sqrt{s^5}$ as $s^{5/2}$. Then by the analog of Theorem 3.3 for linear combinations of three functions and by Theorem 3.2 with $n = 0$, $n = 1$, and $n = \frac{5}{2}$ we have

$$\frac{d}{ds}(1 - s + \sqrt{s^5}) = \frac{d}{ds}(s^0) - \frac{d}{ds}(s^1) + \frac{d}{ds}(s^{5/2}) = 0 - s^0 + \frac{5}{2}s^{3/2} = -1 + \frac{5}{2}s^{3/2}.$$

Because $s^{5/2}$ is not defined for negative s (due to the even root), the differentiation is valid only for $s > 0$.

(11) $F'(2) = [\frac{d}{dx}(6x^3 - x^{-1})]_{x=2} = [6\frac{d}{dx}x^3 - \frac{d}{dx}x^{-1}]_{x=2} = [6(3)x^2 - (-1)x^{-2}]_{x=2}$

$= [18x^2 + x^{-2}]_{x=2} = 18(2)^2 + (2)^{-2} = 72 + \frac{1}{4} = \frac{289}{4}$

(15) $f'(x) = 3g'(x) - 4h'(x)$; $f'(10) = 3g'(10) - 4h'(10) = 3(7) - 4(-3) = 33$

(17) The point on the curve $y = x^3 - 4x$ at $x = 2$ has y-coordinate $(2)^3 - 4(2) = 0$. The tangent line passes through the point $(2,0)$. Its slope is $[\frac{d}{dx}(x^3 - 4x)]_{x=2}$

$= [3x^2 - 4]_{x=2} = 3(2)^2 - 4 = 8$. By the point slope formula the tangent line has the equation $y - 0 = 8(x - 2)$ or $y = 8x - 16$.

(21) Since $1 + kx - kx^2$ and x^4 both have the value 1 at $x = 1$ for any value of k, the curves $y = 1 + x - kx^2$ and $y = x^4$ intersect at $(1,1)$. For them to be tangent the derivatives $\frac{d}{dx}(1 + kx - kx^2) = k - 2kx$ and $\frac{d}{dx}x^4 = 4x^3$ must be equal at $x = 1$. This gives the equation $k - 2k = 4$, which has the solution $k = -4$.

SECTION 3.4

(5)   First write $\frac{1}{w^2}$ as w^{-2}; then use the product rule:

$\frac{d}{dw}[(w^2 + w^{-2})(2 + 3w)] = (w^2 + w^{-2})\frac{d}{dw}(2 + 3w) + (2 + 3w)\frac{d}{dw}(w^2 + w^{-2})$

$= (w^2 + w^{-2})(3) + (2 + 3w)(2w - 2w^{-3})$

(11)
$$\frac{dV}{dy}(y) = \frac{[y - T(y)]\frac{d}{dy}(y^2) - y^2\frac{d}{dy}[y - T(y)]}{[y - T(y)]^2} = \frac{[y - T(y)](2y) - y^2[1 - \frac{dT}{dy}(y)]}{[y - T(y)]^2}$$

Therefore

$$\frac{dV}{dy}(7) = \frac{[7 - T(7)](2(7)) - (7)^2[1 - \frac{dT}{dy}(7)]}{[7 - T(7)]^2} = \frac{14[7 - T(7)] - 49[1 - \frac{dT}{dy}(7)]}{[7 - T(7)]^2}$$

Since $T(7) = -3$ and $\frac{dT}{dy}(7) = -5$, we have

$$\frac{dV}{dy}(7) = \frac{14[7 - (-3)] - 49[1 - (-5)]}{[7 - (-3)]^2} = \frac{14(10) - 49(6)}{10^2} = -\frac{77}{50}.$$

(14)   The point at $x = -2$ on the curve $y = \frac{2}{2 - x}$ has y-coordinate $\frac{2}{2 - (-2)} = \frac{1}{2}$.
The derivative $\frac{dy}{dx} = \frac{2}{(x - 2)^2}$ equals $\frac{1}{8}$ at $x = -2$. The tangent line passes
through $(-2, \frac{1}{2})$ and has slope $\frac{1}{8}$. Its equation is $y - \frac{1}{2} = \frac{1}{8}[x - (-2)]$ or
$y = \frac{1}{8} x + \frac{3}{4}$.

SECTION 3.5

(7a)   The upward velocity is the rate of change (derivative) of the distance
above the ground with respect to time: Upward velocity $= \frac{d}{dt}(48 + 32t - 16t^2)$
$= 32 - 32t$ feet/second. At $t = 0$ the upward velocity is $[32 - 32t]_{t=0}$ $= 32$ feet/second.

(7b)   The velocity $32 - 32t$ feet/second computed in part (a) is 0 for $t = 1$,
is positive for $t < 1$, and is negative for $t > 1$.

(7c)   The ball is at its maximum height at $t = 1$ (when its velocity is zero) since
for $-1 < t < 1$ is is going up (its upward velocity is positive) and for $1 < t < 3$
it is going down (its upward velocity is negative). Its maximum height is its height
$[48 + 32 - 16t^2]_{t=1}$ $= 48 + 32 - 16 = 64$ feet at $t = 1$.

(8a)   The car's velocity (toward the east) is the derivative $\frac{d}{dt}(10t^{3/2} - 15t + 10)$
$= 15t^{1/2} - 15$ miles/hour. At $t = \frac{1}{4}$ this velocity is $15(\frac{1}{4})^{1/2} - 15 = -\frac{15}{2}$ miles/hour
Because the velocity is negative, the car is traveling west.

(8b) The velocity $15t^{1/2} - 15$ miles/hour is zero at $t = 1$. The car's distance east

of the rest stop at that time is $[10t^{3/2} - 15t + 10]_{t=1} = 10 - 15 + 10 = 5$ miles.

SECTION 3.6

(3a)   The average rate of change of the force is the difference quotient $\dfrac{F(100) - F(5,}{100 - 5}$

$\dfrac{1}{95}[(\dfrac{1}{10000}) - (\dfrac{1}{25})] = -\dfrac{399}{950000}$ dynes/centimeter or -0.00042 dynes/centimeter .

(3b)   We calculate $\dfrac{dF}{dr} = \dfrac{d}{dr}(r^{-2}) = -2r^{-3}$ dynes/centimeter and substitute $r = 10$:

$\dfrac{dF}{dr} = -2(10)^{-3} = -\dfrac{1}{500}$ dynes/centimeter   or -0.002 dynes/centimeter

(10a) The revenue is the amount obtained from the sale of the donuts:

$R(x) = [x \text{ dozen}][0.75 \text{ dollars/dozen}] = 0.75x$ dollars. The profit is the revenue minus

the cost: $P(x) = R(x) - C(x) = 0.75x - (50 + \dfrac{1}{4} x - \dfrac{1}{30} x^2) = -50 + \dfrac{1}{2} x + \dfrac{1}{30} x^2$ dollars.

(10b) The average profit on x dozen donuts is $A(x) = \dfrac{P(x) \text{ dollars}}{x \text{ dozen}} = \dfrac{P(x)}{x} \dfrac{\text{dollars}}{\text{dozen}}$.

The formula from part (a) for $P(x)$ yields $A(x) = -\dfrac{50}{x} + \dfrac{1}{2} + \dfrac{1}{30} x \dfrac{\text{dollars}}{\text{dozen}}$. For 30

dozen the average profit is $A(30) = -\dfrac{50}{30} + \dfrac{1}{2} + \dfrac{1}{30}(30) = -\dfrac{1}{6}$ dollars/dozen. The marginal

profit is $P'(x) = \dfrac{d}{dx}(-50 + \dfrac{1}{2} x + \dfrac{1}{30} x^2) = \dfrac{1}{2} + \dfrac{1}{15}x$ dollars/dozen. For 30 dozen the

marginal profit is $P'(30) = \dfrac{1}{2} + \dfrac{1}{15}(30) = \dfrac{5}{2}$ dollars/dozen.

SECTION 3.7

(2) We use formula (10) with $s(t) = t^3 + 2$ and $n = \dfrac{1}{2}$: $f'(t) = \dfrac{d}{dt}(t^3 + 2)^{1/2}$

$= \dfrac{1}{2}(t^3 + 2)^{-1/2} \dfrac{d}{dt}(t^3 + 2) = \dfrac{1}{2}(t^3 + 2)^{-1/2} (3t^2) = \dfrac{3}{2} t^2(t^3 + 2)^{-1/2}$.

(7) By formula (10), $\dfrac{dW}{dt}(t) = \dfrac{d}{dt} v(t)^5 = 5 v(t)^4 \dfrac{dv}{dt}(t)$. Since $v(0) = 2$ and $\dfrac{dv}{dt}(0) = -4$,

we obtain $\dfrac{dW}{dt}(0) = 5 v(0)^4 \dfrac{dv}{dt}(0) = 5(2)^4(-4) = -320$.

(16) By formula (9), $C'(x) = \dfrac{d}{dx} B(A(x)) = B'(A(x))A'(x)$, so $C'(-1) = B'(A(-1))A'(-1)$

$= B'(-3)A'(-1) = (9)(-4) = -36$. (Notice that we do not need the value $B(-3) = -6$, which

is also given.)

(20) The rate of change of the drag with respect to velocity is $\frac{dD}{dv} = \frac{d}{dv}\left(\frac{1}{30}\,v^2\right)$

$= \frac{1}{15}\,v\,\frac{\text{pounds}}{\text{miles per hour}}$. The rate of change of the velocity with respect to time

is the acceleration $\frac{dv}{dt} = 2\,\frac{\text{miles per hour}}{\text{second}}$. The rate of change of the drag with respect

to time is the product $\frac{dD}{dt} = \frac{dD}{dv}\frac{dv}{dt} = \left[\frac{1}{15}\,v\,\frac{\text{pounds}}{\text{miles per hour}}\right]\left[2\,\frac{\text{miles per hour}}{\text{second}}\right]$

$= \frac{2}{15}\,v\,\frac{\text{pounds}}{\text{second}}$. When the velocity is 50 miles per hour, this rate of change is

$\frac{dD}{dt} = \left[\frac{2}{15}\,v\right]_{v=50} = \frac{20}{3}$ pounds per second.

SECTION 3.8

(1b) The angle 135° is drawn in Fig. 3.8.1b. To convert 135° to radian measure we

multiply it by $\frac{\pi}{180}$: (135 degrees)$\left(\frac{\pi}{180}\,\frac{\text{radians}}{\text{degree}}\right) = \frac{3}{4}\,\pi$ radians. To determine the sine

and cosine we consider the point P one unit from the origin on the terminal side

of the angle as in Fig. 3.8.1b. A vertical line through P, the terminal side of the

angle, and the horizontal u-axis form an isosceles right triangle with hypotenuse of

length 1 (Fig. 3.8.1bi). We let s denote the lengths of the legs of the triangle.

Then, by the Pythagorean theorem, $s^2 + s^2 = 1^2$ and therefore $s = 1/\sqrt{2}$. Because P

has a negative u-coordinate and a positive v-coordinate, its coordinates are

$(-1/\sqrt{2},\,1/\sqrt{2})$ and $\cos(\frac{3}{4}\pi) = -1/\sqrt{2}$, $\sin(\frac{3}{4}\pi) = 1/\sqrt{2}$.

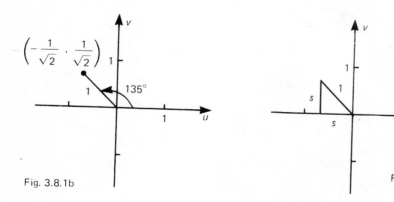

Fig. 3.8.1b　　　　　　　　　　　　　　　　　　　　Fig. 3.8.1bi

(2b) The angle is drawn in Fig. 3.8.2b. To convert $-\frac{10\pi}{3}$ radians to degree measure, we multiply by $\frac{180}{\pi}$: $(-\frac{10\pi}{3}$ radians$)(\frac{180}{\pi}\,\frac{degrees}{radian}) = -600$ degrees. To find the sine and cosine, we consider the point P on the terminal side of the angle a distance 1 from the origin as in Fig. 3.8.2b. The vertical line through P, the terminal side of the angle, and the u-axis form a 30^0-60^0-right triangle (Fig. 3.8.2bi) with hypotenuse of length 1. The base of the triangle is of length $\frac{1}{2}$ because the triangle is half of an equilateral triangle (Fig. 3.8.2bi). We let s denote the length of the other side, and the Pythagorean theorem gives $s^2 + (\frac{1}{2})^2 = 1^2$. Hence $s = \sqrt{3}/2$ and P has coordinates $(-\frac{1}{2}, \frac{\sqrt{3}}{2})$, so that $\cos(-\frac{10\pi}{3}) = -\frac{1}{2}$ and $\sin(-\frac{10\pi}{3}) = \frac{\sqrt{3}}{2}$.

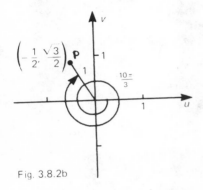

Fig. 3.8.2b

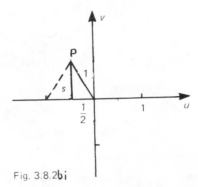

Fig. 3.8.2bi

(7) A positive angle of x radians with its vertex at the center of a circle of radius r subtends an arc of length rx. If the arc is ten feet long and the angle is 4 radians, then $10 = 4r$ and the radius of the circle is $r = \frac{10}{4} = \frac{5}{2}$ feet.

(11) We draw the unit circle and the line $u = -1$ in a uv-plane (Fig. 3.8.11). The line and circle intersect at the one point $(-1,0)$ on the negative u-axis so the angles θ with $\cos\theta = -1$ are those whose terminal sides are along the negative u-axis. These are the angles $\theta = (2k + 1)\pi$ ($k = 0, \pm1, \pm2, \pm3,...$) that are odd multiples of π . Hence the solutions of $\cos(\frac{x}{7}) = -1$ are given by $\frac{x}{7} = (2k + 1)\pi$ or $x = 7(2k + 1)\pi$ with k any integer.

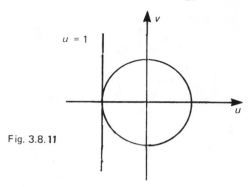

Fig. 3.8.11

(24)   We have -5 sin(-2x) + 5 cos(-2x) = A sin(-2x) + B cos(-2x) with A = -5
and B = 5. We factor out $C = \sqrt{A^2 + B^2} = \sqrt{5^2 + 5^2} = 5\sqrt{2}$:

(*)   -5 sin(-2x) + 5 cos(-2x) = $5\sqrt{2}[-\frac{1}{\sqrt{2}}$ sin(-2x) $+ \frac{1}{\sqrt{2}}$ cos(-2x)].

We want an angle ψ such that cosψ = $-\frac{1}{\sqrt{2}}$ and sinψ = $\frac{1}{\sqrt{2}}$. We can take $\psi = \frac{3\pi}{4}$

(Fig. 3.8.24) and then (*) gives

$$-5 \sin(-2x) + 5 \cos(-2x) = 5\sqrt{2}[\cos(\tfrac{3\pi}{4}) \sin(-2x) + \sin(\tfrac{3\pi}{4}) \cos(-2x)]$$

$$= 5\sqrt{2} \sin(-2x + \tfrac{3\pi}{4}).$$

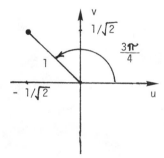

Fig. 3.8.24

(30)   By the law of sines (Fig. 3.8.30), we have

$$\frac{\overline{AB}}{\sin \gamma} = \frac{\overline{AC}}{\sin \beta} ,$$

where $\overline{AC}$ = 100, α = 1.9, γ = 0.8, and because the sum of the interior angles of
a triangle is π , $\beta = \pi - 1.9 - 0.8 = \pi - 2.7 \approx 0.44$. Therefore

$$\overline{AB} = \frac{\overline{AC} \sin \gamma}{\sin \beta} = \frac{100 \sin(0.8)}{\sin(\pi - 2.7)} \approx \frac{100 \sin(0.8)}{\sin(0.44)} \approx \frac{100(0.717)}{0.426} \approx 168.4 \text{ meters.}$$

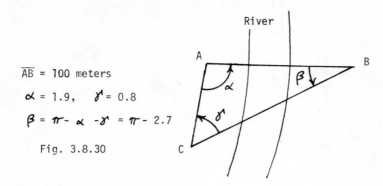

$\overline{AB}$ = 100 meters

α = 1.9, γ = 0.8

$\beta = \pi - \alpha - \gamma = \pi - 2.7$

Fig. 3.8.30

SECTION 3.9

(6)   The last step in computing $\frac{\sin x}{\cos x}$ is division. Therefore, we compute the derivative by first using the quotient rule:

$$\frac{d}{dx}\left[\frac{\sin x}{\cos x}\right] = \frac{(\cos x)\frac{d}{dx}\sin x - (\sin x)\frac{d}{dx}\cos x}{\cos^2 x} = \frac{\cos^2 x + \sin^2 x}{\cos^2 x} = \frac{1}{\cos^2 x} \; .$$

(9)   To compute $w\cos(w^2)$ we first compute w^2, then the cosine, and then the product. Therefore, we compute the derivative by first applying the product rule, then rule (18) for differentiating cosines of functions, and finally the rules for differentiating w and w^2:

$$\frac{d}{dw}[w\cos(w^2)] = w\frac{d}{dw}\cos(w^2) + \cos(w^2)\frac{d}{dw}(w) = w[-\sin(w^2)\frac{d}{dw}w^2] + \cos(w^2)\frac{d}{dw}(w)$$

$$= -w\sin(w^2)(2w) + \cos(w^2) = -2w^2\sin(w^2) + \cos(w^2).$$

(16)   If x is one of the (positive) acute angles in the triangle $(0 < x < \frac{\pi}{2})$ as in Fig. 3.9.16, then the legs of the triangle are of lengths $b = 6\cos x$ and $h = 6\sin x$. The area of the triangle is $A = \frac{1}{2}bh = 18(\cos x)(\sin x)$ and its rate of change with respect to x is

$$\frac{dA}{dx} = \frac{d}{dx}[18(\cos x)(\sin x)] = 18(\cos x)\frac{d}{dx}\sin x + 18(\sin x)\frac{d}{dx}\cos x$$

$$= 18(\cos^2 x - \sin^2 x).$$

Fig. 3.9.16

6

$h = 6\sin x$

x

$b = 6\cos x$

SECTION 4.1

(1) Set $f(x) = x^2 - 4x + 5$. Then $f'(x) = 2x - 4$ is zero at $x = 2$, which is the one critical point of $f(x)$. At $x = 0$ the derivative $f'(0) = -4$ is negative, so the derivative is negative and the function is decreasing for all $x < 2$. At $x = 3$ the derivative $f'(3) = 2(3) - 4 = 2$ is positive, so the derivative is positive and the function is increasing for all $x > 2$. In sketching the graph (Fig. 4.1.1) we plot the points in the following table, which includes the point at the critical point and points on either side of it.

x	0	2	4
$y = x^2 - 4x + 5$	5	1	5

(9) The derivative is $\frac{d}{dx}(\cos x - \sin x) = -\sin x - \cos x$ and has the value $-\sin(\frac{\pi}{6}) - \cos(\frac{\pi}{6}) = -\frac{1}{2} - \frac{1}{2}\sqrt{3}$ at $x = \frac{\pi}{6}$. The derivative is negative, so the function is decreasing at $x = \frac{\pi}{6}$.

(15) We write $\frac{1}{\sqrt{5 - x^2}} = (5 - x^2)^{-1/2}$ and use the rule for differentiating a power of a function: $\frac{d}{dx}(5 - x^2)^{-1/2} = -\frac{1}{2}(5 - x^2)^{-3/2}\frac{d}{dx}(5 - x^2) = -\frac{1}{2}(5 - x^2)^{-3/2}(-2x) = x(5 - x^2)^{-3/2}$. At $x = 1$ the derivative has the value $(1)(5 - 1^2)^{-3/2} = \frac{1}{4^{3/2}} = \frac{1}{8}$. The derivative is positive, so the function is increasing at $x = 1$.

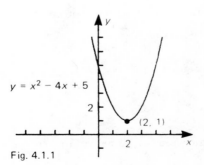

$y = x^2 - 4x + 5$

$(2, 1)$

Fig. 4.1.1

SECTION 4.2

(4) The last step in computing a value of $\dfrac{1}{t^2 + 1} = (t^2 + 1)^{-1}$ is the computation of the -1 power. Accordingly, we differentiate the -1 power first, using the rule for differentiating powers of functions:

(*) $\quad \dfrac{d}{dt}(t^2 + 1)^{-1} = (-1)(t^2 + 1)^{-2} \dfrac{d}{dt}(t^2 + 1) = (-1)(t^2 + 1)^{-2}(2t) = -2t(t^2 + 1)^{-2}.$

The last step in computing the first derivative (*) is the taking of the product. Hence, the first step in computing the second derivative requires the **product** rule:

$$\dfrac{d^2}{dt^2}(t^2 + 1)^{-1} = \dfrac{d}{dt}[-2t(t^2 + 1)^{-2}] = [\dfrac{d}{dt}(-2t)](t^2 + 1)^{-2} + [-2t]\dfrac{d}{dt}(t^2 + 1)^{-2}$$

$$= -2(t^2 + 1)^{-2} - 2t(-2)(t^2 + 1)^{-3}\dfrac{d}{dt}(t^2 + 1)$$

$$= -2(t^2 + 1)^{-2} + 4t(t^2 + 1)^{-3}(2t) = -2(t^2 + 1)^{-2} + 8t^2(t^2 + 1)^{-3}$$

$$= \dfrac{-2}{(t^2 + 1)^2} + \dfrac{8t^2}{(t^2 + 1)^3} = \dfrac{-2(t^2 + 1) + 8t^2}{(t^2 + 1)^3} = \dfrac{6t^2 - 2}{(t^2 + 1)^3}$$

(8) The last step in computing $\cos(x^3)$ is computing the cosine, so we first differentiate the cosine by using the rule for differentiating cosines of functions:

(*) $\quad \dfrac{d}{dx}\cos(x^3) = -\sin(x^3)\dfrac{d}{dx}(x^3) = -\sin(x^3)(3x^2) = -3x^2 \sin(x^3).$

The last step in computing the derivative (*) is finding the product, so the first step in finding the second derivative requires the product rule:

$$\dfrac{d^2}{dx^2}\cos(x^3) = \dfrac{d}{dx}[-3x^2 \sin(x^3)] = [\dfrac{d}{dx}(-3x^2)]\sin(x^3) + [-3x^2]\dfrac{d}{dx}\sin(x^3)$$

$$= -6x \sin(x^3) - 3x^2 \cos(x^3)\dfrac{d}{dx}(x^3)$$

$$= -6x \sin(x^3) - 3x^2 \cos(x^3)(3x^2) = -6x \sin(x^3) - 9x^4 \cos(x^3)$$

(12) The first derivative is $\quad$ (*) $\dfrac{d}{dx}(\dfrac{2}{3}x^3 - \dfrac{1}{5}x^5) = 2x^2 - x^4 = x^2(2 - x^2)$ and is zero at $x = 0, \sqrt{2},$ and $-\sqrt{2}.$ These three critical points of the function divide the x-axis into the four open intervals shown in Fig. 4.2.12a. The point $x = -2$ is in the interval $x < -\sqrt{2}$ and the derivative (*) at $x = -2$ equals $(-2)^2[2 - (-2)^2] = 4(2 - 4) = -8$ and is negative, so the function is decreasing for $x < -\sqrt{2}.$ The point $x = -1$ is in the interval

$-\sqrt{2} < x < 0$ and the derivative (*) at $x = -1$ is $(-1)^2[2 - (-1)^2] = 1$ and is positive, so the function is increasing for $-2 < x < 0$. The point $x = 1$ is in the interval $0 < x < \sqrt{2}$, and the derivative at $x = 1$ is $(1)^2[2 - (1)^2] = 2$, which is positive. Hence the function is increasing for $0 < x < \sqrt{2}$. The point $x = 2$ is in the interval $x > \sqrt{2}$ and the derivative at $x = 2$ is $(2)^2[2 - (2)^2] = 4(2 - 4) = -8$, which is negative. Hence the function is decreasing for $x > \sqrt{2}$. The results of the first-derivative test are summarized in Fig. 4.2.12b. The function has a local minimum at $x = -\sqrt{2}$ and a local maximum at $x = \sqrt{2}$.

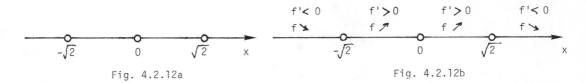

Fig. 4.2.12a   Fig. 4.2.12b

The second derivative is

$$(**) \qquad \frac{d}{dx}(2x^2 - x^4) = 4x - 4x^3 = 4x(1 - x^2)$$

and is zero at $x = 0, 1$ and -1. These points divide the x-axis into the open intervals $x < -1$, $-1 < x < 0$, $0 < x < 1$, and $x > 1$. The second derivative (**) has the value 24 at $x = -2$, the value $-\frac{3}{2}$ at $x = -\frac{1}{2}$, the value $\frac{3}{2}$ at $x = \frac{1}{2}$, and the value -24 at $x = 2$. Consequently, the second derivative is positive and the graph is concave up for $x < -1$ and $0 < x < 1$; the second derivative is negative and the graph is concave down for $-1 < x < 0$ and $x > 1$ (Fig. 4.2.12c). The graph has inflection points at $x = -1$ and $x = 1$. In sketching the graph (Fig. 4.2.12) we plot the points at the critical points and inflection points and at $x = \pm 2$, as given in the following table.

x	-2	$-\sqrt{2}$	-1	0	1	$\sqrt{2}$	2
$y = \frac{2}{3}x^3 - \frac{1}{5}x^5$	$\frac{16}{15}$	$-\frac{8}{15}\sqrt{2}$	$-\frac{7}{15}$	0	$\frac{7}{15}$	$\frac{8}{15}\sqrt{2}$	$-\frac{16}{15}$

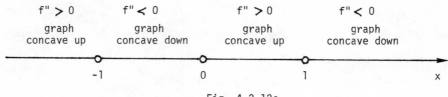

Fig. 4.2.12c

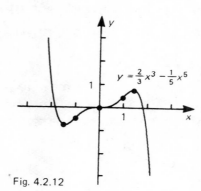

Fig. 4.2.12

(19) The first derivative $\frac{d}{dx}(x^3 + x - 5) = 3x^2 + 1$ is positive for all x, so the function has no critical points and is increasing for all x. The second derivative $\frac{d}{dx}(3x^2 + 1) = 6x$ is positive for x > 0 and negative for x < 0. Hence the graph is concave up for x > 0 and concave down for x < 0. It has an inflection point at x = 0. In sketching its graph (Fig. 4.2.19) we plot the inflection point and the points whose coordinates are given in the following table.

x	-2	-1	0	1	2
$y = x^3 + x - 5$	-15	-7	-5	-3	5

(22) The first derivative is $\frac{d}{dx}(x^4 - 4x^3 - 2x^2 + 12x) = 4x^3 - 12x^2 - 4x + 12$ and is zero at x = -1, so x = -1 is a criticial point as stated in the problem. The second derivative

$$\frac{d}{dx}(4x^3 - 12x^2 - 4x + 12) = 12x^2 - 24x - 4$$

has the value $12(-1)^2 - 24(-1) - 4 = 32$ at x = -1. Because the second derivative is positive, the function has a local minimum at x = -1.

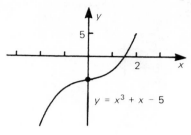

$y = x^3 + x - 5$

Fig. 4.2.19

SECTION 4.3

(2) The function $\dfrac{5}{x^2 + 1}$ has the same limits as $x \longrightarrow \pm\infty$ as the function $\dfrac{5}{x^2}$, so it tends to zero and the x-axis is a horizontal asymptote of its graph. Neither the numerator nor the denominator of $\dfrac{5}{x^2 + 1}$ is ever zero, so the graph does not intersect the x-axis nor does it have any vertical asymptotes; the function is positive for all x.

The derivative

$$(*) \quad \frac{d}{dx}\Big[\frac{5}{x^2 + 1}\Big] = 5\frac{d}{dx}(x^2 + 1)^{-1} = -5(x^2 + 1)^{-2}\frac{d}{dx}(x^2 + 1) = -5(x^2 + 1)^{-2}(2x) = \frac{-10x}{(x^2 + 1)^2}$$

is zero at $x = 0$, is negative for $x > 0$, and is positive for $x < 0$; the function is

increasing for $x < 0$ and decreasing for $x > 0$ (Fig. 4.3.2a).

The second derivative

$$(**) \quad \frac{d^2}{dx^2}\Big[\frac{5}{x^2 + 1}\Big] = \frac{d}{dx}[-10x(x^2 + 1)^{-2}] = \Big[\frac{d}{dx}(-10x)\Big](x^2 + 1)^{-2} + [-10x]\frac{d}{dx}(x^2 + 1)^{-2}$$

$$= -10(x^2 + 1)^{-2} - 10x(-2)(x^2 + 1)^{-3}\frac{d}{dx}(x^2 + 1)$$

$$= -10(x^2 + 1)^{-2} + 20x(x^2 + 1)^{-3}(2x) = \frac{-10}{(x^2 + 1)^2} + \frac{40x^2}{(x^2 + 1)^3}$$

$$= \frac{-10(x^2 + 1) + 40x^2}{(x^2 + 1)^3} = \frac{30x^2 - 10}{(x^2 + 1)^3} = \frac{10(3x^2 - 1)}{(x^2 + 1)^3}$$

is zero at $x = \pm\dfrac{1}{\sqrt{3}}$. It is positive at $x = \pm 1$ and negative at $x = 0$, so it is positive and the graph is concave up for $x < -\dfrac{1}{\sqrt{3}}$ and for $x > \dfrac{1}{\sqrt{3}}$; it is negative and the graph is concave down for $-\dfrac{1}{\sqrt{3}} < x < \dfrac{1}{\sqrt{3}}$ (Fig. 4.3.2b). In sketching the graph (Fig. 4.3.2) we plot the points at the critical point, $x = 0$, the inflection points, and the points at $x = \pm 2$.

x	0	$\pm \dfrac{1}{\sqrt{3}}$	± 2
$y = \dfrac{5}{x^2 + 1}$	5	$\dfrac{15}{4}$	1

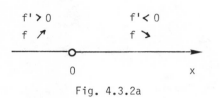

$f' > 0$

$f \nearrow$

$f' < 0$

$f \searrow$

Fig. 4.3.2a

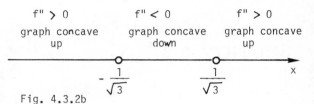

$f'' > 0$

graph concave up

$f'' < 0$

graph concave down

$f'' > 0$

graph concave up

$-\dfrac{1}{\sqrt{3}}$ $\dfrac{1}{\sqrt{3}}$

Fig. 4.3.2b

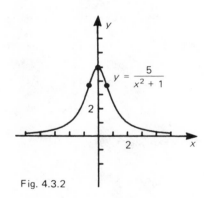

$y = \dfrac{5}{x^2 + 1}$

Fig. 4.3.2

(10) We combine the terms into   one   fraction : $\dfrac{1}{x} - \dfrac{1}{x - 1} = \dfrac{(x - 1) - x}{x(x - 1)} = \dfrac{-1}{x(x - 1)}$

The functions limits as $x \longrightarrow \pm\infty$ are both 0 because it has the same limits as $\dfrac{-1}{x^2}$.

The x-axis is a horizontal asymptote of the graph. The numerator -1 of $\dfrac{-1}{x(x - 1)}$ is never

zero, so the graph does not intersect the x-axis. The denominator $x(x - 1)$ is zero at $x = 0$

and $x = 1$ so the lines $x = 0$ (the y-axis) and $x = 1$ are horizontal asymptotes of the

graph. The function can change sign only at $x = 0$ and $x = 1$. Its value at $x = -1$ is

$\dfrac{-1}{-1(-1 - 1)} = -\dfrac{1}{2}$; its value at $x = \dfrac{1}{2}$ is $\dfrac{-1}{\frac{1}{2}(\frac{1}{2} - 1)} = 4$; and its value at $x = 2$ is

$\dfrac{-1}{2(2 - 1)} = -\dfrac{1}{2}$. Therefore the function is negative for $x < 0$, positive for $0 < x < 1$, and negative for $x > 1$ (Fig. 4.3.10a). The graph goes down on the left of the y-axis and on the right of the line $x = 1$; it goes up on the right of the y-axis and on the left of the line $x = 1$.

To compute the derivatives we use the original formula for the function. The first derivative is

$$(*)\quad \frac{d}{dx}(\frac{1}{x} - \frac{1}{x-1}) = \frac{d}{dx}[x^{-1} - (x-1)^{-1}] = -x^{-2} - (-1)(x-1)^{-2}\frac{d}{dx}(x-1) = -x^{-2} + (x-1)^{-2}$$

$$= -\frac{1}{x^2} + \frac{1}{(x-1)^2} = \frac{-(x-1)^2 + x^2}{x^2(x-1)^2} = \frac{-(x^2 - 2x + 1) + x^2}{x^2(x-1)^2} = \frac{2x-1}{x^2(x-1)^2}$$

and can change sign at $x = \frac{1}{2}$ where its numerator is zero. It does not change sign at $x = 0$ or at $x = 1$ where the denominator is zero because x^2 does not change sign at $x = 0$ and $(x-1)^2$ does not change sign at $x = 1$. (The squares are always nonnegative.) The derivative $(*)$ is negative at $x = 0$ and positive at $x = 1$, so it is negative and the function is decreasing for $x < \frac{1}{2}$; it is positive and the function is increasing for $x > \frac{1}{2}$ (Fig. 4.3.10b). In making the sketch (Fig. 4.3.10) we plot the points at the critical point and at the points $x = -1$ and $x = 2$ which we considered in obtaining Fig. 4.3.10a.

x	$\frac{1}{2}$	-1	2
$y = \frac{1}{x} - \frac{1}{x-1}$	4	$-\frac{1}{2}$	$-\frac{1}{2}$

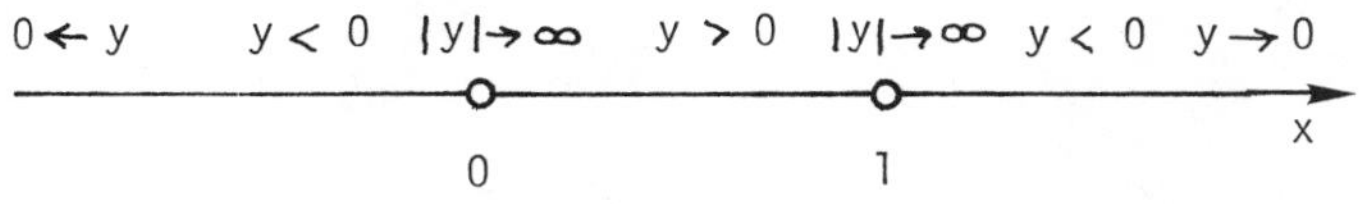

$0 \leftarrow y \quad y < 0 \; |y| \to \infty \quad y > 0 \; |y| \to \infty \; y < 0 \; y \to 0$

Fig. 4.3.10a

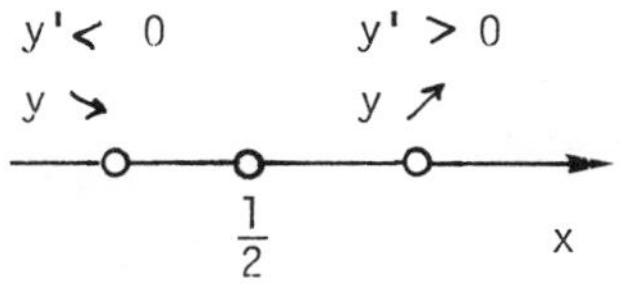

$y' < 0 \qquad y' > 0$

$y \searrow \qquad y \nearrow$

Fig. 4.3.10b

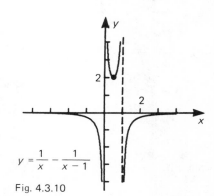

$y = \frac{1}{x} - \frac{1}{x-1}$

Fig. 4.3.10

SECTION 4.4

(4) The function $y = x^{3/4} - 8$ is defined and continuous for $x \geq 0$ and has the derivative

$\frac{dy}{dx} = \frac{3}{4} x^{-1/4}$ **and the second** derivative $\frac{d^2y}{dx^2} = -\frac{3}{16} x^{-5/4}$ for $x > 0$. The derivative is

positive and the second derivative is negative, so the function is increasing and its graph

is concave down for all $x > 0$. (We do not consider the graph to have a vertical tangent line

at $x = 0$ even though $\frac{dy}{dx}$ tends to ∞ as $x \longrightarrow 0^+$ because the function is not

defined for $x < 0$.) In making the sketch (Fig. 4.4.4) we plot the points whose coordinates

are given in the following table.

x	0	1	16
$y = x^{3/4} - 8$	-8	-7	0

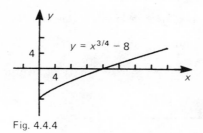

Fig. 4.4.4

(7) The function $y = \sqrt{9 + x^2}$ is defined and continuous **and has** derivatives for all x.

The first derivative $\frac{d}{dx} (9 + x^2)^{1/2} = \frac{1}{2}(9 + x^2)^{-1/2} \frac{d}{dx}(9 + x^2) = \frac{1}{2}(9 + x^2)^{-1/2} (2x) =$

$= \frac{x}{\sqrt{9 + x^2}}$ is zero at $x = 0$. It is negative and the function is decreasing for

$x < 0$; it is positive and the function is increasing for $x > 0$. The second derivative

$\frac{d^2}{dx^2}(9 + x^2)^{1/2} = \frac{d}{dx}[x(9 + x^2)^{-1/2}] = [\frac{d}{dx} x](9 + x^2)^{-1/2} + x \frac{d}{dx}(9 + x^2)^{-1/2}$

$= (9 + x^2)^{-1/2} + x(-\frac{1}{2})(9 + x^2)^{-3/2} \frac{d}{dx}(9 + x^2)$

$= (9 + x^2)^{-1/2} - \frac{1}{2} x(9 + x^2)^{-3/2} (2x) = (9 + x^2)^{-1/2} - x^2(9 + x^2)^{-3/2}$

$= \frac{(9 + x^2) - x^2}{(9 + x^2)^{3/2}} = \frac{9}{(9 + x^2)^{3/2}}$

is positive and the graph is concave up for all x. We plot the points in the following

table (Fig. 4.4.7).

x	0	4	-4
$y = \sqrt{9 + x^2}$	3	5	5

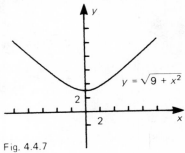

Fig. 4.4.7

(12) We rewrite the definition of the function in the form

$$y = (|x| - 2)^2 = \begin{cases} (x - 2)^2 & \text{for} \quad x > 0 \\ (-x - 2)^2 & \text{for} \quad x < 0. \end{cases}$$

For $x > 0$ it has the derivative $\frac{dy}{dx} = \frac{d}{dx}(x - 2)^2 = 2(x - 2)\frac{d}{dx}(x - 2) = 2(x - 2)$, which

is negative for $0 < x < 2$ and positive for $x > 2$. For $x < 0$ the derivative is

$\frac{dy}{dx} = \frac{d}{dx}(-x - 2)^2 = 2(-x - 2)\frac{d}{dx}(-x - 2) = -2(-x - 2) = 2(x + 2)$ and is negative for $x < -2$,

positive for $-2 < x < 0$ (Fig. 4.4.12a). The second derivative is $\frac{d}{dx}[2(x - 2)] = 2$ for

$x > 0$ and is $\frac{d}{dx}[2(x + 2)] = 2$ for $x < 0$, so the graph is concave up for all $x \neq 0$.

In sketching the graph (Fig. 4.4.12), we plot the following points.

x	0	± 2	± 5
$y = (|x| - 2)^2$	4	0	9

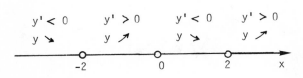

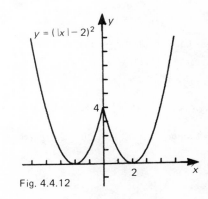

Fig. 4.4.12a

$y = (|x| - 2)^2$

Fig. 4.4.12

SECTION 4.5

(2) Write g for g(x) and differentiate both sides of the equation $xg^3 + xg = 6$ with respect to x:

$$\frac{d}{dx}(xg^3) + \frac{d}{dx}(xg) = \frac{d}{dx}(6)$$

$$(\frac{d}{dx} x)g^3 + x \frac{d}{dx} g^3 + (\frac{d}{dx} x)g + x \frac{d}{dx} g = 0$$

$$g^3 + 3xg^2 \frac{dg}{dx} + g + x \frac{dg}{dx} = 0.$$

Setting x = 3 and g = 1 yields $1^3 + 3(3)(1)^2 \frac{dg}{dx} + 1 + 3 \frac{dg}{dx} = 0$ or

$1 + 9 \frac{dg}{dx} + 1 + 3 \frac{dg}{dx} = 0.$ We solve for $\frac{dg}{dx} = g'(3) = -\frac{1}{6}$.

(8)   We write $(x + y)^{1/2}$ for $\sqrt{x + y}$ and differentiate the equation

$\sqrt{x + y}$ + xy = 17   with respect to x, considering y as a function of x:

$$\frac{d}{dx}(x + y)^{1/2} + \frac{d}{dx}(xy) = \frac{d}{dx}(17)$$

$$\frac{1}{2}(x + y)^{-1/2} \frac{d}{dx}(x + y) + (\frac{d}{dx} x)y + x(\frac{d}{dx} y) = 0$$

$$\frac{1}{2}(x + y)^{-1/2}(1 + \frac{dy}{dx}) + y + x \frac{dy}{dx} = 0$$

$$\frac{1 + \frac{dy}{dx}}{2\sqrt{x + y}} + y + x\frac{dy}{dx} = 0$$

We set x = 2 and y = 7 to obtain

$$\frac{1 + \frac{dy}{dx}}{2(3)} + 7 + 2 \frac{dy}{dx} = 0$$

$$1 + \frac{dy}{dx} + 42 + 12 \frac{dy}{dx} = 0$$

showing that $\frac{dy}{dx} = y'(2) = -\frac{43}{6}$.

(15) We consider y = y(x) to be defined implicitly by the equation $x = \frac{\sin y}{\cos y}$ and the condition y(0) = 0. Then the graph of y(x) is a portion of the curve $x = \frac{\sin y}{\cos y}$ containing the point (0,0) and the slope of the tangent line at (0,0) is the derivative $\frac{dy}{dx}(0)$.

To find the derivative, we differentiate the equation $x = \dfrac{\sin y}{\cos y}$ with respect to x:

$$\frac{d}{dx}(x) = \frac{d}{dx}\left[\frac{\sin y}{\cos y}\right]$$

$$1 = \frac{\cos y[\frac{d}{dx}\sin y] - \sin y[\frac{d}{dx}\cos y]}{\cos^2 y}$$

$$1 = \frac{\cos y[\cos y]\frac{dy}{dx} - \sin y[-\sin y]\frac{dy}{dx}}{\cos^2 y}$$

$$1 = \left[\frac{\cos^2 y + \sin^2 y}{\cos^2 y}\right]\frac{dy}{dx} \quad \text{or} \quad 1 = \left[\frac{1}{\cos^2 y}\right]\frac{dy}{dx}$$

We set $y = 0$ and use the fact that $\cos(0) = 1$ to obtain $1 = \dfrac{dy}{dx}$. (Since x does not appear in the differentiated expression, we do not need to use its value, $x = 0$, here.) The tangent line has slope 1 and passes through $(0,0)$, so its equation is $y = x$.

(22a) We write $y^{2/3} = 1 - x^{2/3}$. Then we cube both sides to obtain $y^2 = (1 - x^{2/3})^3$. Finally, we take the square root to obtain $y = \pm (1 - x^{2/3})^{3/2}$.

(22b) Differentiating $x^{2/3} + y^{2/3} = 1$ with respect to x with y a function of x gives

$$\frac{d}{dx}x^{2/3} + \frac{d}{dx}y^{2/3} = \frac{d}{dx}(1)$$

$$\frac{2}{3}x^{-1/3} + \frac{2}{3}y^{-1/3}\frac{dy}{dx} = 0$$

$$\frac{1}{x^{1/3}} + \frac{1}{y^{1/3}}\frac{dy}{dx} = 0$$

$$\frac{dy}{dx} = -\frac{y^{1/3}}{x^{1/3}}$$

We substitute the formulas $y = \pm (1 - x^{2/3})^{3/2}$ from Exercise 22a to obtain

$$\frac{dy}{dx} = \mp \frac{(1 - x^{2/3})^{1/2}}{x^{1/3}} .$$

(22c) $\dfrac{dy}{dx} = \pm \dfrac{d}{dx}(1 - x^{2/3})^{3/2} = \pm \dfrac{3}{2}(1 - x^{2/3})^{1/2}\dfrac{d}{dx}(1 - x^{2/3}) = \pm \dfrac{3}{2}(1 - x^{2/3})^{1/2}\left(-\dfrac{2}{3}x^{-1/3}\right)$

$\qquad = \mp (1 - x^{2/3})^{1/2}x^{-1/3} = \mp \dfrac{(1 - x^{2/3})^{1/2}}{x^{1/3}}$

(24) For x in the domain of the differentiable function $y = y(x)$, we
have $x^2 - 5xy + y^2 = 4$ and hence

$$\frac{d}{dx}(x^2) - 5\frac{d}{dx}(xy) + \frac{d}{dx}(y^2) = \frac{d}{dx}(4)$$

$$2x - 5[(\frac{d}{dx}x)y + x\frac{dy}{dx}] + 2y\frac{dy}{dx} = 0$$

$$2x - 5y - 5x\frac{dy}{dx} + 2y\frac{dy}{dx} = 0$$

$$(2y - 5x)\frac{dy}{dx} = 5y - 2x$$

$$\frac{dy}{dx} = \frac{5y - 2x}{2y - 5x} \ .$$

SECTION 4.6

(5) To solve $y = 1 + (x + 4)^{3/4}$ for x, we first write the equation in the form
$(x + 4)^{3/4} = y - 1$. Taking the fourth power of each side yields $(x + 4)^3 = (y - 1)^4$, and
then taking cube roots gives $x + 4 = (y - 1)^{4/3}$. Finally, we subtract 4 from each side
to obtain the result $x = (y - 1)^{4/3} - 4$. (We do not obtain a $\pm$ when we take cube roots
because each real number has only one cube root.)

(16) Cubing both sides of the equation $y = (2x - 3)^{2/3}$ gives
$y^3 = (2x - 3)^2$. Here we must have $y^3 \geq 0$, which means $y \geq 0$. Taking square
roots of both sides yields $y^{3/2} = \pm(2x - 3)$ and then $2x - 3 = \pm y^{3/2}$
or $x = \pm\frac{1}{2}y^{3/2} + \frac{3}{2}$.

(18) Because we want x to be the variable of the inverse function, we first
interchange x and y in the equation $y = (x - 2)^{-1/2}$. This gives
$x = (y - 2)^{-1/2}$, from which we obtain $x^{-2} = y - 2$ and then $y = 2 + x^{-2}$.

SECTION 4.7

(5) Introduce xy-axes with the x-axis along the east-west road, the y-axis along the
north-south road, with the positive y-axis pointing north, and with the scales measured
in miles. Let $x = x(t)$ be the coordinate of the bicycle on the east-west road, $y = y(t)$
be the coordinate of the bicycle on the north-south road, and $D = D(t)$ the distance

between them at time t (hours). The functions are related by the equation $D(t)^2 = x(t)^2 + y(t)^2$. Differentiating with respect to t yields

$$\frac{d}{dt} D^2 = \frac{d}{dt} x^2 + \frac{d}{dt} y^2$$

$$2D \frac{dD}{dt} = 2x \frac{dx}{dt} + 2y \frac{dy}{dt}$$

$$(*) \quad D \frac{dD}{dt} = x \frac{dx}{dt} + y \frac{dy}{dt} .$$

At the time in question the first bicycle is 4 miles east of the intersection and is traveling west at 9 miles/hour, so $x = 4$ and $\frac{dx}{dt} = -9$. The second bicylce is 3 miles south of the intersection and is traveling south at 10 miles/hour, so $y = -3$ and $\frac{dy}{dt} = -10$. At that moment $D = \sqrt{x^2 + y^2} = \sqrt{4^2 + (-3)^2} = \sqrt{25} = 5$, so equation (*) gives

$$5 \frac{dD}{dt} = (4)(-9) + (-3)(-10)$$

$$5 \frac{dD}{dt} = -36 + 30$$

which shows that $\frac{dD}{dt} = -\frac{6}{5}$ miles/hour and the distance is decreasing at the rate of $\frac{6}{5}$ miles per hour.

(8) If D(t) (feet) is the man's distance to the lamppost and s(t) (feet) the length of his shadow (Fig. 4.7.8), then because the triangles PQS and PRT are similar, we have $\frac{\overline{PQ}}{\overline{QS}} = \frac{\overline{PR}}{\overline{RT}}$. Since $\overline{PQ} = s(t)$, $\overline{QS} = 7$, $\overline{PR} = s(t) + D(t)$, and $\overline{RT} = 28$, we obtain $\frac{s(t)}{7} = \frac{s(t) + D(t)}{28}$. Solving for s(t) gives $s(t) = \frac{1}{3} D(t)$, and then differentiating yields the relation $\frac{ds}{dt} = \frac{1}{3} \frac{dD}{dt}$. Since the man is walking toward the post at the rate of 4 feet/second, we have $\frac{dD}{dt} = -4$, so that $\frac{ds}{dt} = -\frac{4}{3}$ and the shadow is shrinking at the rate of $\frac{4}{3}$ feet/second.

(15a) We let $s = s(t)$ denote the length of the sides of the equilateral triangle (Fig. 4.7.15). Half of the equilateral triangle is a right triangle of base $\frac{1}{2} s$ and hypotenuse s. By the Pythagorean Theorem its height is $\sqrt{s^2 - (\frac{1}{2} s)^2} = s\sqrt{\frac{3}{4}} = \frac{s\sqrt{3}}{2}$. The area of the equilateral triangle is one half its base times its height, which is $A = \frac{1}{2}(s)(\frac{s\sqrt{3}}{2}) = \frac{\sqrt{3}}{4} s^2$. Hence, $\frac{dA}{dt} = \frac{\sqrt{3}}{4} \frac{d}{dt} s^2 = \frac{\sqrt{3}}{4} (2s \frac{ds}{dt}) = \frac{\sqrt{3}}{2} s \frac{ds}{dt}$. At the moment in question, $s = 10$ and $\frac{ds}{dt} = 5$, so $\frac{dA}{dt} = \frac{\sqrt{3}}{2}(10)(5) = 25\sqrt{3}$ inches per second.

(15b) The perimeter of the equilateral triangle in Fig. 4.7.15 is P = 3s. Hence, $\frac{dP}{dt} = 3\frac{ds}{dt}$, and when s is increasing at the rate of 5 inches per second, P is increasing at the rate of 15 inches per second.

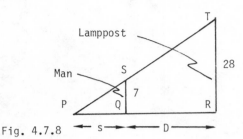

Fig. 4.7.8

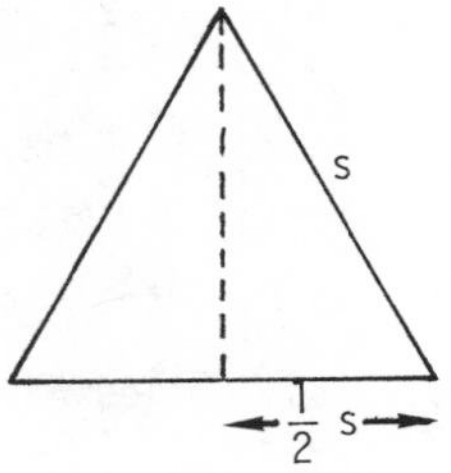

Fig. 4.7.15

(19a) From Figure 4.47 (shown below) we see that $v \approx 5$ feet/second at t = 8. The equation $\frac{1}{2}p + v^2 = 50$ gives $p = 100 - 2v^2 \approx 100 - 2(5)^2 = 50$ pounds/square inch.

(19b) We draw a plausible tangent line to the graph of v(t) at t = 8 as in Figure 4.47 (shown below) and note that its slope is approximately $\frac{1}{2}$. Hence $\frac{dv}{dt}(8) \approx \frac{1}{2}$ feet/second^2. If we differentiate the equation $\frac{1}{2}p + v^2 = 50$ with respect to t, we obtain

$$\frac{1}{2}\frac{dp}{dt} + \frac{d}{dt}v^2 = \frac{d}{dt}(50)$$

$$\frac{1}{2}\frac{dp}{dt} + 2v\frac{dv}{dt} = 0 \qquad \text{or} \qquad \frac{dp}{dt} = -4v\frac{dv}{dt}.$$

Setting v = 5 and $\frac{dv}{dt} = \frac{1}{2}$ gives the approximate value $\frac{dp}{dt} \approx -4(5)(\frac{1}{2}) = -10$ pounds per square inch per second for the rate of change of the pressure at time t = 8.

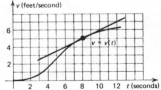

Figure 4.47

SECTION 4.8

(10) Because the square has the largest area of all rectangles with the same perimeter, the box with square ends will have the maximum volume among all boxes with the same length and girth. (The girth is the perimeter of the end.) We let L (inches) be the length of

the box and s (inches) be the width of its square ends. Then its volume is $V = Ls^2$ and

its girth is 4s. The box of maximum volume will have length plus girth equal to 84 inches,

so we will have $L + 4s = 84$ or $L = 84 - 4s$. The volume is then $V = Ls^2 = (84 - 4s)s^2 =$

$= 84s^2 - 4s^3$. Since the girth cannot be negative nor greater than 84, we consider s in

the interval $0 \le s \le 21$. The derivative $\frac{dV}{ds} = \frac{d}{ds}(84s^2 - 4s^3) = 168s - 12s^2 = 12s(14 - s)$

is zero at $s = 0$ and $s = 14$. The maximum of V for $0 \le s \le 21$ occurs either at $s = 0$,

$s = 14$, or $s = 21$. The volume is zero for $s = 0$ and $s = 21$, so the maximum volume occurs

for $s = 14$, for which $L = 84 - 4(14) = 28$. The length of the box should be twice the width

of its square ends.

(17) Let L (inches) be the length of the box and w (inches) the width of its square ends

(Fig. 4.8.17). Then the ends each have area w^2; the bottom, **front, and** back each have area

wL. The volume is $V = [\text{Area of base}][\text{Height}] = w^2L$ and the box requires

$A = 2[\text{Area of each end}] + [\text{Area of bottom}] + [\text{Area of front}] + [\text{Area of back}] = 2w^2 + 3wL$

square inches of material. Since the boy has 600 square inches of material, we will have

$2w^2 + 3wL = 600$ or $L = \frac{600 - 2w^2}{3w}$. The volume is given as a function of w by the formula

$V = [\frac{600 - 2w^2}{3w}]w^2 = 200w - \frac{2}{3}w^3$. Because the width of the box can be no more than 11 inches

we want the maximum of V for $0 \le w \le 11$. The derivative $\frac{dV}{dw} = 200 - 2w^2 = 2(100 - w^2)$ is

zero at $w = \pm 10$, the maximum for $0 \le w \le 11$ occurs either at $w = 0$, $w = 10$, or $w = 11$.

The volume $V = 2w(100 - \frac{1}{3}w^2)$ is zero for $w = 0$, is $\frac{4000}{3}$ for $w = 10$, and is $\frac{3938}{3}$ for

$w = 11$. The volume is a maximum for $w = 10$, for which $L = \frac{600 - 2(10)^2}{3(10)} = \frac{40}{3} = 13\frac{1}{3}$.

(22) Let x be the distance from the point on the fence to which the child runs to the point

opposite the point P (see Figure 4.53 in the text). Then the distance to the point opposite

the point Q is 25 - x and the total distance traveled by the child is

$D = \sqrt{x^2 + (20)^2} + \sqrt{(25 - x)^2 + (30)^2}$. The derivative

$$\frac{dD}{dx} = \frac{d}{dx}(x^2 + 400)^{1/2} + \frac{d}{dx}[(25 - x)^2 + 900]^{1/2}$$

$$= \frac{1}{2}(x^2 + 400)^{-1/2}\frac{d}{dx}(x^2 + 400) + \frac{1}{2}[(25 - x)^2 + 900)]^{-1/2}\frac{d}{dx}[(25 - x)^2 + 900]$$

$$= \frac{1}{2}(x^2 + 400)^{-1/2}(2x) + \frac{1}{2}[(25 - x)^2 + 900]^{-1/2}[2(25 - x)\frac{d}{dx}(25 - x)]$$

$$= \frac{x}{\sqrt{x^2 + 400}} - \frac{25 - x}{\sqrt{(25 - x)^2 + 900}}$$

is zero for x such that

$$\frac{x}{\sqrt{x^2 + 400}} = \frac{25 - x}{\sqrt{(25 - x)^2 + 900}}$$

or

$$\frac{x^2}{x^2 + 400} = \frac{(25 - x)^2}{(25 - x)^2 + 900} \, .$$

We multiply the last equation by $(x^2 + 400)[(25 - x)^2 + 900]$ to obtain

$$x^2(25 - x)^2 + 900x^2 = x^2(25 - x)^2 + 400(25 - x)^2.$$

We subtract $x^2(25 - x)^2$ from each side and take square roots to obtain $30x = 20(25 - x)$.

(We do not have to include any $\pm$ signs when we take square roots because we know that

$0 \le x \le 25$ so that x and 25 - x are both nonnegative.) Solving the last equation yields

x = 10 feet.

(24) From Exercise 23 (Snell's law) we have $\frac{\sin \Theta}{\sin \Psi} = \frac{v_a}{v_w}$. We are given $\frac{v_a}{v_w} = 1.33$ and

that $\Theta = \frac{1}{4}\pi$ and hence $\sin \Theta = \frac{1}{\sqrt{2}}$ and $\sin \Psi = \frac{\sin \Theta}{1.33} = \frac{1}{1.33\sqrt{2}} \approx 0.531$. The

reference table gives the approximate value $\sin(0.56) \approx 0.5312$, so Ψ is approximately

0.56 radians.

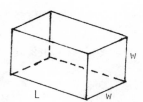

Fig. 4.8.17   L   W

(26)   Set $f(x) = x + 4x^{-1}$. Then $f'(x) = \frac{d}{dx}(x + 4x^{-1}) = 1 - 4x^{-2}$

$= 1 - \frac{4}{x^2} = \frac{x^2 - 4}{x^2}$ is zero at $x = \pm 2$. The one critical point of f in the

interval $1 \le x \le 3$ is at x = 2, so the maximum and minimum of f for

$1 \le x \le 3$ must occur at x = 1, x = 2, or x = 3. We have $f(1) = 1 + 4(1)^{-1} = 5$,

$f(2) = 2 + 4(2)^{-2} = 4$,   and $f(3) = 3 + 4(3)^{-2} = \frac{13}{3}$. The maximum is 5 at

x = 1 and the minimum is 4 at x = 2.

SECTION 4.9

(3) The derivative of $\dfrac{2x^{1/2}}{x + 1}$ is $\dfrac{(x + 1)x^{-1/2} - 2x^{1/2}}{(x + 1)^2} = \dfrac{x + 1 - 2x}{x^{1/2}(x + 1)^2} = \dfrac{1 - x}{x^{1/2}(x + 1)^2}$

and is zero at $x = 1$. The derivative is positive for $0 < x < 1$ and negative for $x > 1$,

so the function has a maximum at $x = 1$, where its value is $\dfrac{2(1)^{1/2}}{1 + 1} = 1$. The function is

0 at $x = 0$ and positive for all $x > 0$, so its minimum value for $x \geq 0$ is 0.

(9) If the length of the barrel is L (feet) and its radius is r (feet), then its bung

stick measurement M is the length of the hypotenuse of a right triangle with legs of

lengths $\frac{1}{2} L$ and $2r$ (Fig. 4.9.9). Hence, $M^2 = (\frac{1}{2} L)^2 + (2r)^2 = \frac{1}{4} L^2 + 4r^2$. The volume of

the barrel is the area of its base times its height or $V = \pi r^2 L$. For the volume to be

8π, we must have $\pi r^2 L = 8\pi$ or $L = \dfrac{8}{r^2}$. With this formula for L, the formula

for M^2 reads $M^2 = 16r^{-4} + 4r^2$. The derivative of M^2 with respect to r is

$-64r^{-5} + 8r = \dfrac{8}{r^5}(-8 + r^6)$. It is negative for $0 < r < 8^{1/6}$, zero for $r = 8^{1/6}$, and

positive for $r > r^{1/6}$. The minimum bungstick measurement is obtained for $r = 8^{1/6}$ feet,

for which $L = 8r^{-2} = 8^{2/3}$ feet.

(16) The radius of the circular piece of paper is 4 inches and its circumference is

8π. An angle of x radians at the center of the circle subtends an arc of length $4x$

on the circle, so the base of the cone has circumference $8\pi - 4x$. The radius of the

base of the cone is, hence, $r = \dfrac{8\pi - 4x}{2\pi}$. The lateral height of the cone is 4, so its

vertical height is $h = \sqrt{16 - r^2}$ (Fig. 4.9.16) and its volume is $V = \frac{1}{3}\pi r^2 h$

$= \frac{1}{3}\pi r^2 \sqrt{16 - r^2}$. Because of the complexity of the expression for r in terms of x,

we will first find the r for which the volume is a maximum and then find the x. We have

$\dfrac{dV}{dr} = \frac{1}{3}\pi \dfrac{d}{dr}[r^2\sqrt{16 - r^2}] = \frac{1}{3}\pi [2r(16 - r^2)^{1/2} - r^3(16 - r^2)^{-1/2}] = \frac{1}{3}\pi\left[\dfrac{2r(16 - r^2) - r^3}{(16 - r^2)^{1/2}}\right]$

$= \frac{1}{3}\pi\left[\dfrac{32r - 3r^2}{(16 - r^2)^{1/2}}\right]$. This derivative is positive for $0 < r < \sqrt{\dfrac{32}{3}}$, zero for $r = \sqrt{\dfrac{32}{3}}$,

and negative for $r > \sqrt{\dfrac{32}{3}}$. The maximum volume occurs for $r = \sqrt{\dfrac{32}{3}}$. When we solve the

equation $r = \dfrac{8\pi - 4x}{2\pi}$ for x, we obtain $x = \frac{\pi}{2}(4 - r)$. Accordingly, the volume is maximized

with $x = \frac{\pi}{2}(4 - \sqrt{\dfrac{32}{3}}) = 2\pi(1 - \sqrt{\dfrac{2}{3}})$ radians.

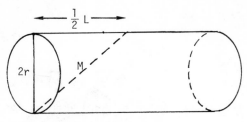

Fig. 4.9.9

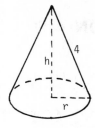

Fig. 4.9.16

(18) Let x (cents) be the fare charged by the railroad. For every cent the fare is less than 200¢ the number of passengers increases by 10, so the number of passengers on the train is N = 1200 + 10(200 - x) = 3200 - 10x. These passangers provide a revenue of $R = Nx = 3200x - 10x^2$. We have $\frac{dR}{dx} = 3200 - 20x$, which is positive for $0 \le x < 160$, is zero at x = 160, and is negative for x > 160. The revenue is maximized when the fare is 160 cents or $1.60.

(26) Let r (inches) be the radius of the base of the can and h (inches) be its height. The volume of the can is V = [Area of base][Height] = $\pi r^2 h$. The area of the top is πr^2, as is the area of the bottom. The lateral surface area is [Circumference][Height] = $2\pi rh$, so the material for the can costs

$$C = [2\pi r^2 \text{ square inches}][\frac{1}{10}\frac{cent}{square\ inch}] + [2\pi rh \text{ square inches}][\frac{1}{20}\frac{cents}{square\ inch}]$$

$$= \frac{1}{5}\pi r^2 + \frac{1}{10}\pi rh \quad \text{cents.}$$

For the volume to be 100 cubic inches we must have $\pi r^2 h = 100$ or $h = \frac{100}{\pi r^2}$. Consequently, the cost is $C = \frac{1}{5}\pi r^2 + \frac{1}{10}\pi r[\frac{100}{\pi r^2}] = \frac{1}{5}\pi r^2 + 10r^{-1}$. The derivative $\frac{dC}{dr} = \frac{2}{5}\pi r - 10r^{-2}$

$= \frac{2}{5}[\pi r - \frac{25}{r^2}] = \frac{2}{5r^2}(\pi r^3 - 25)$ is negative for $0 < r < (\frac{25}{\pi})^{1/3}$, is zero at $r = (\frac{25}{\pi})^{1/3}$,

and is positive for $r > (\frac{25}{\pi})^{1/3}$, so the cost is minimized by taking $r = (\frac{25}{\pi})^{1/3}$, for which

$h = \frac{100}{\pi r^2} = \frac{100}{\pi}(\frac{\pi}{25})^{2/3} = 4(\frac{25}{\pi})^{1/3}$.

(29)   The derivative $\frac{d}{dx}(x^3 + 1) = 3x^2$ is positive except at the one point x = 0 where it is zero. Therefore the function $x^3 + 1$ is increasing for all x.

Its maximum in the interval $-1 < x \le 2$ is its value $2^3 + 1 = 9$ at x = 2. It has no minimum in the interval because the interval does not include the left endpoint x = -1.

SECTION 4.10

(2) Set $y = x^{5/4}$. Then $\frac{dy}{dx} = \frac{5}{4} x^{1/4}$, and at $x = 16$ we have $y = (16)^{5/4} = 2^5 = 32$ and

$\frac{dy}{dx} = \frac{5}{4}(16)^{1/4} = \frac{5}{4}(2) = \frac{5}{2}$. The tangent line at $x = 16$ has the equation $y = 32 + \frac{5}{2}(x - 16)$

and for x near 16 we have $x^{5/4} \approx 32 + \frac{5}{2}(x - 16)$. For $x = 15.9$ we obtain

$(15.9)^{5/4} \approx 32 + \frac{5}{2}(15.9 - 16) = 32 + \frac{5}{2}(-\frac{1}{10}) = 31.75$. This approximation is less than the

actual value of $(15.9)^{5/4}$ because $y'' = \frac{5}{16} x^{-3/4}$ is positive for all $x > 0$ and the graph,

which is concave up, lies above its tangent lines.

(5) Set $y = (1 + x)^{-1}$. Then $\frac{dy}{dx} = -(1 + x)^{-2} \frac{d}{dx}(1 + x) = -(1 + x)^{-2}$ and at $x = 0$ we

have $y = 1$ and $\frac{dy}{dx} = -1$. The tangent line has the equation $y = 1 - x$ and, therefore, for

x near 0, we have $\frac{1}{1 + x} \approx 1 - x$. In particular $\frac{1}{1.03} = \frac{1}{1 + 0.03} \approx 1 - 0.03 = 0.97$.

This approximation is less than the actual value because $y'' = 2(1 + x)^{-3}$ is positive and

the graph is concave up and lies above its tangent lines for $x > -1$.

(12a) The curve $y = \frac{2}{x}$ has no vertical tangent lines, so we can study them all by taking

the derivative $\frac{dy}{dx} = \frac{d}{dx}(2x^{-1}) = -2x^{-2} = \frac{-2}{x^2}$. We view $\frac{dy}{dx}$ as the ratio of differentials on

the tangent line and multiply both sides of the last equation by x^2 and dx to obtain the

equation $x^2 dy = -2 dx$ relating the differe tials on the tangent line at x. At $x = 2$,

we have $4dy = -2 dx$ or $dx + 2 dy = 0$.

(12b) The formula $x^2 dy = -2\,dx$ from Exercise 12a gives $4\,dy = -2\,dx$ or $dx + 2\,dy = 0$

at $x = -2$.

(17) Set $f(x) = (11 + x^2)^{1/2}$. Then $\frac{df}{dx} = \frac{d}{dx}(11 + x^2)^{1/2}$

$= \frac{1}{2}(11 + x^2)^{-1/2} \frac{d}{dx}(11 + x^2) = \frac{1}{2}(11 + x^2)^{-1/2}(2x) = x(11 + x^2)^{-1/2}$. At $x = 5$

the derivative is

$$\frac{df}{dx} = 5(11 + 5^2)^{-1/2} = 5(36)^{-1/2} = \frac{5}{6}$$

and $df = \frac{5}{6} dx$. An error of dx with $|dx| \leq 0.005$ in the measurement of x

would yield the possible error of approximately $|df| = \frac{5}{6}|dx| \leq \frac{5}{6}(0.005) \approx 0.00417$.

(20) Differentiating the equation $x^3 + y^3 = 1$ with respect to x with $y = y(x)$

gives

$$\frac{d}{dx}(x^3) + \frac{d}{dx}(y^3) = \frac{d}{dx}(1) \qquad \text{or} \quad 3x^2 + 3y^2 \frac{dy}{dx} = 0,$$

Dividing by 3 and multiplying by dx yields $x^2 dx + y^2 dy = 0$.

SECTION 4.11

(4) Set $f(x) = \sin x + \cos x$ so that $f'(x) = \cos x - \sin x$ and formula (2) of Section 4.11 gives

$$x_{n+1} = x_n - \frac{\sin(x_n) + \cos(x_n)}{\cos(x_n) - \sin(x_n)} \; .$$

We are to take $x_0 = -1$, so we have

$$x_1 = -1 - \left[\frac{\sin(-1) + \cos(-1)}{\cos(-1) - \sin(-1)}\right] = -1 - \left[\frac{(-0.8415) + 0.5403}{0.5403 - (-0.8415)}\right] = -1 + 0.218 = -0.782$$

$$x_2 = -0.782 - \left[\frac{\sin(-0.782) + \cos(-0.782)}{\cos(-0.782) - \sin(-0.782)}\right] = -0.782 - \left[\frac{-0.704 + 0.709}{0.709 + 0.704}\right]$$

$$= -0.782 - 0.003 = -0.785$$

$$x_3 = -0.785 - \left[\frac{-0.707 + 0.707}{0.707 + 0.707}\right] = -0.785$$

(7) The function $f(x) = x^4 + 4x - 1$ has a negative minimum at $x = -1$ and its graph intersects the x-axis once for $x < -1$ and once for $x > -1$. We anticipate that Newton's method with $x_0 = -1.5$ and with $x_0 = -0.5$ will provide approximate values for the two solutions of $x^4 + 4x - 1 = 0$.

We set $f(x) = x^4 + 4x - 1$. Then $f'(x) = 4x^3 + 4$ and formula (2) of Section 4.11 gives

$$x_{n+1} = x_n - \frac{x_n^4 + 4x_n - 1}{4x_n^3 + 4}$$

With $x_0 = -1.5$ we obtain (with three decimal place accuracy)

$$x_1 = -1.5 - \frac{5.0625 - 6 - 1}{-13.5 + 4} = -1.5 - 0.204 = -1.704$$

$$x_2 = -1.704 - \frac{0.615}{-15.8} = -1.665$$

$$x_3 = -1.665 - \frac{0.025}{-14.5} = -1.663.$$

Taking the initial guess $x_0 = 0.5$ yields

$$x_1 = 0.5 - \frac{1.6025}{4.5} = 0.264; \quad x_2 = 0.264 - \frac{0.061}{4.07} = 0.249; \quad x_3 = 0.249 - \frac{-0.00015}{4.06} = 0.249.$$

SECTION 4.12

(1) Set $f(x) = \sqrt{x}$. Then $f'(x) = \frac{d}{dx} x^{1/2} = \frac{1}{2} x^{-1/2} = \frac{1}{2\sqrt{x}}$ and the equation

$$f'(c) = \frac{f(9) - f(1)}{9 - 1}$$

reads

$$\frac{1}{2\sqrt{c}} = \frac{\sqrt{9} - \sqrt{1}}{8}.$$

To satisfy this equation, we must have $\sqrt{c} = 2$ and hence $c = 4$. Because 4 lies between 1 and 9, this shows that the conclusion of the Mean Value Theorem is satisfied.

(5) For $f(x) = x^3 + x + 7$ we have $f'(x) = 3x^2 + 1$ and the equation

$$f'(c) = \frac{f(3) - f(0)}{3 - 0}$$

reads

$$3c^2 + 1 = \frac{37 - 7}{3}.$$

This is satisfied for $c = \pm\sqrt{3}$. To obtain the value of c between 0 and 3, we take $c = \sqrt{3}$.

(9) Set $f(x) = x^{1/4}$. Then $f'(x) = \frac{1}{4} x^{-3/4}$ tends to 0 as $x \to \infty$. By the Mean Value Theorem there is for each x a number c with $x < c < x + 1$ such that

$$f'(c) = \frac{f(x + 1) - f(x)}{(x + 1) - x} = f(x + 1) - f(x) = (x + 1)^{1/4} - x^{1/4}$$

Because the c tends to ∞ as x tends to ∞ , this shows that $(x + 1)^{1/4} - x^{1/4}$ tends to 0 as $x \to \infty$.

SECTION 4.13

(3) Because $- \cos x$ is an antiderivative of $\sin x$ and $\frac{1}{5} x^5$ is an antiderivative of x^4, $-3 \cos x - \frac{2}{5} x^5$ is an antiderivative of $3 \sin x - 2x^4$. By Theorem 4.10, all antiderivatives of $3 \sin x - 2x^4$ are $-3 \cos x - \frac{2}{5} x^5 + C$ with arbitrary constants C.

SECTION 5.1

(3) The integrand in the integral $\int_{-10}^{-5} 6 \, dx$ is the constant function 6 whose graph is the horizontal line $y = 6$. The lower limit of integration is less than the upper, so

the integral equals the area of the shaded rectangle in Figure 5.1.3. The rectangle is 5

units wide and 6 units high, so the area and the integral are both 30.

(7) In the integral $\int_0^{-4}$ -4 dx the lower limit is greater than the upper limit, so we first

use Definition 5.2 and write $\int_0^{-4}$ -4 dx = $-\int_{-4}^0$ -4 dx. The integrand -4 is negative

so the integral $\int_{-4}^0$ -4 dx is equal to the negative of the area of the **shaded** square in

Fig. 5.1.7. The square is 4 units wide and 4 units high, so $\int_{-4}^0$ -4 dx = -16 and

$\int_0^{-4}$ -4 dx = 16.

(13) The integral $\int_2^{12}$ R(x) dx is equal to the area of those shaded regions in Fig. 5.1.13

that lie above the x-axis minus the area of those that lie below the x-axis. The two regions

above the x-axis have combined area of approximately 3 and the three regions below the

x-axis have combined area of approximately 12. The integral, therefore, is approximately

equal to 3 - 12 = -9, and -10 is the closest of the given values.

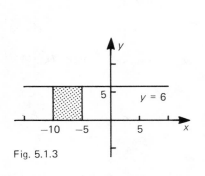

Fig. 5.1.3

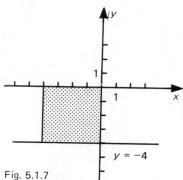

Fig. 5.1.7

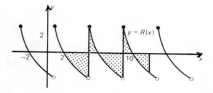

Fig. 5.1.13

SECTION 5.2

(4) The jth interval is $x_{j-1} \leq x \leq x_j$ for $j = 1, 2, 3, \ldots, 20$. Its length is $x_j - x_{j-1}$ and the value of the integrand at its right endpoint is $2x_j^3 - 3x_j^2$. Hence, the Riemann sum is

$$\sum_{j=1}^{20} (2x_j^3 - 3x_j^2)(x_j - x_{j-1}).$$

(8) The partition $\frac{0}{10} < \frac{1}{10} < \frac{2}{10} < \frac{3}{10} < \cdots < \frac{49}{10} < \frac{50}{10}$ of the interval $0 \leq x \leq 5$ is formed by the points $\frac{j}{10}$ for $j = 0, 1, 2, \ldots, 50$. The jth subinterval is $\frac{j-1}{10} \leq x \leq \frac{j}{10}$; its length is $\frac{1}{10}$; and the value of the integrand at its right endpoint is $\cos(\frac{j}{10})$. Consequently, the Riemann sum is

$$\sum_{j=1}^{50} \cos\left(\frac{j}{10}\right)\left(\frac{1}{10}\right) = \frac{1}{10} \sum_{j=1}^{50} \cos\left(\frac{j}{10}\right).$$

(11) The partition $\frac{5}{5} < \frac{6}{5} < \frac{7}{5} < \cdots < \frac{19}{5} < \frac{20}{5}$ of the interval $1 \leq x \leq 4$ is formed by the points $x = \frac{j}{5}$ for $j = 5, 6, 7, \ldots, 20$. The jth subinterval is $\frac{j-1}{5} \leq x \leq \frac{j}{5}$ for $j = 6, 7, 8, \ldots, 20$; its length is $\frac{1}{5}$; and the value of the integrand at its right endpoint is $\sqrt{\frac{j}{5}}$. The Riemann sum is

$$\sum_{j=6}^{20} \sqrt{\frac{j}{5}} \left(\frac{1}{5}\right) = \frac{1}{5} \sum_{j=6}^{20} \sqrt{\frac{j}{5}}.$$

(13a) The region is sketched in Fig. 5.2.13a.

(13b) The partition $1 < \frac{4}{3} < \frac{5}{3} < 2 < \frac{7}{3} < \frac{8}{3} < 3$ is into 6 subintervals of length $\frac{1}{3}$, so there are 6 rectangles of width $\frac{1}{3}$. The function $\frac{3}{x}$ is positive for $1 \leq x \leq 3$, so the rectangles all have their bases on the x-axis and touch the graph $y = \frac{3}{x}$ at their upper right corners (Fig. 5.2.13b).

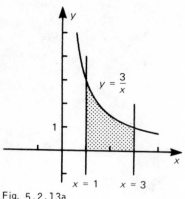

Fig. 5.2.13a

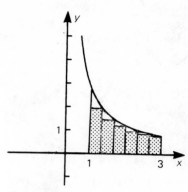

Fig. 5.2.13b

(13c) The function $\frac{3}{x}$ has the values $\frac{3}{4/3}$, $\frac{3}{5/3}$, $\frac{3}{2}$, $\frac{3}{7/3}$, $\frac{3}{8/3}$, and $\frac{3}{3}$ at the

right endpoints of the subintervals and the subintervals are each $\frac{1}{3}$ unit long. Hence the

Riemann sum (which is the sum of the areas of the rectangles in Fig. 5.2.13b) equals

$$\frac{1}{3}[\frac{3}{4/3} + \frac{3}{5/3} + \frac{3}{2} + \frac{3}{7/3} + \frac{3}{8/3} + \frac{3}{3}] = \frac{1}{3}[\frac{9}{4} + \frac{9}{5} + \frac{3}{2} + \frac{9}{7} + \frac{9}{8} + 1]$$

$$= \frac{3}{4} + \frac{3}{5} + \frac{1}{2} + \frac{3}{7} + \frac{3}{8} + \frac{1}{3} \approx 2.987 .$$

(17) Because the partition $0 = x_0 < x_1 < x_2 < \cdots < x_{N-1} < x_N = 3$ is of the interval

$0 \leq x \leq 3$, the integral is over that interval. The sum is the value $\sin(x_j)$ of $\sin x$

at the right endpoint of the jth subinterval multiplied by the length $x_j - x_{j-1}$ of the

j^{th} subinterval, so the sum is a Riemann sum for the integral $\int_0^3 \sin x \, dx$.

(21) The integral is over the interval $0 \leq x \leq 4$ because the partition

$0 = x_0 < x_1 < x_2 < \cdots < x_{N-1} < x_N = 4$ is of that interval. The sum is the value of the

function $5 - (x^2 + 2)^2$ evaluated at the right endpoint x_j of the jth subinterval

multiplied by the length Δx of that subinterval. The sum is a Riemann sum for the

integral $\int_0^4 [5 - (x^2 + 2)^2] \, dx$.

(38)   Because the partition $0 < \frac{1}{N} < \frac{2}{N} < \cdots < \frac{N-1}{N} < 1$ divides the

interval $0 \leq x \leq 1$ into N subintervals of length $\frac{1}{N}$ and the right

endpoint of the jth subinterval of that partition is $\frac{j}{N}$. The sum

$$\frac{1}{N} \sum_{j=1}^{N} (\tfrac{j}{N}) \sin(\tfrac{j}{N}) \quad \text{is a Riemann sum for the integral} \quad \int_{0}^{1} x \sin x \, dx \quad \text{and}$$

tends to that integral as N tends to ∞.

SECTION 5.3

(3) Here y is the independent variable and x is the dummy variable in the integral.
By Theorem 5.1 with x replaced by y and t replaced by x, we have

$$\frac{d}{dy} \int_{3}^{y} f(x) \, dx = f(y) \quad \text{for continuous functions} \quad f(x).$$

Here $f(x) = \dfrac{x}{x^2 + 4}$, so the derivative of the integral is $\dfrac{y}{y^2 + 4}$.

(6a) For $x > 0$ the integral $\displaystyle\int_{0}^{x} (3t + 6)dt$ is equal to the area of the trapezoid in
Fig. 5.3.6a. The parallel sides of the trapezoid have lengths 6 and $3x + 6$ and its
perpendicular dimension is x, so its area and the integral are equal to $\frac{1}{2}[6 + (3x + 6)](x)$
$= 6x + \frac{3}{2}x^2$. For $-2 < x < 0$ the integral is equal to the negative of the area of the
trapezoid shown in Fig. 5.3.6b. The parallel sides of that trapezoid have lengths 6 and
 $x + 6$ and its perpendicular dimension is $-x$. The area of the trapezoid is
$\frac{1}{2}[6 + (3x + 6)](-x) = -6x - \frac{3}{2}x^2$, and the integral equals $6x + \frac{3}{2}x^2$. Thus, for any $x > -2$
the integral equals $6x + \frac{3}{2}x^2$.

(6b) By Theorem 5.1 the function $6x + \frac{3}{2}x^2$ is an antiderivative of $3x + 6$ for
all $x > -2$. (It is in fact an antiderivative for all x since $\frac{d}{dx}(6x + \frac{3}{2}x^2) = 3x + 6$
for all x.) By Theorem 4.10 all antiderivatives of $3x + 6$ are the functions $6x + \frac{3}{2}x^2 + C$.

(6c) For $x < -2$ the integral $\displaystyle\int_{x}^{0} (3t + 6) \, dt$ is equal to the area of triangle I
in Figure 5.3.6c minus the area of triangle II. Triangle I has base of length 2 and
height 6, so its area is $\frac{1}{2}(2)(6) = 6$. Triangle II has base of length $-2 - x$ and
height $-(3x + 6)$, so its area is $\frac{1}{2}(-2 - x)(-3x - 6) = \frac{1}{2}(x + 2)(3x + 6) = \frac{1}{2}(3x^2 + 12x + 12)$
$= \frac{3}{2}x^2 + 6x + 6$. Therefore, $\displaystyle\int_{x}^{0} (3t + 6)dt = (6) - (\frac{3}{2}x^2 + 6x + 6) = -\frac{3}{2}x^2 - 6x$ and
$\displaystyle\int_{0}^{x} (3t + 6)dt = \frac{3}{2}x^2 + 6x$ (the same formula as we obtained for $x > -2$ in Exercise 6a).

(10)   By Theorem 5.2, $\displaystyle\int_0^9 2x\cos(x^2)\,dx = \int_0^9 \frac{d}{dx}[\sin(x^2)]\,dx = [\sin(x^2)]\Big|_0^9$

$= [\sin(9^2)] - [\sin(0^2)] = \sin(81) - \sin(0) = \sin(81).$

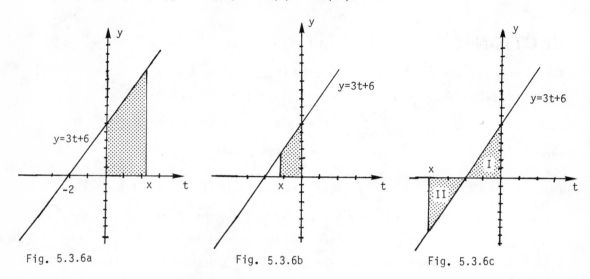

Fig. 5.3.6a   Fig. 5.3.6b   Fig. 5.3.6c

SECTION 5.4

(7)   By Theorem 5.3 with $n = -\dfrac{1}{2}$ and $n + 1 = \dfrac{1}{2}$, we have

$$\int \frac{1}{\sqrt{x}}\,dx = \int x^{-1/2}\,dx = \frac{1}{1/2}\,x^{1/2} + C = 2x^{1/2} + C.$$

Hence

$$\int_1^9 \frac{1}{\sqrt{x}}\,dx = [2x^{1/2}]\Big|_1^9 = [2(9)^{1/2}] - [2(1)^{1/2}] = 2(3) - 2(1) = 4$$

(10)   Since $\displaystyle\int \sin x\,dx = -\cos x + C,$ we have $\displaystyle\int_{\frac{3}{4}\pi}^{\frac{1}{4}\pi} \sin x\,dx = [-\cos x]\Big|_{\frac{3}{4}\pi}^{\frac{1}{4}\pi}$

$= [-\cos(\tfrac{1}{4}\pi)] - [-\cos(\tfrac{3}{4}\pi)] = \cos(\tfrac{3}{4}\pi) - \cos(\tfrac{1}{4}\pi) = -\dfrac{1}{\sqrt{2}} - \dfrac{1}{\sqrt{2}} = -\dfrac{2}{\sqrt{2}} = -\sqrt{2}.$

(15)   Because the function x^3 is negative for $-2 \leq x \leq -1$, the region lies beneath the x-axis (Fig. 5.4.15) and its area equals

$$-\int_{-2}^{-1} x^3\,dx = [-\tfrac{1}{4}x^4]\Big|_{-2}^{-1} = [-\tfrac{1}{4}(-1)^4] - [-\tfrac{1}{4}(-2)^4] = -\tfrac{1}{4} - (-4) = 4 - \tfrac{1}{4} = \tfrac{15}{4}.$$

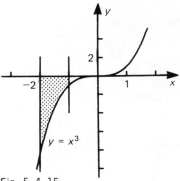

Fig. 5.4.15

SECTION 5.5

(5) $\int_0^{\pi/4} (\cos x - 3)dx = [\sin x - 3x]_0^{\pi/4} = [\sin(\frac{\pi}{4}) - 3(\frac{\pi}{4})] - [\sin(0) - 3(0)]$

$= [\frac{1}{\sqrt{2}} - \frac{3}{4}\pi] - [0] = \frac{1}{\sqrt{2}} - \frac{3}{4}\pi$

(13) $\int_{-4}^{-1} (\frac{2}{y^3} - \frac{3}{y^4})dy = \int_{-4}^{-1} (2y^{-3} - 3y^{-4})dy = [\frac{2}{-2} y^{-2} - \frac{3}{-3} y^{-3}]_{-4}^{-1} = [- y^{-2} + y^{-3}]_{-4}^{-1}$

$= [-(-1)^{-2} + (-1)^{-3}] - [-(-4)^{-2} + (-4)^{-3}] = [-1 - 1] - [- \frac{1}{16} - \frac{1}{64}]$

$= -1 - 1 + \frac{1}{16} + \frac{1}{64} = \frac{-64 - 64 + 4 + 1}{64} = - \frac{123}{64}$

(15) To evaluate the integral, we multiply out the square:

$\int_0^1 (1 + 3t^2)^2 dt = \int_0^1 (1 + 6t^2 + 9t^4)dt = [t + 6(\frac{1}{3} t^3) + 9(\frac{1}{5} t^5)]_0^1$

$= [t + 2t^3 + \frac{9}{5} t^5]_0^1 = [1 + 2(1)^3 + \frac{9}{5}(1)^5] - [0 + 2(0)^3 + \frac{9}{5}(0)^5]$

$= 1 + 2 + \frac{9}{5} = \frac{5 + 10 + 9}{5} = \frac{24}{5}$

(17) We write the integrand as a difference of powers of w:

$$\int_2^1 \frac{1-w}{w^3}\,dw = \int_2^1 \left(\frac{1}{w^3} - \frac{1}{w^2}\right) dw = \int_2^1 (w^{-3} - w^{-2})\,dw = \left[\frac{1}{-2}w^{-2} - \frac{1}{-1}w^{-1}\right]_2^1$$

$$= \left[-\frac{1}{2}w^{-2} + w^{-1}\right]_2^1 = \left[-\frac{1}{2}(1)^{-2} + (1)^{-1}\right] - \left[-\frac{1}{2}(2)^{-2} + (2)^{-1}\right]$$

$$= \left[-\frac{1}{2} + 1\right] - \left[-\frac{1}{8} + \frac{1}{2}\right] = -\frac{1}{2} + 1 + \frac{1}{8} - \frac{1}{2} = \frac{-4 + 8 + 1 - 4}{8} = \frac{1}{8} \ .$$

(22) We write the integral of h(x) from 0 to 3 as the sum of integrals over the three intervals on which h(x) is given by different algebraic expressions:

$$\int_0^3 h(x)\,dx = \int_0^1 h(x)\,dx + \int_1^2 h(x)\,dx + \int_2^3 h(x)\,dx$$

$$= \int_0^1 3x^2\,dx + \int_1^2 4x^3\,dx + \int_2^3 5x^4\,dx = [x^3]_0^1 + [x^4]_1^2 + [x^5]_2^3$$

$$= [1^3 - 0^3] + [2^4 - 1^4] + [3^5 - 2^5] = [1 - 0] + [16 - 1] + [243 - 32] = 227$$

(27) The integrand $f(x) = \dfrac{x}{1 + x^2}$ is an odd function: $f(-x) = \dfrac{-x}{1 + (-x)^2} = \dfrac{-x}{1 + x^2} = -f(x).$.

The graph of the function is symmetric about the origin, so the region set off by the graph, the x-axis, and the lines x = -7 and x = 7 has equal areas above and below the x-axis, and the integral $\int_{-7}^{7} f(x)\,dx$ is zero.

(31) The integrand $t^{1/3} - 5$ is negative for $-1 < t < 0$, so the integral $\int_{-1}^{0} (t^{1/3} - 5)dt$ is negative. Hence, the integral $\int_0^{-1} (t^{1/3} - 5)dt = -\int_{-1}^{0} (t^{1/3} - 5)dt$ is positive.

(36) Because the region is bounded on the bottom by the graph of $x^3 - 1$, on the top by the x-axis, and on the left by x = -2, and because it extends to x = 1 on the right (Fig. 5.5.36), its area equals

$$-\int_{-2}^{1} (x^3 - 1)dx = -\left[\frac{1}{4}x^4 - x\right]_{-2}^{1} = -\left[\frac{1}{4}(1)^4 - 1\right] + \left[\frac{1}{4}(-2)^4 - (-2)\right]$$

$$= -\left[\frac{1}{4} - 1\right] + [4 + 2] = -\frac{1}{4} + 1 + 4 + 2 = \frac{-1 + 4 + 16 + 8}{4} = \frac{27}{4} \ .$$

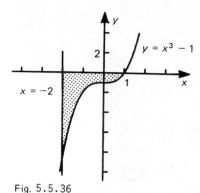

Fig. 5.5.36

SECTION 5.6

(4) The integrand $\sin(3t + 1)$ is of the form $\sin u$ with $u = 3t + 1$, for which $du = \frac{d}{dt}(3t + 1)dt = 3dt$. We can change the variable of integration to u by adjusting a constant factor in the integral. To convert the dt to $du = 3dt$, we multiply the integrand by 3 and compensate by multiplying the integral by $\frac{1}{3}$:

$$\int \sin(3t + 1)dt = \frac{1}{3}\int \sin(3t + 1)(3dt) = \frac{1}{3}\int \sin u \, du = -\frac{1}{3}\cos u + C = -\frac{1}{3}\cos(3t + 1) + C$$

Check: $\frac{d}{dt}[-\frac{1}{3}\cos(3t + 1)] = -\frac{1}{3}[-\sin(3t + 1)]\frac{d}{dt}(3t + 1) = \frac{1}{3}\sin(3t + 1)(3)$

$$= \sin(3t + 1)$$

The derivative of our answer is the original integrand, so the evaluation of the indefinite integrand was correct.

(11) The substitution $u = 3y - 4$ for which $du = \frac{d}{dy}(3y - 4) \, dy = 2dy$, transforms the integral into an integral of a linear combination of powers of u. We have $3y = u + 4$ and consequently $y = \frac{1}{3}u + \frac{4}{3}$, and $dy = \frac{1}{3}du$. With these substitutions, we obtain

$$\int \frac{y}{(3y-4)^3} \, dy = \int \frac{\frac{1}{3}u + \frac{4}{3}}{u^3} \left(\frac{1}{3} \, du\right) = \frac{1}{9} \int \frac{u+4}{u^3} \, du = \frac{1}{9} \int (u^{-2} + 4u^{-3}) \, du$$

$$= \frac{1}{9}\left[\frac{1}{-1} u^{-1} + \frac{4}{-2} u^{-2}\right] + C = -\frac{1}{9} u^{-1} - \frac{2}{9} u^{-2} + C$$

$$= -\frac{1}{9}(3y-4)^{-1} - \frac{2}{9}(3y-4)^{-2} + C$$

Check: $\frac{d}{dy}\left[-\frac{1}{9}(3y-4)^{-1} - \frac{2}{9}(3y-4)^{-2}\right]$

$$= -\frac{1}{9}(-1)(3y-4)^{-2}\frac{d}{dy}(3y-4) - \frac{2}{9}(-2)(3y-4)^{-3}\frac{d}{dy}(3y-4)$$

$$= \frac{1}{9}(3y-4)^{-2}(3) + \frac{4}{9}(3y-4)^{-3}(3) = \frac{1}{3(3y-4)^2} + \frac{4}{3(3y-4)^3} = \frac{(3y-4)+4}{3(3y-4)^3}$$

$$= \frac{3y}{3(3y-4)^3} = \frac{y}{(3y-4)^3} \, .$$

The derivative of our answer is the original integrand, so the indefinite integral was correctly evaluated.

(15) We set $u = 1 - t$, for which $du = \frac{d}{dt}(1-t) \, dt = -dt$, and evaluate the indefinite integral:

$$\int (1-t)^{12} \, dt = -\int (1-t)^{12}(-dt) = -\int u^{12} \, du = -\frac{1}{13}u^{13} + C = -\frac{1}{13}(1-t)^{13} + C$$

Check:

$$\frac{d}{dt}\left[-\frac{1}{13}(1-t)^{13}\right] = -\frac{1}{13}(13)(1-t)^{12}\frac{d}{dt}(1-t) = -(1-t)^{12}(-1) = (1-t)^{12}$$

Then, we evaluate the definite integral:

$$\int_0^1 (1-t)^{12} \, dt = \left[-\frac{1}{13}(1-t)^{13}\right]_0^1 = \left[-\frac{1}{13}(1-1)^{13}\right] - \left[-\frac{1}{13}(1-0)^{13}\right]$$

$$= [0] - \left[-\frac{1}{13}\right] = \frac{1}{13}$$

(18) If we set $u = \sin(3x)$, then $du = \frac{d}{dx}\sin(3x) \, dx = \cos(3x)\frac{d}{dx}(3x) \, dx = 3\cos(3x) \, dx.$

so we can transform the integral into the integral of $\frac{1}{u^2}$ by adjusting a constant factor:

$$\int \frac{\cos(3x)}{\sin^2(3x)} \, dx = \frac{1}{3}\int \frac{1}{\sin^2(3x)} \cdot (3\cos(3x) \, dx) = \frac{1}{3}\int \frac{1}{u^2} \, du = \frac{1}{3}\int u^{-2} \, du = \frac{1}{3}\left(\frac{1}{-1} u^{-1}\right) + C$$

$$= -\frac{1}{3} u^{-1} + C = -\frac{1}{3}[\sin(3x)]^{-1} + C$$

Check:

$$\frac{d}{dx}\left\{-\frac{1}{3}[\sin(3x)]^{-1}\right\} = -\frac{1}{3}(-1)[\sin(3x)]^{-2}\frac{d}{dx}\sin(3x) = \frac{1}{3}[\sin(3x)]^{-2}\cos(3x)\frac{d}{dx}(3x)$$

$$= \frac{1}{3}[\sin(3x)]^{-2}\cos(3x)(3) = \frac{\cos(3x)}{\sin^2(3x)}.$$

This is the original integrand, so our evaluation of the indefinite integral is correct.

SECTION 6.1

(8) We draw the lines $y = 4 - x$, $y = -5x$ and $y = x$ to see that the region is the triangle

shown in Fig. 6.1.8. To find the upper left vertex of the triangle we solve the simultaneous

equations

$$(*) \begin{cases} y = 4 - x \\ y = -5x . \end{cases}$$

Equating the expressions for y gives the equation $4 - x = -5x$ for the x-coordinate

of the intersection. Adding x to both sides of that equation gives $4 = -4x$ to show

that the intersection is at $x = -1$. Equations (*) then show that the y-coordinate is 5.

To find the upper right vertex we solve

$$\begin{cases} y = 4 - x \\ y = x. \end{cases}$$

These equations give first $4 - x = x$, which implies that $x = 2$, and then $y = 2$. The upper

left vertex of the triangle is $(-1,5)$, the upper right vertex is $(2,2)$, and the lower

vertex is the origin $(0,0)$.

Because the two pieces of the bottom of the triangle are given by different equations,

we have to apply Rule 6.1 to the portion of the triangle for $-1 \leq x \leq 0$ and then to the

portion for $0 \leq x \leq 2$ and add the result:

$$\text{Area} = \int_{-1}^{0} [(4 - x) - (-5x)]dx + \int_{0}^{2} [(4 - x) - x] \, dx = \int_{-1}^{0} (4 + 4x) \, dx + \int_{0}^{2} (4 - 2x) \, dx$$

$$= [4x + 4(\tfrac{1}{2} x^2)]_{-1}^{0} + [4x - 2(\tfrac{1}{2} x^2)]_{0}^{2} = [4x + 2x^2]_{-1}^{0} + [4x - x^2]_{0}^{2}$$

$$= [4(0) + 2(0)^2] - [4(-1) + 2(-1)^2] + [4(2) - 2^2] - [4(0) - 0^2]$$

$$= [0] - [-4 + 2] + [8 - 4] - [0] = 2 + 4 = 6$$

(11) We sketch the cubic $y = \tfrac{1}{4} x^3$ and the line $y = 2x$ (Fig. 6.1.11). To find their

points of intersection we solve the simultaneous equations

$$(*) \begin{cases} y = \tfrac{1}{4} x^3 \\ y = 2x . \end{cases}$$

Equating the two expressions for y gives the equation $\tfrac{1}{4} x^3 = 2x$ for the x-coordinates of the intersection points. The equation has the solution $x = 0$. To find its other solutions, we **divide** both sides by x to obtain $\frac{1}{4} x^2 = 2$, which may be written $x^2 = 8$ and has the solutions $x = \pm\sqrt{8}$. For the portion of the region for $-\sqrt{8} \le x \le 0$, the cubic $y = \frac{1}{4} x^3$ forms the top of the region and the line $y = 2x$ forms the bottom. For the portion of the region for $0 \le x \le \sqrt{8}$, the top is formed by the line and the bottom by the cubic. We apply Rule 6.1 to the two portions separately and add the result:

$$\text{Area} = \int_{-\sqrt{8}}^{0} [\tfrac{1}{4} x^3 - 2x] dx + \int_{0}^{\sqrt{8}} [2x - \tfrac{1}{4} x^3] dx = [\tfrac{1}{16} x^4 - x^2]_{-\sqrt{8}}^{0} + [x^2 - \tfrac{1}{16} x^4]_{0}^{\sqrt{8}}$$

$$= [\tfrac{1}{16}(0)^4 - (0)^2] - [\tfrac{1}{16}(-\sqrt{8})^4 - (-\sqrt{8})^2] + [(\sqrt{8})^2 - \tfrac{1}{16}(\sqrt{8})^4] - [0^2 - \tfrac{1}{16}(0)^4]$$

$$= [0] - [4 - 8] + [8 - 4] - [0] = -[-4] + [4] = 8$$

Alternate procedure: Because the region is symmetric about the origin, its area is twice that of the portion for $0 \le x \le \sqrt{8}$:

$$\text{Area} = 2 \int_{0}^{\sqrt{8}} [2x - \tfrac{1}{4} x^3] dx = 2(4) = 8$$

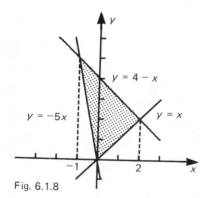

Fig. 6.1.8

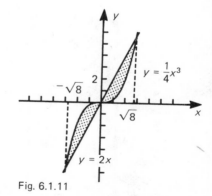

Fig. 6.1.11

(19)   The region is sketched in Fig. 6.1.19. Because the curve $y = \sin(3x)$ is above the line $y = -2$, the area is

$$\int_{0}^{\pi/2} [\sin(3x) - (-2)] dx = \int_{0}^{\pi/2} [\sin(3x) + 2] dx = [-\tfrac{1}{3} \cos(3x) + 2x]_{0}^{\pi/2}$$

$$= [-\tfrac{1}{3} \cos(\tfrac{3\pi}{2}) + 2(\tfrac{\pi}{2})] - [-\tfrac{1}{3} \cos(0) + 2(0)] = [-\tfrac{1}{3}(0) + \pi] - [-\tfrac{1}{3}] = \pi + \tfrac{1}{3}.$$

Here we have made the substitution u = 3x,   du = 3dx   in mentally evaluating the indefinite integral

$$\int \sin(3x)\ dx = \frac{1}{3} \int \sin(3x)(3dx) = \frac{1}{3} \int \sin u\ du = -\frac{1}{3} \cos u + C = -\frac{1}{3} \cos(3x) + C.$$

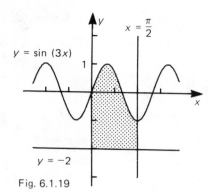

Fig. 6.1.19

(21) The region shown in Fig. 6.1.21 consists of four equal pieces, each of area equal to the area under the graph of sin x and above the x-axis for $0 \leq x \leq \pi$. The area of the entire region is therefore

$$4 \int_0^\pi \sin x\ dx = 4[- \cos x]_0^\pi = 4[- \cos \pi] - 4[- \cos(0)] = 4[-(-1)] - 4[-1] = 8$$

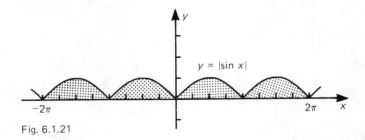

Fig. 6.1.21

(25) The region is shown in Fig. 6.1.25. The coordinates of the intersections of the curves are given by the simultaneous equations

$$(*) \quad \begin{cases} y = x^2 \\ y = x^3. \end{cases}$$

Equating the expressions for y gives the equation $x^2 = x^3$ for the x-coordinates of the intersection points. This equation has $x = 0$ as one solution. Dividing each side by x^2 gives the other solution $x = 1$. Equations (*) show that the intersection points are $(0,0)$ and $(1,1)$.

The top of the region is formed by the curve $y = x^2$ and the bottom by $y = x^3$ because for $0 < x < 1$ we have $x^2 > 0$ and multiplying both sides of the inequality $x < 1$ by x^2 gives $x^3 < x^2$. The region extends from $x = 0$ on the left to $x = 1$ on the right so its area is

$$\int_0^1 [x^2 - x^3]dx = [\tfrac{1}{3}x^3 - \tfrac{1}{4}x^4]_0^1 = [\tfrac{1}{3}(1)^3 - \tfrac{1}{4}(1)^4] - [\tfrac{1}{3}(0)^3 - \tfrac{1}{4}(0)^4] = \tfrac{1}{3} - \tfrac{1}{4} = \tfrac{1}{12}.$$

To compute the area by a y-integration, we first solve the equations $y = x^2$ and $y = x^3$ for x. We obtain $x = \pm y^{1/2}$ and $x = y^{1/3}$. The curve $x = y^{1/2}$ is the right half of the parabola $y = x^2$ and $x = -y^{1/2}$ is the left half. Therefore, the right side of the region is formed by the curve $x = y^{1/3}$ and the left side by $x = y^{1/2}$. The region extends from $y = 0$ on the bottom to $y = 1$ on the top, so its area is

$$\int_0^1 [y^{1/3} - y^{1/2}]dy = [\frac{1}{4/3}y^{4/3} - \frac{1}{3/2}y^{3/2}]_0^1 = [\tfrac{3}{4}y^{4/3} - \tfrac{2}{3}y^{3/2}]_0^1$$

$$= [\tfrac{3}{4}(1)^{4/3} - \tfrac{2}{3}(1)^{3/2}] - [\tfrac{3}{4}(0)^{4/3} - \tfrac{2}{3}(0)^{3/2}] = \tfrac{3}{4} - \tfrac{2}{3} = \tfrac{1}{12}.$$

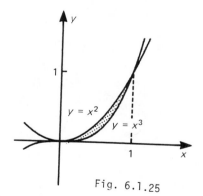

Fig. 6.1.25

SECTION 6.2

(5) If a regular hexagon is inscribed in a circle of radius r (Fig. 6.2.5a), then it
consists of 6 equilateral triangles with sides of length r. The area of each triangle
is $\frac{\sqrt{3}}{4} r^2$, so the area of the hexagon is $6(\frac{\sqrt{3}}{4})r^2 = \frac{3\sqrt{3}}{2} r^2$. The horizontal cross section
of the stool at y $(-1 \leq y \leq 1)$ can be inscribed in a circle of radius $r = \sqrt{2 - y^2}$
(Fig. 6.2.5b), so its area is $A(y) = \frac{3\sqrt{3}}{2}(\sqrt{2 - y^2})^2 = \frac{3\sqrt{3}}{2}(2 - y^2)$ and the volume of the
stool is

$$\int_{-1}^{1} A(y)dy = \int_{-1}^{1} \frac{3\sqrt{3}}{2}(2 - y^2)dy = \frac{3\sqrt{3}}{2}[2y - \frac{1}{3} y^3]_{-1}^{1}$$

$$= \frac{3\sqrt{3}}{2}[2(1) - \frac{1}{3}(1)^3] - \frac{3\sqrt{3}}{2}[2(-1) - \frac{1}{3}(-1)^3] = \frac{3\sqrt{3}}{2}[2 - \frac{1}{3}] - \frac{3\sqrt{3}}{2}(-2 + \frac{1}{3}]$$

$$= \frac{3\sqrt{3}}{2}[2 - \frac{1}{3} + 2 - \frac{1}{3}] = 5\sqrt{3}.$$

Note: We could simplify the calculations a bit by recognizing that the stool is symmetric
about its cross section at y = 0, so A(-y) = A(y) and the volume is

$$2 \int_{0}^{1} A(y) \, dy = 2(\frac{5\sqrt{3}}{2}) = 5\sqrt{3}.$$

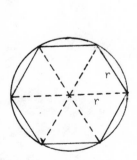

Fig. 6.2.5a

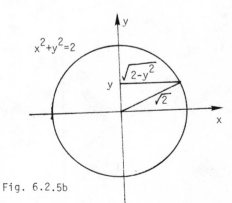

Fig. 6.2.5b

(7) Imagine the axes of the cylinders to be horizontal and a vertical h-axis with its
origin at the intersection of the axes of the cylinders (Fig. 6.2.7a). The horizontal cross

sections of the cylinder are pairs of parallel lines, so the horizontal cross sections of the solid we are considering (the region inside both cylinders) are squares. To compute the width s of the cross section at h, we take an end view of one cylinder, which gives us an edge view of the cross section (Fig. 6.2.7b). The width of the cross section at h is $2\sqrt{16 - h^2}$, its area is $A(h) = 4(16 - h^2)$, so the volume of the solid is

$$\int_{-4}^{4} A(h)\ dh = \int_{-4}^{4} 4(16 - h^2)dh = 2\int_{0}^{4} 4(16 - h^2)dh = 8[16h - \frac{1}{3}h^3]_{0}^{4}$$

$$= 8[16(4) - \frac{1}{3}(4)^3] - 8[16(0) - \frac{1}{3}(0)^3] = 8[64 - \frac{1}{3}(64)] = 8[\frac{2}{3}(64)] = \frac{1024}{3}.$$

Here we have used the fact that $A(h) = 4(16 - h^2)$ is an even function and replaced the integral from -4 to 4 with twice the integral from 0 to 4.

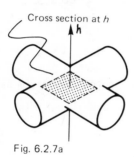

Cross section at h

Fig. 6.2.7a

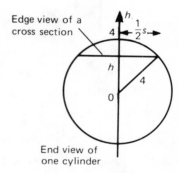

Edge view of a cross section

End view of one cylinder

Fig. 6.2.7b

SECTION 6.3

(2) The top of the region is formed by the axis of revolution $y = 1$, so we use the method of disks. The bottom is formed by the parabola $y = \frac{1}{2} x^2$ (Fig. 6.3.2). The coordinates of the corners of the region are given by the simultaneous equations $y = 1$ and $y = \frac{1}{2} x^2$. Equating the expressions for y gives the equation $1 = \frac{1}{2} x^2$ for the x-coordinates, which has the solutions $x = \pm\sqrt{2}$. The radius of the disk at x is the distance $1 - \frac{1}{2} x^2$ between

the top and the bottom at x. Hence the area of the disk at x is $A(x) = \pi r^2 = \pi(1 - \frac{1}{2}x^2)^2$

and the volume of the solid of revolution is

$$\int_{-\sqrt{2}}^{\sqrt{2}} A(x) \, dx = \int_{-\sqrt{2}}^{\sqrt{2}} \pi(1 - \frac{1}{2}x^2)^2 \, dx = 2\pi \int_{0}^{\sqrt{2}} (1 - \frac{1}{2}x^2)^2 \, dx = 2\pi \int_{0}^{\sqrt{2}} (1 - x^2 + \frac{1}{4}x^4) \, dx$$

$$= 2\pi[x - \frac{1}{3}x^3 + \frac{1}{20}x^5]_0^{\sqrt{2}} = 2\pi[\sqrt{2} - \frac{1}{3}(\sqrt{2})^3 + \frac{1}{20}(\sqrt{2})^5] - 2\pi[0 - \frac{1}{3}(0)^3 + \frac{1}{20}(0)^5]$$

$$= 2\pi[\sqrt{2} - \frac{2}{3}\sqrt{2} + \frac{1}{5}\sqrt{2}] = 2\pi\sqrt{2}[1 - \frac{2}{3} + \frac{1}{5}] = 2\pi\sqrt{2}[\frac{15 - 10 + 3}{15}] = \frac{16}{15}\pi\sqrt{2}.$$

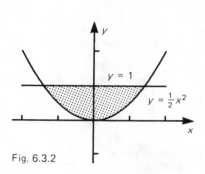

Fig. 6.3.2

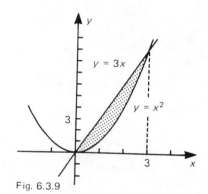

Fig. 6.3.9

(9) The region is bounded on the top by the line $y = 3x$ and on the bottom by the parabola $y = x^2$ (Fig. 6.3.9). The intersections of the top and bottom are given by the simultaneous equations $y = 3x$ and $y = x^2$. Equating the expressions for y gives the equation $3x = x^2$ for the x-coordinates which has the solutions $x = 0$ and $x = 3$. The axis of rotation is the x-axis and we use the method of washers with an x-integration. The outer radius of the washer at x is the distance $3x - 0 = 3x$ between the line and the x-axis; the inner radius is the distance $x^2 - 0 = x^2$ between the parabola and the x-axis. Therefore, the area of the washer at x is

$$A(x) = \pi[\text{Outer radius}]^2 - \pi[\text{Inner radius}]^2 = \pi(3x)^2 - \pi(x^2)^2 = \pi(9x^2 - x^4).$$

The region extends from $x = 0$ to $x = 3$, so the volume of the solid of revolution is

$$\int_{0}^{3} A(x) \, dx = \pi \int_{0}^{3} (9x^2 - x^4) \, dx = \pi[\frac{9}{3}x^3 - \frac{1}{5}x^5]_0^3 = \pi[3x^3 - \frac{1}{5}x^5]_0^3$$

$$= \pi\{[3(3)^3 - \frac{1}{5}(3)^5] - [3(0)^3 - \frac{1}{5}(0)^5]\} = \pi[81 - \frac{1}{5}(243)] = \frac{162}{5}\pi.$$

(13) The region is bounded by the line $x = y - 2$ and the parabola $x = -y^2$ (Fig. 6.3.13).

Equating the expressions for x in the equations $x = y - 2$ and $x = -y^2$ gives $y - 2 = -y^2$, which may be written $y^2 + y - 2 = 0$ or $(y + 2)(y - 1) = 0$. This equation has the solutions $y = -2$ and $y = 1$, which are the y-coordinates of the intersections of the line and the parabola.

The axis of the solid is the vertical line $x = 1$ on the right of the region, and we use the method of washers with a y-integration. The outer radius of the cross section at y is the distance $1 - (y - 2) = 3 - y$ between the line $x = 1$ and the line $x = y - 2$. The inner radius is the distance $1 - (- y^2) = 1 + y^2$ between the line $x = 1$ and the parabola $x = -y^2$. The area of the washer at y is

$$A(y) = \pi \left[\begin{matrix}\text{Outer}\\\text{radius}\end{matrix}\right]^2 - \pi \left[\begin{matrix}\text{Inner}\\\text{radius}\end{matrix}\right]^2 = \pi(3 - y)^2 - \pi(1 + y^2)^2$$

and the volume of the solid of revolution is

$$\int_{-2}^{1} A(y)\, dy = \int_{-2}^{1} \pi[(3 - y)^2 - (1 + y^2)^2]dx = \pi\int_{-2}^{1} [(9 - 6y + y^2) - (1 + 2y^2 + y^4)]dy$$

$$= \pi\int_{-2}^{1} (8 - 6y - y^2 - y^4)dy = \pi[8y - 3y^2 - \tfrac{1}{3}y^3 - \tfrac{1}{5}y^5]\Big|_{-2}^{1}$$

$$= \pi[8(1) - 3(1)^2 - \tfrac{1}{3}(1)^3 - \tfrac{1}{5}(1)^5] - \pi[8(-2) - 3(-2)^2 - \tfrac{1}{3}(-2)^3 - \tfrac{1}{5}(-2)^5]$$

$$= \pi[8 - 3 - \tfrac{1}{3} - \tfrac{1}{5}] - \pi[-16 - 12 + \tfrac{8}{3} + \tfrac{32}{5}] = \pi[33 - \tfrac{9}{3} - \tfrac{33}{5}] = \pi[30 - \tfrac{33}{5}] = \tfrac{117}{5}\pi.$$

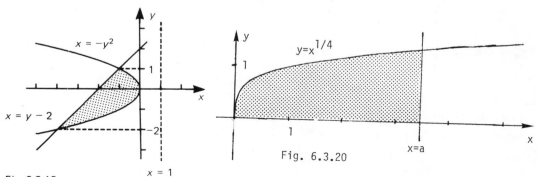

$x = -y^2$

$x = y - 2$

$x = 1$

Fig. 6.3.13

$y = x^{1/4}$

$x = a$

Fig. 6.3.20

(20) The region to be rotated is bounded by the x-axis, the vertical line $x = a$, and by the portion of the curve $x = y^4$ with $y \geq 0$ (Fig. 6.3.20). The top of the region also has the equation $y = x^{1/4}$, so by the method of disks the volume of the bullet is

$$\int_0^a \pi (x^{1/4})^2 \, dx = \pi \int_0^a x^{1/2} \, dx = \pi [\tfrac{1}{3/2} x^{3/2}]_0^a = \pi [\tfrac{2}{3} x^{3/2}]_0^a = \tfrac{2}{3} \pi a^{3/2}.$$

For this to equal 12π, we must have $\tfrac{2}{3} a^{3/2} = 12$, which implies that $a^{3/2} = 18$ and $a = 18^{2/3}$. This is the length of the bullet. The radius of its base is $a^{1/4} = 18^{1/6}$ in.

SECTION 6.4

(6) The region is drawn in Fig.6.4.6. It lies to the left of the vertical axis of the solid of revolution, and we compute the volume by using the method of cylinders with an x-integration. The height of the cylinder at x is the length $x^3 - 0 = x^3$ of the vertical cross section of the region at x. The radius of the cylinder is the distance $3 - x$ from the axis of the solid to the vertical cross section at x. The region extends from $x = 0$ on the left to $x = 2$ on the right, so the volume of the solid is

$$\int_0^2 2\pi \left[\begin{smallmatrix}\text{Radius of the}\\\text{cylinder at } x\end{smallmatrix}\right]\left[\begin{smallmatrix}\text{Height of the}\\\text{cylinder at } x\end{smallmatrix}\right] dx = 2\pi \int_0^2 (3 - x)(x^3) dx$$

$$= 2\pi \int_0^2 (3x^3 - x^4) dx = 2\pi [\tfrac{3}{4} x^4 - \tfrac{1}{5} x^5]_0^2 = 2\pi [\tfrac{3}{4}(2)^4 - \tfrac{1}{5}(2)^5] - 2\pi [\tfrac{3}{4}(0)^4 - \tfrac{1}{5}(0)^5]$$

$$= 2\pi [12 - \tfrac{32}{5}] - 2\pi [0] = 2\pi [\tfrac{60 - 32}{5}] = \tfrac{56}{5} \pi.$$

(9) The region and the axis of revolution are shown in Fig. 6.4.9. Because the boundaries of the region are given by equations expressing x in terms of y, it is easiest to compute the volume by a y-integration. Because the axis is vertical, we use the method of washers. The outer radius of the washer at y is the distance $(2 - y^2) - (-1) = 3 - y^2$ from the right of the region to the axis. The inner radius is the distance $y^2 - (-1) = y^2 + 1$ from the left of the region to the axis. The region extends from $y = -1$ to $y = 1$, so the volume of the solid is

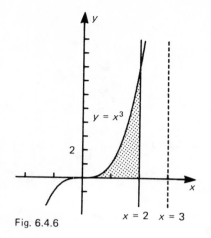

Fig. 6.4.6 $x = 2$ $x = 3$

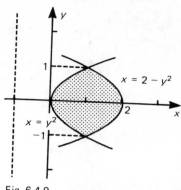

Fig. 6.4.9

$$\int_{-1}^{1} \pi \, [(3 - y^2)^2 - (y^2 + 1)^2] dy = \int_{-1}^{1} \pi [(9 - 6y^2 + y^4) - (y^4 + 2y^2 + 1)] dy$$

$$= \int_{-1}^{1} \pi (8 - 8y^2) dy = 2\pi \int_{0}^{1} (8 - 8y^2) dy = 16 \pi \int_{0}^{1} (1 - y^2) dy$$

$$= 16 \pi \left[y - \frac{1}{3} y^3 \right]_{0}^{1} = 16 \pi \left[1 - \frac{1}{3}(1)^3 \right] - 16 \pi \left[0 - \frac{1}{3}(0)^3 \right] = 16 \pi (\frac{2}{3}) = \frac{32}{3} \pi.$$

Here we used the fact that $8 - 8y^2$ is an even function to replace its integral from
-1 to 1 with twice the integral from 0 to 1.

Note. If we use the method of cylinders and an x-integration (and take advantage of the
symmetry of the solid), we obtain the volume as the sum of integrals

(*)
$$2 \int_{0}^{1} 2\pi [x + 1][\sqrt{x}] dx + 2 \int_{1}^{2} 2\pi [x + 1][\sqrt{2 - x}] dx$$

$$= 4\pi \int_{0}^{1} (x^{3/2} + x^{1/2}) dx + 4\pi \int_{1}^{2} (x + 1)\sqrt{2 - x} \, dx.$$

To evaluate the second indefinite integral, we make the substitution $u = 2 - x$, $du = -dx$:
for which $x = 2 - u$ and $x + 1 = 3 - u$:

$$\int (x + 1)\sqrt{2 - x} \, dx = -\int (3 - u)\sqrt{u} \, du = -\int (3u^{1/2} - u^{3/2}) \, du = -\frac{3}{3/2} u^{3/2} + \frac{1}{5/2} u^{5/2} + C$$

$$= -2u^{3/2} + \frac{2}{5} u^{5/2} + C = -2(2 - x)^{3/2} + \frac{2}{5}(2 - x)^{5/2} + C$$

The volume (*) therefore equals

$$4\pi \left[\tfrac{2}{5} x^{5/2} + \tfrac{2}{3} x^{3/2}\right]_0^1 + 4\pi \left[-2(2 - x)^{3/2} + \tfrac{2}{5}(2 - x)^{5/2}\right]_1^2$$

$$= 4\pi \left[\tfrac{2}{5} + \tfrac{2}{3}\right] - 4\pi\left[-2 + \tfrac{2}{5}\right] = 4\pi\left[\tfrac{2}{5} + \tfrac{2}{3} + 2 - \tfrac{2}{5}\right] = 4\pi \left[\tfrac{8}{3}\right] = \tfrac{32}{3}\pi .$$

SECTION 6.5

(1) The derivative is $\dfrac{dy}{dx} = \dfrac{d}{dx}\left[\tfrac{1}{3}(x^2 + 2)^{3/2}\right] = \tfrac{1}{3}\left(\tfrac{3}{2}\right)(x^2 + 2)^{1/2}\dfrac{d}{dx}(x^2 + 2) = x(x^2 + 2)^{1/2}$,

so the length of the curve is

$$\int_{-2}^3 \sqrt{1 + \left(\tfrac{dy}{dx}\right)^2}\ dx = \int_{-2}^3 \sqrt{1 + x^2(x^2 + 2)}\ dx = \int_{-2}^3 \sqrt{x^4 + 2x^2 + 1}\ dx$$

$$= \int_{-2}^3 \sqrt{(x^2 + 1)^2}\ dx = \int_{-2}^3 (x^2 + 1)dx = \left[\tfrac{1}{3} x^3 + x\right]_{-2}^3 = \left[\tfrac{1}{3}(3)^3 + 3\right] - \left[\tfrac{1}{3}(-2)^3 + (-2)\right]$$

$$= [9 + 3] - \left[-\tfrac{8}{3} - 2\right] = 14 + \tfrac{8}{3} = \tfrac{42 + 8}{3} = \tfrac{50}{3}.$$

(7) The maximum value of x^2 for points on the ellipse $x^2 + 9y^2 = 36$ occurs for $y = 0$ and is 36. The maximum value of y^2 occurs for $x = 0$ and is 4. The ellipse extends from $x = -6$ on the left to $x = 6$ on the right and from $y = -2$ on the bottom to $y = 2$ on the top, and the portion of the ellipse for $1 \le y \le 2$ is the portion for $y \ge 1$. The points at $y = 1$ on the ellipse have x-coordinates given by $x^2 + 9(1)^2 = 36$, which yields $x^2 = 27$ and then $x = \pm 3\sqrt{3}$. The equation for the ellipse gives $9y^2 = 36 - x^2$ or $y^2 = 4 - \tfrac{1}{9} x^2$, so the upper half of the ellipse has the equation $y = \sqrt{4 - \tfrac{1}{9} x^2}$ and the portion for $y \ge 1$ is obtained by taking $-3\sqrt{3} \le x \le 3\sqrt{3}$. The derivative is

$$\dfrac{dy}{dx} = \dfrac{d}{dx}(4 - \tfrac{1}{9} x^2)^{1/2} = \tfrac{1}{2}(4 - \tfrac{1}{9} x^2)^{-1/2}\dfrac{d}{dx}(4 - \tfrac{1}{9} x^2) = \tfrac{1}{2}(4 - \tfrac{1}{9} x^2)^{-1/2}(-\tfrac{2}{9} x)$$

$$= -\tfrac{1}{9} x(4 - \tfrac{1}{9} x^2)^{-1/2} = \dfrac{-x}{9\sqrt{4 - \tfrac{1}{9} x^2}} .$$

Hence

$$1 + \left(\tfrac{dy}{dx}\right)^2 = 1 + \dfrac{x^2}{81(4 - \tfrac{1}{9} x^2)} = 1 + \dfrac{x^2}{324 - 9x^2} = \dfrac{324 - 9x^2 + x^2}{324 - 9x^2} = \dfrac{324 - 8x^2}{324 - 9x^2}$$

and the length of the portion of the ellipse is

$$\int_{-3\sqrt{3}}^{3\sqrt{3}} \sqrt{1 + (\frac{dy}{dx})^2} \; dx = \int_{-3\sqrt{3}}^{3\sqrt{3}} \sqrt{\frac{324 - 8x^2}{324 - 9x^2}} \; dx.$$

SECTION 6.6

(3) The curve $y = x^3$ lies above the x-axis for $0 < x \le 2$, so the radius of the surface at x is $x^3 - 0 = x^3$. We have $\frac{dy}{dx} = 3x^2$, so the area of the surface is

$$\int_0^2 2\pi[x^3]\sqrt{1 + (3x^2)^2} \; dx = 2\pi \int_0^2 x^3 \sqrt{1 + 9x^4} \; dx.$$

To evaluate the indefinite integral, we make the substitution $u = 1 + 9x^4$, $du = 36x^3 \; dx$:

$$2\pi \int x^3 \sqrt{1 + 9x^4} \; dx = \frac{2\pi}{36} \int (1 + 9x^4)^{1/2}(36x^3 dx) = \frac{\pi}{18} \int u^{1/2} \; du = \frac{\pi}{18}(\frac{1}{3/2} u^{3/2}) + C$$

$$= \frac{\pi}{27}(1 + 9x^4)^{3/2} + C.$$

Hence the area of the surface is

$$[\frac{\pi}{27}(1 + 9x^4)^{3/2}]_0^2 = \frac{\pi}{27}[1 + 9(2)^4]^{3/2} - \frac{\pi}{27}[1 + 9(0)^4]^{3/2} = \frac{\pi}{27}[(145)^{3/2} - 1].$$

(6) Because the axis of the surface of revolution is the vertical line $x = -1$, we have to use an integral with respect to y. We solve the equation $y = x^3$ for $x = y^{1/3}$ and note that the portion of the curve for $1 \le x \le 2$ is obtained for $1 \le y \le 8$. The radius of the surface at y is the horizontal distance $y^{1/3} - (-1) = y^{1/3} + 1$ between the point at y on the curve to the axis. We have $\frac{dx}{dy} = \frac{1}{3} y^{-2/3}$ so the area of the surface is

$$\int_1^8 2\pi[\begin{smallmatrix}\text{Radius of the}\\\text{surface at } y\end{smallmatrix}]\sqrt{1 + (\frac{dx}{dy})^2} \; dy = \int_1^8 2\pi[y^{1/3} + 1]\sqrt{1 + \frac{1}{9} y^{-4/3}} \; dy.$$

SECTION 6.7

(5) Because $\frac{dv}{dt} = a$, we have

$$v(t) = \int a(t)\, dt = \int (2 - t^2)\, dt = 2t - \frac{1}{3} t^3 + C$$

and then the condition $v(0) = 15$ implies that $C = 15$ and $v(t) = 2t - \frac{1}{3} t^3 + 15$.

Next, we have

$$s(t) = \int v(t)\, dt = \int (2t - \frac{1}{3} t^3 + 15)\, dt = t^2 - \frac{1}{12} t^4 + 15t + C_1.$$

The condition $s(0) = 3$ implies that $C_1 = 3$ and $s(t) = t^2 - \frac{1}{12} t^4 + 15t + 3$.

(8) The rate of **income** is $10t - t^2$ dollars per hour, so the amount taken in from $t = 0$ to $t = 10$ is

$$\int_0^{10} (10t - t^2)\, dt = [5t^2 - \frac{1}{3} t^3]_0^{10} = [5(10)^2 - \frac{1}{3}(10)^3] - [5(0)^2 - \frac{1}{3}(0)^3]$$

$$= [500 - \frac{1000}{3}] - [0] = \frac{1500 - 1000}{3} = \frac{500}{3} \text{ dollars.}$$

(11a) The velocity $v = t^2 - t = t(t - 1)$ is zero at $t = 0$ and $t = 1$. At $t = 0$ the object is at $s(0) = 10$ and at $t = 1$ it is at

$$s(10) = s(0) + \int_0^1 \frac{ds}{dt}(t)\, dt = s(0) + \int_0^1 v(t)\, dt = 10 + \int_0^1 (t^2 - t)\, dt$$

$$= 10 + [\frac{1}{3} t^3 - \frac{1}{2} t^2]_0^1 = 10 + [\frac{1}{3}(1)^3 - \frac{1}{2}(1)^2] - [\frac{1}{3}(0)^3 - \frac{1}{2}(0)^2]$$

$$= 10 + [\frac{1}{3} - \frac{1}{2}] - [0] = \frac{60 + 2 - 3}{6} = \frac{59}{6} \text{ yards.}$$

(11b) At time T the object is at

$$s(T) = s(0) + \int_0^T v(t)\, dt = 10 + \int_0^T (t^2 - t)\, dt = 10 + \frac{1}{3} T^3 - \frac{1}{2} T^2.$$

The object is at $s = 10$ at times T such that $10 + \frac{1}{3} T^3 - \frac{1}{2} T^2 = 10$. Subtracting 10 from each side of the equation gives $\frac{1}{3} T^3 - \frac{1}{2} T^2 = 0$, which may be written $T^2(\frac{1}{3} T - \frac{1}{2}) = 0$. The solutions are $T = 0$ and $T = \frac{3}{2}$ seconds.

(15) Because the only force on the ball is that of gravity, its upward acceleration is $a = -32$ feet/second^2. Its upward velocity at time t (seconds) is

$$v(t) = \int a\ dt = -32t + v_0 = -32t + 96 .$$

The constant of integration v_0 is 96 because that is its upward velocity at $t = 0$. The object's height above the ground at time t is

$$s(t) = \int v(t)\ dt = \int (-32t + 96)dt = -16t^2 + 96\ t + s_0 = -16t^2 + 96t .$$

The constant of integration here is zero because the object is on the ground at $t = 0$.

(15b) The ball is at its highest point when its velocity $v = -32t + 96$ is zero. This occurs at $t = 3$ seconds. Its height above the ground at that moment is

$$s(3) = [-16t^2 + 96t]_{t=3} = -16(3)^2 + 96(3) = 144\ \text{feet above the ground.}$$

(15c) The ball is on the ground when $s = -16t^2 + 96t$ is zero. The equation $-16t^2 + 96t = 0$ may be written $-16t(t - 6) = 0$, so the ball hits the ground at $t = 6$ when its velocity is $v(6) = [-32t + 96]_{t=6} = -32(6) + 96 = -96$ feet per second. This is its upward velocity. Its speed is 96 feet per second.

(16) The golf ball's height above the ground at time t is $s = -16t^2 + v_0t + s_0$ $= -16t^2 + s_0$, where v_0 its upward velocity at $t = 0$ is zero and s_0 is the height of the window (the ball's height at $t = 0$). The ball hits the ground at $t = 3$, so $0 = [-16t^2 + s_0]_{t=3} = -144 + s_0$ and $s_0 = 144$ feet.

(20) The object's velocity at time t is

$$v(t) = \int a(t)\ dt = \int 6t\ dt = 3t^2 + v_0 = 3t^2 - 48\ \text{centimeters/second.}$$

The constant of integration v_0 is -48 because that is the velocity at $t = 0$. We have $v = 3(t^2 - 16)$, so the velocity is negative for $0 \le t < 4$ and is positive for $t > 4$. The total distance traveled in the time interval $0 \le t \le 5$ is

$$\int_0^5 |v(t)|\,dt = \int_0^5 |3t^2 - 48|\,dt = \int_0^4 (48 - 3t^2)\,dt + \int_4^5 (3t^2 - 48)\,dt$$

$$= [48t - t^3]_0^4 + [t^3 - 48t]_4^5$$

$$= [48(4) - (4)^3] - [48(0) - (0)^3] + [(5)^3 - 48(5)] - [(4)^3 - 48(4)]$$

$$= [192 - 64] - [0] + [125 - 240] - [64 - 192] = 141 \text{ centimeters.}$$

(24) The object's mass is its weight divided by the acceleration of gravity:

$m = \dfrac{128}{32} = 4$ slugs. By Newton's law (F = ma) the object's acceleration in the

positive direction at time t is equal to the force in the positive direction divided by

the object's mass: $a(t) = \dfrac{24t + 96 \quad \text{pounds}}{4 \text{ slugs}} = 6t + 24$ feet/second^2. Its velocity in the

positive direction at time t is

$$v(t) = \int a(t)\,dt = \int (6t + 24)\,dt = 3t^2 + 24t + v_0 = 3t^2 + 24t.$$

The constant of integration v_0 is zero because the object is at rest at t = 0. In the

time interval $0 \le t \le 10$ the object travels

$$\int_0^{10} v(t)\,dt = \int_0^{10} (3t^2 + 24t)\,dt = [t^3 + 12t^2]_0^{10}$$

$$= [(10)^3 + 12(10)^2] - [(0)^3 + 12(0)^2] = 1000 + 1200 = 2200 \text{ feet.}$$

SECTION 6.8

(4) We assume that the spring lies along an s-axis as in Figure 6.46 in the text

and that the spring satisfies Hooke's law so that the force exerted by the spring

toward the right is F = -ks pounds when the end of the spring is s feet to the right of

its rest position. The spring is stretched 2 feet toward the right when its length is

12 feet, and we are told that in that position the spring exerts a force of 12 pounds. The

force is toward the left, so we have F = -12 when s = 2. The equation -12 = -k(2)
implies that k = 6 and F = -6s.

The force on the spring toward the right is the negative 6s of the force by the spring
toward the right, so the amount of work done on the spring in stretching it from its natural
length, where s = 0, to a length of 14 feet, where s = 4, is

$$\int_{0}^{4} 6s \ dx = [3s^2]_{0}^{4} = [3(4)^2] - [3(0)^2] = 48 \text{ foot-pounds.}$$

(8) Introduce a vertical s-axis with its scale measured in feet and so the bag of sand
is at s = 0 when t = 0 (seconds). Because the bag is lifted 2 feet per second, at
time t it is at s = 2t $(0 \le t \le 10)$. Because the bag weighs 100 pounds at t = 0
and loses 3 pounds per second, it weighs 100 - 3t pounds at time t. The upward force
required to lift the bag is equal to its weight F = 100 - 3t, but to calculate the work
we need to have the force expressed as a function of the distance s. We have $t = \frac{1}{2} s$
and therefore $F = 100 - \frac{3}{2} s$. At t = 10 the bag is at s = 20, so the work done is

$$\int_{0}^{20} F \ ds = \int_{0}^{20} (100 - \frac{3}{2} s) ds = [100s - \frac{3}{4} s^2]_{0}^{20} = [100(20) - \frac{3}{4}(20)^2] - [100(0) - \frac{3}{4}(0)^2]$$

$$= 2000 - 300 = 1700 \text{ foot-pounds.}$$

(9a) We introduce a vertical s-axis with s = 0 at the bottom of the bowl (Fig.6.8.9a)
and consider a partition $0 = s_0 < s_1 < s_2 < \cdots < s_N = 1$ of the interval $0 \le s \le 1$. (Note
that the top of the bowl is at s = 1.) We approximate the portion of the bowl for
$s_{j-1} \le s \le s_j$ by a circular disk which extends from $s = s_{j-1}$ on the bottom to $s = s_j$
on the top and whose top is the cross section of the bowl at $s = s_j$ (Fig. 6.8.9a).
The radius r_j of the jth disk satisfies $r_j^2 + (1 - s_j)^2 = 1$ (Fig. 6.8.9b), so the
area of the top of the jth disk is $\pi r_j^2 = \pi[1 - (1 - s_j)^2]$. Because the disk is
$s_j - s_{j-1}$ feet thick, its volume is $\pi[1 - (1 - s_j)^2](s_j - s_{j-1})$ and, if it were filled
with water, it would weigh $62.4\pi [1 - (1 - s_j)^2](s_j - s_{j-1})$ pounds. The distance from

the top of the jth disk to the point 3 feet above the top of the bowl is $4 - s_j$, so it would require approximately

$$62.4 \pi [1 - (1 - s_j)^2][4 - s_j](s_j - s_{j-1}) \quad \text{foot-pounds}$$

of work to lift the water in the jth disk. The work to empty the bowl is approximately

$$\sum_{j=1}^{N} 62.4 \pi [1 - (1 - s_j)^2][4 - s_j](s_j - s_{j-1}) \quad \text{foot pounds.}$$

This is a Riemann sum for the integral that gives the exact amount of work required:

$$\int_0^1 62.4\pi[1 - (1 - s)^2][4 - s]ds = 62.4 \pi \int_0^1 [1 - (1 - 2s + s^2)](4 - s)ds$$

$$= 62.4 \pi \int_0^1 (2s - s^2)(4 - s)ds = 62.4\pi \int_0^1 (8s - 2s^2 - 4s^2 + s^3)ds$$

$$= 62.4 \pi \int_0^1 (8s - 6s^2 + s^3)ds = 62.4 \pi \left[4s^2 - 2s^3 + \frac{1}{4} s^4\right]_0^1$$

$$= 62.4 \pi[4(1)^2 - 2(1)^3 + \frac{1}{4}(1)^4] - 62.4 \pi[4(0)^2 - 2(0)^3 + \frac{1}{4}(0)^4]$$

$$= 62.4 \pi[4 - 2 + \frac{1}{4}] = 62.4 \pi[\frac{9}{4}] = 140.4 \pi \quad \text{foot-pounds.}$$

(9b) If the pump does work at the rate of 55 foot-pounds per second, it will empty the bowl in $\frac{140.4}{55}\pi \approx 8.02$ seconds.

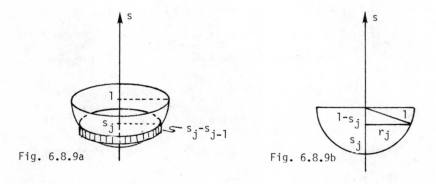

Fig. 6.8.9a   Fig. 6.8.9b

SECTION 6.9

(1) The end of the trough is an equilateral triangle with sides of length 4. By the
Pythagorean Theorem applied to one half of that triangle (Fig. 6.9.1a), the altitude h
of the triangle satisfies $h^2 + 2^2 = 4^2$. Therefore $h = 2\sqrt{3}$ feet.

We introduce a vertical y-axis with its scale measured in feet and its zero at the
bottom of the triangle. We consider a partition $0 = y_0 < y_1 < y_2 < \cdots < y_N = 2\sqrt{3}$ of
the interval $0 \le y \le 2\sqrt{3}$ and approximate the portion of the triangle for $y_{j-1} \le y \le y_j$
by a rectangle whose top is the cross section of the triangle at $y = y_j$ and whose
bottom is at height $y = y_{j-1}$ (Fig. 6.9.1b). If we let r denote half the width of
the jth rectangle, then by the Pythagorean Theorem again (Fig. 6.9.1c), we have
$r^2 + y_j^2 = (2r)^2$ and hence $r = \sqrt{3}\ y_j$. The width of the jth rectangle is $2\sqrt{3}\ y_j$ feet and its
area is $2\sqrt{3}\ y_j(y_j - y_{j-1})$ square feet. The top of the rectangle is $2\sqrt{3} - y_j$ feet beneath
the surface of the water, so the pressure at the top of the rectangle is $62.4(2\sqrt{3} - y_j)$
pounds per square foot. Because the rectangle is narrow, this is the approximate pressure
over all of it and the force on it is approximately

$$[\text{Pressure}][\text{Area}] = [62.4(2\sqrt{3} - y_j)\ \frac{\text{pounds}}{\text{square feet}}][2\sqrt{3}\ y_j(y_j - y_{j-1})\ \text{square feet}]$$

$$= 124.8\sqrt{3}(2\sqrt{3} - y_j)y_j(y_j - y_{j-1})\ \text{pounds}.$$

The force on the end of the trough is approximately

$$\sum_{j=1}^{N} 124.8\sqrt{3}(2\sqrt{3} - y_j)y_j(y_j - y_{j-1})\ \text{pounds},$$

and the exact force is given by the corresponding integral

$$124.8\sqrt{3} \int_0^{2\sqrt{3}} (2\sqrt{3} - y)y\ dy = 124.8\sqrt{3} \int_0^{2\sqrt{3}} (2\sqrt{3}\ y - y^2)dy = 124.8\sqrt{3}[\sqrt{3}\ y^2 - \frac{1}{3}\ y^3]_0^{2\sqrt{3}}$$

$$= 124.8\sqrt{3}[\sqrt{3}\ (2\sqrt{3})^2 - \frac{1}{3}(2\sqrt{3})^3] - 124.8\sqrt{3}[\sqrt{3}(0)^2 - \frac{1}{3}(0)^3]$$

$$= 124.8\sqrt{3}[\sqrt{3}\ (4)(3) - \frac{1}{3}(4)(3)(2\sqrt{3})] = 124.8\sqrt{3}\ (12)[\sqrt{3} - \frac{2}{3}\sqrt{3}] = 499.2\ \text{pounds}$$

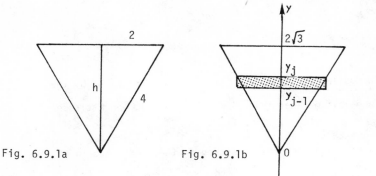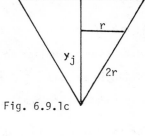

Fig. 6.9.1a   Fig. 6.9.1b   Fig. 6.9.1c

(5) Introduce a vertical y-axis with its scale measured in feet and its zero at the bottom of the can (Fig. 6.9.5). By Rule 6.11 with the density of the oil replacing that of water, the force of the oil on the top third of one side of the can is

$$\int_{1}^{3/2} 59.3 \begin{bmatrix}\text{Depth of the}\\ \text{oil at } y\end{bmatrix}\begin{bmatrix}\text{Width of}\\ \text{the can}\end{bmatrix} dy = 59.3 \int_{1}^{3/2} (\tfrac{3}{2} - y)(2)\, dy$$

$$= 59.3(2)[\tfrac{3}{2} y - \tfrac{1}{2} y^2]_{1}^{3/2} = 59.3[3y - y^2]_{1}^{3/2} = 59.3\left\{[3(\tfrac{3}{2}) - (\tfrac{3}{2})^2] - [3(1) - (1)^2]\right\}$$

$$= 59.3\,[\tfrac{9}{4}] - [2] = \frac{59.3}{4} = 14.825 \quad \text{pounds.}$$

The pressure at y for $0 \le y \le 1$ is due to a one-half foot layer of oil plus a layer of water $1 - y$ feet deep. The pressure is therefore

$$(*) \qquad \frac{59.3}{2} + 62.4(1 - y) = 92.05 - 62.4y \quad \text{pounds per square foot.}$$

The quantity $62.4[\text{Depth of the water at } y]$ in formula (3) of Rule 6.11 is the water pressure at y. Similarly, we obtain the integral that gives the force on the bottom two thirds of one side of the can in this exercise:

$$\int_{0}^{1} [\text{Pressure at } y][\text{Width of the can}]dy = \int_{0}^{1} (92.05 - 62.4\, y)(2)dy$$

$$\int_{0}^{1} (184.1 - 124.8y)dy = [184.1y - 62.4y^2]_{0}^{1}$$

$$= [184.1(1) - 62.4(1)^2] - [184.1(0) - 62.4(0)^2] = 121.7 \quad \text{pounds.}$$

The total force on one side of the can is 14.825 + 121.7 = 136.525 pounds and the force on all
four sides is 4(136.525) = 546.1 pounds.

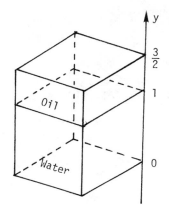

Fig. 6.9.5

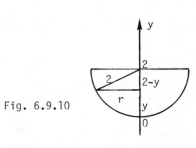

Fig. 6.9.10

(10) Introduce a vertical y-axis with scales measured in feet and with its zero at the
bottom of the semi-circular disk (Fig. 6.9.10). If r is half the width of the disk
at height y, then by the Pythagorean Theorem we have $r^2 + (2 - y)^2 = 2^2$. Therefore
$r = \sqrt{4 - (2 - y)^2} = \sqrt{4y - y^2}$ and the width of the plate at height y is $2\sqrt{4y - y^2}$ feet.
The point at y on the y-axis is 2 - y feet beneath the surface of the water, so by
Rule 6.11 the force of water on one side of the plate is

$$\int_0^2 62.4[2 - y][2\sqrt{4y - y^2}]\, dy = 124.8 \int_0^2 \sqrt{4y - y^2}\,(2 - y)dy \quad \text{pounds.}$$

To evaluate the indefinite integral, we use the substitution $u = 4y - y^2$, $du = (4 - 2y)dy$:

$$124.8 \int \sqrt{4y - y^2}\,(2 - y)dy = 62.4 \int (4y - y^2)^{1/2}(4 - 2y)dy$$

$$= 62.4 \int u^{1/2}\, du = \frac{62.4}{3/2} u^{3/2} + C = \frac{124.8}{3}(4y - y^2)^{3/2} + C.$$

The force on one side of the plate is

$$\frac{124.8}{3}\left[(4y - y^2)^{3/2}\right]_0^2 = \frac{124.8}{3}\left[4(2) - (2)^2\right]^{3/2} - \left[4(0) - (0)^2\right]^{3/2}$$

$$= \frac{124.8}{3}(4)^{3/2} = 41.6(8) = 332.8 \quad \text{pounds.}$$

SECTION 6.10

(3a) The rod's weight is

$$\int_{-3}^{3} [(3 + x^2) \frac{pounds}{foot}][dx \text{ feet}] = [3x + \frac{1}{3} x^3]_{-3}^{3} \text{ pounds}$$

$$= [3(3) + \frac{1}{3}(3)^3] - [3(-3) + \frac{1}{3}(-3)^3] = [18] - [-18] = 36 \text{ pounds}.$$

Its moment about the origin is

$$\int_{-3}^{3} (3 + x^2)x \, dx = \int_{-3}^{3} (3x + x^3)dx$$

and is zero because $3x + x^3$ is an odd function and the interval of integration is symmetric about the origin. The center of gravity is at the origin. (We could have seen this directly because the rod is symmetric about the origin.)

(6a) The plate is shown in Fig. 6.10.6. Its top is formed by the curve $y = x^2$ and its bottom by the curve $y = x^3$ and it. extends from $x = 0$ to $x = 1$. By Rule 6.15 its weight is

$$\text{Weight} = \int_{0}^{1} (x^2 - x^3)\sqrt{x} \, dx = \int_{0}^{1} (x^{5/2} - x^{7/2})dx = [\frac{1}{7/2} x^{7/2} - \frac{1}{9/2} x^{9/2}]_{0}^{1}$$

$$= [\frac{2}{7} x^{7/2} - \frac{2}{9} x^{9/2}]_{0}^{1} = [\frac{2}{7}(1)^{7/2} - \frac{2}{9}(1)^{9/2}] - [\frac{2}{7}(0)^{7/2} - \frac{2}{9}(0)^{9/2}]$$

$$= \frac{2}{7} - \frac{2}{9} = \frac{18 - 14}{63} = \frac{4}{63} \text{ pounds}.$$

The moment about the y-axis is

$$\int_{0}^{1} (x^2 - x^3)\sqrt{x} \, x \, dx = \int_{0}^{1} (x^{7/2} - x^{9/2})dx$$

$$= [\frac{2}{9} x^{9/2} - \frac{2}{11} x^{11/2}]_{0}^{1} = \frac{2}{9} - \frac{2}{11} = \frac{22 - 18}{99} = \frac{4}{99} \text{ foot-pounds}.$$

The moment about the x-axis is

$$\frac{1}{2} \int_{0}^{1} [(x^2)^2 - (x^3)^2]\sqrt{x} \, dx = \frac{1}{2} \int_{0}^{1} (x^{9/2} - x^{13/2})dx$$

$$= \frac{1}{2}[\frac{2}{11} x^{11/2} - \frac{2}{15} x^{15/2}]_0^1 = \frac{1}{2}(\frac{2}{11} - \frac{2}{15}) = \frac{1}{2}(\frac{30 - 22}{165}) = \frac{4}{165}$$ foot-pounds.

The center of gravity is $(\bar{x}, \bar{y})$ where

$$\bar{x} = \frac{\text{Moment about the y-axis}}{\text{Weight}} = \frac{\frac{4}{99}}{\frac{4}{63}} = \frac{63}{99} = \frac{7}{11}$$

$$\bar{y} = \frac{\text{Moment about the x-axis}}{\text{Weight}} = \frac{\frac{4}{165}}{\frac{4}{63}} = \frac{63}{165} = \frac{21}{55} .$$

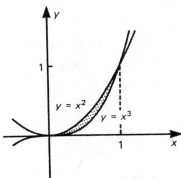

Fig. 6.10.6

(12a) By symmetry the x-coordinate $\bar{x}$ of the center of gravity is 0. When the region is rotated about the x-axis it generates a sphere of radius r and volume $V = \frac{4}{3}\pi r^3$. The region is a semi-circle of area $A = \frac{1}{2}\pi r^2$. By Pappus' First Theorem, the y-coordinate of the center of gravity satisfies $V = (2\pi\bar{y})A$. Hence, we have $\frac{4}{3}\pi r^3 = (2\pi\bar{y})(\frac{1}{2}\pi r^2)$ and $\bar{y} = \frac{4r}{3\pi}$.

SECTION 6.11

(1c) The interval $0 \leq x \leq \pi$ is of length π, so the average value of $\sin x$ in that interval is

$$\frac{1}{\pi} \int_0^\pi \sin x \, dx = \frac{1}{\pi} [- \cos x]_0^\pi = \frac{1}{\pi}[\cos(\pi)] - \frac{1}{\pi}[\cos(0)] = \frac{1}{\pi}(1 + 1) = \frac{2}{\pi} .$$

(2a) By the Mean Value Theorem for Integrals, there should be a number c with

$-3 < c < -1$ such that

$$(*) \qquad \int_{-3}^{-1} x^{-2}\, dx = (c^{-2})[-1 - (-3)]$$

The integral on the left of (*) equals

$$[\frac{1}{-1}\, x^{-1}]_{-3}^{-1} = [-\frac{1}{x}]_{-3}^{-1} = 1 - \frac{1}{3} = \frac{2}{3}\,.$$

The quantity on the right of (*) is $\frac{2}{c^2}$. We therefore want c such that $\frac{2}{c^2} = \frac{2}{3}$.

We must take c so that $c^2 = 3$, and to have c in the interval $-3 < c < -1$, we

take $c = -\sqrt{3}$.

SECTION 7.1

(1a) The equation $y = \log_4(2)$ means that $4^y = 2$. This occurs for $y = \frac{1}{2}$.

(2c) The equation $2\log_{10}(\frac{x}{3}) = 1$ implies that $\log_{10}(\frac{x}{3}) = \frac{1}{2}$, which means that $10^{1/2} = \frac{x}{3}$. Therefore, $x = 3\sqrt{10}$.

(2e) We write the equation in the form $\log_{10}[(x)(x)(\sqrt{x})] = -10$, and then $\log_{10}(x^{5/2}) = -10$. This means that $10^{-10} = x^{5/2}$ and consequently $x = (10^{-10})^{2/5} = 10^{-20/5} = 10^{-4}$

(2j) The equation $\log_6(4x) = \frac{1}{5}$ means that $6^{1/5} = 4x$ and hence $x = \frac{1}{4}(6^{1/5})$.

(3e) $\log_{10}(0.0034) = \log_{10}(3.4 \times 10^{-3}) = -3 + \log_{10}(3.4) \approx -3 + 0.5315$

(5d) $\log_{10}[(8.62)^{1/5}] = \frac{1}{5}\log_{10}(8.62) \approx \frac{1}{5}(0.9355) = 0.1871 \approx \log_{10}(1.54)$. Hence $(8.62)^{1/5} \approx 1.54$.

(5f) $\log_{10}[(1560)^{11}] = 11\log_{10}(1.56 \times 10^3) = 11[3 + \log_{10}(1.56)] \approx 11(3.1931) = 35.1241$.

   $\approx 35 + \log_{10}(1.33) = \log_{10}(1.33 \times 10^{35})$. Hence $(1560)^{11} \approx 1.33 \times 10^{35}$.

(5h) $\log_{10}[(0.0123)^{1/4}] = \frac{1}{4}\log_{10}(0.0123) = \frac{1}{4}\log_{10}(1.23 \times 10^{-2}) = \frac{1}{4}[\log_{10}(1.23) - 2]$

$\approx \frac{1}{4}(0.0899 - 2)$. Here 0.0899 is the mantissa and -2 the characteristic. To simplify the division by 4, we subtract 2 from the characteristic and add it to the mantissa. We obtain

$$\log_{10}[(0.0123)^{1/4}] \approx \frac{1}{4}(2.0899 - 4) = 0.5225 - 1 \approx \log(3.33 \times 10^{-1}).$$

Hence, $(0.0123)^{1/4} \approx 3.33 \times 10^{-1} = 0.33$.

(15a) The graph of $\log_{10}[f(x)]$ is a straight line provided $\log_{10}[f(x)] = mx + b$ for some constants m and b, which means that $f(x) = 10^{mx+b} = 10^b(10^m)^x = Ck^x$ with $C = 10^b$ and $k = 10^m$. Thus, the functions whose graphs are straight lines when a logarithmic scale is used on the y-axis are functions of the form Ck^x with positive constants C and k.

(15b) The graph of $f(x)$ is a straight line when logarithmic scales are used on both the x- and y-axes provided $\log_{10}[f(x)] = m[\log_{10}(x)] + b$. This means that $\log_{10}[f(x)] = \log_{10}(x^m) + \log_{10}(k) = \log_{10}[kx^m]$ with $k = 10^b$, and, consequently, $f(x) = kx^m$. Thus, these are the functions of the form kx^m with k a positive constant and m an arbitrary real constant.

(16)   Since $\frac{1}{8}$ is 2^{-3}, the equation $2^{3x} = \frac{1}{8}$ may be written $2^{3x} = 2^{-3}$. This equation is equivalent to the equation $3x = -3$ because the exponential function 2^t is increasing for all t and does not have the same value for two different values of t. Finally, the one solution of $3x = -3$ is $x = -1$.

(17) First solution: We rewrite $3^x = 4^x$ as $(\frac{3}{4})^x = 1$, which implies that $x = 0$. Second solution: Taking logarithms gives $\log_{10}(3^x) = \log_{10}(4^x)$ and then $x \log_{10}(3) = x \log_{10}(4)$ or $x[\log_{10}(3) - \log_{10}(4)] = 0$. This implies that $x = 0$.

(27)   Taking logarithms of both sides of $4^{\sqrt{x}} = 5$ gives $\log_2(4^{\sqrt{x}}) = \log_2(5)$ and then· $\sqrt{x} \log_2(4) = \log_2(5)$. Since $\log_2(4) = 2$, this simplifies to $\sqrt{x} = \frac{1}{2} \log_2(5)$ and finally $x = \frac{1}{4}[\log_2(5)]^2$.

(32)   We take logarithms of both sides of $(0.001)^x = 2$ to obtain $\log_{10}[(0.001)^x]$ $= \log_{10}(2)$ or $x \log_{10}(0.001) = \log_{10}(2)$. Because $\log_{10}(0.001) = \log_{10}(10^{-3})$ is -3, we obtain $x = -\frac{1}{3} \log_{10}(2)$.

(38)   The equation $\log_4(x^5) = -6$ is equivalent to $x^5 = 4^{-6}$. Taking fifth roots then yields $x = 4^{-6/5}$.

(40)   We rewrite $\log_7(x^2) = 3 \log_7(2x)$ in the form $\log_7(x^2) = \log_7[(2x)^3]$. Because $\log_7 t$ is an increasing function for $t > 0$, the last equation is equivalent to the equation $x^2 = (2x)^3$ with the requirement that x be positive. Cancelling x^2 yields $1 = 8x$ and then $x = \frac{1}{8}$.

SECTION 7.2

(5b) $\log_{1.9}(9.1) = \dfrac{\ln(9.1)}{\ln(1.9)} \approx \dfrac{2.20827}{0.64185} \approx 3.4405$

(6) $L'(x) = \dfrac{d}{dx} \ln x = \dfrac{1}{x}$ for all $x > 0$, so $L'(300) = \dfrac{1}{300}$.

(7) $M'(x) = \dfrac{d}{dx} \log_{10} x = \dfrac{d}{dx}[\dfrac{\ln x}{\ln(10)}] = \dfrac{1}{x \ln(10)}$ for all $x > 0$, so $M'(100) = \dfrac{1}{100 \ln(10)}$.

(11) $\dfrac{d}{dx}[\ln(x^{1/2}) + (\ln x)^{1/2}] = \dfrac{1}{x^{1/2}} \dfrac{d}{dx}(x^{1/2}) + \dfrac{1}{2}(\ln x)^{-1/2} \dfrac{d}{dx} \ln x$

$\qquad = \dfrac{1}{x^{1/2}}(\dfrac{1}{2} x^{-1/2}) + \dfrac{1}{2}(\ln x)^{-1/2}(\dfrac{1}{x}) = \dfrac{1}{2x} + \dfrac{1}{2x}(\ln x)^{-1/2} = [1 + (\ln x)^{-1/2}]/2x$

(15) $\dfrac{d}{dy}[\ln(y^{1/2})]^{1/2} = \dfrac{1}{2}[\ln(y^{1/2})]^{-1/2} \dfrac{d}{dy} \ln(y^{1/2}) = \dfrac{1}{2}[\ln(y^{1/2})]^{-1/2} \dfrac{1}{y^{1/2}} \dfrac{d}{dy} y^{1/2}$

$\qquad = \dfrac{1}{2}[\ln(y^{1/2})]^{-1/2} \dfrac{1}{y^{1/2}}(\dfrac{1}{2} y^{-1/2}) = \dfrac{1}{4y}[\ln(y^{1/2})]^{-1/2} = 1/[4y\sqrt{\ln(\sqrt{y})}]$

(17) $\dfrac{d}{dx}[\log_{10}(x)]^{10} = 10[\ln_{10}(x)]^9 \dfrac{d}{dx} \log_{10}(x) = 10[\ln_{10}x]^9 \dfrac{d}{dx}[\dfrac{\ln x}{\ln(10)}] = 10[\ln_{10}x]^9/[x \ln(10)]$

(19) $y = \dfrac{\ln x}{x}$ is zero at $x = 1$, positive for $x > 1$, and negative for $0 < x < 1$. The derivative

$$\dfrac{dy}{dx} = \dfrac{x \dfrac{d}{dx}(\ln x) - (\ln x)\dfrac{d}{dx} x}{x^2} = \dfrac{x(\dfrac{1}{x}) - (\ln x)(1)}{x^2} = \dfrac{1 - \ln x}{x^2}$$

is zero at $x = e$ where $\ln x = 1$, is positive for all x such that $\ln x < 1$, which is all x with $0 < x < e$, and is negative for all x such that $\ln x > 1$, which is all x with $x > e$. The function has a local maximum at $x = e$, where it has the value $\dfrac{\ln(e)}{e} = \dfrac{1}{e}$. The graph is shown in Fig. 7.2.19.

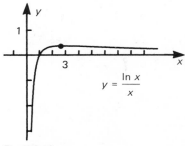

$y = \dfrac{\ln x}{x}$

Fig. 7.2.19

(26) The slope of $y = \log_b x$ at x is $\frac{dy}{dx} = \frac{d}{dx} \log_b x = \frac{d}{dx}[\frac{\ln x}{\ln b}] = \frac{1}{x \ln b}$. Its slope at

$x = 1$ is $\frac{1}{\ln b}$. For this to have the value 2, we must have $\ln b = \frac{1}{2}$, which means that

$e^{1/2} = b$.

(29) Because $\ln t$ is increasing for $t > 0$, the equation $\ln(x + 4) = \ln(x^2 + x)$

is equivalent to $x + 4 = x^2 + x$ with the requirement that $x + 4$ be positive.

The last equation gives $x^2 = 4$ and then $x = \pm 2$.

(32) Squaring both sides of $\sqrt{\ln(x^2)} = 5$ gives $\ln(x^2) = 25$, which is equivalent

to $x^2 = e^{25}$. We then take square roots to obtain $x = \pm e^{25/2}$.

(39) Because $t^{1/3}$ is defined for all t, the domain of $[\ln(x^3)]^{1/3}$ is the same

as the domain of $\ln(x^3)$. This consists of all x such that x^3 is positive, which is

the set of all $x > 0$.

$$\frac{d}{dx}[\ln(x^3)]^{1/3} = \frac{1}{3}[\ln(x^3)]^{-2/3} \frac{d}{dx} \ln(x^3) = \frac{1}{3}[\ln(x^3)]^{-2/3} \frac{1}{x^3} \frac{d}{dx}(x^3)$$

$$= \frac{1}{3}[\ln(x^3)]^{-2/3} \frac{3x^2}{x^3} = \frac{1}{x}[\ln(x^3)]^{-2/3}.$$

SECTION 7.3

(4) Make the substitution $u = x + 2$, $du = dx$ in the indefinite integral:

$$\int \frac{1}{x + 2} dx = \int \frac{1}{u} du = \ln|u| + C = \ln|x + 2| + C$$

Then evaluate the definite integral:

$$\int_0^6 \frac{1}{x + 2} dx = [\ln|x + 2|]_0^6 = \ln|6 + 2| - \ln|2| = \ln(8) - \ln(2) = \ln(\frac{8}{2}) = \ln(4)$$

(7) Make the substitution $u = \ln x$, $du = \frac{d}{dx}(\ln x) dx = \frac{1}{x} dx$:

$$\int \frac{\sqrt{\ln x}}{x} dx = \int (\ln x)^{1/2}(\frac{1}{x} dx) = \int u^{1/2} du = \frac{1}{3/2} u^{3/2} + C = \frac{2}{3}(\ln x)^{3/2} + C.$$

Check:

$$\frac{d}{dx}[\frac{2}{3}(\ln x)^{3/2}] = \frac{2}{3}(\frac{3}{2})(\ln x)^{1/2} \frac{d}{dx} \ln x = (\ln x)^{1/2} (\frac{1}{x}) = \frac{\sqrt{\ln x}}{x}$$

(9) Make the substitution $u = 1 + x^{4/3}$, $du = \frac{d}{dx}(1 + x^{4/3})dx = \frac{4}{3}x^{1/3}$ dx in the indefinite integral:

$$\int \frac{x^{1/3}}{1 + x^{4/3}}\, dx = \frac{3}{4}\int \frac{1}{1 + x^{4/3}}\,(\frac{4}{3}x^{1/3}\, dx) = \frac{3}{4}\int \frac{1}{u}\, du = \frac{3}{4}\ln|u| + C$$

$$= \frac{3}{4}\ln|1 + x^{4/3}| + C$$

Check:

$$\frac{d}{dx}[\frac{3}{4}\ln|1 + x^{4/3}|] = (\frac{3}{4})\,\frac{1}{1 + x^{4/3}}\,\frac{d}{dx}(1 + x^{4/3}) = (\frac{3}{4})\,\frac{1}{1 + x^{4/3}}\,(\frac{4}{3}x^{1/3}) = \frac{x^{1/3}}{1 + x^{4/3}}$$

Evaluate the definite integral:

$$\int_1^8 \frac{x^{1/3}}{1 + x^{4/3}}\, dx = [\frac{3}{4}\ln|1 + x^{4/3}|]_1^8 = \frac{3}{4}\ln(1 + 8^{4/3}) - \frac{3}{4}\ln(1 + 1^{4/3})$$

$$= \frac{3}{4}\ln(1 + 16) - \frac{3}{4}\ln(1 + 1) = \frac{3}{4}[\ln(17) - \ln(2)] = \frac{3}{4}\ln(\frac{17}{2})$$

(14) The region is shown in Fig. 7.3.14. We use the method of cylinders and a y-integration.

We write the equation of the hyperbola $y = \frac{1}{x}$ in the form $x = \frac{1}{y}$. The horizontal cross

section of the region at y extends from $x = 0$ on the left to $x = \frac{1}{y}$ on the right, so

its length is $\frac{1}{y} - 0 = \frac{1}{y}$. This is the height of the cylinder at y. The radius of the

cylinder at y is the distance $y - (-1) = y + 1$ between the cross section at y and the

axis of revolution $y = -1$. Therefore the volume of the solid of revolution is

$$\int_1^4 2\pi [\substack{\text{Radius of the} \\ \text{cylinder at } y}][\substack{\text{Height of the} \\ \text{cylinder at } y}]\, dy = \int_1^4 2\pi [y + 1][\frac{1}{y}]\, dy$$

$$= 2\pi \int_1^4 (1 + \frac{1}{y})dy = 2\pi [y + \ln y\,]_1^4 = 2\pi[4 + \ln(4)] - 2\pi[1 + \ln(1)]$$

$$= 2\pi[4 + \ln(4) - 1] = 6\pi + 2\pi\ln(4)$$

(17a) By formula (2) and the chain rule

$$\frac{d}{dx}\ln|x^2 - 9| = \frac{1}{x^2 - 9}\,\frac{d}{dx}(x^2 - 9) = \frac{2x}{x^2 - 9}\quad .$$

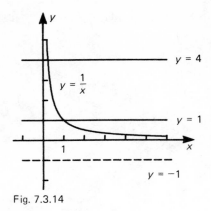

Fig. 7.3.14

(20)   The region extends from x = 0 on the left to x = 2 on the right and

from $y = \frac{1}{8}$ on the bottom to $y = (x^2 + 4)^{-1}$ on the top   (Fig. 7.3.20). By the

method of cylinders the volume generated by rotating the region about the y-axis is

$$\int_0^2 2\pi \left[\begin{matrix}\text{Radius of the}\\\text{cylinder at}\ x\end{matrix}\right]\left[\begin{matrix}\text{Height of the}\\\text{cylinder at}\ x\end{matrix}\right]\ dx = \int_0^2 2\pi [x][\frac{1}{x^2 + 4} - \frac{1}{8}]\ dx$$

$$= \pi \int_0^2 \frac{2x\ dx}{x^2 + 4} - \frac{\pi}{4} \int_0^2 x\ dx.$$

To evaluate the first integral, we set

$u = x^2 + 4,\quad du = 2x\ dx$ and obtain

$$\int \frac{2x\ dx}{x^2 + 4} = \int \frac{1}{u}\ du = \ln|u| + C$$

$$= \ln(x^2 + 4) + C.$$

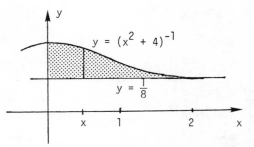

Fig. 7.3.20

The volume is

$$\left[\pi \ln(x^2 + 4)\right]_0^2 - \left[\frac{1}{8}\pi x^2\right]_0^2 = [\pi \ln(8)] - [\pi \ln(4)] - [\frac{1}{8}\pi 2^2] + [0]$$

$$= \pi \ln(2) - \frac{1}{2}\pi .$$

SECTION 7.4

(3) Set $f(x) = [\frac{x^2 + 1}{x^2 - 1}]^{1/2}$. We must assume that $x^2 - 1$ is positive so the function

is defined . Then we have

$$\ln[f(x)] = \ln[\frac{x^2 + 1}{x^2 - 1}]^{1/2} = \frac{1}{2} \ln[\frac{x^2 + 1}{x^2 - 1}]$$

and hence

$$\ln[f(x)] = \frac{1}{2} \ln(x^2 + 1) - \frac{1}{2} \ln(x^2 - 1).$$

Taking the derivative of both sides of the last equation yields

$$\frac{f'(x)}{f(x)} = \frac{1}{2} \frac{1}{x^2 + 1} \frac{d}{dx}(x^2 + 1) - \frac{1}{2} \frac{1}{x^2 - 1} \frac{d}{dx}(x^2 - 1)$$

$$= \frac{x}{x^2 + 1} - \frac{x}{x^2 - 1} .$$

When we multiply both sides by $f(x)$, we obtain

$$\frac{d}{dx} [\frac{x^2 + 1}{x^2 - 1}]^{1/2} = f'(x) = f(x)\left\{\frac{x}{x^2 + 1} - \frac{x}{x^2 - 1}\right\} = [\frac{x^2 + 1}{x^2 - 1}]^{1/2}\left\{\frac{x}{x^2 + 1} - \frac{x}{x^2 - 1}\right\}.$$

(5) Set $f(x) = x^x$ (defined for $x > 0$). Then $\ln[f(x)] = \ln(x^x) = x \ln x$ and differentiating

both sides of this equation gives

$$\frac{f'(x)}{f(x)} = \frac{d}{dx}[x \ln x] = x[\frac{d}{dx} \ln x] + [\ln x]\frac{d}{dx} x = x(\frac{1}{x}) + \ln x = 1 + \ln x.$$

If we multiply both sides by $f(x)$, we obtain

$$\frac{d}{dx}(x^x) = f'(x) = f(x)[1 + \ln x] = x^x[1 + \ln x].$$

Note: Rather than use logarithmic differentiation to compute derivatives of functions of

the form $g(x)^{h(x)}$, we can use the identity $u = e^{\ln(u)}$ to express the **function in terms**

of the exponential function e^v: In this case we have $x^x = e^{\ln(x^x)} = e^{x(\ln x)}$ and hence

$$\frac{d}{dx} x^x = \frac{d}{dx} e^{x(\ln x)} = e^{x(\ln x)} \frac{d}{dx}[x \ln x] = x^x \frac{d}{dx}[x \ln x] = x^x[x \frac{d}{dx}(\ln x) + (\ln x)\frac{d}{dx} x]$$

$$= x^x[x(\frac{1}{x}) + (\ln x)(1)] = x^x(1 + \ln x). \text{ (This is discussed in Section 7.5.)}$$

SECTION 7.5

(1b) $\ln(e^{-x^2}) = -x^2 \ln(e) = -x^2$

(2b) $\ln(1 + x) = 5$ means $e^5 = 1 + x$ and hence $x = e^5 - 1$.

(5) $\frac{d}{dx}(xe^{-x}) = x(\frac{d}{dx} e^{-x}) + e^{-x}(\frac{d}{dx} x) = x[e^{-x} \frac{d}{dx}(-x)] + e^{-x} = -xe^{-x} + e^{-x} = e^{-x}(1 - x)$

(9) $\frac{d}{dx}[\frac{e^x}{x + 3}] = \frac{(x + 3)(\frac{d}{dx} e^x) - e^x \frac{d}{dx}(x + 3)}{(x + 3)^2} = \frac{(x + 3)e^x - e^x(1)}{(x + 3)^2} = \frac{e^x(x + 2)}{(x + 3)^2}$

(13) $\frac{d}{dx}(e^x + x^e) = \frac{d}{dx} e^x + \frac{d}{dx} x^e = e^x + ex^{e-1}$

(17) We write $(3 + x)^{3-x} = e^{\ln[(3+x)^{3-x}]} = e^{(3-x)\ln(3+x)}$ to obtain

$\frac{d}{dx}(3 + x)^{3-x} = \frac{d}{dx} e^{(3-x)\ln(3+x)} = e^{(3-x)\ln(3+x)} \frac{d}{dx}[(3 - x)\ln(3 + x)]$

$= (3 + x)^{3-x} \frac{d}{dx}[(3 - x)\ln(3 + x)]$

$= (3 + x)^{3-x}[(3 - x)\frac{d}{dx} \ln(3 + x) + \ln(3 + x) \frac{d}{dx}(3 - x)]$

$= (3 + x)^{3-x}[\frac{3 - x}{3 + x} \frac{d}{dx}(3 + x) + \ln(3 + x)(-1)] = (3 + x)^{3-x}[\frac{3 - x}{3 + x} - \ln(3 + x)]$.

(22) The rate of change of the pressure with respect to height at height h meters is

$\frac{dP}{dh} = \frac{d}{dh}[10^4 e^{-0.00012\,h}] = 10^4 e^{-0.00012\,h} \frac{d}{dh}(-0.00012\,h) = -0.00012(10^4) e^{-0.00012\,h}$

$= -1.2 e^{-0.00012\,h}$ kilograms per cubic meter.

At $h = 1000$ this equals $-1.2 e^{-0.12}$ kilograms per cubic meter.

(26) Make the substitution $u = -3t, du = -3dt$ in the indefinite integral:

$\int e^{-3t} dt = -\frac{1}{3} \int e^{-3t}(-3 dt) = -\frac{1}{3} \int e^u du = -\frac{1}{3} e^u + C = -\frac{1}{3} e^{-3t} + C$

Check:

$\frac{d}{dt}[-\frac{1}{3} e^{-3t}] = -\frac{1}{3} e^{-3t} \frac{d}{dt}(-3t) = -\frac{1}{3} e^{-3t}(-3) = e^{-3t}$

Evaluate the definite integral:

$\int_0^2 e^{-3t} dt = [-\frac{1}{3} e^{-3t}]_0^2 = [-\frac{1}{3} e^{-3(2)}] - [-\frac{1}{3} e^{-3(0)}] = [-\frac{1}{3} e^{-6}] - [-\frac{1}{3}]$

$= -\frac{1}{3} e^{-6} + \frac{1}{3} = \frac{1}{3}(1 - e^{-6})$

(28) Make the substitution $u = e^t$, $du = e^t \, dt$:

$$\int e^t \cos(e^t) \, dt = \int \cos(e^t)(e^t \, dt) = \int \cos u \, du = \sin u + C = \sin(e^t) + C$$

(30) Use Theorem 7.7 to find the indefinite integral of π^x:

$$\int (x^\pi - \pi^x) \, dx = \frac{1}{\pi + 1} x^{\pi+1} - \frac{1}{\ln(\pi)} \pi^x + C.$$

Then evaluate the definite integral:

$$\int_1^\pi (x^\pi - \pi^x) \, dx = \left[\frac{1}{\pi + 1} x^{\pi+1} - \frac{1}{\ln(\pi)} \pi^x \right]_1^\pi$$

$$= \left[\frac{1}{\pi + 1} \pi^{\pi+1} - \frac{1}{\ln(\pi)} \pi^\pi \right] - \left[\frac{1}{\pi + 1} 1^{\pi+1} - \frac{1}{\ln(\pi)} \pi^1 \right]$$

$$= \frac{1}{\pi + 1} (\pi^{\pi+1} - 1) - \frac{1}{\ln(\pi)} (\pi^\pi - \pi) = \frac{1}{\pi+1}(\pi^{\pi+1} - 1) - \frac{\pi}{\ln(\pi)}(\pi^{\pi-1} - 1)$$

(32) Use $u = \cos(7x)$, $du = \left[\frac{d}{dx} \cos(7x) \right] dx = [- \sin(7x) \frac{d}{dx}(7x)] dx = -7 \sin(7x) \, dx$ to evaluate the indefinite integral:

$$\int \sin(7x) \, e^{\cos(7x)} \, dx = -\frac{1}{7} \int e^{\cos(7x)}[- 7 \sin(7x) \, dx] = -\frac{1}{7} \int e^u \, du$$

$$= -\frac{1}{7} e^u + C = -\frac{1}{7} e^{\cos(7x)} + C$$

Check:

$$\frac{d}{dx}\left[-\frac{1}{7} e^{\cos(7x)} \right] = -\frac{1}{7} e^{\cos(7x)} \frac{d}{dx} \cos(7x) = -\frac{1}{7} e^{\cos(7x)}[- \sin(7x) \frac{d}{dx}(7x)]$$

$$= -\frac{1}{7} e^{\cos(7x)}(-7) \sin(7x) = \sin(7x) \, e^{\cos(7x)}$$

Evaluate the definite integral:

$$\int_0^1 \sin(7x) \, e^{\cos(7x)} \, dx = \left[-\frac{1}{7} e^{\cos(7x)} \right]_0^1 = \left[-\frac{1}{7} e^{\cos[7(1)]} \right] - \left[-\frac{1}{7} e^{\cos[7(0)]} \right]$$

$$= \left[-\frac{1}{7} e^{\cos(7)} \right] - \left[-\frac{1}{7} e^{\cos(0)} \right] = -\frac{1}{7} e^{\cos(7)} + \frac{1}{7} e^1 = \frac{1}{7}(e - e^{\cos(7)})$$

(38) If a is positive, the area is

$$\int_0^a e^{-x} \, dx = [-e^{-x}]_0^a = [-e^{-a}] - [-e^{-0}] = 1 - e^{-a}.$$

For this to equal 0.99, we must have $1 - e^{-a} = 0.99$, which implies that $e^{-a} = 0.01$.
We take logarithms to obtain $\ln(e^{-a}) = \ln(0.01)$ or $-a = \ln(0.01)$. Thus, we obtain a
positive solution a by taking $a = -\ln(0.01) = \ln(100)$.

If a is negative, the area is

$$\int_a^0 e^{-x}\, dx = [-e^{-x}]_a^0 = [-e^{-0}] - [-e^{-a}] = e^{-a} - 1.$$

For the area to be 0.99, we must have $e^{-a} - 1 = 0.99$, which gives $e^{-a} = 1.99$ and then
$-a = \ln(1.99)$. The negative solution is $a = -\ln(1.99)$.

(44) Because x and $1 - e^x$ are defined for all x, the function $\dfrac{x}{1 - e^x}$ is
defined for all x such that the denominator $1 - e^x$ is not zero. This is for all
$x \neq 0$, since e^x equals 1 only at $x = 0$.

The last step in computing a value of $\dfrac{x}{1 - e^x}$ is to compute the quotient,
so the first step in finding the derivative is to use the quotient rule:

$$\frac{d}{dx}\left[\frac{x}{1 - e^x}\right] = \frac{(1 - e^x)\frac{d}{dx}(x) - x\frac{d}{dx}(1 - e^x)}{(1 - e^x)^2} = \frac{(1 - e^x)(1) - x(-e^x)}{(1 - e^x)^2}$$

$$= \frac{1 - e^x + xe^x}{(1 - e^x)^2}\ .$$

SECTION 7.6

(7) Let $P(t)$ (millions of people) be the population in year t. Then $\dfrac{dP}{dt} = rP$, $P(1790) = 4$,
and $P(1960) = 180$. The differential equation gives $P = Ce^{rt}$ with constants C and r
to be determined. The condition $P(1790) = 4$ gives the equation $4 = Ce^{1790r}$, which
implies that $C = 4e^{-1790r}$ and therefore $P = Ce^{rt} = 4e^{-1790r}\, e^{rt} = 4e^{(t-1790)r}$. Setting
$P = 180$ and $t = 1960$ in the last equation gives $180 = 4e^{(1960-1790)r}$. If we divide both

sides of the equation by 4 and perform the subtraction in the exponent, we obtain

$45 = e^{170r}$, which implies that $170r = \ln(45)$ and $r = \dfrac{\ln(45)}{170} \approx 0.0224$. Here we have

calculated $\ln(45)$ by writing it in the form $\ln(45) = \ln(10) + \ln(4.5)$

$\approx$ $2.30258 + 1.50408 = 3.80666.$

(8) By formula (6) in Section 7.6 of the text, if there were C grams of C^{14} in

the sample when it was formed, then there were $y(t) = C(\frac{1}{2})^{t/5700}$ grams t years later.

If 20% has decomposed after T years, then four fifths is left and $y(T) = \frac{4}{5}$, and, hence,

$\frac{4}{5} = (\frac{1}{2})^{T/5700}$. Taking natural logarithms of both sides of the last equation gives

$\ln(\frac{4}{5}) = \ln[(\frac{1}{2})^{T/5700}] = \frac{T}{5700} \ln(\frac{1}{2})$, so that

$$T = 5700 \left\{ \frac{\ln(\frac{4}{5})}{\ln(\frac{1}{2})} \right\}.$$

The table in the text gives values of $\ln x$ for $x \geq 1$, so we rewrite the formula for T as

$$T = 5700 \left\{ \frac{-\ln(\frac{5}{4})}{-\ln(2)} \right\} = 5700 \left\{ \frac{\ln(1.25)}{\ln(2)} \right\} \approx 5700[\frac{0.22314}{0.69315}] \approx 1835 \text{ years.}$$

(11) This exercise can be worked without calculus: If the number of bacteria in the test

tube triples every 10 hours and there are 30,000 after 10 hours, then there were 10,000

initially.

(To find the number at arbitrary times, we note that the number of bacteria at time t

(hours) is given by a formula of the form $y = C(3)^{t/10}$. Since there were 10,000 initially

(which we take to be at t = 0), the constant C is 10,000 and $y = 10,000(3)^{t/10}$.)

(13) By Theorem 7.8 the solutions of the differential equations are $N(t) = Ce^{-0.0005t}$

with C = N(0) the amount of the sample at t = 0. After 1000 seconds we have

$N(1000) = Ce^{-0.5}$ and the fraction that has decomposed is

$$\frac{N(0) - N(1000)}{N(0)} = \frac{C - Ce^{-0.5}}{C} = 1 - e^{-0.5} \approx 0.39347.$$

(19)   Newton's law of cooling gives the differential equation $\frac{dT}{dt} = k(70 - T)$

for the temperature $T = T(t)$ (degrees Fahrenheit). Setting $y = T - 70$ gives

$\frac{dy}{dt} = \frac{dT}{dt} = -ky$, so $y = Ce^{-kt}$ and hence $T = 70 + Ce^{-kt}$ for certain constants k and C.

If we let $t = 0$ (minutes) be the time when the temperature is $50°$, then $T(0) = 50$ and

$T(2) = 60$. Setting $t = 0$ and $T = 50$ in the equation $T = 70 + Ce^{-kt}$ gives

$50 = 70 + C$ to show that $C = -20$. Then setting $t = 2$ and $T = 60$ in the equation

$T = 70 - 20e^{-kt}$ yields $60 = 70 - 20e^{-2k}$ so that $20e^{-2k} = 10$, $e^{-2k} = \frac{1}{2}$, and

$e^{-kt} = (e^{-2k})^{t/2} = (\frac{1}{2})^{t/2}$. Thus, $T = 70 - 20(\frac{1}{2})^{t/2}$ and five minutes after the

box is placed in the room its temperature is $T(5) = 70 - 20(\frac{1}{2})^{5/2} = 70 - 5(\frac{1}{2})^{1/2} \approx 66.46°F$.

SECTION 7.7

(5) By Theorem 7.9 an initial deposit of C dollars grows into $C[1 + \frac{0.1}{2}]^{2N} = C(1.05)^{2N}$

dollars after N years. Here N can take the values $\frac{1}{2}$, 1, $\frac{3}{2}$, 2,... We want the least

of these numbers such that $(1.05)^{2N}$ is greater than or equal to 2. The equation

$(1.05)^{2N} = 2$ is equivalent to the equation $2N \ln(1.05) = \ln(2)$, which has the solution

$N = \frac{1}{2} \frac{\ln(2)}{\ln(1.05)} \approx 7.1$. The least integer or half integer greater than 7.1 is 7.5, so

the account will double in seven and a half years.

(7) The present value of the profit is $f(t) = 5000 \, e^{\sqrt{t}} e^{-0.1t} = 5000 \, e^{\sqrt{t}-0.1t}$. To find

its maximum value we compute its derivative

$$f'(t) = \frac{d}{dt}(5000 \, e^{\sqrt{t}-0.1t}) = 5000 \, e^{\sqrt{t}-0.1t} \frac{d}{dt}(t^{1/2} - 0.1t)$$

$$= 5000 \, e^{\sqrt{t}-0.1t} \, (\frac{1}{2} t^{-1/2} - 0.1) = 5000 \, e^{\sqrt{t}-0.1t} \, (\frac{1}{2})(t^{-1/2} - 0.2).$$

The derivative is zero for t such that $t^{-1/2} = 0.2$, which means that $t = (0.2)^{-2} = \frac{1}{0.04} = 25$.

The derivative is positive for $t < 25$ and negative for $t > 25$. The present value is

a maximum for $t = 25$; the trees should be cut in 25 years.

(11)   The present value Q is the amount that would yield \$15,000 in four years

if it earned 3.5% interest compounded annually.   Hence $Q(1 + 0.035)^4 = 15,000$

and $Q = 15,000(1.035)^{-4} \approx \$13,071.63$.

SECTION 7.8

(1a) The point $(\cos(\frac{7\pi}{4}), \sin(\frac{7\pi}{4}))$ is a distance 1 from the origin along the terminal

side of the angle $\frac{7\pi}{4}$ (Fig. 7.8.1a). The terminal side of the angle, the vertical line

through the point, and the u-axis form an isosceles right triangle with hypotenuse of

length 1. The length of the other sides is $\frac{1}{\sqrt{2}}$, so the point is $(\frac{1}{\sqrt{2}}, -\frac{1}{\sqrt{2}})$ and

$\sin(\frac{7\pi}{4}) = -\frac{1}{\sqrt{2}}$.

(1c) The terminal side of the angle -3π is the negative u-axis, so $\sin(-3\pi) = 0$,

$\cos(-3\pi) = -1$, and $\tan(-3\pi) = \frac{\sin(-3\pi)}{\cos(-3\pi)} = 0$.

(1d) The point on the unit circle at the terminal side of the angle $\frac{4\pi}{3}$ has coordinates

$(\cos(\frac{4\pi}{3}), \sin(\frac{4\pi}{3}))$ (Fig. 7.8.1d). The terminal side of the angle, the u-axis, and the

vertical line through the point form at $30°-60°$-right triangle with hypotenuse of length 1

The triangle is $\frac{1}{2}$ unit wide and $\frac{\sqrt{3}}{2}$ units high, so the point has coordinates $(-\frac{1}{2}, -\frac{\sqrt{3}}{2})$

and $\cos(\frac{4\pi}{3}) = -\frac{1}{2}$, $\sin(\frac{4\pi}{3}) = -\frac{\sqrt{3}}{2}$. Therefore, $\sec(\frac{4\pi}{3}) = \frac{1}{\cos(\frac{4\pi}{3})} = -2$.

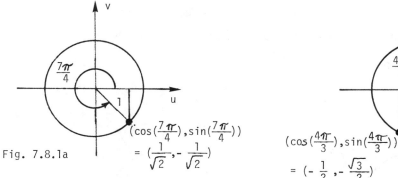

Fig. 7.8.1a

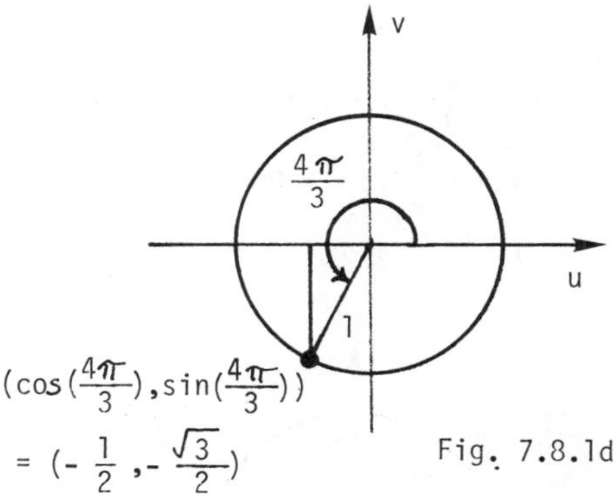

$(\cos(\frac{7\pi}{4}), \sin(\frac{7\pi}{4}))$
$= (\frac{1}{\sqrt{2}}, -\frac{1}{\sqrt{2}})$

$(\cos(\frac{4\pi}{3}), \sin(\frac{4\pi}{3}))$
$= (-\frac{1}{2}, -\frac{\sqrt{3}}{2})$

Fig. 7.8.1d

(2a) Table IV in the text gives the values of tan x for selected values of x in the

interval $0 \le x \le \frac{1}{2}\pi$. We use the facts that tan x is periodic of period

(tan x = tan(x + nπ) for integers n) and is odd (tan(-x) = - tan x) to express

$\tan(\frac{5\pi}{7})$ in terms of the tangent of an angle in the interval considered in the table:

$$\tan(\frac{5\pi}{7}) = \tan(\frac{5\pi}{7} - \pi) = \tan(-\frac{2\pi}{7}) = -\tan(\frac{2\pi}{7}) \approx -\tan(0.90) \approx -1.260.$$

(2d) Because sin x is periodic of period 2π and is odd, we have

$$\sin(5) = \sin(5 - 2\pi) \approx \sin(-1.28) = -\sin(1.28) \approx -0.958.$$

Therefore, $\cos(5) = \dfrac{1}{\sin(5)} \approx \dfrac{1}{-0.958} \approx -1.04.$

(3a) The equation $\sec(3x) = \sqrt{2}$ means $\cos(3x) = \dfrac{1}{\sqrt{2}}$. The vertical line $u = \dfrac{1}{\sqrt{2}}$

intersects the unit circle at the terminal sides of the angles whose cosines are $\dfrac{1}{\sqrt{2}}$

(Fig. 7.8.3a). Those angles are $\dfrac{1}{4}\pi + 2n\pi$ and $-\dfrac{1}{4}\pi + 2n\pi$ with integers n. Hence,

the solutions of the original equation are given by $3x = \pm\dfrac{1}{4}\pi + 2n\pi$ and are

$x = \pm\dfrac{1}{12}\pi + \dfrac{2}{3}n\pi$ with integers n.

(3g) We use the direct definition of the tangent described at the end of this section.
We plot the point at $v = \sqrt{3}$ on the vertical line $u = 1$. The angles whose terminal sides,
extended forward or backward, pass through that point are the angles whose tangents are $\sqrt{3}$
(Fig. 7.8.3g). The line through that point and the origin, the vertical line through that
point, and the u-axis form a right triangle of width 1 and height $\sqrt{3}$. Because its
hypotenuse has length $\sqrt{1^2 + (3)^2} = 2$, it is a 30°-60°-right triangle and its angle
at the origin is 60° or $\dfrac{1}{3}\pi$ radians. Hence the angles whose tangents are $\sqrt{3}$ are
the angles $\dfrac{1}{3}\pi + n\pi$ with integers n. The solutions of $\tan(10x) = \sqrt{3}$ are
given by $10x = \dfrac{1}{3}\pi + n\pi$ and are $x = \dfrac{1}{30}\pi + \dfrac{1}{10}n\pi$ with integers n.

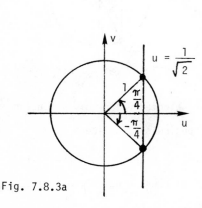

Fig. 7.8.3a

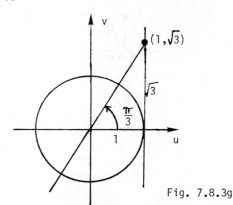

Fig. 7.8.3g

(4b) The angles x such that sec x = -4 are those such that cos x = $-\frac{1}{4}$ = - 0.25. These

are the angles whose terminal sides intersect the unit circle on the vertical line u = -0.25

(Fig. 7.8.4b). The table of cosines gives cos(1.32) $\approx$ 0.25, so the acute angles $\ominus$ in

Figure 7.84b are approximately 1.32 radians and the angles x shown in the figure are

approximately π - 1.32 and π + 1.32 radians. The other angles x with the same

cosine and secant differ from these by integer multiples of 2π. The solutions are

x = π $\pm$ 1.32 + 2nπ with integers n.

(4d) The angles 2x such that tan(2x) = $-\frac{1}{4}$ are those whose terminal sides,extended

forward or backward, intersect the vertical line u = 1 at v = $-\frac{1}{4}$. These are the angle

shown in Fig. 7.8.4d and angles that differ from it by multiples of π. The positive acute

angle $\ominus$ in the figure (which equals -2x for the angle 2x shown there) has tangent

equal to $\frac{1}{4}$ = 0.25, and the table gives tan(0.25) $\approx$ 0.25, so $\ominus$ $\approx$ 0.25 and the solutions

of tan(2x) = $-\frac{1}{4}$ are given by   2x $\approx$ - 0.25 + 2nπ and are x $\approx$ - 0.125 + nπ

with integers n.

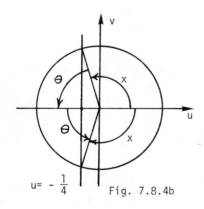

u= $-\frac{1}{4}$ Fig. 7.8.4b

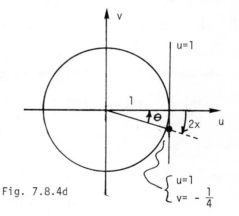

Fig. 7.8.4d

(7) $[\frac{d}{dx} \cot x]_{x=\pi/4}$ = $[- \csc^2 x]_{x=\pi/4}$ = $- \csc^2(\frac{\pi}{4})$ = $- \frac{1}{\sin^2(\frac{\pi}{4})}$ = $- \frac{1}{(\frac{1}{\sqrt{2}})^2}$ = -2

(10) $\frac{d}{dt} \tan(4t) = \sec^2(4t) \frac{d}{dt}(4t) = 4 \sec^2(4t)$

(12) $\frac{d}{dy} \cot^2 y = \frac{d}{dy}(\cot y)^2 = 2(\cot y)\frac{d}{dy} \cot y = 2 \cot y (- \csc^2 y) = -2 \cot y \csc^2 y$

(18) $\frac{dy}{dx} = \frac{d}{dx} \sec(3x) = \sec(3x) \tan(3x) \frac{d}{dx}(3x) = 3 \sec(3x) \tan(3x)$. At x = $\frac{\pi}{12}$ we have

$\sin(3x) = \sin(\frac{\pi}{4}) = \frac{1}{\sqrt{2}}$ and $\cos(3x) = \cos(\frac{\pi}{4}) = \frac{1}{\sqrt{2}}$, so $\sec(3x) = \frac{1}{\cos(3x)} = \sqrt{2}$,

$\tan(3x) = \frac{\sin(3x)}{\cos(3x)} = 1$, $y = \sec(3x) = \sqrt{2}$, and $\frac{dy}{dx} = 3\sec(3x)\tan(3x) = 3\sqrt{2}$. The tangent

line passes through the point $(\frac{\pi}{12}, \sqrt{2})$ and has slope $3\sqrt{2}$. It has the equation

$y - \sqrt{2} = 3\sqrt{2}(x - \frac{\pi}{12})$.

(20) Make the substitution $u = 2x$, $du = 2\,dx$ and use formula (17) in the text:

$$\int \sec(2x)\,\tan(2x)\,dx = \frac{1}{2}\int \sec(2x)\,\tan(2x)\,(2\,dx) = \frac{1}{2}\int \sec u\,\tan u\,du$$

$$= \frac{1}{2}\sec u + C = \frac{1}{2}\sec(2x) + C$$

(22) Make the substitution $u = \tan x$, $du = \sec^2 x\,dx$:

$$\int \sqrt{\tan x}\,\sec^2 x\,dx = \int \sqrt{u}\,du = \int u^{1/2}\,du = \frac{1}{3/2}u^{3/2} + C = \frac{2}{3}u^{3/2} + C$$

$$= \frac{2}{3}(\tan x)^{3/2} + C$$

(26) $\displaystyle\int_0^{\pi/4} \sec^2 t\,dt = [\tan t]_0^{\pi/4} = \tan(\frac{\pi}{4}) - \tan(0) = 1 - 0 = 1$

(34) The derivative of the function is $\frac{d}{dx}[\sqrt{3}\cos(2x) - \sin(2x)] = -2\sqrt{3}\sin(2x) - 2\cos(2x)$

$= -2[\sqrt{3}\sin(2x) + \cos(2x)]$ and is zero at values of x such that $\sqrt{3}\sin(2x) + \cos(2x) = 0$,

which means that $\tan(2x) = -\frac{1}{\sqrt{3}}$. These are the values of x where $2x = -\frac{\pi}{6} + n\pi$ with

integers n (Fig. 7.8.34). For even integers n we have $\sin(2x) = \sin(-\frac{\pi}{6}) = -\frac{1}{2}$,

$\cos(2x) = \cos(-\frac{\pi}{6}) = \frac{\sqrt{3}}{2}$, and $\sqrt{3}\cos(2x) - \sin(2x) = \sqrt{3}(\frac{\sqrt{3}}{2}) - (\frac{1}{2}) = \frac{3}{2} + \frac{1}{2} = 2$. For odd

integers n, we have $\sin(2x) = \sin(\frac{5\pi}{6}) = -\sin(-\frac{\pi}{6}) = \frac{1}{2}$, $\cos(2x) = \cos(\frac{5\pi}{6}) = -\cos(-\frac{\pi}{6})$

$= -\frac{\sqrt{3}}{2}$, and $\sqrt{3}\cos(2x) - \sin(2x) = \sqrt{3}(-\frac{\sqrt{3}}{2}) - (\frac{1}{2}) = -\frac{3}{2} - \frac{1}{2} = -2$. Because the function

$3\cos(2x) - \sin(2x)$ is continuous for all x and is periodic, its maxima and minima

must occur at its critical points. Its maximum value is 2 and its minimum value is -2.

(36) The object's distance to the origin at time t is $[(2 \cos t)^2 + (3 \sin t)^2]^{1/2}$

$= [4 \cos^2 t + 9 \sin^2 t]^{1/2}$ and has the derivative

$$\frac{d}{dt}[4 \cos^2 t + 9 \sin^2 t]^{1/2} = \frac{1}{2}[4 \cos^2 t + 9 \sin^2 t]^{-1/2} \frac{d}{dt}[4 \cos^2 t + 9 \sin^2 t]$$

$$= \frac{1}{2}[4 \cos^2 t + 9 \sin^2 t]^{-1/2}[4(2) \cos t \frac{d}{dt} \cos t + 9(2) \sin t \frac{d}{dt} \sin t]$$

(*) $$= \frac{1}{2}[4 \cos^2 t + 9 \sin^2 t]^{-1/2} [-8 \cos t \sin t + 18 \sin t \cos t]$$

$$= [4 \cos^2 t + 9 \sin^2 t]^{-1/2}(5 \sin t \cos t).$$

The sine and cosine of $\frac{\pi}{4}$ are both $\frac{1}{\sqrt{2}}$, so at $t = \frac{\pi}{4}$, the derivative (*) of the distance

is $[4(\frac{1}{\sqrt{2}})^2 + 9(\frac{1}{\sqrt{2}})^2]^{-1/2}(5)(\frac{1}{\sqrt{2}})(\frac{1}{\sqrt{2}}) = [2 + \frac{9}{2}]^{-1/2}(\frac{5}{2}) = (\frac{13}{2})^{-1/2}(\frac{5}{2}) = \frac{5\sqrt{2}}{2\sqrt{13}} = \frac{5}{\sqrt{26}}$.

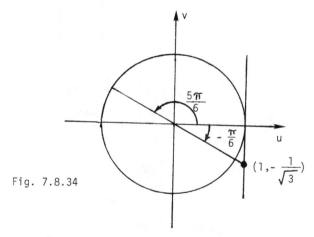

Fig. 7.8.34

(39c) $\frac{d}{dx}[x^2 \sin x] = [\frac{d}{dx} x^2][\sin x] + [x^2][\frac{d}{dx} \sin x] = 2x \sin x + x^2 \cos x$

$$\frac{d^2}{dx^2}[x^2 \sin x] = \frac{d}{dx}[2x \sin x + x^2 \cos x]$$

$$= [\frac{d}{dx}(2x)][\sin x] + [2x][\frac{d}{dx} \sin x] + [\frac{d}{dx} x^2][\cos x] + [x^2][\frac{d}{dx} \cos x]$$

$$= 2 \sin x + 2x \cos x + 2x \cos x - x^2 \sin x = 2 \sin x + 4x \cos x - x^2 \sin x$$

(43)   We write the equation $\tan^3 x = 3 \tan x$ as $\tan^3 x - 3 \tan x = 0$ and then as $(\tan x)(\tan^2 x - 3) = 0$. The solutions are those numbers x such that $\tan x = 0$ or $\tan x = \pm\sqrt{3}$. The solutions of $\tan x = 0$ are $x = k\pi$ for integers k; the solutions of $\tan x = \sqrt{3}$ are $x = \frac{1}{3}\pi + k\pi$ (Fig. 7.8.43a); and the solutions of $\tan x = -\sqrt{3}$ are $x = -\frac{1}{3}\pi + k\pi$ (Fig. 7.8.43b). Combining these three sets of numbers, we obtain the solutions $x = \frac{1}{3} n\pi$ with n an arbitrary integer.

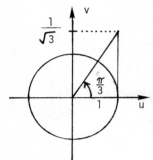

Fig. 7.8.43a

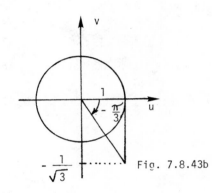

Fig. 7.8.43b

(65)   We let Θ_1 be the angle of inclination of the tangent line to $y = x^2$ (Fig. 7.8.65a)   and Θ_2 the angle of inclination of the tangent line to $y = 16x^{-2}$ (Fig. 7.8.65b). The slope of the first tangent line is $\tan\Theta_1 = [\frac{d}{dx} x^2]_{x=-2}$

$= [2x]_{x=-2} = -4$ and the slope of the second is $\tan\Theta_2 = [\frac{d}{dx}(16x^{-2})]_{x=-2} = [-32x^{-3}]_{x=-2}$

$= 4$. One of the angles between the tangent lines is $\Theta = \Theta_1 - \Theta_2$, where

$$\tan\Theta = \tan(\Theta_1 - \Theta_2) = \frac{\tan\Theta_1 - \tan\Theta_2}{1 + \tan\Theta_1 \tan\Theta_2} = \frac{-4 - 4}{1 + (-4)(4)} = \frac{8}{15} \, .$$

Since Fig. 7.8.65a and Fig. 7.8.65b show that Θ is a positive acute angle, we have

$\Theta = \arctan(\frac{8}{15}) \approx 0.49$ radians. (The other angles between the lines are of the form $\pm\Theta + n\pi$ with integers n.)

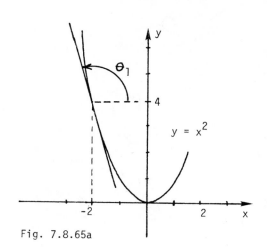

Fig. 7.8.65a

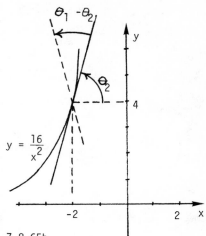

Fig. 7.8.65b

SECTION 7.9

(1b) Because $\frac{4\pi}{5}$ is in the interval $0 \leq \theta \leq \pi$, $\arccos[\cos(\frac{4\pi}{5})] = \frac{4\pi}{5}$.

(1e) The angle $\theta = \arcsin(-\frac{1}{4})$ is shown in Figure 7.9.1e. Its sine is $-\frac{1}{4}$ and its cosine is positive, so $\cos\theta = \sqrt{1 - \sin^2\theta} = \sqrt{1 - (\frac{1}{4})^2} = \sqrt{\frac{15}{16}} = \frac{1}{4}\sqrt{15}$. Hence

$$\tan[\arcsin(-\frac{1}{4})] = \tan\theta = \frac{\sin\theta}{\cos\theta} = \frac{-\frac{1}{4}}{\frac{\sqrt{15}}{4}} = -\frac{1}{\sqrt{15}}$$

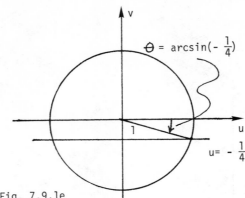

$\theta = \arcsin(-\frac{1}{4})$

$u = -\frac{1}{4}$

Fig. 7.9.1e

(1g) The tangent of arctan x is x for any x, so $\tan[\arctan(-5)] = -5$.

(3) $\dfrac{d}{dx}\arcsin(x^2) = \dfrac{1}{\sqrt{1 - (x^2)^2}}\ \dfrac{d}{dx}(x^2) = \dfrac{2x}{\sqrt{1 - x^4}} = 2x(1 - x^4)^{-1/2}$

(9) $\dfrac{d}{dz}\arctan(7\sec z) = \dfrac{1}{1 + (7\sec z)^2}\ \dfrac{d}{dz}(7\sec z) = \dfrac{7\sec z\ \tan z}{1 + 49\sec^2 z}$

(14) Make the substitution $u = x^3$, $du = 3x^2\ dx$:

$$\int \frac{x^2}{1 + x^6}\ dx = \frac{1}{3}\int \frac{1}{1 + (x^3)^2}\ (3x^2\ dx) = \frac{1}{3}\int \frac{1}{1 + u^2}\ du = \frac{1}{3}\arctan u + C$$

$$= \frac{1}{3}\arctan(x^3) + C$$

Check:

$$\frac{d}{dx}[\frac{1}{3}\arctan(x^3)] = \frac{1}{3}\ \frac{1}{1 + (x^3)^2}\ \frac{d}{dx}(x^3) = \frac{1}{3}\ \frac{1}{1 + (x^3)^2}\ (3x^2) = \frac{x^2}{1 + x^6}$$

(17) By formula (14) in this section of the text with $a = 2$

$$\int \frac{1}{\sqrt{4 - x^2}}\ dx = \arcsin(\frac{x}{2}) + C$$

Therefore,

$$\int_0^1 \frac{1}{\sqrt{4 - x^2}}\ dx = [\arcsin(\frac{x}{2})]_0^1 = \arcsin(\frac{1}{2}) - \arcsin(0) = \frac{\pi}{6} - 0 = \frac{\pi}{6}$$

(19) Make the substitution $u = \arctan x$, $du = \dfrac{1}{1 + x^2}\, dx$:

$$\int \frac{\arctan x}{1 + x^2}\, dx = \int \arctan x\ \left(\frac{1}{1 + x^2}\, dx\right) = \int u\ du = \tfrac{1}{2}\, u^2 + C = \tfrac{1}{2}(\arctan x)^2 + C$$

(24) At $x = \dfrac{1}{2}$ we have $y = \arcsin\left(\tfrac{1}{2}\right) = \dfrac{\pi}{6}$ and $\dfrac{dy}{dx} = \left[\dfrac{1}{\sqrt{1 - x^2}}\right]_{x = \frac{1}{2}} = \dfrac{1}{\sqrt{1 - \frac{1}{4}}} = \dfrac{2}{\sqrt{3}}$.

The tangent line passes through the point $\left(\tfrac{1}{2}, \tfrac{\pi}{6}\right)$ and has slope $\dfrac{2}{\sqrt{3}}$. It has the equation

$y - \dfrac{\pi}{6} = \dfrac{2}{\sqrt{3}}\left(x - \tfrac{1}{2}\right)$.

(32) $\dfrac{dF}{d\theta} = \dfrac{d}{d\theta}\left[\mu W(\cos\theta + \mu\sin\theta)^{-1}\right] = -\mu W(\cos\theta + \mu\sin\theta)^{-2}\,\dfrac{d}{d\theta}(\cos\theta + \mu\sin\theta)$

$\quad = \dfrac{-\mu W}{(\cos\theta + \mu\sin\theta)^2}(-\sin\theta + \mu\cos\theta) = \dfrac{\mu W\cos\theta}{(\cos\theta + \mu\sin\theta)^2}(\tan\theta - \mu)$

The derivative is zero for $\tan\theta = \mu$, negative for $\tan\theta < \mu$, and positive for

$\tan\theta > \mu$. Hence, the derivative is zero for $\theta = \arctan\mu$, negative for $\theta < \arctan\mu$,

and positive for $\theta > \arctan\mu$. The force F is a minimum for $\theta = \arctan\mu$.

SECTION 7.10

(4) To compute a value of $\cosh^3(x^{1/3})$ we first find the cube root of x, then we

compute the hyperbolic cosine, and finally we take the third power. Therefore, in computing

the derivative, we first differentiate the third power, then the hyperbolic cosine, and

finally the cube root:

$$\frac{d}{dx}\cosh^3(x^{1/3}) = \frac{d}{dx}[\cosh(x^{1/3})]^3 = 3[\cosh(x^{1/3})]^2\,\frac{d}{dx}\cosh(x^{1/3})$$

$$= 3\cosh^2(x^{1/3})\,\sinh(x^{1/3})\,\frac{d}{dx}x^{1/3} = 3\cosh^2(x^{1/3})\,\sinh(x^{1/3})\left(\tfrac{1}{3}x^{-2/3}\right)$$

$$= x^{-2/3}\cosh^2(x^{1/3})\,\sinh(x^{1/3})$$

(6) $\dfrac{d}{dx}\ln(\cosh x) = \dfrac{1}{\cosh x}\,\dfrac{d}{dx}\cosh x = \dfrac{\sinh x}{\cosh x} = \tanh x$

(8) To compute a value of $\sqrt{\sinh^2 x + 1}$, we first find $\sinh x$, then $\sinh^2 x + 1$, and finally compute the square root. In finding the derivative we first differentiate the square root, then the square, and finally the hyperbolic sine:

$$\frac{d}{dx}(\sinh^2 x + 1)^{1/2} = \frac{1}{2}(\sinh^2 x + 1)^{-1/2}\, \frac{d}{dx}(\sinh^2 x + 1)$$

$$= \frac{1}{2}(\sinh^2 x + 1)^{-1/2}(2 \sinh x \frac{d}{dx} \sinh x) = \frac{\sinh x \cosh x}{\sqrt{\sinh^2 x + 1}} = \sinh x.$$

We simplified the answer by using the identity $\cosh x = \sqrt{\sin^2 x + 1}$, which comes from the identity $\cosh^2 x = \sinh^2 x + 1$ and the fact that $\cosh x$ is positive for all x. If we had used the identity at the beginning, we would have obtained the answer more quickly:

$$\frac{d}{dx} \sqrt{\sinh^2 x + 1} = \frac{d}{dx} \cosh x = \sinh x$$

(14) Make the substitution $u = x^{1/2}$, $du = \frac{1}{2} x^{-1/2}\, dx$:

$$\int \frac{\sinh(\sqrt{x})}{\sqrt{x}}\, dx = 2 \int \sinh(x^{1/2})(\frac{1}{2} x^{-1/2}\, dx) = 2 \int \sinh u\, du = 2 \cosh u + C$$

$$= 2 \cosh(\sqrt{x}) + C$$

(20) Make the substitution $u = \ln x$, $du = \frac{1}{x} dx$ in the indefinite integral:

$$\int \frac{1}{x} \cosh(\ln x)\, dx = \int \cosh(\ln x)(\frac{1}{x} dx) = \int \cosh u\, du = \sinh u + C$$

$$= \sinh(\ln x) + C$$

Then evaluate the definite integral:

$$\int_1^{10} \frac{1}{x} \cosh(\ln x)dx = [\sinh(\ln x)]_1^{10} = \sinh(\ln(10)) - \sinh(\ln(1))$$

$$= \sinh(\ln(10)) - \sinh(0) = \sinh(\ln(10)) = \frac{1}{2}[e^{\ln(10)} - e^{-\ln(10)}]$$

$$= \frac{1}{2}[10 - \frac{1}{10}] = \frac{100 - 1}{20} = \frac{99}{20}$$

An alternate procedure: Use the identity

$$\cosh(\ln x) = \frac{1}{2}[e^{\ln x} + e^{-\ln x}] = \frac{1}{2}(x + \frac{1}{x})$$

to obtain

$$\int_1^{10} \frac{1}{x} \cosh(\ln x)\, dx = \int_1^{10} \frac{1}{2}(1 + x^{-2})\, dx = \left[\frac{1}{2}\left(x - \frac{1}{x}\right)\right]_1^{10} = \frac{99}{20}.$$

(22c) $\tanh(-0.5) = \dfrac{e^{-0.5} - e^{0.5}}{e^{-0.5} + e^{0.5}} \approx \dfrac{0.60653 - 1.6487}{0.60653 + 1.6487} \approx -0.4621$

(37)   The x-coordinate $\bar{x}$ of the centroid is zero because the portion of the catenary we are considering is symmetric about the y-axis.

For $y = \cosh x$, we have $\dfrac{dy}{dx} = \sinh x$, so the length of the curve is

$$L = \int_{-1}^1 \sqrt{1 + \left(\frac{dy}{dx}\right)^2}\, dx = \int_{-1}^1 \sqrt{1 + \sinh^2 x}\, dx = \int_{-1}^1 \cosh x\, dx = [\sinh x]_{-1}^1$$

$$= \sinh(1) - \sinh(-1) = 2\sinh(1).$$

By Rule 6.16 the y-coordinate of the centroid is

$$\bar{y} = \frac{1}{L}\int_{-1}^1 y\sqrt{1 + \left(\frac{dy}{dx}\right)^2}\, dx = \frac{1}{L}\int_{-1}^1 \cosh x\sqrt{1 + \sinh^2 x}\, dx = \frac{1}{L}\int_{-1}^1 \cosh^2 x\, dx.$$

We could use the identity $\cosh^2 x = \frac{1}{2}[\cosh(2x) + 1]$ to evaluate this integral (see Exercise 23h). Instead we will express the hyperbolic cosine in terms of the exponential function:

$$\bar{y} = \frac{1}{L}\int_{-1}^1 \cosh^2 x\, dx = \frac{1}{L}\int_{-1}^1 \left[\frac{e^x + e^{-x}}{2}\right]^2 dx = \frac{1}{4L}\int_{-1}^1 \left[(e^x)^2 + 2e^x(e^{-x}) + (e^{-x})^2\right] dx$$

$$= \frac{1}{4L}\int_{-1}^1 (e^{2x} + 2 + e^{-2x})\, dx = \frac{1}{4L}\left[\frac{1}{2}e^{2x} + 2x - \frac{1}{2}e^{-2x}\right]_{-1}^1$$

$$= \frac{1}{4L}\left[\frac{1}{2}e^2 + 2 - \frac{1}{2}e^{-2}\right] - \frac{1}{4L}\left[\frac{1}{2}e^{-2} - 2 - \frac{1}{2}e^2\right] = \frac{1}{4L}\left[e^2 + 4 - e^{-2}\right]$$

Since $L = 2\sinh(1) = e^1 - e^{-1}$, we obtain

$$\bar{y} = \frac{1}{4}\left\{\frac{e^2 + 4 - e^{-2}}{e - e^{-1}}\right\} = \frac{1}{4}\left\{\frac{(e + e^{-1})(e - e^{-1}) + 4}{e - e^{-1}}\right\} = \frac{1}{2}\left\{\frac{e + e^{-1}}{2} + \frac{2}{e - e^{-1}}\right\}$$

$$= \frac{1}{2}\left[\cosh(1) + \frac{1}{\sinh(1)}\right] = \frac{1}{2}[\cosh(1) + \operatorname{csch}(1)].$$

SECTION 8.1

(1a) Because of the expression $\sqrt{x^2 + 6}$ in the integrand, we try the substitution $u = x^2 + 6$, for which $\frac{du}{dx} = 2x$ and $du = 2x\,dx$. This substitution will work because there is an x in the integrand and we can transform the integral into the form $\int u^{1/2}\,du$ by adjusting a constant factor.

(1b) We set $u = x^2 + 6$, $du = 2x\,dx$:

$$\int x\sqrt{x^2 + 1}\,dx = \frac{1}{2}\int (x^2 + 1)^{1/2}(2x\,dx) = \frac{1}{2}\int u^{1/2}\,du = \frac{1}{2}(\frac{1}{3/2})u^{3/2} + C$$

$$= \frac{1}{3}u^{3/2} + C = \frac{1}{3}(x^2 + 1)^{3/2} + C$$

Check:
$$\frac{d}{dx}[\frac{1}{3}(x^2 + 1)^{3/2}] = (\frac{1}{3})(\frac{3}{2})(x^2 + 1)^{1/2}\frac{d}{dx}(x^2 + 1) = \frac{1}{2}(x^2 + 1)^{1/2}(2x) = x\sqrt{x^2 + 1}$$

(5a) The substitution $u = \sec x$ would require $du = \sec x \tan x\,dx$ and would not work in this integral. The substitution $u = \tan x$, however, requires $du = \sec^2 x\,dx$ and puts the integral in the form $\int u^2\,du$:

(5b) With $u = \tan x$, $du = \sec^2 x\,dx$ we obtain

$$\int \tan^2 x\,\sec^2 x\,dx = \int u^2\,du = \frac{1}{3}u^3 + C = \frac{1}{3}\tan^3 x + C.$$

(7a) We have to use one of formulas (1) through (13) with a denominator in it or have the denominator be part of the du in the substitution. We set $u = x + \sin x$, for which $du = (1 + \cos x)dx$ and use formula (1) with $n = -1$.

(7b) The substitution $u = x + \sin x$, $du = (1 + \cos x)dx$ gives

$$\int \frac{1 + \cos x}{x + \sin x}\,dx = \int \frac{1}{x + \sin x}(1 + \cos x)dx = \int \frac{1}{u}\,du = \ln|u| + C = \ln|x + \sin x| + C.$$

(9a) Write $\cot(3x) = \frac{\cos(3x)}{\sin(3x)}$ and use the substitution $u = \sin(3x)$, $du = 3\cos x\,dx$ with integration formula (1).

(9b) With $u = \sin(3x)$, $du = 3\cos(3x)\,dx$ we have

$$\int \cot(3x)\ dx = \int \frac{\cos(3x)}{\sin(3x)}\ dx = \frac{1}{3} \int \frac{1}{\sin(3x)}\,(3\,\cos(3x)\ dx) = \frac{1}{3} \int \frac{1}{u}\ du$$

$$= \frac{1}{3}\ \ln|u| + C = \frac{1}{3}\ \ln|\sin(3x)| + C$$

Check:

$$\frac{d}{dx}[\frac{1}{3}\ \ln|\sin(3x)|\,] = \frac{1}{3}\ \frac{1}{\sin(3x)}\ \frac{d}{dx}\sin(3x) = \frac{1}{3}\ \frac{1}{\sin(3x)}\ \cos(3x)\ \frac{d}{dx}(3x) = \frac{\cos(3x)}{\sin(3x)} = \cot(3x)$$

(13a) Note that $\sqrt{9 - x^4} = \sqrt{3^2 - (x^2)^2}$ and that except for a constant factor the derivative $\frac{d}{dx}(x^2) = 2x$ is the numerator in the integral. Use the substitution $u = x^2$ with integration formula (8).

(13b) With $u = x^2$, $du = 2x\ dx$ and formula (8) with $a = 3$, we obtain

$$\int \frac{x}{\sqrt{9 - x^4}}\ dx = \frac{1}{2} \int \frac{1}{\sqrt{3^2 - (x^2)^2}}\,(2x\ dx) = \frac{1}{2}\int \frac{1}{\sqrt{3^2 - u^2}}\ du = \frac{1}{2}\ \arcsin(\frac{u}{3}) + C$$

$$= \frac{1}{2}\ \arcsin(\frac{x^2}{3}) + C$$

Check:

$$\frac{d}{dx}\ \arcsin(\frac{x^2}{3}) = \frac{1}{2}\ \frac{1}{\sqrt{1 - (\frac{x^2}{3})^2}}\ \frac{d}{dx}(\frac{x^2}{3}) = \frac{1}{2}\ \frac{1}{\sqrt{\frac{9 - x^4}{9}}}\,(\frac{2}{3}\,x) = \frac{x}{\sqrt{9 - x^4}}$$

(This is a case where checking the answer requires more difficult algebra than working the problem. Nevertheless, carrying out the check is a good policy when you have the time and when the accuracy of your answer is important to you.)

(15a) None of the basic formulas involve arcsin x, so we try the substitution $u = \arcsin x$, $du = \frac{1}{\sqrt{1 - x^2}}$. This works with formula (1) and $n = 1$.

(15b) The substitution $u = \arcsin x$ gives

$$\int \frac{\arcsin x}{\sqrt{1 - x^2}}\ dx = \int \arcsin x\ \frac{1}{\sqrt{1 - x^2}}\ dx = \int u\ du = \frac{1}{2}\ u^2 + C = \frac{1}{2}\ [\arcsin x]^2 + C$$

(19a) Rule 8.2 indicates that we should write $\csc(6x) = \dfrac{\csc(6x)[\csc(6x) + \cot(6x)]}{\csc(6x) + \cot(6x)}$ and

use the substitution $u = \csc(6x) + \cot(6x)$ with formula (1) for $n = -1$.

(19b) We have $\dfrac{d}{dx}[\csc(6x) + \cot(6x)] = [-\csc^2(6x) - \csc(6x)\cot(6x)]\dfrac{d}{dx}(6x)$

$= -6[\csc^2(6x) + \csc(6x)\cot(6x)]$, so with $u = \csc(6x) + \cot(6x)$, we have

$du = -6[\csc^2(6x) + \csc(6x)\cot(6x)]$ and

$$\int \csc(6x)\,dx = \int \frac{\csc(6x)[\csc(6x) + \cot(6x)]}{\csc(6x) + \cot(6x)}\,dx$$

$$= -\frac{1}{6}\int \frac{1}{\csc(6x) + \cot(6x)}\,(-6)[\csc^2(6x) + \csc(6x)\cot(6x)]\,dx$$

$$= -\frac{1}{6}\int \frac{1}{u}\,du = -\frac{1}{6}\ln|u| + C = -\frac{1}{6}\ln|\csc(6x) + \cot(6x)| + C$$

(23a) We cannot use formula (8) with $u = x$ and $a = 2$ because of the extra x in the
numerator of the integral. Instead we set $u = 4 - x^2$, $du = -2x\,dx$ and use formula (1) with
$n = -\dfrac{1}{2}$.

(23b) The substitution $u = 4 - x^2$, $du = -2x\,dx$ gives

$$\int \frac{x}{\sqrt{4 - x^2}}\,dx = -\frac{1}{2}\int (4 - x^2)^{-1/2}(-2x\,dx) = -\frac{1}{2}\int u^{-1/2} = -\frac{1}{2}\left(\frac{1}{1/2}\right)u^{1/2} + C$$

$$= -u^{1/2} + C = -(4 - x^2)^{1/2} + C$$

Check:

$$\frac{d}{dx}[-(4 - x^2)^{1/2}] = -\left(\frac{1}{2}\right)(4 - x^2)^{-1/2}\frac{d}{dx}(4 - x^2) = -\frac{1}{2}(4 - x^2)^{-1/2}(-2x) = \frac{x}{\sqrt{4 - x^2}}$$

$$\int_0^1 \frac{x}{\sqrt{4 - x^2}}\,dx = [-(4 - x^2)^{1/2}]\Big|_0^1 = [-(4 - 1^2)^{1/2}] - [-(4 - 0^2)^{1/2}] = 2 - 3^{1/2}$$

(29a) Because $\dfrac{d}{dx}\sqrt{x} = \dfrac{d}{dx}x^{1/2} = \dfrac{1}{2}x^{-1/2} = \dfrac{1}{2\sqrt{x}}$, we see we can use formula (6) with

the substitution $u = \sqrt{x}$.

(29b) We make the substitution $u = \sqrt{x}$, $du = \dfrac{1}{2\sqrt{x}} dx$:

$$\int \frac{1}{\sqrt{x}} \, \sec\sqrt{x} \, \tan\sqrt{x} \, dx = 2 \int \sec(\sqrt{x}) \, \tan(\sqrt{x})(\frac{1}{2\sqrt{x}} dx) = 2 \int \sec u \, \tan u \, du$$

$$= 2 \sec u + C = 2 \sec(\sqrt{x}) + C$$

(31a) We can either use the substitution $u = \sin x$, $du = \cos x \, dx$ or $u = \cos x$, $du = - \sin x \, dx$ along with formula (1) with $n = 1$.

(31b) If we use the substitution $u = \sin x$, $du = \cos x \, dx$ to evaluate the indefinite integral, we obtain

$$(*) \qquad \int \sin x \, \cos x \, dx = \int u \, du = \frac{1}{2} u^2 + C = \frac{1}{2} \sin^2 x + C.$$

If we use $u = \cos x$, $du = - \sin x \, dx$, we have

$$(**) \qquad \int \sin x \, \cos x \, dx = -\int \cos x \, (- \sin x \, dx) = - \int u \, du = - \frac{1}{2} u^2 + C_1 = - \frac{1}{2} \cos^2 x + C_1.$$

(Equations (*) and (**) are equivalent because $\sin^2 x = 1 - \cos^2 x$, so we obtain (**) from (*) by taking $C_1 = C - \frac{1}{2}$.)

Using (*) to evaluate the definite integral gives

$$(***) \int_0^2 \sin x \, \cos x \, dx = [\frac{1}{2} \sin^2 x]_0^2 = \frac{1}{2} \sin^2(2) - \frac{1}{2} \sin^2(0) = \frac{1}{2} \sin^2(2).$$

Using (**) yields

$$(****) \qquad \int_0^2 \sin x \, \cos x \, dx = [- \frac{1}{2} \cos^2 x]_0^2 = - \frac{1}{2} \cos^2(2) + \frac{1}{2} \cos^2(0) = \frac{1}{2} - \frac{1}{2} \cos^2(2).$$

Calculations (***) and (****) give the same result because $\sin^2(2) = 1 - \cos^2(2)$.

(45a) Because $\frac{d}{dx} \tan x = \sec^2 x$, we see we can use formula (8) with $u = \tan x$.

(45b) We set $u = \tan x$, $du = \sec^2 x \, dx$:

$$\int \frac{\sec^2 x}{\sqrt{1 - \tan^2 x}} = \int \frac{1}{\sqrt{1 - u^2}} \, du = \arcsin u + C = \arcsin(\tan x) + C$$

(51a) We make the substitution $u = 1 - 2x$, for which $x = \frac{1}{2} - \frac{1}{2} u$ and $dx = -\frac{1}{2} du$.

to put the high power on u instead of on $1 - 2x$. Then we can use formula (1) with the necessary values of n.

(51b). We set $u = 1 - 2x$, $x = \frac{1}{2} - \frac{1}{2} u$, and $dx = -\frac{1}{2} du$ in the indefinite integral:

$$\int x(1 - 2x)^{30} dx = \int (\frac{1}{2} - \frac{1}{2} u)u^{30}(-\frac{1}{2} du) = -\frac{1}{4} \int (u^{30} - u^{31})du = -\frac{1}{4}[\frac{1}{31} u^{31} - \frac{1}{32} u^{32}] + C$$

$$= -\frac{1}{124} u^{31} + \frac{1}{128} u^{32} + C = -\frac{1}{124}(1 - 2x)^{31} + \frac{1}{128}(1 - 2x)^{32} + C$$

We then evaluate the definite integral:

$$\int_0^1 x(1 - 2x)^{30} dx = [-\frac{1}{124}(1 - 2x)^{31} + \frac{1}{128}(1 - 2x)^{32}]_0^1$$

$$= [-\frac{1}{124}(1 - 2)^{31} + \frac{1}{128}(1 - 2)^{32}] - [-\frac{1}{124}(1 - 0)^{31} + \frac{1}{128}(1 - 0)^{32}]$$

$$= -\frac{1}{124}(-1)^{31} + \frac{1}{128}(-1)^{32} + \frac{1}{124}(1)^{31} - \frac{1}{128}(1)^{32} = \frac{1}{124} + \frac{1}{128} + \frac{1}{124} - \frac{1}{128} = \frac{1}{62}$$

(58) We try the substitution $u = x^{1/4}$ so that $x = u^4$, $x^{3/4} = u^3$ and $dx = 4u^3 du$
all involve integer powers of u:

$$\int \frac{5}{2x^{3/4} - 3x} dx = \int \frac{5}{2u^3 - 3u^4} (4u^3 du) = 20 \int \frac{1}{2 - 3u} du = -\frac{20}{3} \int \frac{1}{2 - 3u} (-3 du)$$

$$= -\frac{20}{3} \int \frac{1}{v} dv = -\frac{20}{3} \ln|v| + C = -\frac{20}{3} \ln|2 - 3u| + C$$

$$= -\frac{20}{3} \ln|2 - 3x^{1/4}| + C .$$

We used the substitution $v = 2 - 3u$ to evaluate the integral of u.

Check:

$$\frac{d}{dx}[-\frac{20}{3} \ln|2 - 3x^{1/4}|] = -\frac{20}{3} \frac{1}{2 - 3x^{1/4}} \frac{d}{dx}(2 - 3x^{1/4}) = -\frac{20}{3} \frac{1}{2 - 3x^{1/4}}(-\frac{3}{4} x^{-3/4})$$

$$= \frac{5}{(2 - 3x^{1/4})(x^{3/4})} = \frac{5}{2x^{3/4} - 3x}$$

(61) We make the substitution $u = e^x - 2$, for which $e^x = u + 2$ and $du = e^x dx = (u + 2)dx$, and hence $dx = \dfrac{1}{u + 2} du$:

$$\int \frac{e^{2x}}{\sqrt{e^x - 2}} dx = \int \frac{(u + 2)^2}{\sqrt{u}}\left(\frac{1}{u + 2} du\right) = \int \frac{u + 2}{\sqrt{u}} du = \int (u^{1/2} + 2u^{-1/2})du$$

$$= \frac{1}{3/2} u^{3/2} + \frac{2}{1/2} u^{1/2} + C = \frac{2}{3} u^{3/2} + 4 u^{1/2} + C$$

$$= \frac{2}{3}(e^x - 2)^{3/2} + 4(e^x - 2)^{1/2} + C$$

SECTION 8.2

(1) To make the substitution $u = \sqrt{x}$, we use $x = u^2$ and $dx = 2u\, du$. As x runs from 0 to 16, u runs from 0 to 4:

$$\int_0^{16} e^{\sqrt{x}}\, dx = \int_0^4 e^u(2u\, du) = 2 \int_0^4 u\, e^u\, du$$

(5) With $u = 9 - 3x$, we have $du = -3\, dx$ and $dx = -\dfrac{1}{3} du$. Also u runs from 9 to 3 as x runs from 0 to 2:

$$\int_0^2 \ln(9 - 3x)\, dx = \int_9^3 \ln u \left(-\frac{1}{3} du\right) = \frac{1}{3} \int_3^9 \ln u\, du$$

(7) With $u = e^x + 3$, we have $du = e^x dx = (u - 3)dx$ and $dx = \dfrac{1}{u - 3} du$. Also as $0 \xrightarrow[x]{} \ln(5)$, we have $4 \xrightarrow[u]{} 8$, since $e^0 + 3 = 4$ and $e^{\ln(5)} + 3 = 5 + 3 = 8$:

$$\int_0^{\ln(5)} \sqrt{e^x + 3}\ dx = \int_4^8 \frac{\sqrt{u}}{u - 3} du$$

SECTION 8.3

(5) When we integrate by parts, integrating the x and differentiating the $\ln x$, we end up with an integral of x, which we can evaluate:

$$\begin{cases} u = \ln x \\ \dfrac{dv}{dx} = x \end{cases} \qquad \begin{cases} \dfrac{du}{dx} = \dfrac{1}{x} \\ v = \dfrac{1}{2} x^2 \end{cases}$$

$$\int x \ln x \, dx = \frac{1}{2} x^2 \ln x - \int \frac{1}{2} x^2 (\frac{1}{x}) dx = \frac{1}{2} x^2 \ln x - \frac{1}{2} \int x \, dx$$

$$= \frac{1}{2} x^2 \ln x - \frac{1}{4} x^2 + C$$

Check:

$$\frac{d}{dx} [\frac{1}{2} x^2 \ln x - \frac{1}{4} x^2] = \frac{1}{2} [\frac{d}{dx} x^2] \ln x + \frac{1}{2} x^2 [\frac{d}{dx} \ln x] - \frac{1}{4} [\frac{d}{dx} x^2]$$

$$= x \ln x + \frac{1}{2} x^2 [\frac{1}{x}] - \frac{1}{4} (2x) = x \ln x.$$

(Notice that here as in any example of integration by parts, checking the integration requires the product rule.)

(7) This integral does not require integration by parts. We use the substitution $u = \ln x$, $du = \frac{1}{x} dx$:

$$\int \frac{1}{x \ln x} dx = \int \frac{1}{u} du = \ln|u| + C = \ln|\ln x| + C$$

(11) We integrate by parts twice, integrating the exponential function and differentiating the trigonometric function each time.

First:
$$\begin{cases} u = \sin x \\ \dfrac{dv}{dx} = e^x \end{cases} \qquad \begin{cases} \dfrac{du}{dx} = \cos x \\ v = e^x \end{cases}$$

$$\int e^x \sin x \, dx = e^x \sin x - \int e^x \cos x \, dx$$

Second:
$$\begin{cases} u = \cos x \\ \dfrac{dv}{dx} = e^x \end{cases} \qquad \begin{cases} \dfrac{du}{dx} = -\sin x \\ v = e^x \end{cases}$$

$$\int e^x \sin x \, dx = e^x \sin x - \left\{ e^x \cos x - \int e^x(-\sin x) \, dx \right\}$$

$$= e^x \sin x - e^x \cos x - \int e^x \sin x \, dx$$

Adding the integral of $e^x \sin x$ to both sides gives

$$2 \int e^x \sin x \, dx = e^x \sin x - e^x \cos x + C_1 = e^x(\sin x - \cos x) + C_1$$

We included the constant of integration C_1 because there is no longer an indefinite integral on the right side of the equation. Dividing by 2 gives

$$\int e^x \sin x = \frac{1}{2} e^x(\sin x - \cos x) + C_1$$

Check:

$$\frac{d}{dx}[\frac{1}{2} e^x(\sin x - \cos x)] = \frac{1}{2}[\frac{d}{dx} e^x](\sin x \quad \cos x) + \frac{1}{2} e^x \frac{d}{dx}(\sin x - \cos x)$$

$$= \frac{1}{2} e^x(\sin x - \cos x) + \frac{1}{2} e^x(\cos x + \sin x) = \frac{1}{2} e^x(2 \sin x) = e^x \sin x$$

(21) To evaluate the indefinite integral we integrate by parts twice, differentiating x^2 and integrating $\sin x$ the first time and differentiating x and integrating $\cos x$, the second. We end up with an integral of $\sin x$, which we can evaluate.

First:

$$\begin{cases} u = x^2 \\ \frac{dv}{dx} = \sin x \end{cases} \qquad \begin{cases} \frac{du}{dx} = 2x \\ v = -\cos x \end{cases}$$

$$\int x^2 \sin x \, dx = x^2(-\cos x) - \int (-\cos x)(2x) \, dx$$

$$= -x^2 \cos x + 2 \int x \cos x \, dx$$

Second:

$$\begin{cases} u = x \\ \frac{dv}{dx} = \cos x \end{cases} \qquad \begin{cases} \frac{du}{dx} = 1 \\ v = \sin x \end{cases}$$

$$\int x^2 \sin x \, dx = -x^2 \cos x + 2 \left\{ x \sin x - \int (\sin x)(1) \, dx \right\}$$

$$= - x^2 \cos x + 2x \sin x - 2 \int \sin x \, dx = - x^2 \cos x + 2x \sin x + 2 \cos x + C$$

Check:

$$\frac{d}{dx}[-x^2 \cos x + 2x \sin x + 2 \cos x]$$

$$= - [\frac{d}{dx} x^2] \cos x - x^2 [\frac{d}{dx} \cos x] + 2[\frac{d}{dx} x] \sin x + 2x[\frac{d}{dx} \sin x] + 2 \frac{d}{dx} \cos x$$

$$= -2x \cos x - x^2(- \sin x) \quad 2\sin x + 2x \cos x - 2 \sin x = x^2 \sin x$$

Then we evaluate the definite integral:

$$\int_0^{\pi/2} x^2 \sin x \, dx = [-x^2 \cos x + 2x \sin x + 2 \cos x]_0^{\pi/2}$$

$$= [-(\tfrac{\pi}{2})^2 \cos(\tfrac{\pi}{2}) + 2(\tfrac{\pi}{2})\sin(\tfrac{\pi}{2}) + 2 \cos(\tfrac{\pi}{2})] - [-(0)^2 \cos(0) + 2(0) \sin(0) + 2 \cos(0)]$$

$$= [-(\tfrac{\pi}{2})^2(0) + \pi + 2(0)] - [0 + 0 + 2] = \pi - 2$$

(31) The hint says to integrate by parts, so we view $\cos(\ln x)$ as the product
of $\cos(\ln x)$ with the function 1; we differentiate $\cos(\ln x)$ and integrate 1:

$$\begin{cases} u = \cos(\ln x) \\ \frac{dv}{dx} = 1 \end{cases} \qquad \begin{cases} \frac{du}{dx} = - \sin(\ln x)(\frac{1}{x}) \\ v = x \end{cases}$$

$$\int \cos(\ln x) \, dx = x \cos(\ln x) - \int -\sin(\ln x)(\tfrac{1}{x})(x) \, dx = x \cos(\ln x) + \int \sin(\ln x) \, dx$$

Next, we differentiate $\sin(\ln x)$ and integrate 1:

$$\begin{cases} u = \sin(\ln x) \\ \frac{dv}{dx} = 1 \end{cases} \qquad \begin{cases} \frac{du}{dx} = \cos(\ln x)(\frac{1}{x}) \\ v = x \end{cases}$$

$$\int \cos(\ln x) \, dx = x \cos(\ln x) + \quad x \sin(\ln x) - \int \cos(\ln x)(\tfrac{1}{x})(x) \, dx$$

$$= x[\cos(\ln x) + \sin(\ln x)] - \int \cos(\ln x) \, dx$$

Solving the last equation for the integral of $\cos(\ln x)$ yields

$$\int \cos(\ln x) \, dx = \tfrac{1}{2} x[\cos(\ln x) + \sin(\ln x)] + C$$

(33) If we are to differentiate x^2 during the integration by parts, as suggested in the hint, we have to integrate $x/\sqrt{1 - x^2}$. We start by evaluating that indefinite integral:

$$\int \frac{x}{\sqrt{1 - x^2}} dx = -\frac{1}{2} \int (1 - x^2)^{-1/2}(-2x \, dx) = -\frac{1}{2} \int u^{-1/2} \, du = -u^{1/2} + C$$

$$= -(1 - x^2)^{1/2} + C \quad \text{where we have made the substitution } u = 1 - x^2.$$

Now we integrate by parts:

$$\begin{cases} u = x^2 \\ \frac{dv}{dx} = \frac{x}{\sqrt{1 - x^2}} \end{cases} \qquad \begin{cases} \frac{du}{dx} = 2x \\ v = -(1 - x^2)^{1/2} \end{cases}$$

$$\int \frac{x^3}{\sqrt{1 - x^2}} \, dx = \int x^2 \frac{x}{\sqrt{1 - x^2}} dx = -x^2(1 - x^2)^{1/2} - \int -(1 - x^2)^{1/2}(2x) \, dx$$

$$= -x^2(1 - x^2)^{1/2} - \int (1 - x^2)^{1/2}(-2x \, dx)$$

$$= -x^2(1 - x^2)^{1/2} - \int u^{1/2} \, du = -x^2(1 - x^2)^{1/2} - \frac{2}{3} u^{3/2} + C$$

$$= -x^2(1 - x^2)^{1/2} - \frac{2}{3}(1 - x^2)^{3/2} + C$$

where again we use $u = 1 - x^2$, $du = -2x \, dx$.

Check:

$$\frac{d}{dx}[- x^2(1 - x^2)^{1/2} - \frac{2}{3}(1 - x^2)^{3/2}]$$

$$= -[\frac{d}{dx} x^2](1 - x^2)^{1/2} - x^2[\frac{d}{dx}(1 - x^2)^{1/2}] - \frac{2}{3} \frac{d}{dx}(1 - x^2)^{3/2}$$

$$= -2x(1 - x^2)^{1/2} - x^2(\frac{1}{2})(1 - x^2)^{-1/2} \frac{d}{dx}(1 - x^2) - \frac{2}{3}(\frac{3}{2})(1 - x^2)^{1/2} \frac{d}{dx}(1 - x^2)$$

$$= -2x(1 - x^2)^{1/2} - x^2(\frac{1}{2})(1 - x^2)^{-1/2}(-2x) - (1 - x^2)^{1/2}(-2x) = \frac{x^3}{\sqrt{1 - x^2}}$$

SECTION 8.4

(1) Use $\sin^2(4x) = 1 - \cos^2(4x)$ and then the substitution $u = \cos(4x)$, $du = -4 \sin(4x) \, dx$:

$$\int \sin^3(4x) \ dx = \int \sin^2(4x) \ \sin(4x) \ dx = \int [1 - \cos^2(4x)]\sin(4x) \ dx$$

$$= -\frac{1}{4}\int [1 - \cos^2(4x)][-4 \ \sin(4x) \ dx] = -\frac{1}{4}\int (1 - u^2)du$$

$$= -\frac{1}{4}(u - \frac{1}{3} u^3) + C = -\frac{1}{4} u + \frac{1}{12} u^3 + C = -\frac{1}{4} \cos(4x) + \frac{1}{12} \cos^3(4x) + C$$

(5) We view $\sin^4 x$ as the square of $\sin^2 x$ and use the identity $\sin^2 x = \frac{1}{2}[1 - \cos(2x)]$
to obtain

$$\sin^4 x = [\sin^2 x]^2 = \ \frac{1}{2}[1 - \cos(2x)]^2 \ = \frac{1}{4}[1 - 2 \cos(2x) + \cos^2(2x)]$$

$$= \frac{1}{4} - \frac{1}{2} \cos(2x) + \frac{1}{4} \cos^2(2x).$$

Then we use the identity $\cos^2(2x) = \ \frac{1}{2}[1 + \cos(4x)]$ to see that

(*)
$$\sin^4 x = \frac{1}{4} - \frac{1}{2} \cos(2x) + \frac{1}{4}(\frac{1}{2})[1 + \cos(4x)] = \frac{1}{4} \ - \frac{1}{2} \cos(2x) + \frac{1}{8} + \frac{1}{8} \cos(4x)$$

$$= \frac{3}{8} \ - \frac{1}{2} \cos(2x) + \frac{1}{8} \cos(4x)$$

Therefore,

$$\int \sin^4 \ dx = \ \int [\frac{3}{8} \ - \frac{1}{2} \cos(2x) + \frac{1}{8} \cos(4x)] \ dx$$

To evaluate the integral of $\cos(2x)$, we make the substitution $u = 2x$, to evaluate the
integral of $\cos(4x)$, we use $w = 4x$.

$$\int \sin^4 \ dx = \ \frac{3}{8} x - \frac{1}{2}(\frac{1}{2}) \int \cos(2x)(2 \ dx) + \frac{1}{8}(\frac{1}{4}) \int \cos(4x)(4 \ dx)$$

$$= \frac{3}{8} x \ - \frac{1}{4}\int \cos u \ du \ + \ \frac{1}{32}\int \cos w \ dw \ = \frac{3}{8} x - \frac{1}{4} \sin u + \frac{1}{32} \sin w \ + \ C$$

$$= \frac{3}{8} x - \frac{1}{4} \sin(2x) + \frac{1}{32} \sin(4x) + C$$

Check:

$$\frac{d}{dx}[\frac{3}{8} x - \frac{1}{4} \sin(2x) + \frac{1}{32} \sin(4x)] = \frac{3}{8} - \frac{1}{4} \cos(2x)\frac{d}{dx}(2x) + \frac{1}{32} \cos(4x) \frac{d}{dx}(4x)$$

$$= \frac{3}{8} - \frac{1}{2} \cos(2x) + \frac{1}{8} \cos(4x)$$

This equals $\sin^4 x$ because of identity (*).

(7) We use the identity $\sin\theta\cos\psi = \frac{1}{2}[\sin(\theta-\psi) + \sin(\theta+\psi)]$ with $\theta = 3x$ and $\psi = x$
to obtain

$$\int \sin(3x)\,\cos x\,dx = \frac{1}{2}\int [\sin(2x) + \sin(4x)]\,dx = \frac{1}{2}[-\frac{1}{2}\cos(2x) - \frac{1}{4}\cos(4x)] + C$$

$$= -\frac{1}{4}\cos(2x) - \frac{1}{8}\cos(4x) + C$$

(15) We follow Rule 8.8 and write $\sec^4 x = (\sec^2 x)(\sec^2 x) = (1 + \tan^2 x)\sec^2 x$. Then we use
the substitution $u = \tan x$, $du = \sec^2 x\,dx$:

$$\int \sec^4 x\,dx = \int (1 + \tan^2 x)(\sec^2 x\,dx) = \int (1 + u^2)\,du = u + \frac{1}{3}u^3 + C$$

$$= \tan x + \frac{1}{3}\tan^3 x + C$$

(17) We integrate by parts, integrating $\csc^2 x$ and differentiating $\csc x$:

$$\begin{cases} u = \csc x \\ \dfrac{dv}{dx} = \csc^2 x \end{cases} \qquad \begin{cases} \dfrac{du}{dx} = -\csc x\,\cot x \\ v = -\cot x \end{cases}$$

$$\int \csc^3 x\,dx = \int \csc x\,\csc^2 x\,dx = -\csc x\,\cot x - \int (-\cot x)(-\csc x\,\cot x)\,dx$$

$$= -\csc x\,\cot x - \int \csc x\,\cot^2 x\,dx$$

We then use the identity $\cot^2 x = \csc^2 x - 1$ to obtain

$$\int \csc^3 x\,dx = -\csc x\,\cot x - \int \csc x(\csc^2 x - 1)\,dx$$

$$= -\csc x\,\cot x + \int \frac{\csc x[\csc x + \cot x]}{\csc x + \cot x}\,dx - \int \csc^3 x\,dx$$

$$= -\csc x\,\cot x - \ln|\csc x + \cot x| - \int \csc^3 x\,dx.$$

Finally, solving for the integral of $\csc^3 x$ yields

$$\int \csc^3 x\,dx = -\frac{1}{2}\csc x\,\cot x - \frac{1}{2}\ln|\csc x + \cot x| + C$$

Check:

$$\frac{d}{dx}[-\frac{1}{2}\csc x\,\cot x - \frac{1}{2}\ln|\csc x + \cot x|]$$

$$= -\frac{1}{2}[\frac{d}{dx}\csc x]\cot x - \frac{1}{2}\csc x[\frac{d}{dx}\cot x] - (\frac{1}{2})\frac{1}{\csc x + \cot x}\frac{d}{dx}(\csc x + \cot x)$$

$$= -\frac{1}{2}[-\csc x \cot x]\cot x - \frac{1}{2}\csc x[-\csc^2 x] - \left(\frac{1}{2}\right)\frac{1}{\csc x + \cot x}(-\csc x \cot x - \csc^2 x)$$

$$= \frac{1}{2}\csc x \cot^2 x + \frac{1}{2}\csc^3 x + \frac{1}{2}\csc x = \frac{1}{2}\csc x(\csc^2 x - 1) + \frac{1}{2}\csc^3 x + \frac{1}{2}\csc x = \csc^3 x$$

Finally, evaluate the definite integral:

$$\int_{\pi/4}^{\pi/2} \csc^3 x \, dx = \left[-\frac{1}{2}\csc x \cot x - \frac{1}{2}\ln\left|\csc x + \cot x\right|\right]_{\pi/4}^{\pi/2}$$

$$= \left[-\frac{1}{2}\csc\left(\frac{\pi}{2}\right)\cot\left(\frac{\pi}{2}\right) - \frac{1}{2}\ln\left|\csc\left(\frac{\pi}{2}\right) + \cot\left(\frac{\pi}{2}\right)\right|\right]$$

$$- \left[-\frac{1}{2}\csc\left(\frac{\pi}{4}\right)\cot\left(\frac{\pi}{4}\right) - \frac{1}{2}\ln\left|\csc\left(\frac{\pi}{4}\right) + \cot\left(\frac{\pi}{4}\right)\right|\right]$$

$$= \left[0 - \frac{1}{2}\ln\left|1 + 0\right|\right] - \left[-\frac{1}{2}(\sqrt{2})(1) - \frac{1}{2}\ln\left|\sqrt{2} + 1\right|\right] = 2^{-1/2} + \frac{1}{2}\ln(\sqrt{2} + 1)$$

since $\csc\left(\frac{\pi}{2}\right) = \frac{1}{\sin\left(\frac{\pi}{2}\right)} = \frac{1}{1} = 1,$ $\cot\left(\frac{\pi}{2}\right) = \frac{\cos\left(\frac{\pi}{2}\right)}{\sin\left(\frac{\pi}{2}\right)} = \frac{0}{1} = 0,$ $\csc\left(\frac{\pi}{4}\right) = \frac{1}{\sin\left(\frac{\pi}{4}\right)} = \sqrt{2}$, and

$\cot\left(\frac{\pi}{4}\right) = \frac{\cos\left(\frac{\pi}{4}\right)}{\sin\left(\frac{\pi}{4}\right)} = 1.$

(28) The reduction formula in Exercise 23 with $n = 4, n - 1 = 3,$ and $n - 2 = 2$

gives

$$\int \tan^4 x \, dx = \frac{1}{3}\tan^3 x - \int \tan^2 x \, dx.$$

Then the reduction formula with $n = 2, n - 1 = 1,$ and $n - 2 = 0$ yields

$$\int \tan^2 x \, dx = \frac{1}{1}\tan x - \int \tan^0 x \, dx = \tan x - \int 1 \, dx = \tan x - x + C_1$$

When we combine the last two equations, we obtain

$$\int \tan^4 x \, dx = \frac{1}{3}\tan^3 x - [\tan x - x + C_1] = \frac{1}{3}\tan^3 x - \tan x + x + C.$$

SECTION 8.5

(5) Because of the $\sqrt{25 - x^2}$ in the integral, we use the substitution $\theta = \arcsin\left(\frac{x}{5}\right),$

for which $x = 5\sin\theta$, $dx = 5\cos\theta \, d\theta,$ and $\sqrt{25 - x^2} = 5\cos\theta$:

$$\int x^2 \sqrt{25 - x^2} \, dx = \int (5 \sin\theta)^2 (5 \cos\theta)(5 \cos\theta \, d\theta) = 625 \int \sin^2\theta \cos^2\theta \, d\theta$$

By formula (19) and the equations $\sin\theta = \frac{1}{5} x$ and $\cos\theta = \frac{1}{5}\sqrt{25 - x^2}$ we have

$$\int x^2 \sqrt{25 - x^2} \, dx = \frac{625}{8}[\theta - \sin\theta \cos^3\theta + \sin^3\theta \cos\theta] + C$$

$$= \frac{625}{8}[\arcsin(\tfrac{x}{5}) - (\tfrac{1}{5} x)(\tfrac{1}{5}\sqrt{25 - x^2})^3 + (\tfrac{1}{5} x)^3(\tfrac{1}{5}\sqrt{25 - x^2})] + C$$

$$= \frac{625}{8} \arcsin(\tfrac{1}{5} x) - \tfrac{1}{8} x (25 - x^2)^{3/2} + x^3(25 - x^2)^{1/2} + C$$

(9) Because of the $\sqrt{x^2 + 1}$ in the integral, we use $\theta = \arctan x$, for which $x = \tan\theta$, $dx = \sec^2\theta \, d\theta$, and $\sqrt{x^2 + 1} = \sec\theta$:

$$\int \frac{x^3}{\sqrt{x^2 + 1}} \, dx = \int \frac{\tan^3\theta}{\sec\theta} (\sec^2\theta \, d\theta) = \int \tan^3\theta \sec\theta \, d\theta$$

By formula (28) we have

$$\int \frac{x^3}{\sqrt{x^2 + 1}} \, dx = \tfrac{1}{3} \sec^3\theta - \sec\theta + C = \tfrac{1}{3}(x^2 + 1)^{3/2} - (x^2 + 1)^{1/2} + C$$

(13) Because $1 - x^2$ is the square of $\sqrt{1 - x^2}$ we use $\theta = \arcsin x$, for which $x = \sin\theta$, $dx = \cos\theta \, d\theta$, and $1 - x^2 = \cos^2\theta$:

$$\int \frac{1}{1 - x^2} \, dx = \int \frac{1}{\cos^2\theta} (\cos\theta \, d\theta) = \int \sec\theta \, d\theta$$

By formula (23) this equals

$$\ln|\sec\theta + \tan\theta| + C = \ln\left|\frac{1}{\sqrt{1 - x^2}} + \frac{x}{\sqrt{1 - x^2}}\right| + C$$

We use Figure 8.1 in the text with $a = 1$ to see that $\sec\theta = 1/\sqrt{1 - x^2}$ and $\tan\theta = x/\sqrt{1 - x^2}$. We simplify the answer by writing it in the form

$$\ln\sqrt{\frac{(1 + x)^2}{1 - x^2}} + C = \tfrac{1}{2} \ln\left[\frac{(1 + x)^2}{1 - x^2}\right] + C = \tfrac{1}{2} \ln\left[\frac{1 + x}{1 - x}\right] + C$$

$$= \tfrac{1}{2} \ln(1 + x) - \tfrac{1}{2} \ln(1 - x) + C$$

(Notice that this calculation is valid only for $x^2 < 1$. In the next section we will learn an easier method for evaluating this particular integral. We will find that it equals

$\frac{1}{2} \ln|x + 1| - \frac{1}{2} \ln|x - 1|$ for all $x \neq \pm 1$.)

(21) We begin by completing the square in the expression inside the square root sign:

$$2x - x^2 = -(x^2 - 2x) = -(x^2 - 2x + 1) + 1 = 1 - (x - 1)^2$$

We use the substitution $\theta = \arcsin(x - 1)$ with $x - 1 = \sin\theta$, $dx = \cos\theta \, d\theta$,

and $\sqrt{2x - x^2} = \sqrt{1 - (x - 1)^2} = \cos\theta$:

$$\int \frac{1}{(2x - x^2)^{3/2}} \, dx = \int \frac{1}{\cos^3\theta} (\cos\theta \, d\theta) = \int \sec^2\theta \, d\theta = \tan\theta + C$$

To express $\tan\theta$ in terms of x we either use the sketch in Fig. 8.5.21 or we write $\tan\theta = \frac{\sin\theta}{\cos\theta}$ and use the formulas for $\sin\theta$ and $\cos\theta$ given above:

$$\int \frac{1}{(2x - x^2)^{3/2}} \, dx = \frac{x - 1}{\sqrt{1 - (1 - x)^2}} + C$$

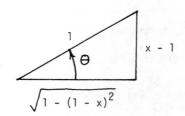

Fig. 8.5.21

SECTION 8.6

(5) We divide $x^2 + 16$ into x^5 to obtain a proper rational function:

$$
\begin{array}{r}
x^3 - 16x \\
x^2 + 16 \overline{\smash{\big)}\ x^5 } \\
\underline{x^5 + 16x^3} \\
- 16x^3 \\
\underline{- 16x^3 - 256x} \\
256x
\end{array}
$$

We obtain $x^3 - 16x$ with a remainder of $256x$:

$$\frac{x^5}{x^2 + 16} = x^3 - 16x + \frac{256x}{x^2 + 16}$$

This is the partial fraction decomposition because the degree of $256x$ is less than the degree of $x^2 + 16$ and because $x^2 + 16$ is irreducible. (In the case of $x^2 + 16$ we have $b^2 - 4ac = 0^2 - 4(1)(16) = -64$, which is negative.

(7) The rational function $\dfrac{x}{(x + 1)^3}$ is proper because the degree of the numerator is 1 and the degree of the denominator is 3. We need to find constants A, B, and C such that

(*) $\qquad \dfrac{x}{(x + 1)^3} = \dfrac{A}{x + 1} + \dfrac{B}{(x + 1)^2} + \dfrac{C}{(x + 1)^3}$

Taking the common denominator on the right (which is the denominator on the left), we obtain

$$\frac{x}{(x + 1)^3} = \frac{A(x + 1)^2 + B(x + 1) + C}{(x + 1)^3}$$

In order for this equation to be valid for all $x \neq -1$ we must have

(**) $\qquad x = A(x + 1)^2 + B(x + 1) + C$

for all x. When we set $x = -1$ in equation (**), we obtain

$$-1 = A(-1 + 1)^2 + B(-1 + 1) + C$$

which reads $-1 = A(0) + B(0) + C$ and shows that $C = -1$. We substitute $C = -1$ in equation (**) and combine the powers of x on the right:

$$x = A(x + 1)^2 + B(x + 1) - 1$$
$$= A(x^2 + 2x + 1) + B(x + 1) - 1$$
$$= Ax^2 + 2Ax + A + Bx + B - 1$$
$$= Ax^2 + (2A + B)x + (A + B - 1)$$

The coefficients of the powers of x on the two sides of the equation must be the same, so we have three equations in the two unknowns A and B:

$$\begin{cases} A = 0 \\ 2A + B = 1 \\ A + B - 1 = 0 \end{cases}$$

The first two equations show that $A = 0$ and $B = 1$. The third equation serves as a check on these calculations. Setting $A = 0$, $B = 1$, and $C = -1$ in equation (*) gives the partial fraction decomposition:

$$\frac{x}{(x + 1)^3} = \frac{1}{(x + 1)^2} - \frac{1}{(x + 1)^3}$$

Check:

$$\frac{1}{(x + 1)^2} - \frac{1}{(x + 1)^3} = \frac{(x + 1) - 1}{(x + 1)^3} = \frac{x}{(x + 1)^3}$$

(13) The rational function is not proper, so we first divide $x^3 + 2x^2 + 5x$ into $x^4 + 3x^3 + 1 = x^4 + 3x^3 + 0x^2 + 0x + 1$:

$$
\begin{array}{r}
x + 1 \\
x^3 + 2x^2 + 5x \,\overline{\smash{\big)}\, x^4 + 3x^3 + 0x^2 + 0x + 1} \\
\underline{x^4 + 2x^3 + 5x^2} \\
x^3 - 5x^2 + 0x + 1 \\
\underline{x^3 + 2x^2 + 5x} \\
- 7x^2 - 5x + 1
\end{array}
$$

Thus,

(*) $$\frac{x^4 + 3x^2 + 1}{x^3 + 2x^2 + 5x} = x + 1 + \frac{-7x^2 - 5x + 1}{x^3 + 2x^2 + 5x}.$$

Next, we factor the denominator:

$$x^3 + 2x^2 + 5x = x(x^2 + 2x + 5)$$

The quadratic polynomial is irreducible because in this case $b^2 - 4ac = (2)^2 - 4(1)(20) = -76$. We need to find constants A, B, and C such that

(**) $$\frac{-7x^2 - 5x + 1}{x(x^2 + 2x + 5)} = \frac{A}{x} + \frac{Bx + C}{x^2 + 2x + 5}$$

This requires that

$$\frac{-7x^2 - 5x + 1}{x(x^2 + 2x + 5)} = \frac{A(x^2 + 2x + 5) + (Bx + C)x}{x(x^2 + 2x + 5)}$$

and hence

$$-7x^2 - 5x + 1 = A(x^2 + 2x + 5) + (Bx + C)x$$

Setting $x = 0$ shows that $1 = 5A$ and $A = \frac{1}{5}$ so the equation may be written

$$-7x^2 - 5x + 1 = \tfrac{1}{5}(x^2 + 2x + 5) + (Bx + C)x$$

We combine like powers of x on the right side of the equation:

$$-7x^2 - 5x + 1 = \tfrac{1}{5}x^2 + \tfrac{2}{5}x + 1 + Bx^2 + Cx$$

$$= (\tfrac{1}{5} + B)x^2 + (\tfrac{2}{5} + C)x + 1$$

We obtain the three equations

$$\begin{cases} -7 = \tfrac{1}{5} + B \\ -5 = \tfrac{2}{5} + C \\ 1 = 1 \end{cases}$$

which show that $B = -\tfrac{36}{5}$ and $C = -\tfrac{27}{5}$. Equations (*) and (**) then yield

$$\frac{x^4 + 3x^2 + 1}{x^3 + 2x^2 + 5x} = x + 1 + \tfrac{1}{5}\left[\tfrac{1}{x} + \frac{-36x - 27}{x^2 + 2x + 5}\right]$$

(21) The rational function is proper and factored. We need to find constants A, B, C, and D such that

$$(*) \quad \frac{2x^3 - 4x^2 + 6}{x(x - 1)(x - 2)(x - 3)} = \frac{A}{x} + \frac{B}{x - 1} + \frac{C}{x - 2} + \frac{D}{x - 3}$$

Taking the common denominator on the right side puts it in the form

$$\frac{A(x - 1)(x - 2)(x - 3) + Bx(x - 2)(x - 3) + Cx(x - 1)(x - 3) + Dx(x - 1)(x - 2)}{x(x - 1)(x - 2)(x - 3)} \ .$$

Therefore, we must have

$$2x^3 - 4x^2 + 6$$

$$= A(x - 1)(x - 2)(x - 3) + Bx(x - 2)(x - 3) + Cx(x - 1)(x - 3) + Dx(x - 1)(x - 2).$$

We set $x = 0$ in the last equation to see that $6 = A(-1)(-2)(-3)$ and hence $A = -1$, Setting $x = 1$ gives $2 - 4 + 6 = B(1)(-1)(-2)$, which shows that $B = 2$. With $x = 2$ we obtain $2(2^3) - 4(2^2) + 6 = C(2)(1)(-1)$ or $6 = -2C$, which shows that $C = -3$. Finally, setting $x = 3$ yields $2(3^3) - 4(3^2) + 6 = D(3)(2)(1)$ which may be written $24 = 6D$ and shows that $D = 4$. We put $A = -1$, $B = 2$, $C = -3$, and $D = 4$ in equation (*) to obtain the partial fraction decomposition

$$\frac{2x^3 - 4x^2 + 6}{x(x - 1)(x - 2)(x - 3)} = -\frac{1}{x} + \frac{2}{x - 1} - \frac{3}{x - 2} + \frac{4}{x - 3} \ .$$

(23) The integrand is a proper rational function. We factor its denominator and then find its partial fraction decomposition:

$$\frac{5x - 1}{x^2 + x} = \frac{5x - 1}{x(x + 1)} = \frac{A}{x} + \frac{B}{x + 1} = \frac{A(x + 1) + Bx}{x(x + 1)}$$

The equation $5x - 1 = A(x + 1) + Bx$ with $x = 0$ gives $A = -1$ and with $x = -1$ gives $5(-1) - 1 = B(-1)$, which shows that $B = 6$. Hence

$$\frac{5x - 1}{x^2 + x} = -\frac{1}{x} + \frac{6}{x + 1} \ .$$

Check:

$$-\frac{1}{x} + \frac{6}{x + 1} = \frac{-(x + 1) + 6x}{x(x + 1)} = \frac{5x - 1}{x^2 + x} \ .$$

We integrate the resulting expression:

$$\int \frac{5x - 1}{x^2 + x} \, dx = -\int \frac{1}{x} \, dx + 6 \int \frac{1}{x + 1} \, dx = -\ln|x| + 6 \ln|x + 1| + C$$

We used the substitution $u = x + 1$, $du = dx$ in evaluating the last integral.

(33) The integrand is a proper rational function. We have

$$\frac{x^2 - 3}{x^3 + x} = \frac{x^2 - 3}{x(x^2 + 1)} = \frac{A}{x} + \frac{Bx + C}{x^2 + 1} = \frac{A(x^2 + 1) + x(Bx + C)}{x(x^2 + 1)} \ .$$

Setting $x = 0$ in the equation

$$x^2 - 3 = A(x^2 + 1) + x(Bx + C)$$

shows that $A = -3$, and making this substitution gives

$$x^2 - 3 = -3(x^2 + 1) + x(Bx + C)$$
$$= -3x^2 - 3 + Bx^2 + Cx$$
$$= (-3 + B)x^2 + Cx - 3.$$

Comparing the coefficients of the powers of x in this equation gives

$$\begin{cases} 1 = -3 + B \\ 0 = C \\ -3 = -3 \end{cases}$$

which shows that $B = 4$ and $C = 0$. With $A = -3$, $B = 4$, and $C = 0$, we have

$$\frac{x^2 - 3}{x^3 + x} = -\frac{3}{x} + \frac{4x}{x^2 + 1} \; .$$

To evaluate the integral of the last term we use the substitution $u = x^2 + 1$, $du = 2x \, dx$ and obtain

$$\int \frac{x^2 - 3}{x^3 + x} \, dx = -3 \int \frac{1}{x} \, dx + 2 \int \frac{1}{x^2 + 1} (2x \, dx) = -3 \int \frac{1}{x} \, dx + 2 \int \frac{1}{u} \, du$$

$$= -3 \ln|x| + 2 \ln|u| + C = -3 \ln|x| + 2 \ln(x^2 + 1) + C$$

We have written $\ln(x^2 + 1)$ in place of $\ln|x^2 + 1|$ because we noted that $x^2 + 1$ is always positive.

Having found the indefinite integral, we evaluate the definite integral:

$$\int_1^5 \frac{x^2 - 3}{x^3 + x} \, dx = \left[-3 \ln x + 2 \ln(x^2 + 1) \right]_1^5$$

$$= [-3 \ln(5) + 2 \ln(5^2 + 1)] - [-3 \ln(1) + 2 \ln(1^2 + 1)]$$

$$= [-3 \ln(5) + 2 \ln(26)] - [2 \ln(2)] = -3 \ln(5) + 2 \ln(26) - 2 \ln(2)$$

(41) We begin by finding the partial fraction decomposition of the proper rational function:

$$\frac{x^2 - 2x + 1}{(x^2 + 1)^2} = \frac{Ax + B}{x^2 + 1} + \frac{Cx + D}{(x^2 + 1)^2}$$

$$= \frac{(Ax + B)(x^2 + 1) + (Cx + D)}{(x^2 + 1)^2}$$

Therefore,

$$x^2 - 2x + 1 = (Ax + B)(x^2 + 1) + (Cx + D)$$

$$= Ax^3 + Ax + Bx^2 + B + Cx + D$$

$$= Ax^3 + Bx^2 + (A + C)x + (B + D)$$

and we must have

$$\begin{cases} A = 0 \\ B = 1 \\ A + C = -2 \\ B + D = 1. \end{cases}$$

These equations give $A = 0$, $B = 1$, $C = -2$, and $D = 0$, and we have

$$\frac{x^2 - 2x + 1}{(x^2 + 1)^2} = \frac{1}{x^2 + 1} - \frac{2x}{(x^2 + 1)^2} .$$

We integrate to obtain

$$\int \frac{x^2 - 2x + 1}{(x^2 + 1)^2} \, dx = \int \frac{1}{x^2 + 1} \, dx - \int \frac{1}{(x^2 + 1)^2}(2x \, dx) = \int \frac{1}{x^2 + 1} \, dx - \int u^{-2} \, du$$

$$= \arctan x + u^{-1} + C = \arctan x + \frac{1}{x^2 + 1} + C.$$

Here we have used the substitution $u = x^2 + 1$, $du = 2x \, dx$.

SECTION 8.7

(5) With $u = \tan(\frac{x}{2})$ we have $\tan x = \dfrac{2u}{1 - u^2}$, $\sin x = \dfrac{2u}{1 + u^2}$, and $du = \dfrac{2}{1 + u^2} \, du$, so that

$$\int \frac{1}{\tan x - \sin x} \, dx = \int \frac{1}{\dfrac{2u}{1 - u^2} - \dfrac{2u}{1 + u^2}} \left[\frac{2}{1 + u^2} \, du \right]$$

$$= \int \frac{2}{2u(1 + u^2) \left[\dfrac{(1 + u^2) - (1 - u^2)}{(1 - u^2)(1 + u^2)} \right]} \, du = \int \frac{1 - u^2}{2u^3} \, du = \frac{1}{2} \int u^{-3} \, du - \frac{1}{2} \int u^{-1} \, du$$

$$= \frac{1}{2}(\frac{1}{-2}) u^{-2} - \frac{1}{2} \ln|u| + C = -\frac{1}{4} u^{-2} - \frac{1}{2} \ln|u| + C = -\frac{1}{4}[\tan(\frac{x}{2})]^{-2} - \frac{1}{2} \ln|\tan(\frac{x}{2})| + C$$

SECTION 8.8

(2) By formula (15) in Table VIII with $a = 2$ we have

$$\int \frac{1}{4 - x^2} \, dx = -\int \frac{1}{x^2 - 2^2} \, dx = -\frac{1}{2(2)} \ln\left|\frac{x - 2}{x + 2}\right| + C = \frac{1}{4} \ln\left|\frac{x + 2}{x - 2}\right| + C.$$

(6) Use formula (25) in Table VIII with $a = 12$:

$$\int \sqrt{x^2 + 144} \, dx = \frac{1}{2} x\sqrt{x^2 + 144} + \frac{1}{2}(144) \ln(x + \sqrt{x^2 + 144}) + C$$

$$= \frac{1}{2} x\sqrt{x^2 + 144} + 72 \ln(x + \sqrt{x^2 + 144}) + C$$

Therefore

$$\int_0^{10} \sqrt{x^2 + 144}\ dx = [\tfrac{1}{2} x \sqrt{x^2 + 144} + 72\ \ln(x + \sqrt{x^2 + 144})]_0^{10}$$

$$= [\tfrac{1}{2}(10)\sqrt{(10)^2 + 144} + 72\ \ln(10 + \sqrt{10^2 + 144})]$$

$$- [\tfrac{1}{2}(0)\sqrt{0^2 + 144} + 72(0 + \sqrt{0^2 + 144})]$$

$$= [5\sqrt{244} + 72\ \ln(10 + \sqrt{244})] - [72\ \ln(12)]$$

$$= 5\sqrt{244} + 72\ \ln[\tfrac{10 + \sqrt{244}}{12}] = 5\sqrt{244} + 72\ \ln[\tfrac{5}{6} + \tfrac{1}{6}\sqrt{61}]$$

(16) Because the denominator of $\dfrac{\sin x}{\cos^2 x + \cos x}$ is constructed from $\cos x$ and the

derivative of $\cos x$ appears in the numerator (except for the constant factor -1), we

make the substitution $u = \cos x$, $du = -\sin x\ dx$:

$$\int \frac{\sin x}{\cos^2 x + \cos x}\ dx = -\int \frac{1}{\cos^2 x + \cos x}\ (-\sin x\ dx) = -\int \frac{1}{u^2 + u}\ du$$

Then we use formula (54) in Table VIII with $a = 1$, $b = 1$, and $c = 0$. (We use formula

(54) rather than (55) because here $b^2 = 1$ is greater than $4ac = 0$.)

$$\int \frac{\sin x}{\cos^2 x + \cos x}\ dx = -\ln\left|\frac{2u + 1 - \sqrt{1}}{2u + 1 + \sqrt{1}}\right| + C = -\ln\left|\frac{2u}{2u + 2}\right| + C = \ln\left|\frac{u + 1}{u}\right| + C$$

$$= \ln\left|\frac{\cos x + 1}{\cos x}\right| + C$$

(28) Formula (42) in Table VIII with $a = 1$ and $n = 2$ gives

$$\int x^2 \sin x\ dx = -x^2 \cos x + 2\int x \cos x\ dx.$$

Then we use formula (41) with $a = 1$ to see that this equals

$$-x^2 \cos x + 2[\cos x + x \sin x] + C = -x^2 \cos x + 2 \cos x + 2x \sin x + C.$$

(38) We use formula (54) in Table VIII with $a = 1$, $b = 1$, and $c = -12$, for which

$b^2 - 4ac = 49$ and $\sqrt{b^2 - 4ac} = 7$:

$$\int \frac{1}{x^2 + x - 12}\ dx = \frac{1}{7}\ \ln\left|\frac{2x + 1 - 7}{2x + 1 + 7}\right| + C = \frac{1}{7}\ \ln\left|\frac{2x - 6}{2x + 8}\right| + C = \frac{1}{7}\ \ln\left|\frac{x - 3}{x + 4}\right| + C$$

(42) Formula (28) in Table VIII reads

$$\int \cos^2 x \, dx = \tfrac{1}{2}(x + \sin x \cos x) + C.$$

Therefore,

$$\int_0^2 \cos^2 x \, dx = [\tfrac{1}{2}(x + \sin x \cos x)]_0^2 = [\tfrac{1}{2}(2 + \sin(2)\cos(2))] - [\tfrac{1}{2}(0 + \sin(0)\cos(0))]$$

$$= 1 + \tfrac{1}{2} \sin(2)\cos(2)$$

(45) By Rule 6.8 in Section 6.5 of the text with $y = x^2$ and $\frac{dy}{dx} = 2x$, the length of the curve is

$$\int_0^3 \sqrt{1 + (\tfrac{dy}{dx})^2} \, dx = \int_0^3 \sqrt{1 + (2x)^2} \, dx.$$

To evaluate the indefinite integral, we first make the substitution $u = 2x$, $du = 2 \, dx$. Then we use formula (25) in Table VIII with $a = 1$:

$$\int \sqrt{1 + (2x)^2} \, dx = \tfrac{1}{2}\int \sqrt{1 + (2x)^2} \, (2 \, dx) = \tfrac{1}{2}\int \sqrt{1 + u^2} \, du$$

$$= \tfrac{1}{2}[\tfrac{1}{2} u\sqrt{u^2 + 1} + \tfrac{1}{2} \ln(u + \sqrt{u^2 + 1})] + C$$

$$= \tfrac{1}{4} u\sqrt{u^2 + 1} + \tfrac{1}{4} \ln(u + \sqrt{u^2 + 1}) + C$$

$$= \tfrac{1}{4}(2x)\sqrt{(2x)^2 + 1} + \tfrac{1}{4} \ln[2x + \sqrt{(2x)^2 + 1}] + C$$

$$= \tfrac{1}{2} x\sqrt{4x^2 + 1} + \tfrac{1}{4} \ln(2x + \sqrt{4x^2 + 1}) + C$$

Hence the length of the curve is

$$\int_0^3 \sqrt{1 + (2x)^2} \, dx = [\tfrac{1}{2} x\sqrt{4x^2 + 1} + \tfrac{1}{4} \ln(2x + \sqrt{4x^2 + 1})]_0^3$$

$$= [\tfrac{1}{2}(3)\sqrt{4(3^2) + 1} + \tfrac{1}{4} \ln(2(3) + \sqrt{4(3^2) + 1})]$$

$$-[\tfrac{1}{2}(0)\sqrt{4(0^2) + 1} + \tfrac{1}{4} \ln(2(0) + \sqrt{4(0^2) + 1})]$$

$$= \tfrac{3}{2}\sqrt{37} + \tfrac{1}{4} \ln(6 + \sqrt{37}).$$

(50) The volume of water is the integral of the rate of flow:

$$\begin{bmatrix} \text{Net volume to flow} \\ \text{out of the pipe} \\ \text{for } 0 \leq t \leq 60 \end{bmatrix} = \int_0^{60} \arctan t \, [\tfrac{\text{gallons}}{\text{minute}}] \, dt[\text{minutes}] = \int_0^{60} \arctan t \, dt \quad \text{gallons}$$

By formula (53) in Table VIII with $a = 1$ this equals

$$[t \arctan t - \tfrac{1}{2} \ln(1 + t^2)]_0^{60}$$

$$= [60 \arctan(60) - \tfrac{1}{2} \ln(1 + 60^2)] - [0 \arctan(0) - \tfrac{1}{2} \ln(1 + 0^2)]$$

$$= 60 \arctan(60) - \tfrac{1}{2} \ln(3601) \quad \text{gallons.}$$

SECTION 8.9

(3a) The interval of integration $0 \leq x \leq 2$ is two units long and $N = 4$, so each subinterval is of length $\frac{1}{2}$ and the partition is $0 < \frac{1}{2} < 1 < \frac{3}{2} < 2$. The midpoints are $\frac{1}{4}$, $\frac{3}{4}$, $\frac{5}{4}$, and $\frac{7}{4}$ so the midpoint rule (equation (4) in the text) gives the approximation

$$\int_0^2 \sin x \, dx \approx [\sin(\tfrac{1}{4}) + \sin(\tfrac{3}{4}) + \sin(\tfrac{5}{4}) + \sin(\tfrac{7}{4})](\tfrac{1}{2})$$

$$\approx \tfrac{1}{2}(0.2474 + 0.6816 + 0.9490 + 0.9837) = \tfrac{1}{2}(2.8617) = 1.43085$$

(3b) The trapezoid rule (equation (5) in the text) with $x_0 = 0$, $x_1 = \frac{1}{2}$, $x_2 = 1$, $x_3 = \frac{3}{2}$, and $x_4 = 1$ gives the approximation

$$\int_0^2 \sin x \, dx \approx [\tfrac{1}{2} \sin(0) + \sin(\tfrac{1}{2}) + \sin(1) + \sin(\tfrac{3}{2}) + \tfrac{1}{2} \sin(2)](\tfrac{1}{2})$$

$$\approx \tfrac{1}{2}[\tfrac{1}{2}(0) + 0.4794 + 0.8415 + 0.9975 + \tfrac{1}{2}(0.9086)] = 1.38635$$

(3c) Simpson's rule (equation (6) in the text) gives

$$\int_0^2 \sin x \, dx \approx \tfrac{1}{3}[\sin(0) + 4 \sin(\tfrac{1}{2}) + 2 \sin(1) + 4 \sin(\tfrac{3}{2}) + \sin(2)](\tfrac{1}{2})$$

$$\approx \tfrac{1}{6}[0 + 4(0.4794) + 2(0.8415) + 4(0.9975) + 0.9086] \approx 1.4165$$

SECTION 9.1

(1) When we separate the variables in the differential equation, we obtain

$$\frac{dy}{y} = \sin t \, dt$$

which gives

$$\int \frac{dy}{y} = \int \sin t \, dt.$$

We evaluate the integrals:

(*) $\ln|y| = -\cos(t) + C.$

The initial condition $y(0) = 1$ determines the constant C of integration: We set $t = 0$
and $y = 1$ in equation (*) to obtain $\ln(1) = -\cos(0) + C$. Since $\ln(1) = 0$ and $\cos(0) = 1$,
we have $C = 1$ and equation (*) gives

(**) $\ln|y| = -\cos(t) + 1.$

If y tends to zero, then $\ln y$ tends to $-\infty$. Therefore, because the right side of (**)
is continuous, y can never change sign. It is positive at $t = 0$, so it is positive for
all t, and we can drop the absolute value signs in (**) to obtain $\ln y = -\cos(t) + 1$.
Then solving for y gives the solution

$$y = e^{1-\cos(t)}.$$

Check:

$$\frac{dy}{dt} = \frac{d}{dt} e^{1-\cos(t)} = e^{1-\cos(t)} \frac{d}{dt}[1 - \cos(t)] = e^{1-\cos(t)} \sin(t) = y \sin(t)$$

$$y(0) = e^{1-\cos(0)} = e^{1-1} = e^0 = 1$$

(5) When we separate the variables and add integral signs, we obtain

$$\int \frac{1}{x^2 + 1} \, dx = -\int y^{-2} \, dy$$

We evaluate the integrals:

$$\arctan x = \frac{1}{y} + C$$

If we are viewing the solutions as curves, we can leave the equation in this form. If we are considering the solutions to be functions $y = y(x)$, we can solve for y. We have first

$$\frac{1}{y} = \arctan x - C$$

and then

$$y = \frac{1}{\arctan x - C}.$$

Check:

$$\frac{dy}{dx} = \frac{d}{dx}(\arctan x - C)^{-1} = -(\arctan x - C)^{-2}\frac{d}{dt}(\arctan x - C)$$

$$= - (\arctan x - C)^{-2}(\frac{1}{x^2 + 1}) = \frac{-y}{x^2 + 1}$$

To put this in the form of the original differential equation, we multiply both sides

by dx and by $x^2 + 1$ to obtain

$$(x^2 + 1)dy = - ydx \quad \text{and then} \quad ydx + (x^2 + 1)dy = 0.$$

(7) When we separate variables and add integral signs, we obtain

$$\int \sec^2 y \, dy = \int dx.$$

We evaluate the integrals and solve for y:

$$\tan y = x + C$$

$$y = \arctan(x + C) + n\pi \qquad \text{for integers} \ n$$

(11) Separating variables gives

$$\int \frac{1}{F^2 + 2^2} \, dF = \int dx,$$

and evaluating the integrals yields

$$\frac{1}{2} \arctan(\frac{F}{2}) = x + C_1$$

or
(*) $$\arctan(\frac{F}{2}) = 2x + C.$$

To satisfy the initial condition $F(0) = 2$, we set $x = 0$ and $F = 2$ in the last equation:

$$\arctan(1) = C$$

Since $\arctan(1) = \frac{\pi}{4}$, the constant C is $\frac{\pi}{4}$ and equation (*) gives $\arctan(\frac{F}{2}) = 2x + \frac{\pi}{4}$.

To solve for F, we take the tangent of both sides: $\frac{F}{2} = \tan(2x + \frac{\pi}{4})$. The solution is

$$F = 2 \tan(2x + \frac{\pi}{4}).$$

Check:

$$\frac{dF}{dx} = \frac{d}{dx}[2 \tan(2x + \frac{\pi}{4})] = 2 \sec^2(2x + \frac{\pi}{4}) \frac{d}{dx}(2x + \frac{\pi}{4}) = 4 \sec^2(2x + \frac{\pi}{4})$$

$$= 4[\tan^2(2x + \frac{\pi}{4}) + 1] = F^2 + 4$$

$$F(0) = 2 \tan(2(0) + \frac{\pi}{4}) = 2 \tan(\frac{\pi}{4}) = 2$$

(16) We first write

(*)
$$\int \frac{1}{(f - 1)(3 - f)} \, df = \int 5 \, dt$$

We can evaluate the integral with respect to f by using a table of integrals or by partial fractions as follows. We have

$$\frac{1}{(f - 1)(3 - f)} = \frac{A}{f - 1} + \frac{B}{3 - f} = \frac{A(3 - f) + B(f - 1)}{(f - 1)(3 - f)}$$

$$1 = A(3 - f) + B(f - 1).$$

Setting $f = 3$ gives $1 = A(0) + B(2)$ and shows that $B = \frac{1}{2}$. Setting $f = 1$ gives $1 = A(2) + B(0)$ and shows that $A = \frac{1}{2}$. Therefore

$$\int \frac{1}{(f - 1)(3 - f)} \, df = \frac{1}{2} \int \frac{1}{f - 1} \, df + \frac{1}{2} \int \frac{1}{3 - f} \, df$$

$$= \frac{1}{2} \ln|f - 1| - \frac{1}{2} \ln|3 - f| + C$$

$$= \frac{1}{2} \ln\left|\frac{f - 1}{3 - f}\right| + C.$$

Because the integral of 5 with respect to t is $5t + C_1$, equation (*) gives

$$\frac{1}{2} \ln\left|\frac{f - 1}{3 - f}\right| = 5t + C_2 \quad \text{or} \quad \ln\left|\frac{f - 1}{3 - f}\right| = 10t + C_3$$

where C, C_1, C_2, and C_3 are related but, as of yet, undetermined constants. To satisfy the initial condition $f(0) = 2$, we set $t = 0$ and $f = 2$ in the last equation:

$$\ln\left|\frac{2 - 1}{3 - 2}\right| = C_3$$

Since $\ln(1) = 0$, this shows that $C_3 = 0$. Also, because $\frac{f - 1}{3 - f}$ is positive at $t = 0$, it is positive for all t and we can drop the absolute value signs from around it. Thus,

$$\ln\left[\frac{f - 1}{3 - f}\right] = 10t \quad \text{and hence} \quad \frac{f - 1}{3 - f} = e^{10t}.$$

Finally, we solve for f:

$$f - 1 = 3e^{10t} - fe^{10t}$$

$$f + fe^{10t} = 1 + 3e^{10t}$$

$$(1 + e^{10t})f = 1 + 3e^{10t}$$

$$f = \frac{1 + 3e^{10t}}{1 + e^{10t}}$$

(18) We separate variables to obtain

$$\int \frac{y - 1}{y} \, dy = -\int \frac{x + 1}{x} \, dx$$

or

$$\int (1 - \frac{1}{y}) dy = -\int (1 + \frac{1}{x}) dx.$$

Then evaluating the integrals gives the solutions

$$y - \ln|y| = -x - \ln|x| + C.$$

SECTION 9.2

(3) The differential equation is

$$\frac{dP}{dt} = \sqrt{P}$$

which gives

$$\int P^{-1/2} \, dP = \int dt$$

and then

$$\frac{1}{1/2} P^{1/2} = t + C \quad \text{or} \quad \sqrt{P} = \frac{1}{2} t + C_1.$$

The condition that $P = 400$ at $t = 0$ implies that $C_1 = 20$, so we have $\sqrt{P} = \frac{1}{2} t + 20$
and $P = (\frac{1}{2} t + 20)^2.$

Check:

$$\frac{dP}{dt} = \frac{d}{dt}(\frac{1}{2} t + 20)^2 = 2(\frac{1}{2} t + 20)\frac{d}{dt}(\frac{1}{2} t + 20) = 2(\frac{1}{2} t + 20)(\frac{1}{2})$$

$$= (\frac{1}{2} t + 20) = \sqrt{P}$$

$$P(0) = (\frac{1}{2}(0) + 20)^2 = 20^2 = 400$$

(5) The derivative of the rate of growth is the second derivative of P:

$$\frac{d}{dt}\left(\frac{dP}{dt}\right) = \frac{d}{dt}[kP(L - P)] = k[\frac{d}{dt}P](L - P) + kP\frac{d}{dt}(L - P)$$

$$= k\frac{dP}{dt}(L - P) + kP(-\frac{dP}{dt}) = k\frac{dP}{dt}(L - P - P) = k\frac{dP}{dt}(L - 2P)$$

In studying the differential equation we consider P with $0 < P < L$ where

$\frac{dP}{dt} = kP(L - P)$ is **positive** (We assume k is a positive constant). Hence $\frac{d}{dt}\left(\frac{dP}{dt}\right)$ is

positive for $0 < P < \frac{1}{2}L$, zero at $P = \frac{1}{2}L$ and negative for $\frac{1}{2}L < P < L$; the rate of

growth is a maximum at $P = \frac{1}{2}L$.

(10) Every mole per liter of NO_2 that is formed takes away one mole per liter of

NO, so at time t, $[NO] = 2a - [NO_2] = 2a - y$. Every mole per liter of NO_2 that is

formed takes away one half mole per liter of O_2. Therefore, at time t, $[O_2] = a - \frac{1}{2}[NO_2]$

$= a - \frac{1}{2}y$. With these expressions for the concentrations the differential equation reads

$$\frac{dy}{dt} = 10^{10}(2a - y)^2(a - \frac{1}{2}y)$$

or

$$\frac{dy}{dt} = \frac{1}{2}(10^{10})(2a - y)^3.$$

Separating variables gives

$$\int \frac{dy}{(2a - y)^3} = \frac{1}{2}(10^{10}) \int dt.$$

Integrate: both sides to obtain

$$(\frac{1}{2})\frac{1}{(2a - y)^2} = \frac{1}{2}(10^{10})t + C \qquad \text{or} \qquad \frac{1}{(2a - y)^2} = 10^{10}t + C_1.$$

Setting $t = 0$ and $y = 0$ shows that $C_1 = \frac{1}{(2a)^2} = \frac{1}{4}a^{-2}$. Hence

$(2a - y)^{-2} = 10^{10}t + \frac{1}{4}a^{-2}$, so that $2a - y = (10^{10}t + \frac{1}{4}a^{-2})^{-1/2}$ and

$y = 2a - (10^{10}t + \frac{1}{4}a^{-2})^{-1/2}$. (Notice that the concentration of NO_2 increases toward

the concentration   that there would be if all the atoms were combined into NO_2.)

(13a) If $y = y(t)$ is the concentration [HI] of hydrogen iodide at time t, then at

that time there are $2a - y$ moles per liter of hydrogen atoms and of oxygen atoms in the forms of H_2 and O_2. Therefore, $[H_2] = a - \frac{1}{2} y$ and $[O_2] = a - \frac{1}{2} y$ at time t and the differential equation gives

$$\frac{dy}{dt} = 0.160(a - \frac{1}{2} y)(a - \frac{1}{2} y) - 0.00253 \ y^2 \ .$$

At equilibrium, $\frac{dy}{dt} = 0$ and

$$0.160(a - \frac{1}{2} y)^2 = 0.00253 \ y^2 \ .$$

This equation gives

$$a - \frac{1}{2} y = \sqrt{\frac{0.00253}{0.160}} \ y \approx 0.126 \ y$$

where we took the positive square root since we must have $0 \le y \le 2a$. Solving this approximate equation for y gives

$$y = [HI] \approx 1.598a$$

at equilibrium. (Notice that the lines in the direction field of Figure 9.15 in the text appear to be horizontal that this value of y.)

(17e) We differentiate the equation $x = cy^4$ for the family of curves with respect to x:

(*) $$1 = 4cy^3 \frac{dy}{dx} \ .$$

We want an expression for $\frac{dy}{dx}$ that involves only the coordinates (x,y) of the point on the curve and not the constant c, which indicates which curve we are on. We solve the original equation $x = cy^4$ for $c = xy^{-4}$ and substitute the result in equation (*):

$$1 = 4(xy^{-4})y^3 \frac{dy}{dx} \qquad \text{or} \qquad 1 = \frac{4x}{y} \frac{dy}{dx}$$

This shows that the original family of curves are solutions of the differential equation

(**) $$\frac{dy}{dx} = \frac{y}{4x} \ .$$

To find a differential equation for the family of orthogonal trajectories, we replace the slope on the right of (**) by its negative reciprocal, which is the slope of perpendicular curves:

$$\frac{dy}{dx} = - \frac{4x}{y}$$

Separating the variables gives

$$\int y \ dy = - 4 \int x \ dx$$

and then $$\frac{1}{2} y^2 = - 2x^2 + C_1 \qquad \text{or} \qquad 4x^2 + y^2 = C.$$ (We will see in Chapter 10 that the family of curves given by this equation consists of ellipses centered at the origin.)

SECTION 10.1

(1) We will give two solutions of this exercise.

Solution based on the definition of a parabola   The distance from (x,y) to the focus

is $\sqrt{x^2 + (y - 4)^2}$ and the distance to the directrix $y = 0$ is $|y|$. The point (x,y)

is on the parabola if the squares of these distances are equal, so the parabola has the

equation $x^2 + (y - 4)^2 = y^2$. We rewrite it first as $x^2 + y^2 - 8y + 16 = y^2$,

as $x^2 + 16 = 8y$ and then $y = \frac{1}{8} x^2 + 2$. The ellipse is sketched in Fig. 10.1.1.

Solution based on formula (1) in Section 10.1 of the text Because the focus is at $(0,4)$

and the directrix is the y-axis (Fig. 10.1.1), the parabola opens upward and its equation

is of the form $y' = \frac{1}{4p}(x')^2$ where x' and y' are translated coordinates with origin

at the vertex of the parabola. The vertex is $(0,2)$ because it is midway between the focus

and the directrix. Hence $x' = x$, $y' = y - 2$, and $p = 2$. The equation is $y - 2 = \frac{1}{4(2)}x^2$

or $y = \frac{1}{8} x^2 + 2$.

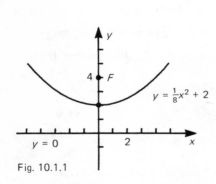

Fig. 10.1.1

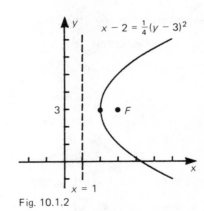

Fig. 10.1.2

(2) Solution based on the definition of a parabola. We set the square of the distance

from (x,y) to the focus $(3,3)$ equal to the square of the distance from (x,y) to the

directrix $x = 1$ and simplify the resulting equation:

$$(x - 3)^2 + (y - 3)^2 = (x - 1)^2$$
$$x^2 - 6x + 9 + (y - 3)^2 = x^2 - 2x + 1$$
$$(y - 3)^2 = 4x - 8$$
$$x - 2 = \frac{1}{4}(y - 3)^2 \quad \text{(Fig. 1.1.2)}$$

<u>Solution based on formula (2) in the text.</u> Because the focus is (3,3) and the

directrix is the vertical line $x = 1$ on its left (Fig. 10.1.2), the parabola opens

toward the right and its equation is of the form $x' = \frac{1}{4p}(y')^2$, where x' and y' are

translated coordinates with origin at the vertex of the parabola. The vertex is $(2,3)$, so

$x' = x - 2$, $y' = y - 3$, and $p = 1$. The parabola has the equation $x - 2 = \frac{1}{4}(y - 3)^2$.

(4) Because the focus at $(4,0)$ is 6 units to the right of the vertex at $(-2,0)$, the

directrix is the line $x = -8$ six units to the left of the vertex (Fig. 10.1.4). We can

obtain the equation from the definition of a parabola as above. Or, we can note that its

equation is of the form $x' = \frac{1}{4p} (y')^2$ with x' and y' translated coordinates with origin

at the vertex $(-2,0)$. Hence $x' = x + 2$, $y' = y$, and $p = 6$. The equation is $x + 2 = \frac{1}{24} y^2$.

(9) Because the y-axis is the axis of the parabola, it has an equation of the form

$y - k = \frac{1}{4p} x^2$. Setting $x = 1$, $y = 4$ in the equation and then $x = 2$, $y = 7$ gives the

simultaneous equations

$$\begin{cases} 4 - k = \dfrac{1}{4p} \\[2mm] 7 - k = \dfrac{1}{p} \end{cases}$$

for the constants k and p. Subtracting the first of these equations from the second gives

$3 = \frac{3}{4p}$ to show that $p = \frac{1}{4}$. Then either equation gives the value $k = 3$. The parabola's

equation is $y - 3 = x^2$. Its vertex is at $(0,3)$, its focus is $\frac{1}{4}$ unit higher at $(0,\frac{13}{4})$, and

its directrix is the horizontal line $y = \frac{11}{4}$, one-fourth unit below the focus (Fig. 10.1.9).

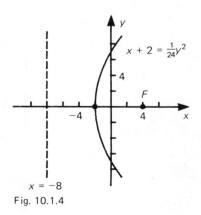

$x = -8$

Fig. 10.1.4

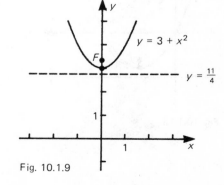

Fig. 10.1.9

(13) We first complete the square in x in the equation $-x^2 + 2x + y = 0$:

$$x^2 - 2x = y$$

$$x^2 - 2x + 1 = y + 1$$

$$(x - 1)^2 = y + 1$$

The last equation is of the form $y' = \frac{1}{4p}(x')^2$ with $x' = x - 1$, $y' = y + 1$, and $p = \frac{1}{4}$.
The parabola's vertex is at $(1,-1)$ (the origin of the x'y'-coordinates), it opens upward
(because p is positive), its focus is at $(1,-\frac{3}{4})$, one fourth unit above the vertex, and
is directrix is the horizontal line $y = -\frac{5}{4}$, one fourth unit below the vertex (Fig. 10.1.13).

(22) The distance from (x,y) to the focus $(0,3)$ is $\sqrt{x^2 + (y - 3)^2}$ and the distance
from (x,y) to the line $y - x = 0$ is   (by formula (9) in the text)

$$\frac{|y - x|}{\sqrt{2}}.$$

Equating the squares of these distances gives $x^2 + (y - 3)^2 = \frac{1}{2}(y - x)^2$, which we simplify
by writing

$$x^2 + y^2 - 6y + 9 = \frac{1}{2}(y^2 - 2xy + x^2)$$

$$\frac{1}{2} x^2 + \frac{1}{2} y^2 + xy - 6y + 9 = 0$$

$$x^2 + 2xy + y^2 - 12y + 18 = 0 \quad \text{(Fig. 10.1.22)}.$$

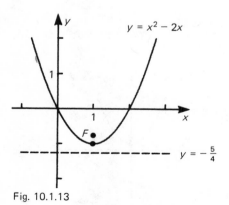

Fig. 10.1.13

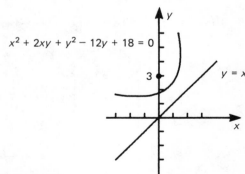

Fig. 10.1.22

(25) Because the line through the focus (-2,0) and the vertex (0,-4) **is the axis of the**
parabola and has slope - 2, the directrix, which is perpendicular to the axis, has slope $\frac{1}{2}$.
The directrix intersects the axis at the point (2,-8) **symmetric to** the focus about the vertex
(Fig. 10.1.25).Hence the directrix has the equation $y + 8 = \frac{1}{2}(x - 2)$ or $x - 2y - 18 = 0$
For (x,y) to be on the parabola, **its** distance to the directrix must equal its distance to
the focus and we must have

$$\frac{|x - 2y - 18|}{\sqrt{5}} = \sqrt{(x + 2)^2 + y^2}.$$

Squaring both sides of the equation yields

$$\frac{1}{5}(x - 2y - 18)^2 = (x + 2)^2 + y^2$$

$$\frac{1}{5}(x^2 + 4y^2 + (18)^2 - 4xy - 36x + 72y) = x^2 + 4x + 4 + y^2$$

$$x^2 + 4y^2 + 324 - 4xy - 36x + 72y = 5x^2 + 20x + 20 + 5y^2$$

$$-4x^2 - 4xy - y^2 + 304 - 56x + 72y = 0$$

and finally $4x^2 + 4xy + y^2 + 56x - 72y - 304 = 0.$ (In this calculation we used the
formula

$$(a + b + c)^2 = a^2 + b^2 + c^2 + 2ab + 2ac + 2bc.)$$

$$4x^2 + 4xy + y^2 + 56x - 72y = 304$$

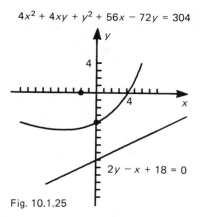

Fig. 10.1.25

SECTION 10.2

(3) We first complete the squares in x and y in the equation $9x^2 + y^2 - 18x + 2y + 1 = 0$:

$$9(x^2 - 2x) + (y^2 + 2y) = -1$$

$$9(x^2 - 2x + 1) + (y^2 + 2x + 1) = -1 + 9 + 1$$

$$9(x - 1)^2 + (y + 1)^2 = 9$$

$$\frac{(x - 1)^2}{1^2} + \frac{(y + 1)^2}{3^2} = 1$$

This is in the form of equation (3) in Section 10.2 of the text with $a = 3$, $b = 1$
and hence $c = \sqrt{a^2 - b^2} = \sqrt{8}$. The center of the ellipse is at $(1,-1)$, its major axis

is vertical and of length $2a = 6$, its minor axis is horizontal and of length $2b = 2$, and
its foci are $(1,-1 -\sqrt{8})$ and $(1,-1 +\sqrt{8})$ a distance $c = \sqrt{8}$ units above and below
the center (Fig. 10.2.3).

(7) We complete the squares in the equation $9x^2 + 25y^2 + 18x + 50y = 191$:

$$9(x^2 + 2x) + 25(y^2 + 2y) = 191$$

$$9(x^2 + 2x + 1) + 25(y^2 + 2y + 1) = 191 + 9 + 25$$

$$9(x + 1)^2 + 25(y + 1)^2 = 225$$

$$\frac{(x + 1)^2}{5^2} + \frac{(y + 1)^2}{3^2} = 1$$

This equation is of the form of equation (1) in the text with $a = 5$, $b = 3$, and hence

$c = \sqrt{a^2 - b^2} = 4$. The center of the ellipse is at $(-1,-1)$, its major axis is horizontal
and of length $2a = 10$, its minor axis is vertical and of length $2b = 6$, and its foci
are $(-5,-1)$ and $(3,-1)$, four units to the left and right of the center (Fig. 10.2.7).

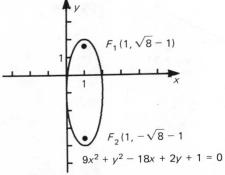

Fig. 10.2.3

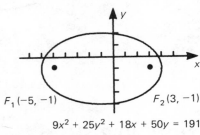

Fig. 10.2.7

(9) The center of the ellipse is midway between the foci $(-3,0)$ and $(3,0)$, so it is

$(0,0)$. The distance from the center to the foci is $c = 3$. Half the length of the major

axis is $a = 5$. Therefore, $b = \sqrt{a^2 - c^2}$ is $\sqrt{5^2 - 3^2} = 4$. The major axis is on the x-axis

so, by equation (1) in the text, the ellipse has the equation

$$\frac{x^2}{5^2} + \frac{y^2}{4^2} = 1 \quad \text{or} \quad \frac{x^2}{25} + \frac{y^2}{16} = 1 \, .$$

(14) Because the center of the ellipse is at $(1,10)$, its major axis is horizontal

and its minor axis is vertical, it has an equation of the form

$$\frac{(x - 1)^2}{a^2} + \frac{(y - 10)^2}{b^2} = 1.$$

Because the major axis is of length 8 and the minor axis is of length 2, we have

$a = 4$ and $b = 1$, and the equation reads

$$\frac{(x - 1)^2}{16} + \frac{(y - 10)^2}{1} = 1$$

(21) If the sum of the distances from (x,y) to $(-1,0)$ and $(0,3)$ is 10, then

$$\sqrt{(x + 1)^2 + y^2} + \sqrt{x^2 + (y - 3)^2} = 10.$$

To put this equation in the desired form (without square root signs), we mimic the proof

of Theorem 10.2. We put one square root on each side of the equation and square both sides:

$$\sqrt{(x + 1)^2 + y^2} = 10 - \sqrt{x^2 + (y - 3)^2}$$

$$(x + 1)^2 + y^2 = 100 - 20\sqrt{x^2 + (y - 3)^2} + x^2 + (y - 3)^2$$

Then we isolate the remaining square root on one side and simplify the other side of the

equation:

$$(x + 1)^2 + y^2 - x^2 - (y - 3)^2 - 100 = -20\sqrt{x^2 + (y - 3)^2}$$

$$x^2 + 2x + 1 + y^2 - x^2 - y^2 + 6y - 9 - 100 = -20\sqrt{x^2 + (y - 3)^2}$$

$$2x + 6y - 108 = -20\sqrt{x^2 + (y - 3)^2}$$

Next, we square both sides and simplify again:

$$(2x + 6y - 108)^2 = 400[x^2 + (y - 3)^2]$$

$$4x^2 + 36y^2 + (108)^2 + 24xy - 432x - 1296y = 400x^2 + 400y^2 - 2400y + 3600$$

$$- 396x^2 + 24xy - 364y^2 - 432x + 1104y + 8064 = 0$$

Finally, we divide the equation by -4 to obtain

$$99x^2 - 6xy + 91y^2 + 108x - 276y - 2016 = 0.$$

(23) The top half of the ellipse is the graph of $y = b\sqrt{1 - (\frac{x}{a})^2}$, so the area of the entire ellipse is

$$\text{Area} = 4 \int_0^a b\sqrt{1 - (\frac{x}{a})^2}\ dx = \frac{4b}{a} \int_0^a \sqrt{a^2 - x^2}\ dx.$$

We evaluate the indefinite integral by using the substitution $\theta = \arcsin(\frac{x}{a})$, $x = a\sin\theta$, $\sqrt{a^2 - x^2} = a\cos\theta$, $dx = a\cos\theta$, or by using formula (24) in Table VIII of integrals. Then we have

$$\text{Area} = \frac{4b}{a}[\ \frac{1}{2}\ x\sqrt{a^2 - x^2} + \frac{1}{2}\ a^2\ \arcsin(\frac{x}{a})]_0^a = \frac{4b}{a}[\frac{1}{2}\ a^2\ \arcsin(1)] - \frac{4b}{a}[0]$$

$$= \frac{4b}{a}(\frac{1}{2})\ a^2(\frac{\pi}{2}) = \pi ab.$$

(27) The solution given in the back of the text uses the equation for the ellipse. We will use here the geometric definition of the ellipse and the properties of light that reflects off straight lines. Consider an ellipse with foci F_1 and F_2 and a point P on the ellipse (Fig. 10.2.27). A point Q is on the ellipse if and only if $\overline{QF_1} + \overline{QF_2} = \overline{PF_1} + \overline{PF_2}$. A point Q is inside the ellipse if $\overline{QF_1} + \overline{QF_2} < \overline{PF_1} + \overline{PF_2}$ and outside it if $\overline{QF_1} + \overline{QF_2} > \overline{PF_1} + \overline{PF_2}$. Because all points on the tangent at P are outside the ellipse except for the point P itself, the minimum of $\overline{QF_1} + \overline{QF_2}$ for Q on the tangent line occurs for $Q = P$. By Fermat's principle (p. 163 of the text), light shining from F_1 and reflecting off the tangent line will pass through F_2 . For light reflecting off a straight line the angle of incidence equals the angle of reflection (by Snell's law, see p. 164 of the text). Therefore, the tangent line makes equal angles with the focal radii at P.

Fig. 10.2.27

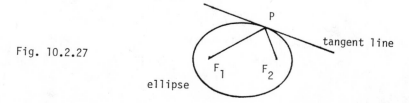

SECTION 10.3

(3) Complete the squares in x and y in the equation $x^2 - y^2 + 2x + 2y = 1$:

$$(x^2 + 2x) - (y^2 - 2y) = 1$$
$$(x^2 + 2x + 1) - (y^2 - 2y + 1) = 1 + 1 - 1$$
$$(x + 1)^2 - (y - 1)^2 = 1$$

We introduce new coordinates $x' = x + 1$, $y' = y - 1$ to put the equation in the form

(*) $(x')^2 - (y')^2 = 1$,

which is of the form of equation (1) in Section 10.3 in the text with x and y
replaced by x' and y', with a = 1, and with b = 1. The center of the hyperbola is
at x = -1, y = 1, which is the origin of the x'y'-coordinates. Because x' can never
be zero in equation (*), the hyperbola does not intersect the y'-axis and it opens to the
right and left. To find the vertices, we set y' = 0 in equation (*): the vertices are
at $x' = \pm 1$, y' = 0, which are the points (0,1) and (-2,1) in xy-coordinates. Because
a and b are 1, we have $c = \sqrt{a^2 + b^2} = \sqrt{2}$, and the foci are at $(-1-\sqrt{2},1)$ and
$(-1+\sqrt{2},1)$, a distance $\sqrt{2}$ to the left and right of the center. The asymptotes have the
equations $y' = \pm x'$ in the translated coordinates, or $y - 1 = \pm (x + 1)$ in the
original coordinates. These equations simplify to y = -x and y = x + 2 (Fig. 10.3.3).

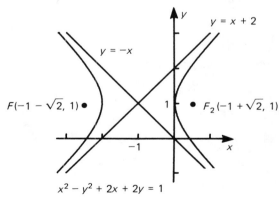

Fig. 10.3.3

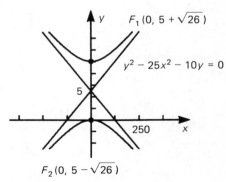

Fig. 10.3.5

(5) We complete the square in y in the equation $y^2 - 10y - 25x^2 = 0$;

$$(y^2 - 10y + 25) - 25x^2 = 0 + 25$$

$$(y - 5)^2 - 25x^2 = 25$$

$$\frac{(y - 5)^2}{5^2} - \frac{x^2}{1^2} = 1$$

We set x' = x and y' = y - 5 to put the equation in the form

(*) $$\frac{(y')^2}{5^2} - \frac{(x')^2}{1^2} = 1.$$

The center of the hyperbola is at x = 0, y = 5, where x' and y' are zero. Because y'
cannot be zero in equation (*), the hyperbola does not cross the x-axis and the hyperbola
opens upward and downward. Setting x' = 0 in equation (*) shows that y' = ± 5 at the
vertices of the hyperbola. They are the points with **xy-coordinates** (0,0) and (0,10).
In equation (*) we have a = 5 and b = 1. Hence, c is $\sqrt{a^2 + b^2} = 26$ and the foci
are $(0,5+\sqrt{26})$ and $(0,5-\sqrt{26})$. The asymptotes are $y' = \pm (\frac{a}{b})x'$ or y - 5 = ± 5x. The

hyperbola is shown in Fig. 10.3.5, where unequal scales have been used on the x- and
y-axes to make the sketch clearer.

(11) The center of the hyperbola is at (0,0), midway between the foci. Because the
foci are (± 4,0), we have c = 4. Because the vertices are (± 3,0), we have a = 3.
Therefore, we have $b = \sqrt{c^2 - a^2} = \sqrt{7}$. The hyperbola opens to the right and left, so
its equation is in the form of equation (1) in Section 10.3 of the text. The equation is

$$\frac{x^2}{9} - \frac{y^2}{7} = 1.$$

(16) Because the foci of the hyperbola are (± 3,0), its equation is of the form of equation
(1) in Section 10.3 in the text and c = 3. Because the asymptotes are y = ± x, we have
a = b. Since c equals $\sqrt{a^2 + b^2}$, a and b are both $\frac{3}{\sqrt{2}}$ and the hyperbola has the

equation

$$\frac{x^2}{\frac{9}{2}} - \frac{y^2}{\frac{9}{2}} = 1 \qquad \text{or} \qquad \frac{2}{9} x^2 - \frac{2}{9} y^2 = 1.$$

(23) If the difference between the distances from (x,y) to (4,4) and (-4,-4) is 8, then

$$\sqrt{(x - 4)^2 + (y - 4)^2} - \sqrt{(x + 4)^2 + (y + 4)^2} = \pm\,8$$

$$\sqrt{(x - 4)^2 + (y - 4)^2} = \pm\,8 + \sqrt{(x + 4)^2 + (y + 4)^2}$$

$$(x - 4)^2 + (y - 4)^2 = 64 \pm 16\sqrt{(x + 4)^2 + (y + 4)^2} + (x + 4)^2 + (y + 4)^2$$

$$x^2 - 8x + 16 + y^2 - 8y + 16 = 64 \pm 16\sqrt{(x + 4)^2 + (y + 4)^2} +$$
$$+ x^2 + 8x + 16 + y^2 + 8y + 16$$

$$-16x - 16y - 64 = \pm 16\sqrt{(x + 4)^2 + (y + 4)^2}$$

$$x + y + 4 = \mp\sqrt{(x + 4)^2 + (y + 4)^2}$$

$$(x + y + 4)^2 = (x + 4)^2 + (y + 4)^2$$

$$x^2 + y^2 + 16 + 2xy + 8x + 8y = x^2 + 8x + 16 + y^2 + 8y + 16$$

This simplifies to the final form of the equation of the hyperbola

$$xy = 8.$$

(30)　We must show that the vertical distance between the points at x on a branch
of the hyperbola and the point on the corresponding asymptote tends to zero as $x \to \pm\infty$.
On the upper half of the hyperbola $\left(\frac{x}{a}\right)^2 - \left(\frac{y}{b}\right)^2 = 1$ we have $y^2 = b^2\left[\left(\frac{x}{a}\right)^2 - 1\right]$ and

$$y = b\sqrt{\left(\frac{x}{a}\right)^2 - 1} = \left|\frac{bx}{a}\right|\sqrt{1 - \left(\frac{a}{x}\right)^2}\,.$$

On the corresponding asymptote we have $y = \left|\frac{bx}{a}\right|$, so

(*)　　　　$$\left|\frac{bx}{a}\right| - \left|\frac{bx}{a}\right|\sqrt{1 - \left(\frac{a}{x}\right)^2} = \left|\frac{bx}{a}\right|\left[1 - \sqrt{1 - \left(\frac{a}{x}\right)^2}\right]$$

is the distance between the points at x on the hyperbola and the asymptote. A similar
calculation shows that (*) equals that distance on the lower part of the hyperbola as well.

To show that (*) tends to zero as $x \to \pm\infty$, we multiply and divide it by
$1 + \sqrt{1 - \left(\frac{a}{x}\right)^2}$ (as in the rationalization process we used to compute derivatives of
square roots of functions). The distance (*) equals

$$\left|\frac{bx}{a}\right|\,\frac{1^2 - \left[\sqrt{1 - \left(\frac{a}{x}\right)^2}\,\right]^2}{1 + \sqrt{1 - \left(\frac{a}{x}\right)^2}} = \left|\frac{bx}{a}\right|\,\frac{\left(\frac{a}{x}\right)^2}{1 + \sqrt{1 - \left(\frac{a}{x}\right)^2}} = \frac{\left|\frac{ba}{x}\right|}{1 + \sqrt{1 - \left(\frac{a}{x}\right)^2}}$$

and therefore tends to zero as $x \to \pm\infty$.

SECTION 10.4

(1) In the equation $x^2 + 3xy - y^2 + 6x - 6 = 0$ we have $A = 1$, $B = 3$, $C = -1$, and $B^2 - 4AC = (3)^2 - 4(1)(-1) = 13$, so the curve is a hyperbola.

(3) In the equation $-x^2 + 4xy - 4y^2 + x = 1$ we have $A = -1$, $B = 4$, $C = -4$ and $B^2 - 4AC = (4)^2 - 4(-1)(-4) = 0$, so the curve is a parabola.

(8) In the equation $2x^2 + \sqrt{3}\ xy + y^2 = 2$ we have $A = 2$, $B = \sqrt{3}$, and $C = 1$, so

$$\cot(2\alpha) = \frac{A - C}{B} = \frac{1}{\sqrt{3}} .$$

We can satisfy this equation by taking $2\alpha = \frac{\pi}{3}$ (Fig. 10.4.8a), for which $\alpha = \frac{\pi}{6}$, $\cos \alpha = \frac{\sqrt{3}}{2}$, and $\sin \alpha = \frac{1}{2}$. By formulas (2) of Section 10.4 we can eliminate the xy-term in the equation by changing to x'y'-coordinates where

(*)
$$x = \frac{\sqrt{3}}{2} x' - \frac{1}{2} y'$$
$$y = \frac{1}{2} x' + \frac{\sqrt{3}}{2} y'.$$

We make the substitutions (*) in the equation $2x^2 + \sqrt{3}\ xy + y^2 = 2$, compute the products, combine terms, and simplify:

$$2[\frac{\sqrt{3}}{2} x' - \frac{1}{2} y']^2 + \sqrt{3}\ [\frac{\sqrt{3}}{2} x' - \frac{1}{2} y'][\frac{1}{2} x' + \frac{\sqrt{3}}{2} y'] + [\frac{1}{2} x' + \frac{\sqrt{3}}{2} y']^2 = 2$$

$$\frac{1}{2}(\sqrt{3}\ x' - y')^2 + \frac{\sqrt{3}}{4}(\sqrt{3}\ x' - y')(x' + \sqrt{3}\ y') + \frac{1}{4}(x' + \sqrt{3}\ y')^2 = 2$$

$$\frac{1}{2}[3(x')^2 - 2\sqrt{3}\ x'y' + (y')^2] + \frac{\sqrt{3}}{4}[\sqrt{3}(x')^2 + 2x'y' - \sqrt{3}(y')^2] + \frac{1}{4}[(x')^2 + 2\sqrt{3}x'y' + 3(y')^2]$$

$$(x')^2[\frac{3}{2} + \frac{3}{4} + \frac{1}{4}] + x'y'[-\sqrt{3} + \frac{\sqrt{3}}{2} + \frac{\sqrt{3}}{2}] + (y')^2[\frac{1}{2} - \frac{3}{4} + \frac{3}{4}] = 2$$

$$\frac{5}{2}(x')^2 + \frac{1}{2}(y')^2 = 2$$

$$\frac{(x')^2}{\frac{4}{5}} + \frac{(y')^2}{4} = 1$$

The resulting equation is of the form of equation (3) of Section 4.2 in the text with $a = 2$ and $b = \sqrt{\frac{4}{5}}$, for which $c = \sqrt{a^2 - b^2}$ is $\sqrt{4 - \frac{4}{5}} = \frac{4}{\sqrt{5}}$. The vertices of the ellipse are at $x' = 0$, $y' = \pm 2$ and the foci are at $x' = 0$, $y' = \pm\frac{4}{\sqrt{5}}$.

Equations (*) give the xy-coordinates of the vertices as $(1, -\sqrt{3})$ and $(-1, \sqrt{3})$ and the xy-coordinates of the foci as $(\frac{2}{\sqrt{5}}, -2\sqrt{\frac{3}{5}})$ and $(-\frac{2}{\sqrt{5}}, 2\sqrt{\frac{3}{5}})$. The ellipse is sketched in Fig. 10.4.8.

$\cot(2\alpha) = \frac{1}{\sqrt{3}}$

$2\alpha = \frac{\pi}{3}$

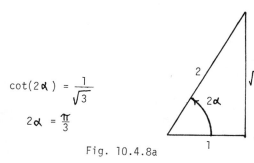

Fig. 10.4.8a

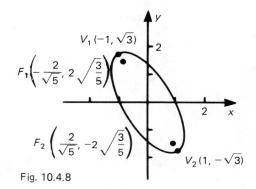

Fig. 10.4.8

(12) In the equation $x^2 + 2xy + y^2 = 4\sqrt{2}\,y$ we have $A = 1$, $B = 2$, and $C = 1$ so that

$$\cot(2\alpha) = \frac{A - C}{B} = 0.$$

We can satisfy this equation by taking $2\alpha = \frac{\pi}{2}$ and $\alpha = \frac{\pi}{4}$. Then $\sin\alpha$ and $\cos\alpha$ are $\frac{1}{\sqrt{2}}$ and equations (2) of Section 10.4 in the text give

(*)
$$x = \frac{1}{\sqrt{2}}(x' - y')$$

$$y = \frac{1}{\sqrt{2}}(x' + y').$$

When we make these substitutions in the equation for the curve, compute the squares and products, and simplify, we obtain

$$\frac{1}{2}(x' - y')^2 + (x' - y')(x' + y') + \frac{1}{2}(x' + y') = \frac{4\sqrt{2}}{\sqrt{2}}(x' + y')$$

$$\frac{1}{2}[(x')^2 - 2x'y' + (y')^2] + (x')^2 - (y')^2 + \frac{1}{2}[(x')^2 + 2x'y' + (y')^2] = 4x' + 4y'$$

$$(x')^2[\frac{1}{2} + 1 + \frac{1}{2}] + x'y'[-1 + 1] + (y')^2[\frac{1}{2} - 1 + \frac{1}{2}] = 4x' + 4y'$$

$$2(x')^2 = 4x' + 4y'$$

$$y' = \frac{1}{2}[(x')^2 - 2x'].$$

Next, we complete the square in x' to obtain

$$y' + \frac{1}{2} = \frac{1}{2}[(x')^2 - 2x' + 1]$$

and then

(**)
$$y' + \frac{1}{2} = \frac{1}{2}(x' - 1)^2 .$$

Equation (**) is of the form of equation (1) of Section 10.1 with x replaced by x" = x - 1 with y replaced by y" = y' + $\frac{1}{2}$, and with p = $\frac{1}{2}$. The curve is a parabola

with its vertex at the origin of the x"y"-axes, where x' = 1, y' = -$\frac{1}{2}$ and, by equations (**), x = $\frac{1}{\sqrt{2}}(\frac{3}{2})$, y = $\frac{1}{\sqrt{2}}(\frac{1}{2})$. The parabola opens in the direction of the positive y-axis

(Fig. 10.4.12). Because p is $\frac{1}{2}$, the focus is at the point where x" = 0 and y" = $\frac{1}{2}$. Because x" = x' - 1 and y" = y' + $\frac{1}{2}$, this is at x' = 1, y' = 0, where x = $\frac{1}{\sqrt{2}}$, y = $\frac{1}{\sqrt{2}}$. The directrix has the equation y" = -$\frac{1}{2}$ in x"y"-equations and

y' = -1 in x'y'-coordinates. By equation (*) the xy-coordinates of the points on the directrix satisfy the simultaneous equations

$$x = \frac{1}{\sqrt{2}}(x' + 1)$$

$$y = \frac{1}{\sqrt{2}}(x' - 1).$$

Subtracting the second of these equations from the first to eliminate x' shows that the directrix has the equation x - y = $\frac{2}{\sqrt{2}}$ or y = x - $\sqrt{2}$.

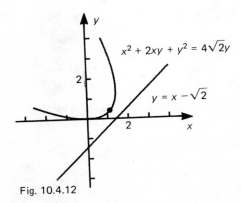

$x^2 + 2xy + y^2 = 4\sqrt{2}y$

$y = x - \sqrt{2}$

Fig. 10.4.12

(24) In the equation $4x^2 - 4xy + 7y^2 = 72$ we have $A = 4$, $B = -4$, and $C = 7$. Hence, by formula (5) in Section 10.4 of the text, we can eliminate the xy-term by rotating the axes through an angle α such that

$$\tan \alpha = \frac{C - A}{B} + \sqrt{\left(\frac{C - A}{B}\right)^2 + 1} = \frac{7 - 4}{-4} + \sqrt{\left(\frac{7 - 4}{-4}\right)^2 + 1} = -\frac{3}{4} + \sqrt{\frac{25}{16}}$$

$$= -\frac{3}{4} + \frac{5}{4} = \frac{1}{2} .$$

we chose the acute positive angle α $(0 < \alpha < \frac{\pi}{2})$ with this tangent. Figure 10.4.24a shows that $\cos \alpha = \frac{2}{\sqrt{5}}$ and $\sin = \frac{1}{\sqrt{5}}$, and equations (2) of Section 10.4 of the text yield

(*)

$$x = \frac{1}{\sqrt{5}}(2x' - y')$$

$$y = \frac{1}{\sqrt{5}}(x' + 2y').$$

When we make these substitutions in the equation for the curve, we obtain

$$\frac{4}{5}(2x' - y')^2 - \frac{4}{5}(2x' - y')(x' + 2y') + \frac{7}{5}(x' + 2y')^2 = 72$$

$$\frac{4}{5}[4(x')^2 - 4x'y' + (y')^2] - \frac{4}{5}[2(x')^2 + 3x'y' - 2(y')^2] + \frac{7}{5}[(x')^2 + 4x'y' + 4(y')^2] = 72$$

$$(x')^2[\frac{16}{5} - \frac{8}{5} + \frac{7}{5}] + x'y'[-\frac{16}{5} - \frac{12}{5} + \frac{28}{5}] + (y')^2[\frac{4}{5} + \frac{8}{5} + \frac{28}{5}] = 72$$

$$3(x')^2 + 8(y')^2 = 72$$

$$\frac{(x')^2}{24} + \frac{(y')^2}{9} = 1.$$

This is in the form of equation (1) of Section 10.2 with x and y replaced by x' and y'. The curve is an ellipse with vertices at $x' = \pm\sqrt{24}$, $y' = 0$, where by (*) $x = \pm \frac{2}{\sqrt{5}}\sqrt{24}$ and $y = \pm \frac{1}{\sqrt{5}}\sqrt{24}$ (Fig. 10.4.24).

$\tan \alpha = \frac{1}{2}$

$\cos \alpha = \frac{2}{\sqrt{5}}$

$\sin \alpha = \frac{1}{\sqrt{5}}$

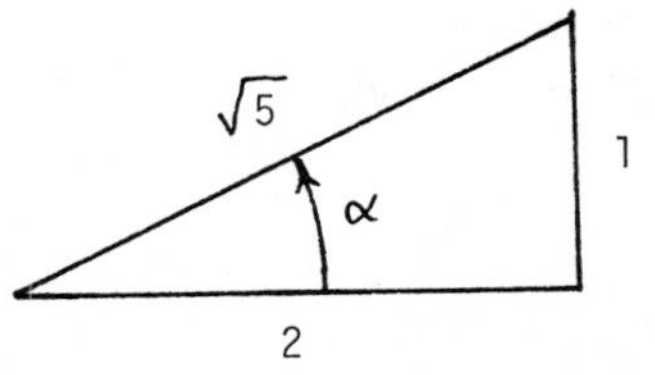

Fig. 10.4.24a

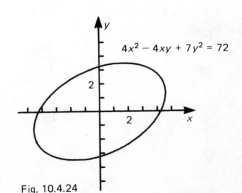

$4x^2 - 4xy + 7y^2 = 72$

Fig. 10.4.24

(35)   In the equation $x^2 - 2xy + y^2 = 0$ we have A = 1, B = -2, C = 1 and

$B^2 - 4AC = (-2)^2 - 4(1)(1) = 0$, so the conic section is a parabola. We can rewrite

the equation in the form $(x - y)^2 = 0$ to see that its graph is the line y = x,

a degenerate parabola (Fig. 10.4.35).

The degenerate parabola

$(x - y)^2 = 0$

Fig. 10.4.35

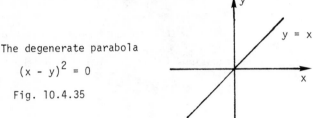

SECTION 10.5

(1a)   Because the foci are $(\pm 1,0)$, the center of the conic section is at (0,0) and

c = 1. Because the eccentricity $e = \frac{1}{3}$ is less than 1, the curve is an ellipse. The

equation $e = \frac{c}{a}$ shows that a = 3, and then the equation $b = \sqrt{a^2 - c^2}$ shows that

$b = \sqrt{3^2 - 1^2} = \sqrt{8}$. The foci lie on the major axis, which is the x-axis, so the equation

of the ellipse is

$$\frac{x^2}{9} + \frac{y^2}{8} = 1 \quad \text{(see Fig. 10.5.1a)}.$$

(1b)   Again, because the foci are $(\pm 1,0)$, the center is at (0,0) and c = 1.   The curve

is a hyperbola because the eccentricity e = 3 is greater than 1.The equation $e = \frac{c}{a}$

implies that $a = \frac{1}{3}$ and the equation $b = \sqrt{c^2 - a^2}$ simplies that

$$b = \sqrt{1 - (\tfrac{1}{3})^2} = \frac{\sqrt{8}}{3}.$$

The axis of the hyperbola is the x-axis because the foci are on it. Hence, the hyperbola

has the equation

$$\frac{x^2}{\frac{1}{9}} - \frac{y^2}{\frac{8}{9}} = 1 \quad \text{or} \quad 9x^2 - \frac{9}{8}y^2 = 1 \quad \text{(see Fig. 10.5.1b)}.$$

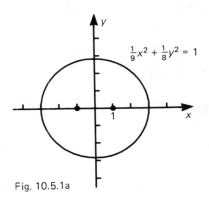

Fig. 10.5.1a

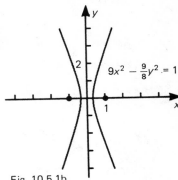

Fig. 10.5.1b

(4) For $0 < e < 1$ the curve is an ellipse with the x-axis as its major axis. It has
an equation of the form

$$\frac{(x')^2}{a^2} + \frac{(y')^2}{b^2} = 1$$

with $x' = x + h$ and $y' = y$ translated to put the origin of the x'y'-coordinates
at the center of the ellipse. Because the foci are at $x' = \pm c$, the **center** has
xy-coordinates $(-c,0)$ and the other focus **has** coordinates $(-2c,0)$ (Fig. 10.5.4a).
The **original and** translated coordinates are related by $x' = x + c, y' = y$. The second
directrix is the line $x = -2c - 1$, the same distance from the center as the **directrix**
$x = 1$. The vertex on the right is at $x' = a, y' = 0$ or $x = a - c, y = 0$.

Equation (9) in Section 10.5 shows that a, c, and e are related by

(*) $c = ae.$

Equation (9) of that section shows that the directrix on the right has the equation
$x' = \frac{a}{e}$, which becomes $x = \frac{a}{e} - c$ in the original coordinates. That directrix also has
the equation $x = 1$, so we have $1 = \frac{a}{e} - c$, which implies that

(**) $c = \frac{a}{e} - 1.$

Equating expressions (*) and (**) for c gives $ae = \frac{a}{e} - 1$, which shows that

$$a = \frac{e}{1 - e^2} \; .$$

Then (*) gives

$$c = \frac{e^2}{1 - e^2} \; .$$

As x $\rightarrow$ 1$^-$, c tends to ∞ , so the focus F(-2c,0) and the directrix x = -2c - 1

tend to - ∞ .

For e = 1 the curve is a parabola with only one focus and directrix.

For e > 1, the conic section is a hyperbola with **an equation of** the form

$$\frac{(x')^2}{a^2} - \frac{(y')^2}{b^2} = 1$$

with x' = x - c, y ' = 0   because the center is to the right of the directrix x = 1.
We again have

(*)   c = ae

but because the directrix x = 1 is now on the left side of the **center,it** has the equation
x' = - $\frac{a}{e}$ or x = - $\frac{a}{e}$ + c, which yields   1 = - $\frac{a}{e}$ + c and then

(***)   c = 1 + $\frac{a}{e}$.

Solving equations (*) and (***) for a yields

$$a = \frac{e}{e^2 - 1}$$

and then (*) gives

$$c = \frac{e^2}{e^2 - 1}$$

The number c decreases toward the number 1 as   e tends to ∞; the focus F(2c,0)

approaches the point (2,0) and the directrix   x = 2c - 1 approaches the fixed directrix
x = 1 (Fig. 10.5.4b).

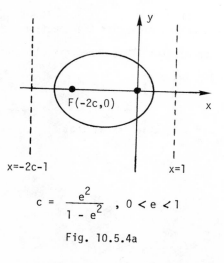

$$c = \frac{e^2}{1 - e^2} , \ 0 < e < 1$$

Fig. 10.5.4a

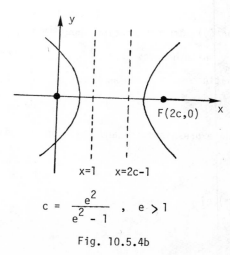

$$c = \frac{e^2}{e^2 - 1} , \ e > 1$$

Fig. 10.5.4b

(8a) The ellipse

$$\frac{x^2}{3^2} + \frac{y^2}{2^2} = 1$$

is of the type in Figure 10.18 in Section 10.2 of the text with $a = 3$, $b = 2$, and $c = \sqrt{a^2 - b^2} = \sqrt{5}$. Its foci are $(\pm\sqrt{5}, 0)$ and its directrices are $x = \pm \frac{a^2}{c} = \pm \frac{9}{\sqrt{5}}$ (Fig. 10.5.8a).

(8b) The hyperbola $x^2 - y^2 = 16$ has the equation

$$\frac{x^2}{4^2} - \frac{y^2}{4^2} = 1$$

so it is of the type in Figure 10.26 in Section 10.3 of the text with $a = 4$, $b = 4$, and $c = \sqrt{a^2 + b^2} = 4\sqrt{2}$. Its foci are $(\pm 4\sqrt{2}, 0)$ and its directrices are $x = \pm \frac{a^2}{c} = \pm \frac{16}{4\sqrt{2}} = \pm 2\sqrt{2}$ (Fig. 10.5.8b).

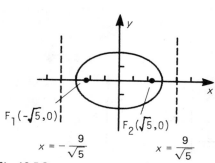

$x = -\frac{9}{\sqrt{5}}$ $x = \frac{9}{\sqrt{5}}$

Fig. 10.5.8a

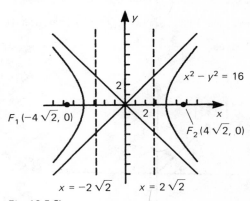

$x = -2\sqrt{2}$ $x = 2\sqrt{2}$

Fig. 10.5.8b

(9) The equation $x^2 - 8y^2 = 8$ can be written $\frac{1}{8}x^2 - y^2 = 1$ which is of the form $\frac{x^2}{a^2} - \frac{y^2}{b^2} = 1$ with $a = \sqrt{8}$ and $b = 1$. The curve is a hyperbola with its center at the origin and its foci at $(\pm c, 0)$ where $c = \sqrt{a^2 + b^2} = \sqrt{8 + 1} = 3$ (Fig. 10.5.9). Its eccentricity is $e = \frac{c}{a} = \frac{3}{\sqrt{8}}$ and its directrices are the vertical lines $x = \pm d$ where $d = \frac{a^2}{c} = \frac{8}{3}$.

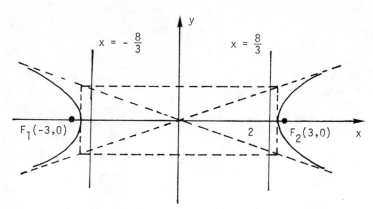

Fig. 10.5.9

SECTION 10.6

(1a) We draw an angle of $\frac{3}{4}\pi$ radians (Fig. 10.6.1a). The point with polar coordinates $[3,\frac{3}{4}\pi]$ is a distance 3 from the origin on the terminal side of that angle. The terminal side of the angle, the x-axis, and the vertical line through the point form an isosceles right triangle with hypotenuse of length 3 (Fig. 10.6.1aᵢ). By the Pythagorean theorem, the legs of the triangle have length $\frac{3}{\sqrt{2}}$. Therefore, the point has rectangular coordinates $(-\frac{3}{\sqrt{2}} , \frac{3}{\sqrt{2}})$.

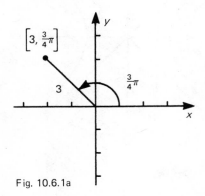

Fig. 10.6.1a

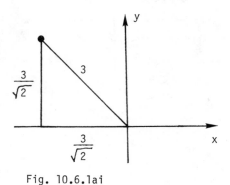

Fig. 10.6.1ai

(1c) We draw an r-axis with its origin at the origin of the rectangular coordinates and with its positive side making an angle of $\frac{\pi}{6}$ radians with the positive x-axis (Fig. 10.6.1c). The point with polar coordinates $[-\frac{1}{2},\frac{\pi}{6}]$ is at $r = -\frac{1}{2}$ on that axis. The x-axis, the r-axis, and the vertical line through the point form a 30°-60°-right triangle with hypotenuse of length $\frac{1}{2}$ (Fig. 10.6.1ci). Because the triangle is half an equilateral triangle, its height is half the length of its hypotenuse, which is $\frac{1}{4}$. By the Pythagorean theorem it is $\frac{\sqrt{3}}{4}$ units wide, and the rectangular coordinates of the point are $(-\frac{\sqrt{3}}{4}, -\frac{1}{4})$.

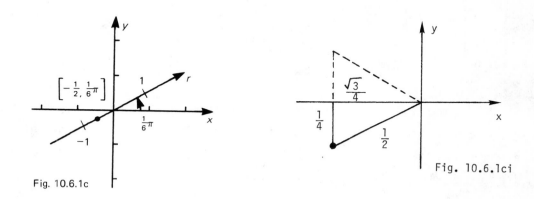

Fig. 10.6.1c

Fig. 10.6.1ci

(1i) Because 3π is approximately $3(3.14) = 9.42$, 10 radians is approximately $3\pi + 0.58$ radians and -10 is approximately $-3\pi - 0.58$. We draw an r-axis with its positive side at the terminal end of such an angle (Fig. 10.6.1i). The point with

polar coordinates $[-4, -10]$ is at $r = -4$ on that axis. Its exact rectangular coordinates are $(-4 \cos(-10), -4 \sin(-10))$. To find approximate values of the coordinates from the table of values of sines and cosines, we note that the r-axis, the x-axis, and the vertical line through the point form a right triangle with an angle of $10 - 3\pi$ radians at the origin (Fig. 10.6.6ii). The height of the triangle is $4 \sin(10 - 3\pi) \approx 4 \sin(0.58)$

$\approx 4(0.5480) \approx 2.19$; its width is $4 \cos(10 - 3\pi) \approx 4 \cos(0.58) \approx 4(0.8365) \approx 3.35$. Hence the point has approximate coordinates $(3.35, -2.19)$. (The coordinates $(3.36, -2.18)$ given as the answer in the text were obtained with more accurate calculations.)

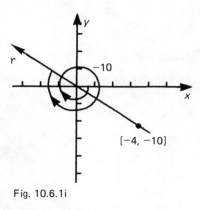

Fig. 10.6.1i

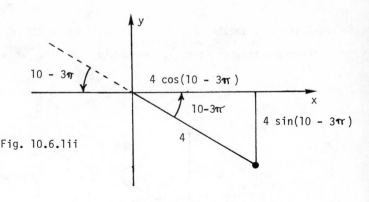

Fig. 10.6.1ii

(2a) We plot the point (-3,-3) and note that the line from it to the origin makes an angle of $\frac{5}{4}\pi$ with the positive x-axis (Fig. 10.6.2a). The point is a distance $3\sqrt{2}$ from the origin, so it has polar coordinates $[3\sqrt{2}, \frac{5}{4}\pi]$. All possible polar coordinates are $[3\sqrt{2}, \frac{5}{4}\pi + 2n\pi]$ and $[-3\sqrt{2}, \frac{1}{4}\pi + 2n\pi]$ with integers n.

(2i) We plot the point (-3,-6) as in Fig. 10.6.2i. The line from the point to the origin, the vertical line through the point, and the x-axis form a right triangle of height 6 and width 3. The angle at the origin in the triangle has tangent equal to 2 and is a positive acute angle, so it is arctan(2). The tables give tan(1.11) $\approx$ 2, so arctan(2) is approximately 1.11 radians. The r-axis in Fig. 10.6.2i makes an angle arctan(2) with the x-axis, and the point (-3,-6) is a distance $\sqrt{3^2 + 6^2} = \sqrt{45} \approx$ 6.708 from the origin. The point has polar coordinates $[-\sqrt{45}, arctan(2)] \approx [-6.708,1.11]$. All possible polar coordinates for it are $[-\sqrt{45}, arctan(2) + 2n\pi] \approx [-6.708, 1.11 + 2n\pi]$ and $[\sqrt{45}, arctan(2) + (2n+1)\pi] \approx [6.708, 1.11 + (2n + 1)\pi]$ with integers n.

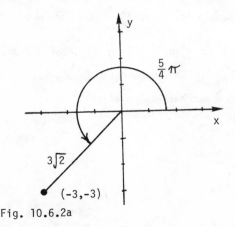

Fig. 10.6.2a

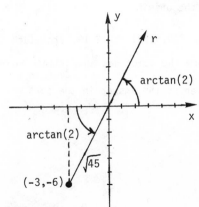

Fig. 10.6.2i

SECTION 10.7

(3) When we replace x by $r\cos\theta$ and y by $r\sin\theta$ in the equation $x = 3y$, we obtain $r\cos\theta = 3r\sin\theta$. We cancel the r, noting that we want to be sure the origin $(r = 0)$ is a solution of the final equation we obtain. We have $\cos\theta = 3\sin\theta$ and hence $\tan\theta = \frac{1}{3}$. We write this as $\theta = \arctan(\frac{1}{3})$. This is an equation of the entire line since we allow r to take any real values.

(5) We replace x by $r\cos\theta$ and y by $r\sin\theta$ in the equation $x^2 - y^2 = 1$. This gives $r^2\cos^2\theta - r^2\sin^2\theta = 1$ or $r^2 = \dfrac{1}{\cos^2\theta - \sin^2\theta}$. We can also use the trigonometric identity $\cos^2\theta - \sin^2\theta = \cos(2\theta)$ to write the equation in any of the forms

$$r^2 = \frac{1}{\cos(2\theta)}, \qquad r^2 = \sec(2\theta), \qquad \text{or} \qquad r = \pm\sqrt{\sec(2\theta)}.$$

(9) We make the substitutions $r^2 = x^2 + y^2$ and $x = r\cos\theta$ in the equation $(x^2 + y^2 - 2x)^2 = 4(x^2 + y^2)$ to obtain $(r^2 - 2r\cos\theta)^2 = 4r^2$ and then $r^2(r - 2\cos\theta)^2 = 4r^2$. We can cancel the r^2 without losing any solutions because $r = 0$ is a solution of the resulting equation $(r - 2\cos\theta)^2 = 4$ for all θ such that $\cos\theta = 1$. Taking square roots gives $r - 2\cos\theta = \pm 2$ and then $r = \pm 2 + 2\cos\theta = 2(\cos\theta \pm 1)$.

(11) We sketch the graph of $r = 1 - 2\sin\theta$ in a θr-plane (Fig. 10.7.11a), noting that $r = 0$ at $\theta = \frac{\pi}{6}$ and $\theta = \frac{5\pi}{6}$ where $\sin\theta = \frac{1}{2}$. As θ increases from 0 to $\frac{\pi}{6}$, r decreases from 1 to 0 and the point on the curve moves from $(1,0)$ to the origin (Fig. 10.7.11). As θ increases from $\frac{\pi}{6}$ to $\frac{\pi}{2}$, r decreases from 0 to -1 and the point on the curve moves from $(0,0)$ to $(0,-1)$. As θ increases from $\frac{\pi}{2}$ to $\frac{5\pi}{6}$, r increases from -1 to 0 and the point on the curve moves from $(0,-1)$ to $(0,0)$. As θ increases from $\frac{5\pi}{6}$ to $\frac{3\pi}{2}$, r increases from 0 to 3 and the point on the curve moves from the origin, through the point $(-1,0)$ and to the point $(0,-3)$. Finally, as θ increases from $\frac{3\pi}{2}$ to 2π, r decreases from 3 to 1 and the point moves from $(0,-3)$ to $(1,0)$ to complete the curve.

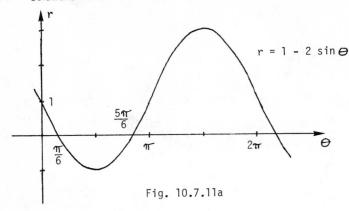

Fig. 10.7.11a

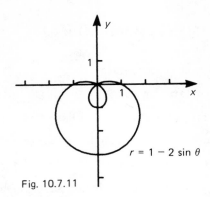

Fig. 10.7.11

(15) We first sketch the curve $r = \cos\left(\frac{\theta}{2}\right)$ in a θr-plane (Fig. 10.7.15a). We plot the portion for $0 \le \theta \le 4\pi$ because $\cos\left(\frac{\theta}{2}\right)$ is periodic of period 4π. As θ increases from 0 to π, r decreases from 1 to 0 and the point on the curve swings around from (1,0) through $(0,\frac{1}{\sqrt{2}})$ to the origin. As θ increases from π to 2π, r decreases from 0 to -1 and the point on the curve swings around from the origin, through the point $(0,\frac{1}{\sqrt{2}})$ to the point (-1,0). As θ increases from 2π to 4π, r increases from -1 to 1 and the point traverses the bottom half of the curve. The curve is symmetric about the x-axis because replacing θ by $-\theta$ in $r = \cos\left(\frac{\theta}{2}\right)$ gives an equivalent equation (Fig. 10.7.15).

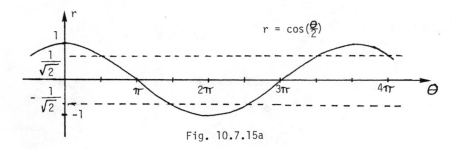

Fig. 10.7.15a

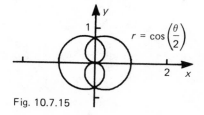

Fig. 10.7.15

(24) The equation $r = \dfrac{3}{1 - \cos\theta}$ is in the form of equation (5) of Section 10.7

in the text with $e = 1$ and $k = 3$. The curve is accordingly a parabola with focus

at the origin and vertical directrix $x = -3$ (Fig. 10.7.24).

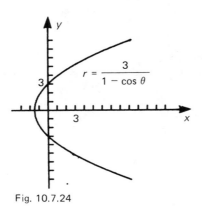

Fig. 10.7.24

SECTION 10.8

(3) We begin by sketching the curve $r = 2\cos(3\theta)$ in a θr-plane (Fig. 10.8.3a).

We obtain one leaf of the rose (Fig. 10.8.3b) by taking θ in the interval $-\dfrac{\pi}{6} \le \theta \le \dfrac{\pi}{6}$.

By formula (1) in Section 10.8 of the text, the area of the leaf is

$$\int_{-\pi/6}^{\pi/6} \tfrac{1}{2}[2\cos(3\theta)]^2 d\theta \;=\; 2\int_{-\pi/6}^{\pi/6}\cos^2(3\theta)\,d\theta \;=\; \int_{-\pi/6}^{\pi/6}[1 + \cos(6\theta)]d\theta$$

$$= [\theta + \tfrac{1}{6}\sin(6\theta)]_{-\pi/6}^{\pi/6} \;=\; [\tfrac{\pi}{6} + \sin(\pi)] - [-\tfrac{\pi}{6} + \tfrac{1}{6}\sin(-\pi)]$$

$$= [\tfrac{\pi}{6} + 0] - [-\tfrac{\pi}{6} + 0] = \tfrac{\pi}{3}.$$

We used the trigonometric identity $\cos^2\alpha = \tfrac{1}{2}[1 + \cos(2\alpha)]$ to evaluate the integral

of $\cos^2(3\theta)$.

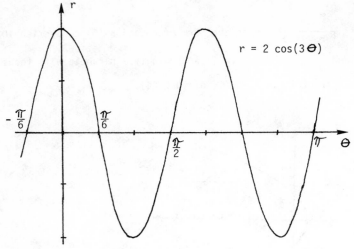

Fig. 10.8.3⌐

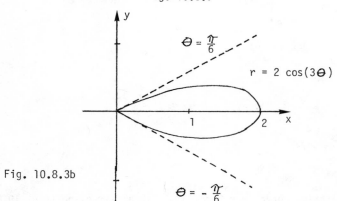

Fig. 10.8.3b

(5) We sketch the graphs of $r = 1 + 2 \sin\theta$ in a θr-plane in Figure 10.8.5a and in an xy-plane in Figure 10.8.5b. We can obtain the outer loop of the limacon by taking $-\frac{\pi}{6} \leq \theta \leq \frac{7\pi}{6}$ and the inner loop by taking $\frac{7\pi}{6} \leq \theta \leq \frac{11\pi}{6}$. The area inside the **outer** loop is

$$\int_{-\pi/6}^{7\pi/6} \frac{1}{2}[1 + 2\sin\theta]^2 \, d\theta = \frac{1}{2}\int_{-\pi/6}^{7\pi/6} [1 + 4\sin\theta + 4\sin^2\theta] \, d\theta$$

$$= \frac{1}{2}\int_{-\pi/6}^{7\pi/6} [1 + 4\sin\theta + 2 - 2\cos(2\theta)] \, d\theta$$

$$= \frac{1}{2}\int_{-\pi/6}^{7\pi/6} [3 + 4\sin\theta - 2\cos(2\theta)] \, d\theta$$

$$= \frac{1}{2}[3\theta - 4\cos\theta - \sin(2\theta)]_{-\pi/6}^{7\pi/6}$$

$$= \frac{1}{2}[\frac{7\pi}{2} - 4\cos(\frac{7\pi}{6}) - \sin(\frac{7\pi}{3})] - \frac{1}{2}[-\frac{\pi}{2} - 4\cos(-\frac{\pi}{6}) - \sin(-\frac{\pi}{3})]$$

$$= \frac{1}{2}[\frac{7\pi}{2} - 4(-\frac{\sqrt{3}}{2}) - \frac{\sqrt{3}}{2}] - \frac{1}{2}[-\frac{\pi}{2} - 4(\frac{\sqrt{3}}{2}) - (-\frac{\sqrt{3}}{2})]$$

(*) $$= \frac{1}{2}[\frac{7\pi}{2} + 2\sqrt{3} - \frac{\sqrt{3}}{2} + \frac{\pi}{2} + 2\sqrt{3} - \frac{\sqrt{3}}{2}] = \frac{1}{2}[4\pi + 3\sqrt{3}]$$

On the other hand, the area inside the inner loop is

$$\int_{7\pi/6}^{11\pi/6} \frac{1}{2}(1 + 2 \sin\Theta)^2 \, d\Theta = \frac{1}{2}[3\Theta - 4 \cos\Theta - \sin(2\Theta)]_{7\pi/6}^{11\pi/6}$$

$$= \frac{1}{2}[\frac{11\pi}{2} - 4 \cos(\frac{11\pi}{6}) - \sin(\frac{11\pi}{3})] - \frac{1}{2}[\frac{7\pi}{2} - 4 \cos(\frac{7\pi}{6}) - \sin(\frac{7\pi}{3})]$$

$$= \frac{1}{2}[\frac{11\pi}{2} - 4(\frac{\sqrt{3}}{2}) - (-\frac{\sqrt{3}}{2})] - \frac{1}{2}[\frac{7\pi}{2} - 4(-\frac{\sqrt{3}}{2}) - \frac{\sqrt{3}}{2}]$$

(**) $$= \frac{1}{2}[2\pi - 3\sqrt{3}].$$

We used the trigonometric identity $\sin^2\Theta = \frac{1}{2} - \frac{1}{2} \cos(2\Theta)$ to evaluate the integrals of $\sin^2\Theta$ in these calculations.

The area between the two loops is the difference between areas (*) and (**). It is

$$\frac{1}{2}[4\pi + 3\sqrt{3}] - \frac{1}{2}[2\pi - 3\sqrt{3}] = \frac{1}{2}[2\pi + 6\sqrt{3}] = \pi + 3\sqrt{3}.$$

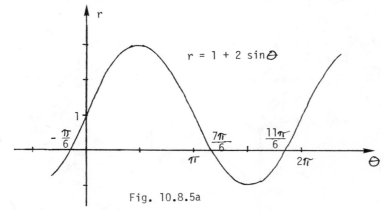

Fig. 10.8.5a

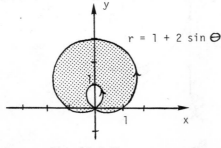

Fig. 10.8.5b

(7) The circle $r = 2 \cos \theta$ has radius 1 and has its center at $(1,0)$. The
line $x = \frac{3}{2}$ has the polar equation $r \cos \theta = \frac{3}{2}$, which we write $r = \frac{3}{2} \sec \theta$.
To find the polar coordinates of the intersections of the line and the circle (Fig. 10.8.7),
we solve the simultaneous equations

$$\begin{cases} r = 2 \cos \theta \\ r = \frac{3}{2} \sec \theta . \end{cases}$$

Equating the two expressions for r in these equations gives the equation $2 \cos \theta = \frac{3}{2} \sec \theta$,
which implies that $\cos^2 \theta = \frac{3}{4}$ and hence $\cos \theta = \pm \frac{\sqrt{3}}{2}$. The intersections are at
$\theta = - \frac{\pi}{6}$ and $\theta = \frac{\pi}{6}$. The area of the region (shaded in Fig. 10.8.7) is

$$\int_{-\pi/6}^{\pi/6} \frac{1}{2}(2 \cos \theta)^2 \, d\theta \quad - \quad \int_{-\pi/6}^{\pi/6} \frac{1}{2}(\frac{9}{4} \sec^2 \theta) d\theta$$

$$= \int_{-\pi/6}^{\pi/6} (2 \cos^2 \theta - \frac{9}{8} \sec^2 \theta) d\theta = \int_{-\pi/6}^{\pi/6} [1 + \cos(2\theta) - \frac{9}{8} \sec^2 \theta] \, d\theta$$

$$= [\theta + \frac{1}{2}\sin(2\theta) - \frac{9}{8} \tan \theta]_{-\pi/6}^{\pi/6}$$

$$= [\frac{\pi}{6} + \frac{1}{2}\sin(\frac{\pi}{3}) - \frac{9}{8} \tan(\frac{\pi}{6})] - [- \frac{\pi}{6} + \frac{1}{2}\sin(- \frac{\pi}{3}) - \frac{9}{8} \tan(- \frac{\pi}{6})]$$

$$= [\frac{\pi}{6} + \frac{\sqrt{3}}{4} - \frac{9}{8}(\frac{1}{\sqrt{3}})] - [- \frac{\pi}{6} - \frac{\sqrt{3}}{4} - \frac{9}{8}(- \frac{1}{\sqrt{3}})] = \frac{\pi}{3} + \frac{\sqrt{3}}{2} - \frac{9}{4}(\frac{\sqrt{3}}{3}) = \frac{\pi}{3} - \frac{\sqrt{3}}{4} .$$

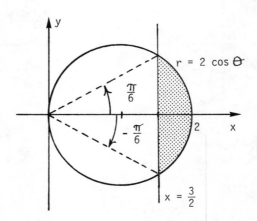

Fig. 10.8.7

SECTION 11.1

(1b) For P(0,-1) and Q(-7,-6) we have $\overrightarrow{PQ}$ = $\langle -7 - 0, -6 - (-1) \rangle$ = $\langle -7, -5 \rangle$.

(2a) $\overrightarrow{A}$ + 2$\overrightarrow{B}$ = $\langle 1,6 \rangle$ + 2$\langle 2,1 \rangle$ = $\langle 1 + 2(2), 6 + 2(1) \rangle$ = $\langle 5,8 \rangle$

$|\overrightarrow{A} + 2\overrightarrow{B}|$ = $\sqrt{5^2 + 8^2}$ = $\sqrt{89}$

The unit vector in the direction of $\overrightarrow{A}$ + 2$\overrightarrow{B}$ is $\dfrac{\overrightarrow{A} + 2\overrightarrow{B}}{|\overrightarrow{A} + 2\overrightarrow{B}|}$ = $\dfrac{\langle 5,8 \rangle}{\sqrt{89}}$ = $\langle \dfrac{5}{\sqrt{89}}, \dfrac{8}{\sqrt{89}} \rangle$.

(6a) Because $\cos(\frac{2\pi}{3})$ = $-\frac{1}{2}$ and $\sin(\frac{2\pi}{3})$ = $\frac{\sqrt{3}}{2}$ (Fig. **11.1.6a**), the vector of length

5 that makes an angle of $\frac{2\pi}{3}$ with the vector $\overrightarrow{i}$ is $\langle 5 \cos(\frac{2\pi}{3}), 5 \sin(\frac{2\pi}{3}) \rangle$ = $\langle -\frac{5}{2}, \frac{5\sqrt{3}}{2} \rangle$.

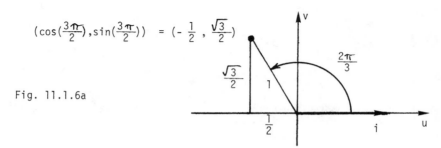

$(\cos(\frac{3\pi}{2}), \sin(\frac{3\pi}{2}))$ = $(-\frac{1}{2}, \frac{\sqrt{3}}{2})$

Fig. 11.1.6a

(9a) For P(2,4) and Q(6,3), we have $\overrightarrow{PQ}$ = $\langle 6 - 2, 3 - 4 \rangle$ = $\langle 4,-1 \rangle$. The position
vector of the point one third of the way from P toward Q is

$$\overrightarrow{OP} + \frac{1}{3}\overrightarrow{PQ} = \langle 2,4 \rangle + \frac{1}{3}\langle 4,-1 \rangle = \langle 2 + \frac{1}{3}(4), 4 + \frac{1}{3}(-1) \rangle = \langle \frac{10}{3}, \frac{11}{3} \rangle.$$

Hence, the point has coordinates $(\frac{10}{3}, \frac{11}{3})$.

(13) The velocity of the ball relative to the ground is the sum of the velocity of the
car relative to the road plus the velocity of the ball relative to the car:

Velocity = $60\overrightarrow{i}$ + $10\overrightarrow{j}$ miles per hour.

The speed is the length of the velocity vector: Speed = $\sqrt{60^2 + 10^2}$ = $\sqrt{3700}$ miles per hour.

(22c)   The vector $\vec{i} - \vec{j}$ makes an angle of $\frac{7}{4}\pi$ radians with the vector $\vec{i}$
(Fig. 11.1.22c).

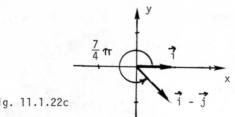

Fig. 11.1.22c

(24)   The velocity of the boat relative to the stationary water is $\vec{v}_1 = -10\vec{j}$ knots,
and the velocity of the wind relative to the boat is $\vec{v}_2 = -2\vec{i}$ knots. Therefore, the
velocity of the wind relative to the water is $\vec{v}_1 + \vec{v}_2 = -2\vec{i} - 10\vec{j}$ knots.

SECTION 11.2

(1a) $\langle 3,1 \rangle \cdot \langle -6,2 \rangle = (3)(-6) + (1)(2) = -16$

(2c)   The angles Θ between the vectors $\vec{A} = 6\vec{i} + \vec{j}$ and $\vec{B} = -6\vec{i} + \vec{j}$ have cosines
given by

$$\cos \Theta = \frac{\vec{A} \cdot \vec{B}}{|\vec{A}||\vec{B}|} = \frac{(6\vec{i} + \vec{j}) \cdot (-6\vec{i} + \vec{j})}{\sqrt{6^2 + 1}\sqrt{6^2 + 1}} = \frac{(6)(-6) + (1)(1)}{37} = -\frac{35}{37} \approx -0.95$$

$$\approx -\cos(0.32) = \cos(\pi - 0.32) \approx \cos(2.82)$$

Hence one such angle (the angle between 0 and π) is approximately 2.82 radians.

(3a)   When we switch the components of the vector $6\vec{i} + 3\vec{j}$ and multiply one component or the
other by -1, we obtain vectors $3\vec{i} - 6\vec{j}$ and $-3\vec{i} + 6\vec{j}$ that have the two directions
perpendicular to $6\vec{i} + 3\vec{j}$. These vectors both have length $\sqrt{3^2 + 6^2} = \sqrt{45}$, so the unit vectors
with the same directions are

$$\frac{3\vec{i} - 6\vec{j}}{\sqrt{45}} = (\frac{1}{\sqrt{5}})\vec{i} - (\frac{2}{\sqrt{5}})\vec{j} \quad \text{and} \quad \frac{-3\vec{i} + 6\vec{j}}{\sqrt{45}} = -(\frac{1}{\sqrt{5}})\vec{i} + (\frac{2}{\sqrt{5}})\vec{j}.$$

(4a)   The component of $\vec{A} = \langle 1,4 \rangle$ in the direction of $\vec{B} = \langle 2,1 \rangle$ is

$$\frac{\vec{A} \cdot \vec{B}}{|\vec{B}|} = \frac{\langle 1,4 \rangle \cdot \langle 2,1 \rangle}{|\langle 2,1 \rangle|} = \frac{(1)(2) + (4)(1)}{\sqrt{2^2 + 1^2}} = \frac{6}{\sqrt{5}}.$$

The projection of $\vec{A}$ along $\vec{B}$ is

$$\frac{\vec{A} \cdot \vec{B}}{|\vec{B}|^2} \vec{B} = \frac{6}{5} \langle 2,1 \rangle = \langle \frac{12}{5} , \frac{6}{5} \rangle . \text{ (See Fig. 11.2.4a)}$$

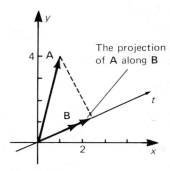

The projection
of **A** along **B**

Fig. 11.2.4a

(6) We introduce xy-coordinates with the positive y-axis pointing north. Then the unit vector pointing northwest is $\vec{u} = \langle - \frac{1}{\sqrt{2}} , \frac{1}{\sqrt{2}} \rangle$ and the force vector is

$$10\vec{u} = \langle - \frac{10}{\sqrt{2}} , \frac{10}{\sqrt{2}} \rangle \text{ pounds. When the man walks 100 feet north he goes from a point } P \text{ to}$$

a point Q where $\vec{PQ} = 100\vec{j}$ feet. The work done by the wind is

$$\vec{F} \cdot \vec{PQ} = \langle - \frac{10}{\sqrt{2}} , \frac{10}{\sqrt{2}} \rangle \cdot \langle 0,100 \rangle = (- \frac{10}{\sqrt{2}})(0) + (\frac{10}{\sqrt{2}})(100) = \frac{1000}{\sqrt{2}} \text{ foot-pounds}$$

(13a) By the formula in Exercise 12 of Section 11.2, the distance from (x_0,y_0) to the line $3x - 4y + 6 = 0$ is

$$\frac{|3x_0 - 4y_0 + 6|}{\sqrt{3^2 + 4^2}} = \frac{|3x_0 - 4y_0 + 6|}{5} .$$

For $(x_0,y_0) = (2,-1)$ the distance is

$$\frac{|3(2) - 4(-1) + 6|}{5} = \frac{16}{5} .$$

(16a) The vector $\langle x,y \rangle$ is perpendicular to $\langle 2,-5 \rangle$ if and only if $\langle x,y \rangle \cdot \langle 2,-5 \rangle = 2x - 5y$ is zero. This occurs for $y = \frac{2}{5} x$, so the vectors are of the form $\langle x, \frac{2}{5} x \rangle$ where x is any number.

(25a) The displacement vector of the object is $\vec{PQ} = \langle 4 - 1, 0 - 1 \rangle = \langle 3,-1 \rangle$, so the work is $\vec{F} \cdot \vec{PQ} = \langle 1,1 \rangle \cdot \langle 3,-1 \rangle = 1(3) + (1)(-1) = 2$ foot-pounds.

SECTION 11.3

(1) We first plot the graph of $x = 6t - \frac{1}{2}t^3$ in a tx-plane and the graph of

$y = \frac{1}{4}t^4 - \frac{13}{4}t^2 + 9$ in a ty-plane (Figs. 11.3.1a and 1.3.1b). To make the sketches

we compute the derivatives $\frac{dx}{dt} = \frac{d}{dt}(6t - \frac{1}{2}t^3) = 6 - \frac{3}{2}t^2$ and $\frac{dy}{dt} = \frac{d}{dt}(\frac{1}{4}t^4 - \frac{13}{4}t^2 + 9)$

$= t^3 - \frac{13}{2}t$. The derivative $\frac{dx}{dt}$ is zero at $t = \pm 2$, negative for $|t| > 2$, and positive

for $|t| > 2$, so $x = x(t)$ is decreasing for $t < -2$ and for $t > 2$ and is increasing

for $-2 < t < 2$. The derivative $\frac{dy}{dt}$ is zero at $t = 0$ and at $t = \pm\sqrt{\frac{13}{2}} \approx \pm 2.55$. It is

negative for $t < -\sqrt{\frac{13}{2}}$ and for $0 < t < \sqrt{\frac{13}{2}}$ and is positive for $-\sqrt{\frac{13}{2}} < t < 0$ and

for $t > \sqrt{\frac{13}{2}}$. Hence, $y = y(t)$ is decreasing for $t < -\sqrt{\frac{13}{2}}$ and for $0 < t < \sqrt{\frac{13}{2}}$ and is

increasing for $-\sqrt{\frac{13}{2}} < t < 0$ and for $t > \sqrt{\frac{13}{2}}$. In drawing the graphs we plot the points in

the following table.

t	-3	-2	-1	0	1	2	3
$x = 6t - \frac{1}{2}t^3$	$-\frac{9}{2}$	-8	$-\frac{11}{2}$	0	$\frac{11}{2}$	8	$\frac{9}{2}$
$y = \frac{1}{4}t^4 - \frac{13}{4}t^2 + 9$	0	0	6	9	6	0	0

Once the graphs of $x(t)$ and $y(t)$ are drawn in tx- and ty-planes, we draw the

curve $x = x(t)$, $y = y(t)$ in the xy-plane by plotting the points at integer values of t

in the above table and by joining the points in a way that reflects whether x and y are

increasing or decreasing as t increases (Fig. 11.3.1c).

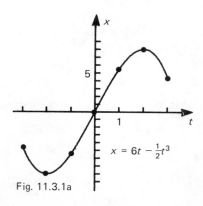

Fig. 11.3.1a

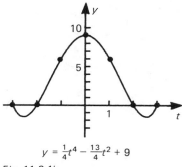

$$y = \frac{1}{4}t^4 - \frac{13}{4}t^2 + 9$$

Fig. 11.3.1b

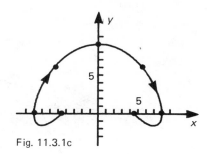

Fig. 11.3.1c

(6)   We first sketch the graph of $x = \cos t + \frac{t}{\pi}$ in a tx-plane and the graph of

$y = \sin t$ in a ty-plane (Figs. 11.3.6a and 11.3.6b). Because $\cos t$ oscillates between

1 and -1, the graph of $x = x(t)$ oscillates between the lines $x = 1 + \frac{t}{\pi}$ and $x = -1 + \frac{t}{\pi}$.

It crosses the line $x = \frac{t}{\pi}$ wherever $\cos t$ is zero. The derivative $\frac{dx}{dt} = -\sin t + \frac{1}{\pi}$

is positive wherever $|\sin t| < \frac{1}{\pi}$ and is negative wherever $|\sin t| > \frac{1}{\pi}$. We sketch

the curves by plotting the points in the following table

t	0	$\frac{\pi}{2}$	π	$\frac{3\pi}{2}$	2π	$\frac{5\pi}{2}$	3π	$\frac{7\pi}{2}$	4π
$x = \cos t + \frac{t}{\pi}$	1	$\frac{1}{2}$	0	$\frac{3}{2}$	3	$\frac{5}{2}$	2	$\frac{7}{2}$	5
$y = \sin t$	0	1	0	-1	0	1	0	-1	0

Then we plot the points in the xy-plane and draw the curve through them (Fig. 11.3.6).

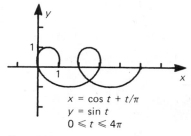

$x = \cos t + t/\pi$
$y = \sin t$
$0 \le t \le 4\pi$

Fig. 11.3.6

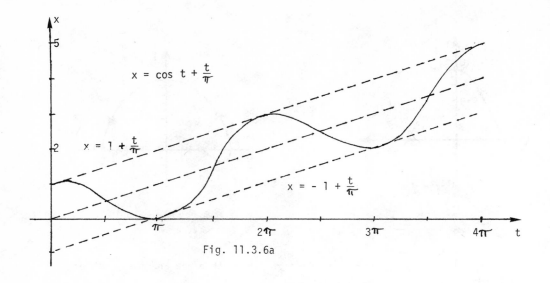

Fig. 11.3.6a

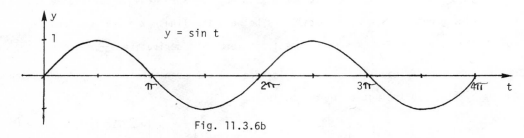

Fig. 11.3.6b

(8) With $x = \frac{1}{3} t^3$, $y = \frac{1}{2} t^2$ we have $\frac{dx}{dt} = t^2$ and $\frac{dy}{dt} = t$, so the length of the curve

is
$$\int_0^2 \sqrt{[\frac{dx}{dt}]^2 + [\frac{dy}{dt}]^2} \; dt = \int_0^2 \sqrt{[t^2]^2 + [t]^2} \; dt = \int_0^2 \sqrt{t^4 + t^2} \; dt$$

To evaluate the indefinite integral, we factor t^2 from inside the square root sign and

use the substitution $u = t^2 + 1$, $du = 2t \; dt$: For $t \geq 0$,

$$\int \sqrt{t^4 + t^2} \; dt = \int t \sqrt{t^2 + 1} \; dt = \frac{1}{2} \int (t^2 + 1)^{1/2}(2t \; dt) = \frac{1}{2} \int u^{1/2} \; du$$

$$= \frac{1}{2} (\frac{1}{3/2} u^{3/2}) + C = \frac{1}{3} u^{3/2} + C = \frac{1}{3}(t^2 + 1)^{3/2} + C$$

Then we compute the definite integral:

$$\int_0^2 \sqrt{t^4 + t^2}\ dt = [\tfrac{1}{3}(t^2 + 1)^{3/2}]_0^2 = [\tfrac{1}{3}(2^2 + 1)^{3/2}] - [\tfrac{1}{3}(0^2 + 1)^{3/2}]$$

$$= \tfrac{1}{3} 5^{3/2} - \tfrac{1}{3} = \tfrac{1}{3}(5^{3/2} - 1)$$

(13a) For $x = 2 \sec t$ and $y = 2 \csc t$ we have

$$\frac{4}{x^2} + \frac{4}{y^2} = \frac{4}{4 \sec^2 t} + \frac{4}{4 \csc^2 t} = \cos^2 t + \sin^2 t = 1.$$

(13b) At $t = -\frac{\pi}{4}$ the point is at $x = 2 \sec(-\frac{\pi}{4}) = \dfrac{2}{\cos(-\frac{\pi}{4})} = 2\sqrt{2}$, $y = 2 \csc(-\frac{\pi}{4})$

$$= \frac{2}{\sin(-\frac{\pi}{4})} = -2\sqrt{2} \text{ because } \cos(-\tfrac{\pi}{4}) = \frac{1}{\sqrt{2}} \text{ and } \sin(-\tfrac{\pi}{4}) = -\frac{1}{\sqrt{2}}.$$

(13c) We have $\dfrac{dx}{dt} = \dfrac{d}{dt}(2 \sec t) = 2 \sec t \tan t$ and $\dfrac{dy}{dt} = \dfrac{d}{dt}(2 \csc t) = -2 \csc t \cot t.$

At $t = -\frac{\pi}{4}$, these derivatives have the values

$$\frac{dx}{dt} = 2 \sec(-\tfrac{\pi}{4}) \tan(-\tfrac{\pi}{4}) = 2(\sqrt{2})(-1) = -2\sqrt{2}$$

$$\frac{dy}{dt} = -2 \csc(-\tfrac{\pi}{4}) \cot(-\tfrac{\pi}{4}) = -2(-\sqrt{2})(-1) = -2\sqrt{2}.$$

The object's speed at that value of t is

$$\text{Speed} = \sqrt{[\tfrac{dx}{dt}]^2 + [\tfrac{dy}{dt}]^2} = \sqrt{[-2\sqrt{2}]^2 + [-2\sqrt{2}]^2} = \sqrt{8 + 8} = 4$$

(17) The derivatives of $x = 7 \cos(\frac{t}{4})$ and $y = 7 \sin(\frac{t}{4})$ with respect to t are

$\dfrac{dx}{dt} = -7 \sin(\tfrac{t}{4}) \dfrac{d}{dt}(\tfrac{t}{4}) = -\tfrac{7}{4} \sin(\tfrac{t}{4})$ and $\dfrac{dy}{dt} = 7 \cos(\tfrac{t}{4}) \dfrac{d}{dt}(\tfrac{t}{4}) = \tfrac{7}{4} \cos(\tfrac{t}{4}).$ If we let $s = s(t)$

be arclength with $s = 0$ at $t = 0$ and with s increasing with increasing t, then

$$s = \int_0^t \sqrt{[\tfrac{dx}{dt}(u)]^2 + [\tfrac{dy}{dt}(u)]^2}\ du = \int_0^t \sqrt{[-\tfrac{7}{4} \sin(\tfrac{u}{4})]^2 + [\tfrac{7}{4} \cos(\tfrac{u}{4})]^2}\ du$$

$$= \int_0^t \sqrt{(\tfrac{7}{4})^2 [\sin^2(\tfrac{u}{4}) + \cos^2(\tfrac{u}{4})]}\ du = \int_0^t \tfrac{7}{4}\ du = \tfrac{7}{4} t.$$

Hence $t = \frac{4}{7} s$ and replacing t by $\frac{4}{7} s$ in the parametric equations yields the equations $x = 7 \cos(\frac{t}{7})$, $y = 7 \sin(\frac{t}{7})$, $0 \le s \le \frac{7\pi}{2}$. The arclength runs from 0 to $\frac{7\pi}{2}$ because t runs from 0 to 2π .

SECTION 11.4

(1a) As t runs from $\frac{1}{2}$ to 2, $x = t^2$ runs from $\frac{1}{4}$ to 4 and $y = -\frac{1}{t^2}$ runs from -4 to $-\frac{1}{4}$. Furthermore, we have $y = -\frac{1}{x}$, so the curve is the portion of the hyperbola $y = -\frac{1}{x}$ for $\frac{1}{4} \le x \le 4$, oriented from left to right (Fig. 11.4.1a).

The velocity vector $\frac{d\vec{R}}{dt} = \frac{d}{dt}(t^2\vec{i} - t^{-2}\vec{j}) = 2t\vec{i} + 2t^{-3}\vec{j}$ is $2(1)\vec{i} + 2(1)^{-3}\vec{j} = 2\vec{i} + 2\vec{j}$ at $t = 1$. We draw whis vector with its base at the point $(1,-1)$ on the curve (Fig. 11.4.1a).

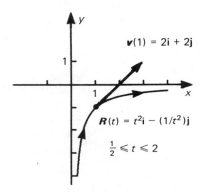

Fig. 11.4.1a

(2c) For $\vec{R}(t) = e^{2t}\vec{i} + t^2\vec{j}$ we have $\frac{d\vec{R}}{dt}(t) = [\frac{d}{dt}e^{2t}]\vec{i} + [\frac{d}{dt}t^2]\vec{j} = 2e^{2t}\vec{i} + 2t\vec{j}$, and at $t = 0$ this tangent vector is $\frac{d\vec{R}}{dt}(0) = [2e^0]\vec{i} + [2(0)]\vec{j} = 2\vec{i}$. The unit tangent vector is

$$\vec{T}(0) = \frac{\frac{d\vec{R}}{dt}(0)}{\left|\frac{d\vec{R}}{dt}(0)\right|} = \frac{2\vec{i}}{2} = \vec{i} = \langle 1,0 \rangle .$$

Because the tangent vector is horizontal, the tangent line is horizontal. Because $\vec{R}(0) = e^0\vec{i} + 0^2\vec{j} = \vec{i}$, the point on the curve at $t = 0$ is $(1,0)$, and the tangent line is the x-axis, $y = 0$.

(4a) $\vec{R}(t) = \int \vec{v}(t)\ dt = [\int t\ dt]\vec{i} - [\int t^2\ dt]\vec{j} = [\frac{1}{2}t^2 + c_1]\vec{i} - [\frac{1}{3}t^3 + c_2]\vec{j}$
(*)
$$= \frac{1}{2}t^2\vec{i} - \frac{1}{3}t^3\vec{j} + \vec{c}$$

where $\vec{c} = \langle c_1, c_2 \rangle$ is a constant vector to be determined from the value of $\vec{R}(t)$ at one point. We are given $\vec{R}(1) = \vec{i}$, and equation (*) yields $\vec{R}(1) = \frac{1}{2}(1)^2\vec{i} - \frac{1}{3}(1)^3\vec{j} + \vec{c}$

$= \frac{1}{2}\vec{i} - \frac{1}{3}\vec{j} + \vec{c}$, so we have $\vec{i} = \frac{1}{2}\vec{i} - \frac{1}{3}\vec{j} + \vec{c}$, which yields $\vec{c} = \frac{1}{2}\vec{i} + \frac{1}{3}\vec{j}$. Therefore,

$\vec{R}(t) = \frac{1}{2}t^2\vec{i} - \frac{1}{3}t^3\vec{j} + \frac{1}{2}\vec{i} + \frac{1}{3}\vec{j} = (\frac{1}{2}t^2 + \frac{1}{2})\vec{i} + (-\frac{1}{3}t^3 + \frac{1}{3})\vec{j}.$

Alternate procedure:

We can deal with x and y separately, rather than together as a vector. Because $\vec{v}(t) = t\vec{i} - t^2\vec{j}$, we have $\frac{dx}{dt} = t$ and $\frac{dy}{dt} = -t^2$. Consequently,

$$(**) \qquad x = \int t\, dt = \frac{1}{2} t^2 + C_1 \qquad \text{and} \quad y = -\int t^2\, dt = -\frac{1}{3} t^3 + C_2.$$

Because $\vec{R}(1) = \vec{i}$, we have $x(1) = 1$ and $y(1) = 0$. By equations $(**)$,

$$1 = x(1) = \frac{1}{2} + C_1 \qquad \text{and} \quad 0 = y(1) = -\frac{1}{3} + C_2.$$

Hence $C_1 = \frac{1}{2}$, $C_2 = \frac{1}{3}$, and by $(**)$ $x = \frac{1}{2} t^2 + \frac{1}{2}$, $y = -\frac{1}{3} t^3 + \frac{1}{3}$, and

$$\vec{R}(t) = (\frac{1}{2} t^2 + \frac{1}{2})\vec{i} + (-\frac{1}{3} t^3 + \frac{1}{3})\vec{j}.$$

(7a) The function $x(t) = 8 \sin(\frac{3}{4} t)$ has periods L_1 where L_1 is such that $8 \sin[\frac{3}{4}(t + L_1)] = 8 \sin(\frac{3}{4} t)$ for all t. The function $y(t) = 7 \sin t$ has periods L_2 where L_2 is such that $7 \sin(t + L_2) = 7 \sin t$ for all t. Because $\sin t$ has period 2π, the periods of $y(t)$ are $L_2 = 2n\pi$ with integers n and the periods of $x(t)$ are given by the equation $\cdot \frac{3}{4} L_1 = 2m\pi$ or $L_1 = \frac{8}{3} m\pi$ with integers m. The curve $x = 8 \sin(\frac{3}{4} t)$, $y = 7 \sin t$ is traversed once as t runs over an interval of length L where L is the smallest positive number that is both a period of $x(t)$ and a period of $y(t)$. To have $L_1 = L_2$ we must have $2n\pi = \frac{8}{3} m\pi$. The smallest positive integers n and m for which this occurs are $n = 4$, $m = 3$, for which $L = L_1 = L_2 = 8\pi$.

(7b) $x = 8 \sin(\frac{3}{4} t)$ is zero when $\frac{3}{4} t = n\pi$ with integers n, which is at $t = \frac{4n\pi}{3}$ with integers n; $y = 7 \sin t$ is zero at $t = m\pi$ with integers m. In the interval $0 \le t < 8\pi$, as the curve is traversed once, x is zero at $t = 0, \frac{4}{3}\pi, \frac{8}{3}\pi, 4\pi, \frac{16}{3}\pi$, and $\frac{20}{3}\pi$, whereas y is zero at $t = 0, \pi, 2\pi, 3\pi, 4\pi, 5\pi, 6\pi$, and 7π. The curve goes through the origin when both x and y are zero, and this occurs at $t = 0$ and $t = 4\pi$. The velocity vector

$$\vec{v} = \frac{d\vec{R}}{dt} = \frac{d}{dt}[8 \sin(\frac{3}{4} t)\vec{i} + 7 \sin(t)\vec{j}] = 8 \cos(\frac{3}{4} t) \frac{d}{dt}(\frac{3}{4} t)\vec{i} + 7 \cos(t)\vec{j}$$

$$= 8(\frac{3}{4}) \cos(\frac{3}{4} t)\vec{i} + 7 \cos(t)\vec{j} = 6 \cos(\frac{3}{4} t)\vec{i} + 7 \cos(t)\vec{j}$$

at $t = 0$ is $\vec{v}(0) = 6 \cos(0)\vec{i} + 7 \cos(0)\vec{j} = 6\vec{i} + 7\vec{j}$ and points up and to the right.

At $t = 4\pi$ it is $\vec{v}(4\pi) = 6 \cos(3\pi)\vec{i} + 7 \cos(4\pi)\vec{j} = -6\vec{i} + 7\vec{j}$ and points up and to the left. The object passes through the origin from the right and toward the left at $t = 4\pi$ when its velocity vector is $-6\vec{i} + 7\vec{j}$.

(7c) The object passes through the origin from the left at $t = 0$, when its velocity vector is $6\vec{i} + 7\vec{j}$.

SECTION 11.5

(1a) The first and second derivatives of $y = \frac{1}{4}x^4 - \frac{1}{2}x^2$ are $y' = x^3 - x$ and $y'' = 3x^2 - 1$. At $x = 0$ they are $y'(0) = 0$ and $y''(0) = -1$. By formula (3) in Section 11.5 of the text the curvature of the curve at $x = 0$ is

$$\mathcal{K}(0) = \frac{y''(0)}{[1 + [y'(0)]^2]^{3/2}} = \frac{-1}{[1 + (0)^2]^{3/2}} = -1.$$

We assume that the curve is oriented with increasing x, from left to right, since nothing is stated to the contrary. The radius of curvature is $\rho = \frac{1}{|\mathcal{K}|} = 1$.

(1b) At $x = 1$ we have $y'(1) = 0$ and $y''(1) = 2$, and the curvature is

$$\mathcal{K}(1) = \frac{y''(1)}{[1 + [y'(1)]^2]^{3/2}} = \frac{2}{[1 + (0)^2]^{3/2}} = 2.$$

The radius of curvature is

$$\rho = \frac{1}{|\mathcal{K}|} = \frac{1}{2}.$$

(6) The ellipse $x = 3 \cos t$, $y = 5 \sin t$ has the equation

$$\frac{x^2}{3^2} + \frac{y^2}{5^2} = \cos^2 t + \sin^2 t = 1$$

in rectangular coordinates. Its major axis is the portion of the y-axis for $-5 \le y \le 5$ and its minor axis is the portion of the x-axis for $-3 \le x \le 3$ (Fig. 11.5.6). The point at $t = \frac{\pi}{2}$ has coordinates $x = 3 \cos(\frac{\pi}{2}) = 0$, $y = 5 \sin(\frac{\pi}{2}) = 5$. The **derivatives** of $x(t)$ and $y(t)$ are

$$x'(t) = -3 \sin t, \quad y'(t) = 5 \cos t$$

$$x''(t) = -3 \cos t, \quad y''(t) = -5 \sin t$$

and at $t = \frac{\pi}{2}$ they have the values

$$x'(\tfrac{\pi}{2}) = -3, \quad y'(\tfrac{\pi}{2}) = 0, \quad x''(\tfrac{\pi}{2}) = 0, \quad y''(\tfrac{\pi}{2}) = -5,$$

so by formula (5) of Section 11.5 in the text, the curvature is

$$\mathcal{K}(\tfrac{\pi}{2}) = \frac{x'(\tfrac{\pi}{2})y''(\tfrac{\pi}{2}) - y'(\tfrac{\pi}{2})x''(\tfrac{\pi}{2})}{[[x'(\tfrac{\pi}{2})]^2 + [y'(\tfrac{\pi}{2})]^2]^{3/2}} = \frac{(-3)(-5) - (0)(0)}{[(-3)^2 + (0)^2]^{3/2}} = \frac{15}{9^{3/2}} = \frac{15}{27} = \frac{5}{9}.$$

Therefore the radius of curvature is $\rho = \frac{1}{|\mathcal{K}|} = \frac{9}{5}$, and the circle of curvature has radius $\frac{9}{5}$ and center at $(0, \frac{16}{5})$, which is $\frac{9}{5}$ units below the point $(0,5)$ on the ellipse (Fig. 11.5.6)

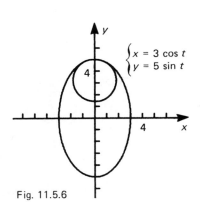

Fig. 11.5.6

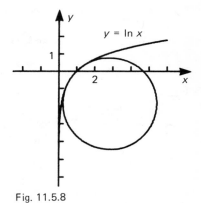

Fig. 11.5.8

(8) If the curve is oriented from right to left, its curvature is positive and if it is oriented from left to right (with increasing x) its curvature is negative. To obtain its maximum (**positive**) curvature when it is oriented from right to left, we can find its minimum (negative) curvature when it is oriented from left to right and take the negative of that number.

If the curve is oriented from left to right, we can use formula (3) of Section 11.5 of the text with $y = \ln x$, $y' = \frac{1}{x}$, and $y'' = -\frac{1}{x^2}$. The curvature at x is

(*) $\mathcal{K}(x) = \dfrac{y''(x)}{(1 + [y'(x)]^2)^{3/2}} = \dfrac{-\frac{1}{x^2}}{[1 + (\frac{1}{x})^2]^{3/2}} = \dfrac{-x}{[x^2 + 1]^{3/2}}.$

The derivative of the curvature is

$$\frac{d\mathcal{K}}{dx}(x) = \frac{[x^2 + 1]^{3/2} \frac{d}{dx}(-x) - (-x)\frac{d}{dx}[x^2 + 1]^{3/2}}{(x^2 + 1)^3} =$$

$$= \frac{[x^2 + 1]^{3/2}(-1) + x(\frac{3}{2})[x^2 + 1]^{1/2}\frac{d}{dx}(x^2 + 1)}{(x^2 + 1)^3} = \frac{-(x^2 + 1)^{3/2} + 3x^2(x^2 + 1)^{1/2}}{(x^2 + 1)^3}$$

$$= \frac{(x^2 + 1)^{1/2}}{(x^2 + 1)^3}[-(x^2 + 1) + 3x^2] = \frac{2x^2 - 1}{(x^2 + 1)^{5/2}}.$$

The derivative is zero at $x = \frac{1}{\sqrt{2}}$, is negative for $0 < x < \frac{1}{\sqrt{2}}$, and is positive for $x > \frac{1}{\sqrt{2}}$. Accordingly, the curvature is a minimum at $x = \frac{1}{\sqrt{2}}$, where by (*) it is

$$\mathcal{K}(\tfrac{1}{\sqrt{2}}) = \frac{-\frac{1}{\sqrt{2}}}{[(\frac{1}{\sqrt{2}})^2 + 1]^{3/2}} = \frac{-\frac{1}{\sqrt{2}}}{(\frac{1}{2} + 1)^2} = \frac{-\frac{1}{\sqrt{2}}}{(\frac{3}{2})^{3/2}} = -(\frac{1}{\sqrt{2}})(\frac{2}{3})^{3/2}$$

$$= -(\frac{1}{\sqrt{2}})[\frac{\sqrt{2}}{\sqrt{3}}]^3 = -\frac{2}{3\sqrt{3}}.$$

For the curve oriented from right to left the maximum curvature is the negative of this amount and is $\frac{2}{3\sqrt{3}}$. The radius of curvature at that point is $\rho = \frac{3\sqrt{3}}{2} \approx 2.60$. We draw a plausible normal line to the curve at $x = \frac{1}{\sqrt{2}} \approx 0.71$ and put the center of the circle of curvature a distance ρ from the curve on that line. (Because the tangent line at $x = \frac{1}{\sqrt{2}}$ has slope $\sqrt{2}$, the normal line has slope $-\frac{1}{\sqrt{2}} \approx -0.71$.)

SECTION 11.6

(2a) Let $\vec{R}(t)$ be the object's position vector at time t. Because the only force on the object is that of gravity, its acceleration is 32 feet per second^2 in the direction of $-\vec{j}$: Its acceleration vector is $\vec{a}(t) = \vec{R}''(t) = -32\vec{j}$. Integrating gives the velocity vector

$$\vec{v}(t) = \int \vec{a}(t) \, dt = \int (-32\vec{j}) dt = -32t\vec{j} + \vec{v}_0,$$

where the constant of integration is the object's velocity $\vec{v}_0$ at $t = 0$. Because the object's speed at $t = 0$ is M and its velocity makes an angle ψ with the vector $\vec{i}$, $\vec{v}_0$ is the vector $M[\cos\psi \, \vec{i} + \sin\psi \, \vec{j}]$ of length M that has that direction. The velocity at time t is

$$\vec{v}(t) = (M \cos \psi)\vec{i} + (M \sin \psi - 32t)\vec{j}.$$

We obtain the position vector by one more integration:

$$\vec{R}(t) = \int \vec{v}(t) \, dt = \int [(M \cos\psi)\vec{i} + (M \sin\psi - 32t)\vec{j}] \, dt$$

$$= Mt \cos \psi \, \vec{i} + (Mt \sin \psi - 16t^2)\vec{j} + \vec{R}_0$$

where $\vec{R}_0 = \vec{R}(0)$ is the object's position vector at $t = 0$. We are told that $\vec{R}(0) = \vec{0}$, so $\vec{R}(t) = Mt \cos\psi \, \vec{i} + (Mt \sin\psi - 16t)\vec{j}$ and the object's coordinates at time t are $x = Mt \cos \psi$ and $y = Mt \sin\psi - 16t^2$.

(3) We introduce xy-coordinates in the plane of the motion of the shell, with the y-axis vertical, and with the origin at the cannon. By Exercise 2a with $M = 400$ feet per second, the shell's coordinates at time t are $x = 400t \cos \psi$, $y = 400t \sin\psi - 16t^2$. The shell hits the ground at the positive time t such that $400t \sin \psi - 16t^2$ is zero. This is at $t = \dfrac{400 \sin \psi}{16} = 25 \sin \psi$, and at that time the shell's x-coordinate is

$$x = 400[25 \sin \psi] \cos\psi = 10{,}000 \sin \psi \cos \psi = 5{,}000 \sin(2\psi).$$

For this to be 2,500, we must have $\sin(2\psi) = \dfrac{1}{2}$. We consider angles ψ between 0 and π, so 2ψ equals $\dfrac{\pi}{6}$ or $\dfrac{5\pi}{6}$ and the two choices of ψ are $\dfrac{\pi}{12}$ and $\dfrac{5\pi}{12}$.

(4) We use the result of Exercise 2a with $y(0) = 3$ instead of $y(0) = 0$, with $M = 30$

feet per second, and with $\psi = \frac{\pi}{4}$ radians (45 degrees): t seconds after the ball is

thrown it is $x = Mt \cos \psi = 30\, t \cos(\frac{\pi}{4}) = \frac{30}{\sqrt{2}}t$ feet from the boy and is

$y = Mt \sin\psi - 16t^2 + 3 = \frac{30}{\sqrt{2}} t - 16t^2 + 3$ feet above the ground. If there were no ground

to hit, the ball would reach $x = 35$ when $35 = \frac{30}{\sqrt{2}} t$, which would be at $t = \frac{7}{6}\sqrt{2}$. However,

at this value of t we have

$$y = \frac{30}{\sqrt{2}}(\tfrac{7}{6}\sqrt{2}) - 16(\tfrac{7}{6}\sqrt{2})^2 + 3 = 35 - 16(\tfrac{49}{18}) + 3 = \frac{315 - 392 + 27}{9} = -\frac{50}{9} ,$$

so the value of y would be negative. Hence, the ball hits the ground before it reaches the

building.

(7) We introduce xy-coordinates in the vertical plane containing the bead's path

and let $\vec{u}$ denote the unit vector pointing down the ramp (Fig. 11.6.7). The acceleration

due to gravity is $-32\vec{j}$ feet per second^2 and makes an angle of 85 degrees $(\frac{85\pi}{180} = \frac{17\pi}{36}$

radians) with $\vec{u}$. The component of the acceleration in the direction of $\vec{u}$ is

$32 \cos(\frac{17\pi}{36})$, so after t seconds the bead's veclocity is $32t \cos(\frac{17\pi}{36})\,\vec{u}$ and it has

traveled $16t^2 \cos(\frac{17\pi}{36})$ feet down the ramp. After 6 seconds it has traveled

$$16(6)^2 \cos(\frac{17\pi}{36}) = 576 \cos(\frac{17\pi}{36}) \approx 576 \cos(1.48) \approx 55 \text{ feet.}$$

(We used the table of values of the cosine in the back of the text to obtain this approximate

answer. The exact answer, 576[Sine of 5^0], given in the back of the text is obtained by

using the equation [Sine of 5^0] = [Cosine of 85^0]. The approximate answer, 50.2 feet,

given in the back of the text is more accurate than the approximate answer given above

because it was obtained by using a calculator.)

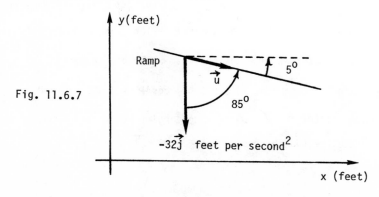

Fig. 11.6.7

(9) We introduce xy-coordinates so the orbit is the circle $x^2 + y^2 = \rho^2$ oriented counterclockwise. We measure the scales in feet, so that

$$\rho = [4400 \text{ miles}][5280 \tfrac{\text{feet}}{\text{mile}}] = 23{,}232{,}000 \text{ feet.}$$

Because the acceleration of gravity is directed toward the center of the earth, which is the origin, we have $\vec{a} = 30 \, \vec{N}$ (see Figure 11.65 in the text). On the other hand, because the satellite has constant speed, we have $\dfrac{d^2s}{dt^2} = 0$ in equation (6) of Section 11.6 in the text, and hence $\vec{a} = \varkappa (\tfrac{ds}{dt})^2 \vec{N}$ with $\varkappa = \dfrac{1}{\rho}$. Comparing the two expressions for $\vec{a}$ shows that $30 = \varkappa (\tfrac{ds}{dt})^2$ and consequently the satellite's constant speed is

$$\frac{ds}{dt} = \sqrt{\frac{30}{\varkappa}} = \sqrt{30\rho} = \sqrt{696{,}960{,}000} = 26{,}400 \text{ feet per second.}$$

(12) Because the speed is the constant $\dfrac{ds}{dt} = 3$ feet per second, the rate of change of the speed $\dfrac{d^2s}{dt^2}$ is zero and formula (6) of Section 11.6 in the text yields $\vec{a} = 9\varkappa\vec{N}$ for the acceleration of the object. Because the object weighs 2 pounds, its mass is $m = \dfrac{2}{32} = \dfrac{1}{16}$ slug and the total force on it is

(*) $\vec{F} = m\vec{a} = \dfrac{1}{16}(9\varkappa\vec{N}) = \dfrac{9}{16}\varkappa\,\vec{N}$ pounds.

The magnitude $|\vec{F}| = \dfrac{9}{16}|\varkappa|$ of the force (*) is greatest when the **absolute value** of the curvature $|\varkappa|$ is greatest. By equation (3) of Section 11.5 in the text with $f(x) = x^2$, $f'(x) = 2x$, and $f''(x) = 2$, we have

$$|\varkappa| = \frac{2}{[1 + 4x^2]^{3/2}} .$$

The maximum value of $|\varkappa|$ is   2 (at x = 0), so the maximum magnitude of the force (*) is $\dfrac{9}{16}(2) = \dfrac{9}{8}$ pounds.

(15) Because the object weighs 16 pounds, its mass is $m = \dfrac{16}{32} = \dfrac{1}{2}$ slug. When it is at the origin, the force on it is $\vec{F} = \vec{i} - 3\vec{j}$ pounds, so its acceleration is $\vec{a} = \dfrac{1}{m}\vec{F} = (\dfrac{1}{1/2})(\vec{i} - 3\vec{j}) = 2(\vec{i} - 3\vec{j}) = 2\vec{i} - 6\vec{j}$ feet per second^2. At that moment its velocity is $\vec{v} = 4\vec{j}$ feet per second. Therefore, its speed is $\dfrac{ds}{dt} = |\vec{v}| = |4\vec{j}| = 4$ feet

per second, the unit tangent vector to its path is $\vec{T} = \vec{j}$, and the unit normal vector is $\vec{N} = -\vec{i}$. With equation (3) of Section 11.6 of the text, we obtain

$$2\vec{i} - 6\vec{j} = (\frac{d^2s}{dt^2})\vec{j} + \kappa(4)^2(-\vec{i}).$$

The coefficients of $\vec{i}$ and $\vec{j}$ on each side of the equation must be equal, so we have $2 = -16\kappa$ and $-6 = \frac{d^2s}{dt^2}$. In particular $\kappa = -\frac{1}{8}$ feet^{-1}.

(21) Because the object is neither speeding up nor slowing down at R, we have $\frac{d^2s}{dt^2} = 0$ at that point. The curvature at R is approximately $\frac{1}{3}$ and the unit normal vector to the path is approximately $\frac{-1}{\sqrt{2}}\vec{i} + \frac{1}{\sqrt{2}}\vec{j}$. With $\frac{d^2s}{dt^2} = 0$, $\frac{ds}{dt} = 3$, $\kappa \approx \frac{1}{3}$, and $\vec{N} \approx \frac{-1}{\sqrt{2}}\vec{i} + \frac{1}{\sqrt{2}}\vec{j}$, equation (6) of Section 11.6 gives

$$\vec{a} = \kappa(\frac{ds}{dt})^2\vec{N} \approx \frac{1}{3}(3)^2(\frac{-1}{\sqrt{2}}\vec{i} + \frac{1}{\sqrt{2}}\vec{j}) = \frac{-3}{\sqrt{2}}\vec{i} + \frac{3}{\sqrt{2}}\vec{j}.$$

(29) We let $\vec{R} = \vec{R}(t)$ meters and $\vec{v} = \vec{v}(t)$ meters/second be the arrow's position and velocity vectors at time t (seconds) with $t = 0$ the time when the arrow is at the origin. Then the arrow's acceleration vector is the constant $-9.8\vec{j}$ and we are given that $\vec{R}(0) = \vec{0}$ and $\vec{R}(5) = \langle 100,0 \rangle$. We have

$$\vec{v} = \int(-9.8\vec{j})dt = -9.8t\vec{j} + \vec{v}_0$$

and

(*) $$\vec{R} = \int\vec{v}\,dt = \int(-9.8t\vec{j} + \vec{v}_0)dt = -4.9t^2\vec{j} + \vec{v}_0 t + \vec{R}_0.$$

The condition $\vec{R}(0) = \vec{0}$ implies that $\vec{R}_0 = \vec{0}$ and then the condition $\vec{R}(5) = \langle 100,0 \rangle$ gives $100\vec{i} = -4.9(5)^2\vec{j} + 5\vec{v}_0$ to show that $5\vec{v}_0 = 100\vec{i} + 4.9(25)\vec{j}$ and hence $\vec{v}_0 = 20\vec{i} + 24.5\vec{j}$. Setting $\vec{v}_0 = 20\vec{i} + 24.5\vec{j}$ and $\vec{R}_0 = \vec{0}$ in (*) yields

$$\vec{R}(t) = -4.9t^2\vec{j} + (20\vec{i} + 24.5\vec{j})t = \langle 20t, -4.9t^2 + 24.5t \rangle$$

which corresponds to the parametric equations $x = 20t$, $y = -4.9t^2 + 24.5t$ for the arrow's path.

SECTION 11.7

(1) With Θ as the parameter t and with $r(\Theta) = \Theta$, we have $\frac{dr}{dt} = 1$, $\frac{d\Theta}{dt} = 1$, and formula (5) of Section 11.7 yields

$$\vec{v} = \vec{u}_r + \theta \vec{u}_\theta .$$

At $\theta = \frac{3\pi}{4}$, the unit vectors $\vec{u}_r$ and $\vec{u}_\theta$ are $\vec{u}_r = -\frac{1}{\sqrt{2}}\vec{i} + \frac{1}{\sqrt{2}}\vec{j}$ and

$\vec{u}_\theta = -\frac{1}{\sqrt{2}}\vec{i} - \frac{1}{\sqrt{2}}\vec{j}$ (Fig. 11.7.1), so formula (8) gives

$$\vec{v} = \vec{u}_r + \frac{3\pi}{4}\vec{u}_\theta = (-\frac{1}{\sqrt{2}}\vec{i} + \frac{1}{\sqrt{2}}\vec{j}) + \frac{3\pi}{4}(-\frac{1}{\sqrt{2}}\vec{i} - \frac{1}{\sqrt{2}}\vec{j})$$

$$= \frac{1}{\sqrt{2}}[(-1 - \frac{3\pi}{4})\vec{i} + (1 - \frac{3\pi}{4})\vec{j}].$$

This is a tangent vector to the curve. To obtain the unit tangent vector, we divide $\vec{v}$

by its length

$$|\vec{v}| = |\vec{u}_r + \frac{3\pi}{4}\vec{u}_\theta| = \sqrt{1^2 + (\frac{3\pi}{4})^2} = \sqrt{1 + \frac{9\pi^2}{16}} = \frac{1}{4}\sqrt{16 + 9\pi^2}.$$

We obtain

$$\vec{T} = \frac{4\vec{u}_r + 3\pi\vec{u}_\theta}{\sqrt{16 + 9\pi^2}} = \frac{(-4 - 3\pi)\vec{i} + (4 - 3\pi)\vec{j}}{\sqrt{32 + 18\pi^2}} .$$

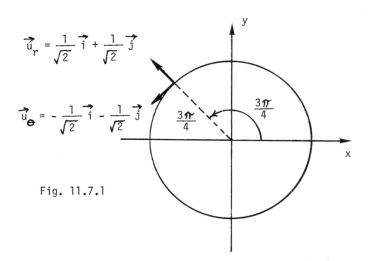

Fig. 11.7.1

(3) Since $r = 3 - 2 \sin \Theta$ and $\frac{d\Theta}{dt} = 5$, we have $\frac{dr}{dt} = -2 \cos\Theta \frac{d\Theta}{dt} = -10 \cos \Theta$.

At the point $(0,1)$, the angle Θ is $\frac{\pi}{2}$ and $\cos \Theta = 0$. Therefore, $\frac{dr}{dt}$ is zero at

that point, and formula (8) in Section 11.7 with $r = 1$, $\frac{dr}{dt} = 0$, and $\frac{d\Theta}{dt} = 5$ gives

$$|\vec{v}| = \sqrt{(\frac{dr}{dt})^2 + r^2(\frac{d\Theta}{dt})^2} = \sqrt{0^2 + 1^2(5)^2} = 5.$$

SECTION 12.1

(14) With $(x,y,z) = (3,-4,-1)$, (a) the distance to the z-axis is $\sqrt{x^2 + y^2} = \sqrt{3^2 + 4^2} = 5$;
(b) the distance to the x-axis is $\sqrt{y^2 + z^2} = \sqrt{4^2 + 1^2} = \sqrt{17}$; (c) the distance to the y-axis
is $\sqrt{x^2 + z^2} = \sqrt{3^2 + 1^2} = \sqrt{10}$; (d) the distance to the xy-plane is $|z| = 1$; (e) the
distance to the xz-plane is $|y| = 4$; (f) the distance to the y-z-plane is $|x| = 3$;
and (g) the distance to the origin is $\sqrt{x^2 + y^2 + z^2} = \sqrt{3^2 + 4^2 + 1^2} = \sqrt{26}$.

(17a) $\vec{A} + 3\vec{B} = \langle 3,1,-2 \rangle + 3\langle -1,6,4 \rangle = \langle 3 + 3(-1),1 + 3(6),-2 + 3(4) \rangle = \langle 0,19,10 \rangle$

(17b) $\vec{A} \cdot \vec{B} = \langle 3,1,-2 \rangle \cdot \langle -1,6,4 \rangle = 3(-1) + 1(6) - 2(4) = -3 + 6 - 8 = -5$

$\vec{A} - (\vec{A} \cdot \vec{B})\vec{B} = \vec{A} + 5\vec{B} = \langle 3,1,-2 \rangle + 5\langle -1,6,4 \rangle = \langle 3 + 5(-1),1 + 5(6),-2 + 5(4) \rangle = \langle -2,31,18 \rangle$

(17c) $|\vec{A}| = \sqrt{3^2 + 1^2 + 2^2} = \sqrt{14}$

(17d) $|\vec{B}| = \sqrt{1^2 + 6^2 + 4^2} = \sqrt{53}$

(17e) $\vec{A} + \vec{B} = \langle 3,1,-2 \rangle + \langle -1,6,4 \rangle = \langle 3 - 1,1 + 6,-2 + 4 \rangle = \langle 2,7,2 \rangle$

$\vec{A} - \vec{B} = \langle 3,1,-2 \rangle - \langle -1,6,4 \rangle = \langle 3 - (-1),1 - 6, -2 - 4 \rangle = \langle 4,-5,-6 \rangle$

$(\vec{A} + \vec{B}) \cdot (\vec{A} - \vec{B}) = \langle 2,7,2 \rangle \cdot \langle 4,-5,-6 \rangle = 2(4) + 7(-5) + 2(-6) = 8 - 35 - 12 = -39$

(17f) $(\vec{A} + \vec{B}) \cdot (\vec{A} - \vec{B}) = \vec{A} \cdot \vec{A} - \vec{A} \cdot \vec{B} + \vec{B} \cdot \vec{A} - \vec{B} \cdot \vec{B} = |\vec{A}|^2 - |\vec{B}|^2$ because $\vec{A} \cdot \vec{B} = \vec{B} \cdot \vec{A}$,

$\vec{A} \cdot \vec{A} = |\vec{A}|^2$, and $\vec{B} \cdot \vec{B} = |\vec{B}|^2$.

(20) Set $P = (1,2,3)$, $Q = (4,0,2)$, and $R = (2,1,3)$ and consider the schematic
sketch in Fig. 12.1.20. We have $\vec{PQ} = \langle 3,-2,-1 \rangle$, $\vec{QR} = \langle -2,1,1 \rangle$, and $\vec{PR} = \langle 1,-1,0 \rangle$
so that $|\vec{PQ}| = \sqrt{3^2 + 2^2 + 1^2} = \sqrt{14}$, $|\vec{QR}| = \sqrt{2^2 + 1^2 + 1^2} = \sqrt{6}$, and $|\vec{PR}| = \sqrt{1^2 + 1^2 + 0^2} = \sqrt{2}$.
By formula (9) of Section 12.1 in the text

$$\cos[\text{the angle at } P] = \frac{\overrightarrow{PQ} \cdot \overrightarrow{PR}}{|\overrightarrow{PQ}||\overrightarrow{PR}|} = \frac{3(1) - 2(-1) - 1(0)}{\sqrt{14}\sqrt{2}} = \frac{5}{\sqrt{28}} \approx 0.945 \approx \cos(0.33).$$

Hence, the angle at P is approximately 0.33 radians. Similarly, we have

$$\cos[\text{the angle at } Q] = \frac{\overrightarrow{QP} \cdot \overrightarrow{QR}}{|\overrightarrow{QP}||\overrightarrow{QR}|} = \frac{-3(-2) + 2(1) + 1(1)}{\sqrt{14}\sqrt{6}} = \frac{9}{\sqrt{14}\sqrt{6}} \approx 0.982 \approx \cos(0.19)$$

and

$$\cos[\text{the angle at } R] = \frac{\overrightarrow{RP} \cdot \overrightarrow{RQ}}{|\overrightarrow{RP}||\overrightarrow{RQ}|} = \frac{-1(2) + 1(-1) + 0(-1)}{\sqrt{2}\sqrt{6}} = \frac{-3}{\sqrt{12}} \approx -0.866$$

$$\approx -\cos(0.52) = \cos(\pi - 0.52) \approx \cos(2.62),$$

so that the angle at Q is approximately 0.33 radians and the angle at R is approximately 2.62 radians.

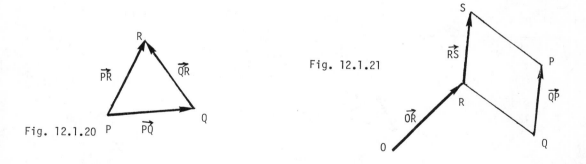

Fig. 12.1.20

Fig. 12.1.21

(21)   Consider the schematic sketch of the parallelogram in Fig. 12.1.21. Because the sides RS and QP of the parallelogram are equal and parallel, the vectors $\overrightarrow{RS}$ and $\overrightarrow{QP}$ are equal: $\overrightarrow{RS} = \overrightarrow{QP} = \langle 6 - 3, 8 - 4, -2 - 0 \rangle = \langle 3, 4, -2 \rangle$. Hence,

$$\overrightarrow{OS} = \overrightarrow{OR} + \overrightarrow{RS} = \langle 4, -7, -10 \rangle + \langle 3, 4, -2 \rangle = \langle 7, -3, -12 \rangle$$

and the point S has coordinates $(7, -3, -12)$. Here O denotes the origin $(0,0,0)$.

(27a) By formula (10) of Section 12.1 the component of $\vec{A} = \langle 4,3,1 \rangle$ in the direction

of $\vec{B} = \langle -1,0,5 \rangle$ is

$$\frac{\vec{A} \cdot \vec{B}}{\cdot |\vec{B}|} = \frac{\langle 4,3,1 \rangle \cdot \langle -1,0,5 \rangle}{\sqrt{1^2 + 0^2 + 5^2}} = \frac{-4 + 0 + 5}{\sqrt{26}} = \frac{1}{\sqrt{26}} \, .$$

(27b) The projection of $\vec{A}$ along $\vec{B}$ is the component of $\vec{A}$ in the direction of $\vec{B}$, which

we found in part (a) of this exercise, multiplied by the unit vector $\dfrac{\vec{B}}{|\vec{B}|}$ in the direction

of $\vec{B}$:

$$\frac{1}{\sqrt{26}} \, \frac{\vec{B}}{|\vec{B}|} = \frac{1}{\sqrt{26}}(\frac{1}{\sqrt{26}}) \langle -1,0,5 \rangle = \frac{1}{26} \langle -1,0,5 \rangle \, .$$

(33) We make a schematic sketch of the triangle (Fig. 12.1.33), where we set P = (3,5,1),

Q = (2,4,3), and R = (5,7,3). We have $\vec{PQ} = \langle 2 - 3, 4 - 5, 3 - 1 \rangle = \langle -1,-1,2 \rangle$,

$\vec{PR} = \langle 5 - 3, 7 - 5, 3 - 1 \rangle = \langle 2,2,2 \rangle$, and $\vec{QR} = \langle 5 - 2, 7 - 4, 3 - 3 \rangle = \langle 3,3,0 \rangle$, so

that $\vec{PQ} \cdot \vec{PR} = (-1)(2) + (-1)(2) + 2(2) = 0$. This shows that the angle at P is a right

angle and the area of the triangle is $\frac{1}{2}(\text{Base})(\text{Height}) = \frac{1}{2}(\vec{PQ})(\vec{PR}) = \frac{1}{2}|\vec{PQ}||\vec{PR}|$

$$= \frac{1}{2} \sqrt{(-1)^2 + (-1)^2 + 2^2} \sqrt{2^2 + 2^2 + 2^2} = \frac{1}{2}\sqrt{6} \sqrt{12} = \frac{1}{2}(\sqrt{6})^2\sqrt{2} = 3\sqrt{2}.$$

Fig. 12.1.33

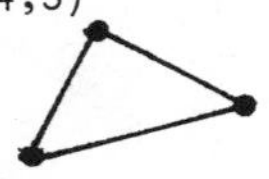

Q(2,4,3)

R(5,7,3)

P(3,5,1)

(37) We let $\langle x,y,z \rangle$ denote the desired vector. Its component in the direction of

$\vec{i}$ is 1, its component in the direction of $\vec{j} + \vec{k}$ is $2\sqrt{2}$, and its component in the

direction of $\vec{i} - 3\vec{j}$ is $\sqrt{10}$ provided

$$\langle x,y,z \rangle \cdot \langle 1,0,0 \rangle = 1$$

$$\frac{\langle x,y,z \rangle \cdot \langle 0,1,1 \rangle}{|\langle 0,1,1 \rangle|} = 2\sqrt{2}$$

$$\frac{\langle x,y,z \rangle \cdot \langle 1,0,-3 \rangle}{|\langle 1,0,-3 \rangle|} = \sqrt{10}.$$

These conditions give the simultaneous equations

$x = 1$, $\dfrac{y + z}{\sqrt{2}} = 2\sqrt{2}$, $\dfrac{x - 3z}{\sqrt{10}} = \sqrt{10}$, which we rewrite as $x = 1$, $y + z = 4$, $x - 3z = 10$.

The first equation gives $x = 1$, the third then gives $z = -3$, and the second yields

$y = 7$. The desired vector is $\langle 1,7,-3 \rangle$.

SECTION 12.2

(1)
$$\begin{vmatrix} 1 & 3 & 0 \\ 2 & -1 & 1 \\ 0 & 4 & 5 \end{vmatrix} = 1 \begin{vmatrix} -1 & 1 \\ 4 & 5 \end{vmatrix} - 3 \begin{vmatrix} 2 & 1 \\ 0 & 5 \end{vmatrix} + 0 \begin{vmatrix} 2 & -1 \\ 0 & 4 \end{vmatrix}$$

$$= (1)[(-1)(5) - (1)(4)] - 3[(2)(5) - (1)(0)] + 0[(2)(4) - (-1)(0)]$$

$$= (-5 - 4) - 3(10 - 0) + 0 = -39$$

(2)
$$\begin{vmatrix} 5 & 0 & 1 \\ 0 & 4 & -2 \\ 1 & 2 & 3 \end{vmatrix} = 5 \begin{vmatrix} 4 & -2 \\ 2 & 3 \end{vmatrix} - 0 \begin{vmatrix} 0 & -2 \\ 1 & 3 \end{vmatrix} + 1 \begin{vmatrix} 0 & 4 \\ 1 & 2 \end{vmatrix}$$

$$= 5[(4)(3) - (-2)(2)] - 0[(0)(3) - (-2)(1)] + 1[(0)(2) - (4)(1)]$$

$$= 5[12 + 4] - 0 + [-4] = 80 - 4 = 76$$

(4)
$$\langle 1,4,-6\rangle \times \langle 3,2,-4\rangle = \begin{vmatrix} \vec{i} & \vec{j} & \vec{k} \\ 1 & 4 & -6 \\ 3 & 2 & -4 \end{vmatrix} = \vec{i} \begin{vmatrix} 4 & -6 \\ 2 & -4 \end{vmatrix} - \vec{j} \begin{vmatrix} 1 & -6 \\ 3 & -4 \end{vmatrix} + \vec{k} \begin{vmatrix} 1 & 4 \\ 3 & 2 \end{vmatrix}$$

$$= [(4)(-4) - (-6)(2)]\vec{i} - [(1)(-4) - (-6)(3)]\vec{j} + [(1)(2) - (4)(3)]\vec{k}$$

$$= -4\vec{i} - 14\vec{j} - 10\vec{k} = \langle -4,-14,-10\rangle$$

(8) For $P(1,4,0)$, $Q(3,2,1)$, and $R(5,2,1)$ we have $\vec{PQ} = \langle 3 - 1, 2 - 4, 1 - 0\rangle = \langle 2,-2,1\rangle$ and $\vec{QR} = \langle 5 - 3, 2 - 2, 1 - 1\rangle = \langle 2,0,0\rangle$. By Theorem 12.4 in the text the area of the parallelogram is $|\vec{PQ} \times \vec{QR}|$ Now

$$\vec{PQ} \times \vec{QR} = \begin{vmatrix} \vec{i} & \vec{j} & \vec{k} \\ 2 & -2 & 1 \\ 2 & 0 & 0 \end{vmatrix} = \vec{i} \begin{vmatrix} -2 & 1 \\ 0 & 0 \end{vmatrix} - \vec{j} \begin{vmatrix} 2 & 1 \\ 2 & 0 \end{vmatrix} + \vec{k} \begin{vmatrix} 2 & -2 \\ 2 & 0 \end{vmatrix}$$

$$= [(-2)(0) - (1)(0)]\vec{i} - [(2)(0) - (1)(2)]\vec{j} + [(2)(0) - (-2)(2)]\vec{k}$$

$$= 2\vec{j} + 4\vec{k}.$$

Hence the area of the parallelogram is $|2\vec{j} + 4\vec{k}| = \sqrt{2^2 + 4^2} = \sqrt{20} = 2\sqrt{5}.$

(12) The cross product

$$\langle 4,3,1 \rangle \times \langle 5,7,2 \rangle = \begin{vmatrix} \vec{i} & \vec{j} & \vec{k} \\ 4 & 3 & 1 \\ 5 & 7 & 2 \end{vmatrix} = \vec{i} \begin{vmatrix} 3 & 1 \\ 7 & 2 \end{vmatrix} - \vec{j} \begin{vmatrix} 4 & 1 \\ 5 & 2 \end{vmatrix} + \vec{k} \begin{vmatrix} 4 & 3 \\ 5 & 7 \end{vmatrix}$$

$$= [(3)(2) - (1)(7)]\vec{i} - [(4)(2) - (1)(5)]\vec{j} + [(4)(7) - (3)(5)]\vec{k}$$

$$= -\vec{i} - 3\vec{j} + 13\vec{k} = \langle -1,-3,13 \rangle$$

is perpendicular to both vectors $\langle 4,3,1 \rangle$ and $\langle 5,7,2 \rangle$. The unit vectors with this property are

$$\pm \frac{\langle -1,-3,13 \rangle}{|\langle -1,-3,13 \rangle|} = \pm \frac{\langle -1,-3,13 \rangle}{\sqrt{1^2 + 3^2 + 13^2}} = \pm \frac{1}{\sqrt{179}} \langle -1,-3,13 \rangle .$$

(20b) For P(1,1,1), Q(0,0,-6), R(8,1,2), and S(-4,3,1), we have

$\vec{PQ} = \langle 0 - 1,0 - 1,-6 - 1 \rangle = \langle -1,-1,-7 \rangle$, $\vec{PR} = \langle 8 - 1,1 - 1,2 - 1 \rangle = \langle 7,0,1 \rangle$,   and

$\vec{PS} = \langle -4 - 1,3 - 1,1 - 1 \rangle = \langle -5,2,0 \rangle$. These vectors form the three edges at P of the parallelopiped, so by Theorem 12.4 its volume is $|\vec{PQ} \cdot (\vec{PR} \times \vec{PS})|$ and

$$\vec{PQ} \cdot (\vec{PR} \times \vec{PS}) = \begin{vmatrix} -1 & -1 & -7 \\ 7 & 0 & 1 \\ -5 & 2 & 0 \end{vmatrix} = -1 \begin{vmatrix} 0 & 1 \\ 2 & 0 \end{vmatrix} - (-1) \begin{vmatrix} 7 & 1 \\ -5 & 0 \end{vmatrix} - 7 \begin{vmatrix} 7 & 0 \\ -5 & 2 \end{vmatrix}$$

$$= -[(0)(0) - (1)(2)] + [(7)(0) - (1)(-5)] - 7[(7)(2) - (0)(-5)]$$

$$= -[-2] + [5] - 7[14] = -91.$$

Hence the volume is $|-91| = 91.$

(22a) For P(1,2,3), Q(3,3,6), R(4,2,-1), and S(6,3,5) we have

$\vec{PQ} = \langle 3 - 1, 3 - 2, 6 - 3 \rangle = \langle 2,1,3 \rangle$, $\vec{PR} = \langle 4 - 1,2 - 2,-1 - 3 \rangle = \langle 3,0,-4 \rangle$,   and

$\vec{PS} = \langle 6 - 1, 3 - 2, 5 - 3 \rangle = \langle 5,1,2 \rangle$. By the formula in Exercise 21 of this section, the volume of the tetrahedron (Fig. 12.2.22a) is $\frac{1}{6} |(\vec{PQ} \times \vec{PR}) \cdot \vec{PS}| = \frac{1}{6} |\vec{PS} \cdot (\vec{PQ} \times \vec{PR})|$. Now, we have

$$\vec{PS} \cdot (\vec{PQ} \times \vec{PR}) = \begin{vmatrix} 5 & 1 & 2 \\ 2 & 1 & 3 \\ 3 & 0 & -4 \end{vmatrix} = 5 \begin{vmatrix} 1 & 3 \\ 0 & -4 \end{vmatrix} - \begin{vmatrix} 2 & 3 \\ 3 & -4 \end{vmatrix} + 2 \begin{vmatrix} 2 & 1 \\ 3 & 0 \end{vmatrix}$$

$$= 5[(1)(-4) - (3)(0)] - [(2)(-4) - (3)(3)] + 2[(2)(0) - (1)(3)]$$

$$= 5(-4) - (-17) + 2(-3) = -9,$$

so the volume of the tetrahedron is $\frac{1}{6}|-9| = \frac{3}{2}$.

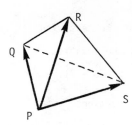

$$\text{Volume} = \frac{1}{6}\left|(\vec{PQ} \times \vec{PR}) \cdot \vec{PS}\right|$$

Fig. 12.2.22a

(24) For P(1,2,-1), Q(3,3,-4), R(2,2,1), and S(5,3,0), we have

$\vec{PQ} = <3 - 1, 3 - 2, -4 + 1> = <2,1,-3>$, $\vec{PR} = <2 - 1, 2 - 2, 1 + 1> = <1,0,2>$, and

$\vec{PS} = <5 - 1, 3 - 2, 0 + 1> = <4,1,1>$, for which

$$\vec{PQ} \cdot (\vec{PR} \times \vec{PS}) = \begin{vmatrix} 2 & 1 & -3 \\ 1 & 0 & 2 \\ 4 & 1 & 1 \end{vmatrix} = 2\begin{vmatrix} 0 & 2 \\ 1 & 1 \end{vmatrix} - \begin{vmatrix} 1 & 2 \\ 4 & 1 \end{vmatrix} - 3\begin{vmatrix} 1 & 0 \\ 4 & 1 \end{vmatrix}$$

$$= 2[(0)(1) - (2)(1)] - [(1)(1) - (2)(4)] - 3[(1)(1) - (0)(4)]$$

$$= 2(-2) - (-7) - 3(1) = 0.$$

Because this triple product is zero, the points P, Q, R, and S are in the same plane.

(37)   For P(1,2,4), Q(5,2,1), and R(0,4,4) we have $\vec{PQ} = <5 - 1, 2 - 2, 1 - 4>$

$= <4,0,-3>$ and $\vec{PR} = <0 - 1, 4 - 2, 4 - 4> = <-1,2,0>$. The cross product is

$$\vec{PQ} \times \vec{PR} = \begin{vmatrix} \vec{i} & \vec{j} & \vec{k} \\ 4 & 0 & -3 \\ -1 & 2 & 0 \end{vmatrix} = \vec{i}\begin{vmatrix} 0 & -3 \\ 2 & 0 \end{vmatrix} - \vec{j}\begin{vmatrix} 4 & -3 \\ -1 & 0 \end{vmatrix} + \vec{k}\begin{vmatrix} 4 & 0 \\ -1 & 2 \end{vmatrix}$$

$$= [(0)(0) - (-3)(2)]\vec{i} - [(4)(0) - (-3)(-1)]\vec{j} + [(4)(2) - (0)(-1)]\vec{k} = 6\vec{i} + 3\vec{j} + 8\vec{k}.$$

(Partial check: $<6,3,8> \cdot <4,0,-3> = 6(4) + 8(-3) = 0$; $<6,3,8> \cdot <-1,2,0> = 6(-1) + 3(2) = 0$.)

The area of the triangle is

$$\frac{1}{2}\left|\vec{PQ} \times \vec{PR}\right| = \frac{1}{2}|<6,3,8>| = \frac{1}{2}\sqrt{6^2 + 3^2 + 8^2} = \frac{1}{2}\sqrt{109}.$$

SECTION 12.3

(2) By formula (1) of Section 12.3 of the text with $(x_0, y_0, z_0) = (2, 4, 3)$ and $\langle a, b, c \rangle = \langle 4, 0, -7 \rangle$, the line has the equations

$$x = 2 + 4t, \quad y = 4, \quad z = 3 - 7t.$$

(4) The coefficients of t in the equations

$$x = 2, \quad y = 3t - 4, \quad z = 5t + 10$$

are the components of a vector $\langle 0, 3, 5 \rangle$ parallel to this line. The parallel line through $(-3, -2, 0)$ has the equations

$$x = -3, \quad y = 3t - 2, \quad z = 5t.$$

(8) The displacement vector from the point $P(6, 2, 3)$ to the point $Q(7, 0, -10)$ is $\vec{PQ} = \langle 7 - 6, 0 - 2, -10 - 3 \rangle = \langle 1, -2, -13 \rangle$ and is parallel to the line. Because the point $P(6, 2, 3)$ is on the line, the line has the equations

(*) $x = 6 + t, \quad y = 2 - 2t, \quad z = 3 - 13t.$

(Notice that as a result of this construction of equations (*), the point $P(6, 2, 3)$ is on the line at $t = 0$ and the point $Q(7, 0, -10)$ is on it at $t = 1$. This serves as a check on our calculations.)

(13) The coefficients of x, y, and z in the equation $2x - y = 3$ are the components of a vector $\vec{n}_1 = \langle 2, -1, 0 \rangle$ perpendicular to that plane. The coefficients in the equation $3y - 4z = 10$ are the components of a vector $\vec{n}_2 = \langle 0, 3, -4 \rangle$ perpendicular to the second plane. The cross product

$$\vec{n}_1 \times \vec{n}_2 = \langle 2, -1, 0 \rangle \times \langle 0, 3, -4 \rangle = \begin{vmatrix} \vec{i} & \vec{j} & \vec{k} \\ 2 & -1 & 0 \\ 0 & 3 & -4 \end{vmatrix}$$

$$= \vec{i} \begin{vmatrix} -1 & 0 \\ 3 & -4 \end{vmatrix} - \vec{j} \begin{vmatrix} 2 & 0 \\ 0 & -4 \end{vmatrix} + \vec{k} \begin{vmatrix} 2 & -1 \\ 0 & 3 \end{vmatrix}$$

$$= [(-1)(-4) - (0)(3)]\vec{i} - [(2)(-4) - (0)(0)]\vec{j} + [(2)(3) - (-1)(0)]\vec{k}$$

$$= 4\vec{i} + 8\vec{j} + 6\vec{k}$$

is perpendicular to both planes and hence parallel to their line of intersection. To find a point on the line of intersection, we find one solution of the simultaneous equations

$$\begin{cases} 2x - y = 3 \\ 3y - 4z = 10. \end{cases}$$

If we set $x = 0$ in these equations, we find that $y = -3$ and then $z = -\frac{19}{4}$, so that the point $(0,-3,-\frac{19}{4})$ is on both planes. The line of intersection has the equations

$$x = 4t, \quad y = -3 + 8t, \quad z = -\frac{19}{4} + 6t.$$

(To obtain the equations $x = 2t$, $y = -3 + 4t$, $z = -\frac{19}{4} + 3t$ that are given as the answer to this exercise in the back of the text, we use the vector $\langle 2,4,3 \rangle$ parallel to the line in place of the vector $\langle 4,8,6 \rangle$.)

(22) Two planes are perpendicular if and only if their normal vectors are perpendicular. We therefore want a plane whose normal vectors are perpendicular to the normal vectors to the planes $y - z = 4$ and $x + z = 3$. The coefficients of x, y, and z in the equation $y - z = 4$ are the components of a normal vector $\vec{n}_1 = \langle 0,1,-1 \rangle$ to the first plane; the coefficients in the equation $x + z = 3$ are the components of a normal vector $\vec{n}_2 = \langle 1,0,1 \rangle$ to the second plane. The cross product

$$\vec{n}_1 \times \vec{n}_2 = \langle 0,1,-1 \rangle \times \langle 1,0,1 \rangle = \begin{vmatrix} \vec{i} & \vec{j} & \vec{k} \\ 0 & 1 & -1 \\ 1 & 0 & 1 \end{vmatrix}$$

$$= \vec{i} \begin{vmatrix} 1 & -1 \\ 0 & 1 \end{vmatrix} - \vec{j} \begin{vmatrix} 0 & -1 \\ 1 & 1 \end{vmatrix} + \vec{k} \begin{vmatrix} 0 & 1 \\ 1 & 0 \end{vmatrix}$$

$$= [(1)(1) - (-1)(0)]\vec{i} - [(0)(1) - (-1)(1)]\vec{j} + [(0)(0) - (1)(1)]\vec{k} = \vec{i} - \vec{j} - \vec{k}$$

is perpendicular to $\vec{n}_1$ and $\vec{n}_2$ and, therefore, is a normal vector to the desired plane. Since the plane contains the point $(5,-1,-2)$ and has normal vector $\langle 1,-1,-1 \rangle$, it has the equation $(x - 5) - (y + 1) - (z + 2) = 0$, which may be simplified to the form $x - y - z = 8$.

(29) To find the x-intercept, we set $y = 0$ and $z = 0$ in the equation $2x - 3y + z = 6$ and solve for $x = 3$. To find the y-intercept, we set $x = 0$ and $z = 0$ and solve for $y = -2$. To find the z-intercept, we set $x = 0$ and $y = 0$ and solve for $z = 6$. We sketch

the plane by drawing the triangle with vertices at the intercepts on the coordinate axes (Fig. 12.3.29).

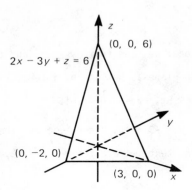

Fig. 12.3.29

(36) The coefficients of x, y, and z in the equation x - 3y = 10 are the components of a normal vector $\underset{\sim}{n} = <1,-3,0>$ to the two planes. We find one point on each plane by y = 0 and z = 0 in each equation and solving for x. The point P(10,0,0) is on the plane x - 3y = 10 and the point Q(-6,0,0) is on the plane x - 3y = -6. By formula (3) of section 10.4 in the text, the distance between the planes is

$$\frac{|\vec{PQ}\cdot\vec{n}|}{|\vec{n}|} = \frac{|<-16,0,0>\cdot<1,-3,0>|}{\sqrt{1^2 + 3^2 + 0^2}} = \frac{|-16|}{\sqrt{10}} = \frac{16}{\sqrt{10}}.$$

(38) The coefficients of t in the equations

(*)   x = 2 - t, y = 3 + 4t, z = 2t

are the components of a vector $\vec{A} = <-1,4,2>$ parallel to the first line. The coefficients of t in the equations

(**)   x = -1 + t, y = 2, z = -1 + 2t

are the components of a vector $\vec{B} = <1,0,2>$ parallel to the second line. The vectors $\vec{A}$ and $\vec{B}$ are not parallel, so the lines are not parallel; their either intersect or are skew. The distance between the lines is the distance between parallel planes containing them. The cross product

$$\vec{A} \times \vec{B} = <-1,4,2> \times <1,0,2> = \begin{vmatrix} \vec{i} & \vec{j} & \vec{k} \\ -1 & 4 & 2 \\ 1 & 0 & 2 \end{vmatrix}$$

$$= \vec{i} \begin{vmatrix} 4 & 2 \\ 0 & 2 \end{vmatrix} - \vec{j} \begin{vmatrix} -1 & 2 \\ 1 & 2 \end{vmatrix} + \vec{k} \begin{vmatrix} -1 & 4 \\ 1 & 0 \end{vmatrix}$$

$$= [(4)(2) - (2)(0)]\vec{i} - [(-1)(2) - (2)(1)]\vec{j} + [(-1)(0) - (4)(1)]\vec{k} = 8\vec{i} + 4\vec{j} - 4\vec{k}$$

is perpendicular to the lines are normal to the parallel lines containing them. To find a point

on each of the lines we set $t = 0$ in equations (*) and (**): The point $P(2,3,0)$ is on the

first line and the point $Q(-1,2,-1)$ is on the second. Hence, the distance between the lines,

which equals the distance between the planes, is

$$\frac{|\overrightarrow{PQ}\cdot\vec{n}|}{|\vec{n}|} = \frac{|<-3,-1,-1>\cdot<8,4,-4>|}{\sqrt{8^2 + 4^2 + 4^2}} = \frac{|-24|}{4\sqrt{2^2 + 1^2 + 1^2}} = \frac{6}{\sqrt{6}} = \sqrt{6}.$$

SECTION 12.4

(3) The position vector of the point on the curve at time t is

$$\vec{R} = (3t^2 + 1)\vec{i} + (\sin t)\vec{j} + (\cos^2 t)\vec{k}.$$

The velocity vector is

$$\vec{v} = \frac{d\vec{R}}{dt} = [\frac{d}{dt}(3t^2 + 1)]\vec{i} + [\frac{d}{dt}\sin t]\vec{j} + [\frac{d}{dt}\cos^2 t]\vec{k}$$

$$= (6t)\vec{i} + (\cos t)\vec{j} - 2\cos t(\sin t)\vec{k}$$

and the acceleration vector is

$$\vec{a} = \frac{d\vec{v}}{dt} = [\frac{d}{dt}(6t)]\vec{i} + [\frac{d}{dt}\cos t]\vec{j} - 2[\frac{d}{dt}(\cos t \sin t)]\vec{k}$$

$$= 6\vec{i} - (\sin t)\vec{j} - 2(\cos^2 t - \sin^2 t)\vec{k}.$$

We can use the trigonometric identities $2\cos t \sin t = \sin(2t)$ and

$\cos^2 t - \sin^2 t = \cos(2t)$ to express the velocity vector as $\vec{v} = <6t, \cos t, -\sin(2t)>$

and the acceleration vector in the form $\vec{a} = <6, -\sin t, -2\cos(2t)>$.

(6) For $x = \sin t$, $y = te^t$, and $z = t^3 - 3t$, we have $\frac{dx}{dt} = \frac{d}{dt}\sin t = \cos t$,

$\frac{dy}{dt} = \frac{d}{dt}(te^t) = (\frac{d}{dt}t)e^t + t(\frac{d}{dt}e^t) = e^t + te^t = (1 + t)e^t$, and $\frac{dz}{dt} = \frac{d}{dt}(t^3 - 3t) = 3t^2 - 3$.

By formula (3) in Section 12.4 of the text, the length of the curve is

$$\int_0^{10} \sqrt{[\tfrac{dx}{dt}]^2 + [\tfrac{dy}{dt}]^2 + [\tfrac{dz}{dt}]^2} \ dt = \int_0^{10} \sqrt{[\cos t]^2 + [(1 + t)e^t]^2 + [3t^2 - 3]^2} \ dt$$

$$= \int_0^{10} \sqrt{\cos^2 t + (1 + t)^2 e^{2t} + (3t^2 - 3)^2} \ dt \ .$$

(11) If the force vector $\vec{F}$ is always directed toward the origin, then the acceleration vector $\vec{a} = \tfrac{1}{m}\vec{F}$ is also directed toward the origin. (Here m is the mass of the object.) Hence, $\vec{a}$ is always parallel to the position vector $\vec{R}$ of the object and $\vec{a} \times \vec{R} = \vec{0}$ for all t. By the product rule for the cross product (Exercise 8a in Section 12.5), we have

(*) $$\frac{d}{dt}[\vec{v} \times \vec{R}] = \frac{d\vec{v}}{dt} \times \vec{R} + \vec{v} \times \frac{d\vec{R}}{dt} = \vec{a} \times \vec{R} + \vec{v} \times \vec{v} = \vec{0}.$$

The vector $\vec{v} \times \vec{v}$ is zero since the cross product of any vector with itself is zero.

Because the derivatives of the components of $\vec{v} \times \vec{R}$ are the components of the derivative (*), they are zero. Consequently, the components of $\vec{v} \times \vec{R}$ are constant and $\vec{v} \times \vec{R}$ is a constant vector $\vec{C}$. If $\vec{C}$ is not $\vec{0}$, then by the definition of the cross product, $\vec{R}$ is perpendicular to $\vec{C}$ for all t. Since the base of the position vector $\vec{R}$ is at the origin, its tip lies in the plane through the origin and perpendicular to $\vec{C}$. The curve lies in that plane.

If $\vec{C}$ is the zero vector, we have to use an argument similar to that in Exercise 12 of Section 12.4. Because $\vec{v}(t) \times \vec{R}(t) = \vec{0}$, the vectors $\vec{v}(t)$ and $\vec{R}(t)$ are parallel and we can write $\vec{v}(t) = f(t)\vec{R}(t)$. We assume that f(t) is continuous and define

$$g(t) = \int_{t_0}^{t} f(u)du.$$

By the Fundamental Theorem of calculus $\frac{dg}{dt}(t) = f(t)$, so that

$$\frac{d}{dt}[e^{-g(t)}\,\vec{R}(t)] = e^{-g(t)}\frac{d\vec{R}}{dt}(t) - e^{-g(t)}\frac{dg}{dt}(t)\,\vec{R}(t) = e^{-g(t)}[\vec{v}(t) - f(t)\vec{R}(t)] = \vec{0}.$$

Hence $e^{-g(t)}\vec{R}(t)$ equals a constant vector $\vec{C}_1$ and $\vec{R}(t) = e^{g(t)}\vec{C}_1$. The motion is in the line through the origin and parallel to the vector $\vec{C}_1$.

(14) The position vector is $\vec{R} = \langle \sin t, \cos t, \frac{1}{3} t^3 \rangle$; its derivative is

$\frac{d\vec{R}}{dt} = \langle \frac{d}{dt} \sin t, \frac{d}{dt} \cos t, \frac{d}{dt} \frac{1}{3} t^3 \rangle = \langle \cos t, -\sin t, t^2 \rangle$,and its second derivative is

$\frac{d^2\vec{R}}{dt^2} = \langle \frac{d}{dt} \cos t, -\frac{d}{dt} \sin t, \frac{d}{dt} t^2 \rangle = \langle -\sin t, -\cos t, 2t \rangle$.   At $t = 1$, we have

$\frac{d\vec{R}}{dt} = \langle \cos(1), -\sin(1), 1 \rangle$ and $\frac{d^2\vec{R}}{dt^2} = \langle -\sin(1), -\cos(1), 2 \rangle$, so that

$$\frac{d\vec{R}}{dt} \times \frac{d^2\vec{R}}{dt^2} = \begin{vmatrix} \vec{i} & \vec{j} & \vec{k} \\ \cos(1) & -\sin(1) & 1 \\ -\sin(1) & -\cos(1) & 2 \end{vmatrix}$$

$$= \vec{i} \begin{vmatrix} -\sin(1) & 1 \\ -\cos(1) & 2 \end{vmatrix} - \vec{j} \begin{vmatrix} \cos(1) & 1 \\ -\sin(1) & 2 \end{vmatrix} + \vec{k} \begin{vmatrix} \cos(1) & -\sin(1) \\ -\sin(1) & -\cos(1) \end{vmatrix}$$

$$= [-2\sin(1) + \cos(1)]\vec{i} - [2\cos(1) + \sin(1)]\vec{j} + [-\cos^2(1) - \sin^2(1)]\vec{k}$$

$$= [\cos(1) - 2\sin(1)]\vec{i} - [2\cos(1) + \sin(1)]\vec{j} - \vec{k}.$$

Therefore, at $t = 1$

$$\left| \frac{d\vec{R}}{dt} \times \frac{d^2\vec{R}}{dt^2} \right|^2 = [\cos(1) - 2\sin(1)]^2 + [2\cos(1) + \sin(1)]^2 + 1^2$$

$$= \cos^2(1) - 4\cos(1)\sin(1) + 4\sin^2(1) + 4\cos^2(1) + 4\cos(1)\sin(1) + \sin^2(1) + 1$$

$$= 5[\cos^2(1) + \sin^2(1)] + 1 = 6$$

and

$$\left| \frac{d\vec{R}}{dt} \right| = \sqrt{\cos^2(1) + \sin^2(1) + 1} = \sqrt{2}.$$

By formula (9) in Section 12.4 of the text, the curvature is

$$\mathcal{K} = \frac{\left| \frac{d\vec{R}}{dt} \times \frac{d^2\vec{R}}{dt^2} \right|}{\left| \frac{d\vec{R}}{dt} \right|^3} = \frac{\sqrt{6}}{(\sqrt{2})^3} = \frac{\sqrt{3}}{2} .$$

(16)   We have $\vec{v}(t) = \int \vec{a}(t)\, dt = \int < t^4, t^3, t^2 > dt = < \frac{1}{5}t^5, \frac{1}{4}t^4, \frac{1}{3}t^3 > + \vec{C}$

for some constant vector $\vec{C}$. The condition $\vec{v}(0) = <1,2,3>$ implies that $\vec{C} = <1,2,3>$

and $\vec{v}(t) = < \frac{1}{5}t^5 + 1, \frac{1}{4}t^4 + 2, \frac{1}{3}t^3 + 3 >$. Then $\vec{R}(t) = \int \vec{v}(t)\, dt$

$= \int < \frac{1}{5}t^5 + 1, \frac{1}{4}t^4 + 2, \frac{1}{3}t^3 + 3 > dt = < \frac{1}{30}t^6 + t, \frac{1}{20}t^5 + 2t, \frac{1}{12}t^4 + 3t > + \vec{C}_1$ for another

constant vector $\vec{C}_1$. Since $\vec{R}(0) = <7,6,5>$, we have $\vec{C}_1 = <7,6,5>$ and

$\vec{R}(t) = < \frac{1}{30}t^6 + t + 7, \frac{1}{20}t^5 + 2t + 6, \frac{1}{12}t^4 + 3t + 5 >$.

(20)   Since $\vec{a}(t) = -32\vec{k}$ feet/second^2, we have $\vec{v}(t) = -32t\vec{k} + \vec{v}_0$ feet/second

and $\vec{R}(t) = -16t^2\vec{k} + \vec{v}_0 t + \vec{R}_0$ feet. Because the ball is at $(4,3,2)$ at $t = 0$,

we have $\vec{R}(0) = \vec{R}_0 = 4\vec{i} + 3\vec{j} + 2\vec{k}$. Its velocity at $t = 0$ is given to be $5\vec{i} + 6\vec{j} + 10\vec{k}$

so $\vec{v}_0 = 5\vec{i} + 6\vec{j} + 10\vec{k}$ and $\vec{R}(t) = -16t^2\vec{k} + (5\vec{i} + 6\vec{j} + 10\vec{k})t + (4\vec{i} + 3\vec{j} + 2\vec{k})$

$= (5t + 4)\vec{i} + (6t + 3)\vec{j} + (-16t^2 + 10t + 2)\vec{k}$.

SECTION 12.5

(2) The variable y does not appear in the equation $x^2 + z^2 = 1$, so the surface
consists of lines parallel to the y-axis. The curve $x^2 + z^2 = 1$ in the xz-plane
is a circle of radius 1 with its center at the origin. The surface is a circular cylinder
of radius 1 with the y-axis as its axis (Fig.12.5.2).

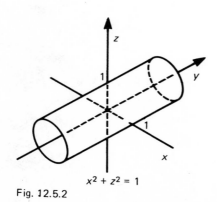

$x^2 + z^2 = 1$

Fig. 12.5.2

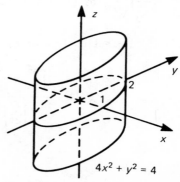

$4x^2 + y^2 = 4$

Fig. 12.5.4

(4) The variable z does not appear in the equation $4x^2 + y^2 = 4$, so the surface consists of lines parallel to the z-axis. The curve $4x^2 + y^2 = 4$ in the xy-plane is an ellipse with its center at the origin. The surface is an elliptical cylinder (Fig. 12.5.4).

(6) The variable y does not appear in the equation $z = x^4 - 2x^2$, so the surface consists of lines parallel to the y-axis. We sketch the curve $z = x^4 - 2x^2$ in the xz-plane (Fig. 12.5.6a). The surface is the cylinder consisting of all lines parallel to the y-axis and passing through that curve Fig. 12.5.6 .

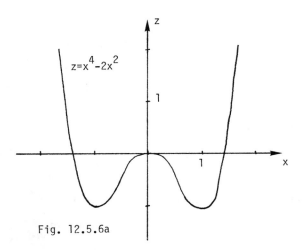

Fig. 12.5.6a

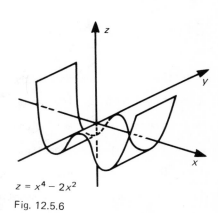

$z = x^4 - 2x^2$

Fig. 12.5.6

(8) If we set $x =$ a constant in the equation $z = 1 - x^2 - y^2$, we obtain an equation $z = $ [Constant] $- y^2$ and if we set $y = $ a constant, we obtain $z = $ [constant] $- z^2$. The intersections of the surface with vertical planes perpendicular to the x- and y-axes are therefore parabolas that open downward. If we set $z = $ a constant, we obtain $x^2 + y^2 = $ [Constant], so the horizontal cross sections of the surface are circles. The surface is a circular paraboloid that opens downward. Its highest point is $(0,0,1)$ on the z-axis (Fig. 12.5.8).

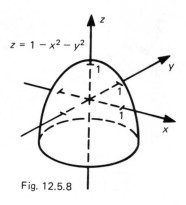

$z = 1 - x^2 - y^2$

Fig. 12.5.8

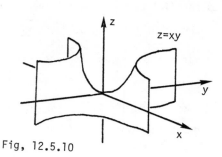

z=xy

Fig. 12.5.10

(10) Setting x = a constant in the equation $z = xy$ gives $z = $ [Constant]y and setting y = a constant gives $z = $ [Constant]x. The intersections of the surface with vertical planes perpendicular to the x- and y-axes are therefore straight lines. If we set $y = mx$ with m a nonzero constant, we obtain $z = mx^2$, so the intersections with other vertical planes through the origin are parabolas. The parabola opens upward if m is positive and downward if m is negative. Setting z = a constant yields $xy = $ Constant, so the horizontal cross sections of the surface are hyperbolas. The surface is a hyperbolic paraboloid (Fig. 12.5.10).

(12) If we set x equal to a constant in the equation $z^2 = x^2 + y^2 + 1$ we obtain $z^2 = y^2 + $ [A positive constant]. If we set y equal to a constant, we obtain $z^2 = x^2 + $ [A positive constant]. The intersections of the surface with vertical planes perpendicular to the x- and y-axes are therefore hyperbolas that open upward and downward. Setting z equal to a constant yields $x^2 + y^2 = $ Constant, so the horizontal cross sections are circles. The surface is a hyperboloid of two sheets (Fig. 12.5.12).

(15) If we set z equal to a constant in the equation $z^2 = x^2 + y^2$, we obtain $x^2 + y^2 = $ Constant, and the horizontal cross sections of the surface are circles. If we set $y = mx$, we obtain $z^2 = (1 + m^2)x^2$, and if we set $x = 0$, we obtain $z^2 = y^2$. The intersections of the surface with vertical planes through the origin are intersecting straight lines. The surface is a (double) circular cone (Fig. 12.5.15).

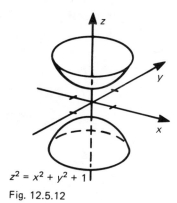

$z^2 = x^2 + y^2 + 1$

Fig. 12.5.12

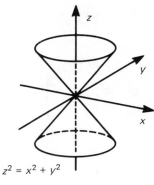

$z^2 = x^2 + y^2$

Fig. 12.5.15

(19) If we set $y = mx$ in the equation $z = -\sqrt{x^2 + y^2}$, we obtain

$$z = -\sqrt{x^2 + m^2 x^2} = -\sqrt{1 + m^2}\,|x|$$

and if we set $x = 0$, we obtain $z = -\sqrt{y^2} = -|y|$. The intersections of the surface
with vertical planes through the origin are V-shaped curves. When we set z equal to a
constant, we obtain $x^2 + y^2 = $ Constant, so the horizontal cross sections are circles.
The surface is a (half) cone with its vertex at the origin (Fig. 12.5.19).

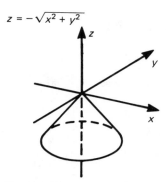

$z = -\sqrt{x^2 + y^2}$

Fig. 12.5.19

APPENDIX TO CHAPTER 12

(1)
$$\begin{vmatrix} 2 & 4 & 2 \\ 0 & 1 & -4 \\ -3 & 0 & 4 \end{vmatrix} = 2 \begin{vmatrix} 1 & -4 \\ 0 & 4 \end{vmatrix} - 4 \begin{vmatrix} 0 & -4 \\ -3 & 4 \end{vmatrix} + 2 \begin{vmatrix} 0 & 1 \\ -3 & 0 \end{vmatrix}$$

$$= 2[(1)(4) - (-4)(0)] - 4[(0)(4) - (-4)(-3)] + 2[(0)(0) - (1)(-3)]$$

$$= 2[4] - 4[-12] + 2[3] = 8 + 48 + 6 = 62$$

(3)
$$\begin{vmatrix} \frac{1}{2} & 2 & 3 \\ 1 & 5 & 0 \\ 0 & 3 & \frac{1}{4} \end{vmatrix} = \frac{1}{2} \begin{vmatrix} 5 & 0 \\ 3 & \frac{1}{4} \end{vmatrix} - 2 \begin{vmatrix} 1 & 0 \\ 0 & \frac{1}{4} \end{vmatrix} + 3 \begin{vmatrix} 1 & 5 \\ 0 & 3 \end{vmatrix}$$

$$= \frac{1}{2}[(5)(\frac{1}{4}) - (0)(3)] - 2[(1)(\frac{1}{4}) - (0)(0)] + 3[(1)(3) - (5)(0)]$$

$$= \frac{1}{2}(\frac{5}{4}) - 2(\frac{1}{4}) + 3(3) = \frac{5}{8} - \frac{1}{2} + 9 = \frac{5 - 4 + 72}{8} = \frac{73}{8}$$

(9) The determinant of the system of equations is

$$D = \begin{vmatrix} 1 & 2 & -1 \\ 2 & -3 & -1 \\ 3 & -1 & -1 \end{vmatrix} = 1 \begin{vmatrix} -3 & -1 \\ -1 & -1 \end{vmatrix} - 2 \begin{vmatrix} 2 & -1 \\ 3 & -1 \end{vmatrix} + (-1) \begin{vmatrix} 2 & -3 \\ 3 & -1 \end{vmatrix}$$

$$= [(-3)(-1) - (-1)(-1)] - 2[(2)(-1) - (-1)(3)] - [(2)(-1) - (-3)(3)]$$

$$= (2) - 2(1) - (7) = -7.$$

This determinant is not zero, so the system of equations has unique solutions x, y, and z,
which are given by Cramer's rule. We have

$$x = \frac{1}{D} \begin{vmatrix} 0 & 2 & -1 \\ 1 & -3 & -1 \\ 2 & -1 & -1 \end{vmatrix} = -\frac{1}{7} \begin{vmatrix} 0 & 2 & -1 \\ 1 & -3 & -1 \\ 2 & -1 & -1 \end{vmatrix} = -\frac{1}{7}(0) \begin{vmatrix} -3 & -1 \\ -1 & -1 \end{vmatrix} + \frac{1}{7}(2) \begin{vmatrix} 1 & -1 \\ 2 & -1 \end{vmatrix} - \frac{1}{7}(-1) \begin{vmatrix} 1 & -3 \\ 2 & -1 \end{vmatrix}$$

$$= 0 + \frac{2}{7}[(1)(-1) - (-1)(2)] + \frac{1}{7}[(1)(-1) - (-3)(2)] = \frac{2}{7}(1) + \frac{1}{7}(5) = 1$$

$$y = \frac{1}{D} \begin{vmatrix} 1 & 0 & -1 \\ 2 & 1 & -1 \\ 3 & 2 & -1 \end{vmatrix} = -\frac{1}{7} \begin{vmatrix} 1 & 0 & -1 \\ 2 & 1 & -1 \\ 3 & 2 & -1 \end{vmatrix} = -\frac{1}{7}(1) \begin{vmatrix} 1 & -1 \\ 2 & -1 \end{vmatrix} + \frac{1}{7}(0) \begin{vmatrix} 2 & -1 \\ 3 & -1 \end{vmatrix} - \frac{1}{7}(-1) \begin{vmatrix} 2 & 1 \\ 3 & 2 \end{vmatrix}$$

$$= -\frac{1}{7}[(1)(-1) - (-1)(2)] + 0 + \frac{1}{7}[(2)(2) - (1)(3)] = -\frac{1}{7}(1) + \frac{1}{7}(1) = 0$$

$$z = \frac{1}{D} \begin{vmatrix} 1 & 2 & 0 \\ 2 & -3 & 1 \\ 3 & -1 & 2 \end{vmatrix} = -\frac{1}{7} \begin{vmatrix} 1 & 2 & 0 \\ 2 & -3 & 1 \\ 3 & -1 & 2 \end{vmatrix} = -\frac{1}{7}(1) \begin{vmatrix} -3 & 1 \\ -1 & 2 \end{vmatrix} + \frac{1}{7}(2) \begin{vmatrix} 2 & 1 \\ 3 & 2 \end{vmatrix} - \frac{1}{7}(0) \begin{vmatrix} 2 & -3 \\ 3 & -1 \end{vmatrix}$$

$$= -\frac{1}{7}[(-3)(2) - (1)(-1)] + \frac{2}{7}[(2)(2) - (1)(3)] - 0 = -\frac{1}{7}(-5) + \frac{2}{7}(1) = 1.$$

SECTION 13.1

(7) $\ln(xy - 1)$ is defined for (x,y) such that $xy - 1 > 0$. We write this inequality in the form $xy > 1$. This has no solutions with $x = 0$. Dividing by x with x positive yields the equivalent inequality $y > \frac{1}{x}$; dividing by x with x negative gives $y < \frac{1}{x}$. The domain consists of the points above the hyperbola $y = \frac{1}{x}$ for $x > 0$ and below it for $x < 0$ (Fig. 13.1.7).

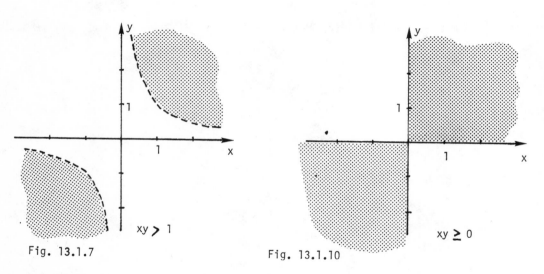

Fig. 13.1.7   Fig. 13.1.10

(10) $\sqrt{xy}$ is defined for $xy \geq 0$. The domain consists of all (x,y) with x or y (or both) equal to zero or with either both x and y positive or both x and y negative. It is the first and third quadrants along with the x- and y-axes (Fig. 13.1.10).

(15) The intersection of the surface $z = xy$ with the horizontal plane $z = c$ is given by the equations $xy = c, z = c$ and is a hyperbola above the first and third quadrants of the xy-plane for c positive and below the second and fourth quadrants of the xy-plane for c negative. The intersections of the surface with vertical planes $x = c$ and $y = c$ perpendicular to the x- and y-axes are straight lines. The other vertical planes have equations of the form $y = ax + b$, and their intersections with the surface are given by the simultaneous equations $y = ax + b$, $z = ax^2 + bx$ and are parabolas that open upward if a is positive and downward if a is negative. The surface is a hyperbolic paraboloid (Fig. 13.1.15).

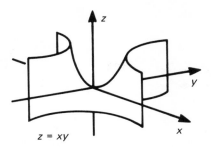

z = xy

Fig. 13.1.15

(21a) The graph of $\sin x + \frac{1}{9} y^3 + \frac{1}{8}$ is the surface $z = \sin x + \frac{1}{9} y^3 + \frac{1}{8}$. Its intersection

with the vertical surface $y = c$ parallel to the x-axis has the equations

$y = c$, $z = \sin x + \frac{1}{9} c^3 + \frac{1}{8}$ and is a sine curve of amplitude 1 (the maximum and

minimum values of z on the curve differ by 2). The intersection with the vertical plane

$x = c$ parallel to the y-axis has the equations $z = \sin(c) + \frac{1}{9} y^3 + \frac{1}{8}$ and is a cubic

that goes up for positive y and down for negative y. The surfaces in Figures 13.20 and

13.23 both have vertical cross sections parallel to the x-axis that are sine curves and

vertical cross sections parallel to the y-axis that are cubics. In Figure 13.20, however,

the sine curves have larger amplitudes the farther they are from the y-axis and some of

the cubics go up and others go down for positive y. The graph of $\sin x + \frac{1}{9} y^3 + \frac{1}{9}$

is shown in Figure 13.23.

(22a) By visualizing the horizontal cross sections of the graph of $\sin x + \frac{1}{9} y^3 + \frac{1}{8}$

in Figure 13.23 we can see that its level curves are those given in Figure 13.26. We can

check this by noting that the level curves have equations of the form $\sin x + \frac{1}{9} y^2 + \frac{1}{8} = c$

or $y = \sqrt[3]{9(c - \frac{1}{8} - \sin x)}$. These modified sine curves are periodic of period 2.

They cross the x-axis for those values of c with $-\frac{7}{8} < c < \frac{9}{8}$, lie entirely above the

x-axis for $c > \frac{9}{8}$, and lie entirely below the x-axis for $c < -\frac{7}{8}$.

(29) The level curve $x^2 + y = c$ is the parabola $y = c - x^2$ with y-intercept c.

These curves for $c = 2, 0,$ and -2 are shown in Fig. 13.1.29.

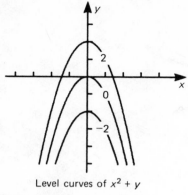

Level curves of $x^2 + y$

Fig. 13.1.29

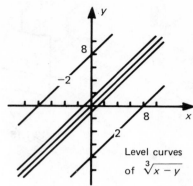

Level curves of $\sqrt[3]{x - y}$

Fig. 13.1.32

(32) The level curve $\sqrt[3]{x - y} = c$ also has the equation $x - y = c^3$ or $y = x - c^3$. It is a line with slope 1 and y-intercept $-c^3$. These lines for $c = 0$, ± 1, and ± 2 are shown in Fig. 13.1.32.

SECTION 13.2

(2) To compute the y-derivative we treat x as a constant:

$$\frac{\partial}{\partial y}(x^2 \sin(xy) + y - x) = x^2 \frac{\partial}{\partial y} \sin(xy) + \frac{\partial}{\partial y}(y) - \frac{\partial}{\partial y}(x) = x^2 \cos(xy) \frac{\partial}{\partial y}(xy) + 1 - 0$$

$$= x^2 \cos(xy)(x) + 1 = x^3 \cos(xy) + 1$$

(6) $\quad G_x(x,y) = \frac{\partial}{\partial x}[\ln(1 - xy)] = \frac{1}{1 - xy} \frac{\partial}{\partial x}(1 - xy) = \frac{-y}{1 - xy}$

$\quad G_y(x,y) = \frac{\partial}{\partial y}[\ln(1 - xy)] = \frac{1}{1 - xy} \frac{\partial}{\partial y}(1 - xy) = \frac{-x}{1 - xy}$

(8) $\quad p_u(u,v) = \frac{\partial}{\partial u}[e^{u^2} \cos(v^2)] = e^{u^2} \cos(v^2) \frac{\partial}{\partial u}(u^2) = 2u \, e^{u^2} \cos(v^2)$

$\quad p_v(u,v) = \frac{\partial}{\partial v}[e^{u^2} \cos(v^2)] = e^{u^2} [- \sin(v^2)] \frac{\partial}{\partial v}(v^2) = -2v \, e^{u^2} \sin(v^2).$

Therefore,

$$p_u(1,2) = [2u\ e^{u^2}\ \cos(v^2)]_{(1,2)} = 2(1)\ e^{1^2}\ \cos(2^2) = 2e\ \cos(4)$$

$$p_v(1,2) = [-2v\ e^{u^2}\ \sin(v^2)]_{(1,2)} = -2(2)\ e^{1^2}\ \sin(2^2) = -4e\ \sin(4)$$

(12) $$\frac{\partial}{\partial r}\left[\frac{r+s}{r-s}\right] = \frac{(r-s)\frac{\partial}{\partial r}(r+s) - (r+s)\frac{\partial}{\partial r}(r-s)}{(r-s)^2} = \frac{(r-s)(1) - (r+s)(1)}{(r-s)^2}$$

$$= \frac{-2s}{(r-s)^2}$$

(15) $$f_x = \frac{\partial}{\partial x}[\ln(2x-3y)] = \frac{1}{2x-3y}\frac{\partial}{\partial x}(2x-3y) = \frac{2}{2x-3y} = 2(2x-3y)^{-1}$$

$$f_y = \frac{\partial}{\partial y}[\ln(2x-3y)] = \frac{1}{2x-3y}\frac{\partial}{\partial y}(2x-3y) = \frac{-3}{2x-3y} = -3(2x-3y)^{-1}$$

$$f_{xx} = \frac{\partial}{\partial x}f_x = \frac{\partial}{\partial x}[2(2x-3y)^{-1}] = 2(-1)(2x-3y)^{-2}\frac{\partial}{\partial x}(2x-3y) = -4(2x-3y)^{-2}$$

$$f_{xy} = \frac{\partial}{\partial y}f_x = \frac{\partial}{\partial y}[2(2x-3y)^{-1}] = 2(-1)(2x-3y)^{-2}\frac{\partial}{\partial y}(2x-3y) = 6(2x-3y)^{-2}$$

$$f_{yx} = \frac{\partial}{\partial x}f_y = \frac{\partial}{\partial x}[-3(2x-3y)^{-1}] = -3(-1)(2x-3y)^{-2}\frac{\partial}{\partial x}(2x-3y) = 6(2x-3y)^{-2}$$

$$f_{yy} = \frac{\partial}{\partial y}f_y = \frac{\partial}{\partial y}[-3(2x-3y)^{-1}] = -3(-1)(2x-3y)^{-2}\frac{\partial}{\partial y}(2x-3y) = -9(2x-3y)^{-2}$$

Because they are continuous for all (x,y) where they are defined, the mixed partial derivatives f_{xy} and f_{yx} are equal. We calculate both of them to have a check on our work.

(22) $\frac{\partial f}{\partial x}(x,y) = \frac{\partial}{\partial x}(x^3y^4) = 3x^2y^4$ (a) $\frac{\partial f}{\partial x}(2,10) = 3(2)^2(10)^4 = 120{,}000$

$\frac{\partial^2 f}{\partial x^2}(x,y) = \frac{\partial}{\partial x}\frac{\partial f}{\partial x}(x,y) = \frac{\partial}{\partial x}(3x^2y^4) = 6xy^4$ (b) $\frac{\partial^2 f}{\partial x^2}(2,10) = 6(2)(10)^4 = 120{,}000$

$\frac{\partial^3 f}{\partial y\partial x^2}(x,y) = \frac{\partial}{\partial y}\frac{\partial^2 f}{\partial x^2}(x,y) = \frac{\partial}{\partial y}(6xy^4) = 24yx^3$ (c) $\frac{\partial^3 f}{\partial y\partial x^2}(2,10) = 24(2)(10)^3 = 48{,}000$

(25)   The rate of change of the volume $V(r,h) = \frac{1}{3}\pi r^2 h$ with respect to the radius r is the partial derivative

$$V_r(r,h) = \frac{\partial}{\partial r}[\frac{1}{3}\pi\ r^2 h] = \frac{2}{3}\pi rh.$$

(28a) The point at t = 4, L = 40 in Fig. 13.2.28 is just above the level curve R(t,L) = 900 and between that level curve and the curve R(t,L) = 800. We estimate that R(4,40) is approximately 890 gram calories.

(28b) We consider the points on either side of (4,40) where the vertical line t = 4 intersectes the level curves R(t,L) = 900 and R(t,L) = 800 (Fig. 13.2.28). The points are approximately 20 degrees apart. The change in R as we go from the lower point to the upper point is ΔR = 800 - 900 = -100 gram-calories. The corresponding change in L is approximately ΔL = 20 degrees. The average rate of change of R(t,L) with respect to L between the two points is approximately

$$\frac{\Delta R}{\Delta L} = \frac{-100 \text{ gram-calories}}{20 \text{ degrees}} = -5 \text{ gram-calories per degree.}$$

This is approximately equal to the instantaneous rate of change $\frac{\partial R}{\partial L}(4,40)$ of R(t,L) with respect to L at (4,40).

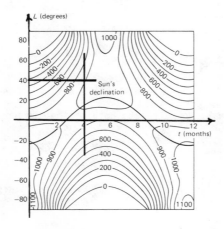

Fig. 13.2.28

(28c) We now consider the points on either side of (4,40) where the horizontal line L = 40 intersects the level curves R(t,L) = 800 and R(t,L) = 900. The points are approximately $\frac{5}{6}$ months apart. The change in R as we go from the point on the left to the point on the right is ΔR = 900 - 800 = 100 gram-calories. The corresponding change in t is approximately $\Delta t = \frac{5}{6}$ months. The average rate of change of $R(t,L)$ with respect to t between the two points is approximately

$$\frac{\Delta R}{\Delta t} = \frac{100 \text{ gram-calories}}{\frac{5}{6} \text{ months}} = 120 \text{ gram-calories per month.}$$

This is approximately equal to the instantaneous rate of change $\frac{\partial R}{\partial t}(4,40)$ of $R(t,L)$ with respect to t at $(4,40)$. (The answer of 130 gram-calories per month given in the back of the text was obtain by taking $t = \frac{10}{13}$ as the approximate distance between the two points on the line $L = 40$.)

SECTION 13.3

(1)   As (x,y) tends to $(-5,3)$, $\dfrac{x^3 y}{x^2 - y}$ tends to $\dfrac{(-5)^3(3)}{(-5)^2 - 3} = -\dfrac{375}{22}$.

(9)   Because $f(x,y)$ equals $x \ln(xy + 1)$, $x(u,v)$ **equals** ue^v, and $y(u,v) = u^2 v^3$, we have

$$f(x(u,v),y(u,v)) = x(u,v) \ln[x(u,v)y(u,v) + 1]$$
$$= ue^v \ln[(ue^v)(u^2 v^3) + 1] = ue^v \ln(u^3 v^3 e^v + 1)$$

(12a) $h(3) = g(3^3 - 5(3), 11(3) - 1) = g(12,32) = 0$

(12b) $\dfrac{dh}{dt}(t) = g_x(t^3 - 5t, 11t - 1) \dfrac{d}{dt}(t^3 - 5t) + g_y(t^3 - 5t, 11t - 1) \dfrac{d}{dt}(11t - 1)$

$$= g_x(t^3 - 5t, 11t - 1)(3t^2 - 5) + g_y(t^3 - 5t, 11t - 1)(11)$$

$\dfrac{dh}{dt}(3) = g_x(3^3 - 5(3), 11(3) - 1)(3(3)^2 - 5) + g_y(3^3 - 5(3), 11(3) - 1)(11)$

$$= 22g_x(12,32) + 11g_y(12,32) = 22(-3) + 11(2) = -44$$

(16a) $F(0,2) = f(2 \sin(0), 0 \sin(2)) = f(0,0) = 4$

(16b) $F_u(u,v) = f_x(v \sin u, u \sin v) \dfrac{\partial}{\partial u}(v \sin u) + f_y(v \sin u, u \sin v) \dfrac{\partial}{\partial u}(u \sin v)$

$\qquad\qquad = f_x(v \sin u, u \sin v)[v \cos u] + f_y(v \sin u, u \sin v)[\sin v]$

$\qquad F_u(0,2) = f_x(2 \sin(0), 0 \sin(2))[2 \cos(0)] + f_y(2 \sin(0), 0 \sin(2))[\sin(2)]$

$\qquad\qquad = f_x(0,0)(2) + f_y(0,0)[\sin(2)] \;\; = 10(2) + 2 \sin(2) = 20 + 2 \sin(2)$

(16c) $F_v(u,v) = f_x(v \sin u, u \sin v) \dfrac{\partial}{\partial v}(v \sin u) + f_y(v \sin u, u \sin v) \dfrac{\partial}{\partial v}(u \sin v)$

$\qquad\qquad = f_x(v \sin u, u \sin v)[\sin u] + f_y(v \sin u, u \sin v)[u \cos v]$

$\qquad F_v(0,2) = f_x(2 \sin(0), 0 \sin(2))[\sin(0)] + f_y(2 \sin(0), 0 \sin(2))[0 \cos(2)]$

$\qquad\qquad = f_x(0,0) \sin(0) + f_y(0,0)(0) = 0$

(22a) We assume that the first order derivatives of $f(x,y)$ and $y(x)$ are continuous.
Differentiating the equation

$$f(x, y(x)) = c$$

with respect to x gives

$$f_x(x, y(x)) \frac{d}{dx}(x) + f_y(x, y(x)) \frac{d}{dx} y(x) = \frac{d}{dx}(c)$$

$$f_x(x, y(x)) + f_y(x, y(x)) \frac{dy}{dx} = 0.$$

Hence

(*) $\qquad\qquad\qquad \dfrac{dy}{dx}(x) = - \; \dfrac{f_x(x, y(x))}{f_y(x, y(x))} \; .$

We also assume that $f_y(x, y(x))$ is not zero for the x's under consideration.

(22b)   We abbreviate notation by writing y for $y(x)$, $\frac{dy}{dx}$ for $\frac{dy}{dx}(x)$, and $\frac{d^2 y}{dx^2}$ for $\frac{d^2 y}{dx^2}(x)$.
Differentiating both sides of equation (*) from the solution of Exercise 22a above yields

$$\frac{d^2 y}{dx^2} = \frac{-f_y(x,y) \frac{d}{dx} f_x(x,y) + f_x(x,y) \frac{d}{dx} f_y(x,y)}{[f_y(x,y)]^2}$$

$$= \frac{-f_y(x,y)[f_{xx}(x,y) \frac{dx}{dx} + f_{xy}(x,y) \frac{dy}{dx}] + f_x(x,y)[f_{yx}(x,y) \frac{dx}{dx} + f_{yy}(x,y) \frac{dy}{dx}]}{[f_y(x,y)]^2}$$

$$= \frac{-f_y f_{xx} - f_y f_{xy} \frac{dy}{dx} + f_x f_{yx} + f_x f_{yy} \frac{dy}{dx}}{[f_y]^2}$$

Here we have abbreviated the notation further by dropping the references to where the derivatives are evaluated. When we use the equation $\frac{dy}{dx} = - f_x/f_y$ again, we obtain

$$\frac{d^2 y}{dx^2} = \frac{-f_y f_{xx} + f_x f_{xy} + f_x f_{yx}}{[f_y]^2} - \frac{[f_x]^2 f_{yy}}{[f_y]^3} = - \frac{f_{yy} f_x^2}{f_y^3} + \frac{2 f_{xy} f_x}{f_y^2} - \frac{f_{xx}}{f_y} .$$

(30)   By Theorem 13.1

$$\lim_{(x,y) \to (0,3)} x^3 = \lim_{x \to 0} x^3 = 0; \qquad \lim_{(x,y) \to (0,3)} x = \lim_{x \to 0} x = 0;$$

$$\lim_{(x,y) \to (0,3)} (2x) = \lim_{x \to 0} (2x) = 0; \quad \text{and} \quad \lim_{(x,y) \to (0,3)} y = \lim_{y \to 3} y = 3.$$

We write $\lim$ for $\lim_{(x,y) \to (0,3)}$. Then by Theorem 13.2,

$$\lim(x^3 y - y) = (\lim x^3)(\lim y) - \lim y = (0)(3) - 3 = -3;$$

$$\lim(2x + y + 1) = \lim(2x) + \lim(y) + \lim(1) = 0 + 3 + 1 = 4;$$

and consequently

$$\lim \frac{x^3 y - y}{2x + y + 1} = \frac{\lim(x^3 y - y)}{\lim(2x) y + 1)} = \frac{-3}{4} .$$

(38)   The function $\sqrt{xy}$ is defined for all (x,y) with $xy \geq 0$, and this consists of all points in the first and third quadrants of the xy-plane including the x- and y-axes. The function $\sqrt{x^2 + y^2}$ is defined for all (x,y) and is zero only at $(0,0)$. Hence the domain of the quotient $\sqrt{xy}/\sqrt{x^2 + y^2}$ consists of all (x,y) in the first and third quadrants, including all of the coordinate axes except the origin.

We can use polar coordinates $x = r \cos \theta$, $y = r \sin \theta$ with r positive to see that for (x,y) in the domain of the function its value is

$$\frac{\sqrt{xy}}{\sqrt{x^2 + y^2}} = \frac{\sqrt{r\cos \theta \; r \sin \theta}}{\sqrt{r^2}} = \sqrt{\cos \theta \; \sin \theta}$$

Hence the function has different limits along rays $\theta =$ constant as $r \to 0$, so its limit as $(x,y) \longrightarrow (0,0)$ does not exist.

SECTION 13.4

(1a) $\vec{\text{grad}}(x^3 y^2) = [\frac{\partial}{\partial x}(x^3 y^2)]\vec{i} + [\frac{\partial}{\partial y}(x^3 y^2)]\vec{j} = 3x^2 y^2 \vec{i} + 2x^3 y \vec{j}$

At $(2,-3)$ the gradient is

$$[\vec{\text{grad}}(x^3 y^2)]_{(2,-3)} = [3(2)^2(-3)^2]\vec{i} + [2(2)^3(-3)]\vec{j} = 108\vec{i} - 48\vec{j}.$$

(1b) The derivative of $x^3 y^2$ at $(2,-3)$ in the direction of a unit vector $\vec{u}$ is the dot product of $\vec{u}$ with the gradient found in exercise 1a. Because $\vec{u} = \frac{3}{5}\vec{i} - \frac{4}{5}\vec{j}$ is a unit vector, the derivative in that direction is

$$(108\vec{i} - 48\vec{j})\cdot(\frac{3}{5}\vec{i} - \frac{4}{5}\vec{j}) = (108)(\frac{3}{5}) + (-48)(-\frac{4}{5}) = \frac{516}{5}$$

(4a) $\vec{\text{grad}}[\arctan(\frac{y}{x})] = [\frac{\partial}{\partial x}\arctan(\frac{y}{x})]\vec{i} + [\frac{\partial}{\partial y}\arctan(\frac{y}{x})]\vec{j}$

$= [\{\frac{1}{1 + (\frac{y}{x})^2}\}\frac{\partial}{\partial x}(\frac{y}{x})]\vec{i} + [\{\frac{1}{1 + (\frac{y}{x})^2}\}\frac{\partial}{\partial y}(\frac{y}{x})]\vec{j} = [\{\frac{x^2}{x^2 + y^2}\}(-\frac{y}{x^2})]\vec{i} + [\{\frac{x^2}{x^2 + y^2}\}(\frac{1}{x})]\vec{j}$

$= \frac{1}{x^2 + y^2}[-y\vec{i} + x\vec{j}]$

At $(-1,-1)$ this gradient vector is $\frac{1}{(-1)^2 + (-1)^2}[\vec{i} - \vec{j}] = \frac{1}{2}\vec{i} - \frac{1}{2}\vec{j}$

(4b) The unit vector in the direction of $-\vec{i} - \vec{j}$ is $\vec{u} = \frac{1}{\sqrt{2}}(-\vec{i} - \vec{j})$, and the directional derivative of $\arctan(\frac{y}{x})$ at $(-1,-1)$ in that direction is the dot product of $\vec{u}$ with the gradient of Exercise 4a. The directional derivative is

$$(\frac{1}{2}\vec{i} - \frac{1}{2}\vec{j})\cdot[\frac{1}{\sqrt{2}}(-\vec{i} - \vec{j})] = \frac{1}{\sqrt{2}}[(\frac{1}{2})(-1) + (-\frac{1}{2})(-1)] = 0$$

(8) At (1,1) the function $\frac{1}{4}x^2 + \frac{1}{4}y^2$ has the value $\frac{1}{4}(1)^2 + \frac{1}{4}(1)^2 = \frac{1}{2}$. At (1,-2)

it has the value $\frac{1}{4}(1)^2 + \frac{1}{4}(-2)^2 = \frac{5}{4}$. At (-3,-1) it has the value $\frac{1}{4}(-3)^2 + \frac{1}{4}(-1)^2 = \frac{5}{2}$.

Consequently, the level curve through (1,1) has the equation $\frac{1}{4}x^2 + \frac{1}{4}y^2 = \frac{1}{2}$ and is the

circle of radius 2 with center at the origin; the level curve through (1,-2) has the

equation $\frac{1}{4}x^2 + \frac{1}{4}y^2 = \frac{5}{4}$ and is the circle of radius 5 with center at the origin;

the level curve through (-3,-1) has the equation $\frac{1}{4}x^2 + \frac{1}{4}y^2 = \frac{5}{2}$ and is the circle of

radius 10 with center at the origin (Fig. 13.4.8).

The gradient

$$\overrightarrow{grad}(\frac{1}{4}x^2 + \frac{1}{4}y^2) = [\frac{\partial}{\partial x}(\frac{1}{4}x^2 + \frac{1}{4}y^2)]\vec{i} + [\frac{\partial}{\partial y}(\frac{1}{4}x^2 + \frac{1}{4}y^2)]\vec{j}$$

$$= (\frac{1}{2}x)\vec{i} + (\frac{1}{2}y)\vec{j}$$

equals $\frac{1}{2}\vec{i} + \frac{1}{2}\vec{j}$ at (1,1), equals $\frac{1}{2}\vec{i} - \vec{j}$ at (1,-2), and equals $-\frac{3}{2}\vec{i} - \frac{1}{2}\vec{j}$ at

(-3,-1). These gradient vectors are also drawn in Fig. 13.4.8. Notice that they are

perpendicular to the corresponding level curves and point in the direction in which the

function increases.

(12a) Set $f(x,y) = 2x - \ln y$. Then $\overrightarrow{grad} f(x,y) = [\frac{\partial}{\partial x}(2x - \ln y)]\vec{i} + [\frac{\partial}{\partial y}(2x - \ln y)]\vec{j}$

$= 2\vec{i} - \frac{1}{y}\vec{j}$ and $\overrightarrow{grad} f(0,3) = 2\vec{i} - \frac{1}{3}\vec{j}$. The maximum directional derivative of $f(x,y)$

at (0,3) is

$$\left|\overrightarrow{grad} f(0,3)\right| = \left|2\vec{i} - \frac{1}{3}\vec{j}\right| = \sqrt{(2)^2 + (-\frac{1}{3})^2} = \sqrt{\frac{37}{9}} = \frac{\sqrt{37}}{3}$$

That derivative occurs in the direction of the gradient. The unit vector in that direction is

$$\frac{\overrightarrow{grad} f(0,3)}{\left|\overrightarrow{grad} f(0,3)\right|} = \frac{2\vec{i} - \frac{1}{3}\vec{j}}{\frac{\sqrt{37}}{3}} = \frac{6}{\sqrt{37}}\vec{i} - \frac{1}{\sqrt{37}}\vec{j} = \langle\frac{6}{\sqrt{37}}, \frac{-1}{\sqrt{37}}\rangle .$$

(12b) The minimum directional derivative of $f(x,y)$ at (0,3) is

$$-\left|\overrightarrow{grad} f(0,3)\right| = -\frac{\sqrt{37}}{3}$$

and it occurs in the direction opposite the gradient. The unit vector in that direction is

$$-\frac{\overrightarrow{grad} f(0,3)}{\left|\overrightarrow{grad} f(0,3)\right|} = \langle\frac{-6}{\sqrt{37}}, \frac{1}{\sqrt{37}}\rangle .$$

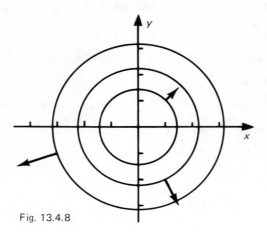

Fig. 13.4.8

(15) By the quotient rule

$$g_x(x,y) = \frac{\partial}{\partial x}\left[\frac{x}{x + y}\right] = \frac{(x + y)\frac{\partial}{\partial x}(x) - x\frac{\partial}{\partial x}(x + y)}{(x + y)^2} = \frac{x + y - x}{(x + y)^2} = \frac{y}{(x + y)^2}$$

$$g_y(x,y) = \frac{\partial}{\partial y}\left[\frac{x}{x + y}\right] = \frac{(x + y)\frac{\partial}{\partial y}(x) - x\frac{\partial}{\partial y}(x + y)}{(x + y)^2} = \frac{-x}{(x + y)^2} \ .$$

Hence,

$$g_x(3,2) = \frac{2}{(3 + 2)^2} = \frac{2}{25} \quad , \quad g_y(3,2) = \frac{-3}{(3 + 2)^2} = \frac{-3}{25} \ , \text{ and}$$

(*) $$\overrightarrow{\text{grad}}\ g(3,2) = \frac{2}{25}\vec{i} - \frac{3}{25}\vec{j}.$$

The vector $\vec{A} = 2\vec{i} - 3\vec{j}$ is parallel to the gradient vector (*). If we switch the components

of $\vec{A}$ and multiply one or the other of the components by -1, we obtain vectors

$$\vec{C} = 3\vec{i} + 2\vec{j} \qquad \text{and} \qquad \vec{D} = -3\vec{i} - 2\vec{j}$$

perpendicular to A and hence to the gradient. The unit vectors in those directions are

$$\frac{\vec{C}}{|\vec{C}|} = \frac{3\vec{i} + 2\vec{j}}{\sqrt{3^2 + 2^2}} = \frac{3}{\sqrt{13}}\vec{i} + \frac{2}{\sqrt{13}}\vec{j} \quad \text{and} \quad \frac{\vec{D}}{|\vec{D}|} = -\frac{3}{\sqrt{13}}\vec{i} - \frac{2}{\sqrt{13}}\vec{j}.$$

(20) **Write** $\overrightarrow{\text{grad}}\ P(0,0) = a\vec{i} + b\vec{j}$, where $a = P_x(0,0)$ and $b = P_y(0,0)$ are to be determined. With $\vec{u} = \frac{\sqrt{3}}{2}\ \vec{i} + \frac{1}{2}\ \vec{j}$, we have

$$D_{\vec{u}}P(0,0) = \overrightarrow{\text{grad}}\ P(0,0)\cdot\vec{u} = (a\vec{i} + b\vec{j})(\frac{\sqrt{3}}{2}\vec{i} + \frac{1}{2}\vec{j}) = \frac{\sqrt{3}}{2}\ a + \frac{1}{2}\ b$$

and with $\vec{v} = -\frac{\sqrt{3}}{2}\ \vec{i} + \frac{1}{2}\ \vec{j}$, we have

$$D_{\vec{v}}P(0,0) = \overrightarrow{\text{grad}}\ P(0,0)\cdot\vec{v} = (a\vec{i} + b\vec{j})\cdot(-\frac{\sqrt{3}}{2}\ \vec{i} + \frac{1}{2}\vec{j}) = -\frac{\sqrt{3}}{2}\ a + \frac{1}{2}\ b.$$

Because $D_uP(0,0) = 2$ and $D_vP(0,0) = 8$, we conclude that

$$\frac{\sqrt{3}}{2}\ a + \frac{1}{2}\ b = 2$$

$$-\frac{\sqrt{3}}{2}\ a + \frac{1}{2}\ b = 8.$$

Adding these equations shows that $b = 10$, and then either equation gives $a = -2\sqrt{3}$

Thus, $P_x(0,0) = -2\sqrt{3}$ and $P_y(0,0) = 10$.

(23) We draw an   s-axis through the point $(-1,1)$ in the direction of the vector

$\vec{u} = \frac{1}{\sqrt{10}}\ \vec{i} - \frac{3}{\sqrt{10}}\ \vec{j}$ (Fig. 13.4.23). We consider the points on either side of $(-1,1)$ where

the   s-axis intersects level curves of the function. The points are approximately $\Delta s = 2$

units apart and the change in the value of the function as we go from the upper to the

lower point (in the direction of increasing s) is $\Delta g = 20 - 30 = -10$. The average

rate of change of $g(x,y)$ with respect to s between those points is approximately

$$\frac{\Delta g}{\Delta s} = \frac{-10}{2} = -5.$$

This is approximately equal to the derivative of $g(x,y)$ at $(-1,1)$ in the direction of $\vec{u}$.

(26) We draw a plausible level curve through $(2,2)$ and an s-axis perpendicular to

the level curve and pointing in the direction of increasing s (Fig. 13.4.26). The

points on either side of $(2,2)$ where the s-axis intersects the level curves are approximately $\Delta s = \frac{3}{4}$ unit apart, and the level curves are shown for increments of $g(x,y)$ of $\Delta g = 10$. Hence, the average rate of change of $g(x,y)$ with respect to s between the two points is approximately

$$\frac{\Delta g}{\Delta s} = \frac{10}{\frac{3}{4}} = \frac{40}{3} \, .$$

This is approximately equal to the maximum directional derivative of $g(x,y)$ at $(2,2)$, which is the length of the gradient vector:

$$\left| \overrightarrow{\text{grad}} \, g(2,2) \right| \approx \frac{40}{3} \, .$$

The s-axis has approximately the direction of the vector $-5\vec{i} - 4\vec{j}$ and the unit vector in that direction is $- \frac{5}{\sqrt{41}} i - \frac{4}{\sqrt{41}} j$. Hence

$$\overrightarrow{\text{grad}} \, g(2,2) \approx \frac{40}{3} \left(- \frac{5}{\sqrt{41}} \vec{i} - \frac{4}{\sqrt{41}} \vec{j} \right) \approx -10.4\vec{i} - 8.3\vec{j} \approx \langle -10, -8 \rangle \, .$$

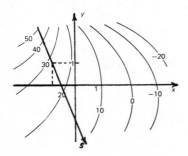

Fig. 13.4.23

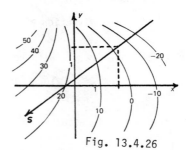

Fig. 13.4.26

SECTION 13.5

(2) The tangent plane to the graph of $f(x,y)$ at $x = 3$, $y = 0$ has the equation

$$z = f(3,0) + f_x(3,0)(x - 3) + f_y(3,0)(y - 0).$$

With $f(x,y) = xe^{-y}$, we have $f(3,0) = 3e^{-0} = 3$, $f_x(3,0) = [e^{-y}]_{(3,0)} = e^{-0} = 1$, and

$f_y(3,0) = [-xe^{-y}]_{(3,0)} = -3e^{-0} = -3$, so the tangent line has the equation

$z = 3 + (1)(x - 3) + (-3)(y - 0)$, which simplifies to $z = x - 3y$.

The vector $\langle f_x(3,0), f_y(3,0), -1 \rangle$ is normal to the graph of $f(x,y)$ at $x = 3$, $y = 0$. In the case of $f(x,y) = xe^{-y}$, we have $f_x(3,0) = 1$ and $f_y(3,0) = -3$, so a suitable normal vector is $\langle 1, -3, -1 \rangle$.

(7) The tangent line to the graph of $f(x,y)$ at $x = 3$, $y = 4$ has the equation

$$z = f(3,4) + f_x(3,4)(x - 3) + f_y(3,4)(y - 4),$$

and the vector $\langle f_x(3,4), f_y(3,4), -1 \rangle$ is normal to the graph at that point. With

$f(x,y) = \ln\sqrt{x^2 + y^2} = \frac{1}{2}\ln(x^2 + y^2)$ we have

$$f_x(x,y) = \frac{\partial}{\partial x}[\frac{1}{2}\ln(x^2 + y^2)] = \frac{1}{2(x^2 + y^2)}\frac{\partial}{\partial x}(x^2 + y^2) = \frac{x}{x^2 + y^2}$$

$$f_y(x,y) = \frac{\partial}{\partial y}[\frac{1}{2}\ln(x^2 + y^2)] = \frac{1}{2(x^2 + y^2)}\frac{\partial}{\partial y}(x^2 + y^2) = \frac{y}{x^2 + y^2}.$$

Hence, $f(3,4) = \ln\sqrt{3^2 + 4^2} = \ln(5)$, $f_x(3,4) = \frac{3}{3^2 + 4^2} = \frac{3}{25}$, and $f_y(3,4) = \frac{4}{3^2 + 4^2} = \frac{4}{25}$.

The tangent plane has the equation

$$z = \ln(5) + \frac{3}{25}(x - 3) + \frac{4}{25}(y - 4)$$

and the vector $\langle \frac{3}{25}, \frac{4}{25}, -1 \rangle$ is normal to the graph at $x = 3$, $y = 4$.

(10) We set $f(x,y) = \sqrt{\dfrac{x}{y}} = x^{1/2} y^{-1/2}$. Then $f_x(x,y) = \dfrac{1}{2} x^{-1/2} y^{-1/2}$ and

$f_y(x,y) = -\dfrac{1}{2} x^{1/2} y^{-3/2}$, so that $f(9,4) = \sqrt{\dfrac{9}{4}} = \dfrac{3}{2}$; $f_x(9,4) = \dfrac{1}{2}(9)^{-1/2}(4)^{-1/2} = \dfrac{1}{12}$;

and $f_y(9,4) = -\dfrac{1}{2}(9)^{1/2}(4)^{-3/2} = -\dfrac{3}{16}$. The tangent line to $z = \sqrt{\dfrac{x}{y}}$ at $(9,4)$ has

the equation

(*) $\qquad\qquad z = \dfrac{3}{2} + \dfrac{1}{12}(x - 9) - \dfrac{3}{16}(y - 4)$.

We approximate $\sqrt{\dfrac{9.003}{3.998}} = f(9.003, 3.998)$ by the value of z at $x = 9.003$, $y = 3.998$ on

the tangent plane (*):

$$\sqrt{\dfrac{9.003}{3.998}} \approx \dfrac{3}{2} + \dfrac{1}{12}(9.003 - 9) - \dfrac{3}{16}(3.998 - 4)$$

$$= 1.5 + \dfrac{1}{12}(0.003) - \dfrac{3}{16}(-0.002) = 1.5 + \left(\dfrac{1}{4} + \dfrac{3}{8}\right)(0.001) = 1.500625.$$

(12) Set $f(x,y) = \ln(x^{75} + y^{100})$. Then $f_x(x,y) = \dfrac{1}{x^{75} + y^{100}} \dfrac{\partial}{\partial x}(x^{75} + y^{100}) = \dfrac{75x^{74}}{x^{75} + y^{100}}$

and $f_y(x,y) = \dfrac{1}{x^{75} + y^{100}} \dfrac{\partial}{\partial y}(x^{75} + y^{100}) = \dfrac{100y^{99}}{x^{75} + y^{100}}$. Because $f(0,1) = \ln(0^{75} + 1^{100})$ is 0,

$f_x(0,1) = \dfrac{75(0)^{74}}{0^{75} + 1^{100}}$ is zero, and $f_y(0,1) = \dfrac{100(1)^{99}}{0^{75} + 1^{100}}$ equals 100, the tangent

plane to the graph of $f(x,y)$ at $x = 0$, $y = 1$ has the equation $z = 0 + 0(x - 0) + 100(y - 1)$

or

$$z = 100(y - 1).$$

This yields the approximation

$\ln[(0.0003)^{75} + (0.9995)^{100}] = f(0.0003, 0.9995) \approx 100(0.9995 - 1) = -0.05.$

(15) If x is the length of the side opposite the angle Θ and y is the length of

the hypotenuse of the right triangle, then $\sin\Theta = \dfrac{x}{y}$, and, because Θ is an acute

angle $\Theta = \Theta(x,y) = \arcsin\left(\dfrac{x}{y}\right)$ (Fig. 13.5.15). We have

$$\Theta_x(x,y) = \dfrac{\partial}{\partial x}\arcsin\left(\dfrac{x}{y}\right) = \dfrac{1}{\sqrt{1 - \left(\dfrac{x}{y}\right)^2}} \dfrac{\partial}{\partial x}\left(\dfrac{x}{y}\right) = \dfrac{y}{\sqrt{y^2 - x^2}}\left(\dfrac{1}{y}\right) = \dfrac{1}{\sqrt{y^2 - x^2}}$$

$$\Theta_y(x,y) = \frac{\partial}{\partial y} \arcsin\left(\frac{x}{y}\right) = \frac{1}{\sqrt{1 - \left(\frac{x}{y}\right)^2}} \; \frac{\partial}{\partial y}(xy^{-1}) = \frac{y}{\sqrt{y^2 - x^2}} (-xy^{-2}) = \frac{-x}{y\sqrt{y^2 - x^2}}$$

Setting $x = 4$ and $y = 8$, we obtain

$$\Theta_x(4,8) = \frac{1}{\sqrt{8^2 - 4^2}} = \frac{1}{\sqrt{48}} \quad \text{and} \quad \Theta_y(4,8) = \frac{-4}{8\sqrt{8^2 - 4^2}} = -\frac{1}{2\sqrt{48}} \; ,$$

so the differentials dx, dy, and $d\Theta$ at $x = 4$, $y = 8$ on the graph of $\Theta(x,y)$ are
related by the equation $d\Theta = \Theta_x(4,8)dx + \Theta_y(4,8)dy$ or

(*) $$d\Theta = \frac{1}{\sqrt{48}} \, dx - \frac{1}{2\sqrt{48}} \, dy$$

For $|dx| \leq 0.01$ and $|dy| \leq 0.01$, we obtain the maximum $|d\Theta|$ by taking $dx = 0.01$
and $dy = -0.01$ or $dx = -0.01$ and $dy = 0.01$. With either of these choices, we obtain

$$|d\Theta| = \frac{1}{\sqrt{48}} (0.01) + \frac{1}{2\sqrt{48}}(0.01) = \frac{3}{2\sqrt{48}} (0.01) = \frac{\sqrt{3}}{8}(0.01) \approx 0.002$$

The maximum possible error in calculating Θ is approximately 0.002 radians.

$$\sin\Theta = \frac{x}{y}$$

$$\Theta = \arcsin\left(\frac{x}{y}\right)$$

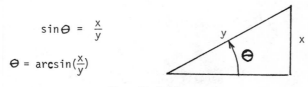

Fig. 13.5.15

(17)   For $f = x^2 y^5$, we have $f_x = \frac{\partial}{\partial x}(x^2 y^5) = 2xy^5$ and $f_y = \frac{\partial}{\partial y}(x^2 y^5) = 5x^2 y^4$, so that $df = 2xy^5\ dx + 5x^2 y^4\ dy$.

(21)   For $A = wh$, we have $A_w = h$ and $A_h = w$, so that $dA = h\,dw + w\,dh$ and at $w = 3$, $h = 5$ the total differential is $dA = 5\,dw + 3\,dh$. For $|dw| \le 0.02$ and $|dh| \le 0.03$, the approximate maximum error is $|dA| = 5(0.02) + 3(0.03) = 0.1 + 0.09 = 0.19$.

SECTION 13.6

(2a) For $f(x,y,z) = x^2 e^{-3y} \sin(4z)$, we have

$$f_x = \frac{\partial}{\partial x}[x^2\ e^{-3y}\ \sin(4z)] = 2x\ e^{-3y}\ \sin(4z)$$

$$f_y = \frac{\partial}{\partial y}[x^2\ e^{-3y}\ \sin(4z)] = x^2(-3\ e^{-3y})\ \sin(4z) = -3x^2\ e^{-3y}\ \sin(4z)$$

$$f_z = \frac{\partial}{\partial z}[x^2\ e^{-3y}\ \sin(4z)] = x^2\ e^{-3y}\ \cos(4z)(4) = 4x^2\ e^{-3y}\ \cos(4z).$$

Therefore,

$$f_{xy} = \frac{\partial}{\partial y}\ f_x = \frac{\partial}{\partial y}[2x\ e^{-3y}\ \sin(4z)] = -6x\ e^{-3y}\ \sin(4z).$$

As a check we compute

$$f_{yx} = \frac{\partial}{\partial x}\ f_y = \frac{\partial}{\partial x}[-3x^2\ e^{-3y}\ \sin(4z)] = -6x\ e^{-3y}\ \sin(4z).$$

(2b) From the calculations in part (a), we have

$$f_{yz} = \frac{\partial}{\partial z}\ f_y = \frac{\partial}{\partial z}[-3x^2\ e^{-3y}\ \sin(4z)] = -3x^2\ e^{-3y}\ \cos(4z)(4) = -12x^2\ e^{-3y}\ \cos(4z).$$

As a check we also compute

$$f_{zy} = \frac{\partial}{\partial y}\ f_z = \frac{\partial}{\partial y}[4x^2\ e^{-3y}\ \cos(4z)] = 4x^2(-3e^{-3y})\cos(4z) = -12x^2\ e^{-3y}\ \cos(4z).$$

(2c) From the calculations of part (a),

$$f_{xz} = \frac{\partial}{\partial z}\ f_x = \frac{\partial}{\partial z}[2x\ e^{-3y}\ \sin(4z)] = 2x\ e^{-3y}\ \cos(4z)(4) = 8xe^{-3y}\ \cos(4z).$$

To check this result we also compute

$$f_{zx} = \frac{\partial}{\partial x}\ f_z = \frac{\partial}{\partial x}[4x^2\ e^{-3y}\ \cos(4z)] = 8x\ e^{-3y}\ \cos(4z).$$

(7) $z_x = \frac{\partial}{\partial x}(x^2 + y^2 - 2xy \cos \Theta)^{1/2} = \frac{1}{2}(x^2 + y^2 - 2xy \cos \Theta)^{-1/2} \frac{\partial}{\partial x}(x^2 + y^2 - 2xy \cos \Theta)$

$$= \frac{1}{2}(x^2 + y^2 - 2xy \cos\Theta)^{-1/2}(2x - 2y \cos\Theta) = \frac{x - y \cos\Theta}{\sqrt{x^2 + y^2 - 2xy \cos\Theta}}$$

$$z_y = \frac{\partial}{\partial y}(x^2 + y^2 - 2xy \cos\Theta)^{1/2} = \frac{1}{2}(x^2 + y^2 - 2xy \cos\Theta)^{-1/2}\frac{\partial}{\partial y}(x^2 + y^2 - 2xy \cos\Theta)$$

$$= \frac{1}{2}(x^2 + y^2 - 2xy \cos\Theta)^{-1/2}(2y - 2x \cos\Theta) = \frac{y - x \cos\Theta}{\sqrt{x^2 + y^2 - 2xy \cos\Theta}}$$

$$z_\Theta = \frac{\partial}{\partial\Theta}(x^2 + y^2 - 2xy \cos\Theta)^{1/2} = \frac{1}{2}(x^2 + y^2 - 2xy \cos\Theta)^{-1/2}\frac{\partial}{\partial\Theta}(x^2 + y^2 - 2xy \cos\Theta)$$

$$= \frac{1}{2}(x^2 + y^2 - 2xy \cos\Theta)^{-1/2}(2xy \sin\Theta) = \frac{xy \sin\Theta}{\sqrt{x^2 + y^2 - 2xy \cos\Theta}}$$

(11a) Set $f(x,y,z) = \ln(xyz)$. Then for positive x, y, and z,

$$f_x(x,y,z) = \frac{\partial}{\partial x}\ln(xyz) = \frac{1}{xyz}\frac{\partial}{\partial x}(xyz) = \frac{yz}{xyz} = \frac{1}{x}$$

$$f_y(x,y,z) = \frac{\partial}{\partial y}\ln(xyz) = \frac{1}{xyz}\frac{\partial}{\partial y}(xyz) = \frac{xz}{xyz} = \frac{1}{y}$$

$$f_z(x,y,z) = \frac{\partial}{\partial z}\ln(xyz) = \frac{1}{xyz}\frac{\partial}{\partial z}(xyz) = \frac{xy}{xyz} = \frac{1}{z}.$$

(We could also compute these derivatives by writing $\ln(xyz) = \ln(x) + \ln(y) + \ln(z)$.)

Hence

$$\overrightarrow{grad}\, f(5,2,6) = \langle f_x(5,2,6), f_y(5,2,6), f_z(5,2,6)\rangle = \langle \frac{1}{5}, \frac{1}{2}, \frac{1}{6}\rangle.$$

(11b) The displacement vector from P(5,2,6) to Q(4,3,7) is

$$\overrightarrow{PQ} = \langle 4 - 5, 3 - 2, 7 - 6\rangle = \langle -1,1,1\rangle$$

and the unit vector in that direction is

$$\vec{u} = \frac{\overrightarrow{PQ}}{|\overrightarrow{PQ}|} = \frac{\langle -1,1,1\rangle}{|\langle -1,1,1\rangle|} = \frac{\langle -1,1,1\rangle}{\sqrt{(-1)^2 + 1^2 + 1^2}} = \frac{1}{\sqrt{3}}\langle -1,1,1\rangle.$$

The derivative of $f(x,y,z) = \ln(xyz)$ at $P(5,2,6)$ in the direction toward $Q(4,3,7)$ is

$$\overrightarrow{\text{grad}}\, f(5,2,6) \cdot \vec{u} = \left\langle \frac{1}{5}, \frac{1}{2}, \frac{1}{6} \right\rangle \cdot \left[\frac{1}{\sqrt{3}} \langle -1,1,1 \rangle \right] =$$

$$= \frac{1}{\sqrt{3}} \left[\left(\frac{1}{5}\right)(-1) + \left(\frac{1}{2}\right)(1) + \left(\frac{1}{6}\right)(1) \right] = \frac{1}{\sqrt{3}} \left(\frac{7}{15}\right) = \frac{7}{45}\sqrt{3}.$$

(13a) For $f(x,y,z) = (x + y)\sinh(y - z)$, we have

$$f_x(x,y,z) = \frac{\partial}{\partial x}[(x + y)\sinh(y - z)] = \sinh(y - z)$$

$$f_y(x,y,z) = \frac{\partial}{\partial y}[(x + y)\sinh(y - z)] = \left[\frac{\partial}{\partial y}(x + y)\right]\sinh(y - z) + (x + y)\left[\frac{\partial}{\partial y}\sinh(y - z)\right]$$

$$= \sinh(y - z) + (x + y)\cosh(y - z)\frac{\partial}{\partial y}(y - z)$$

$$= \sinh(y - z) + (x + y)\cosh(y - z)$$

$$f_z(x,y,z) = \frac{\partial}{\partial z}[(x + y)\sinh(y - z)] = (x + y)\cosh(y - z)\frac{\partial}{\partial z}(y - z)$$

$$= -(x + y)\cosh(y - z).$$

Hence

$$\overrightarrow{\text{grad}}\, f(5,4,4) = \langle f_x(5,4,4), f_y(5,4,4), f_z(5,4,4) \rangle$$

$$= \langle \sinh(4 - 4), \sinh(4 - 4) + (5 + 4)\cosh(4 - 4), -(5 + 4)\cosh(4 - 4) \rangle$$

$$= \langle 0, 0 + 9(1), -9(1) \rangle = \langle 0, 9, -9 \rangle$$

(13b) The displacement vector from $P(5,4,4)$ to $Q(-5,-4,-4)$ is

$$\overrightarrow{PQ} = \langle -5 - 5, -4 - 4, -4 - 4 \rangle = \langle -10, -8, -8 \rangle$$

and the unit vector in that direction is

$$\vec{u} = \frac{\overrightarrow{PQ}}{|\overrightarrow{PQ}|} = \frac{\langle -10,-8,-8 \rangle}{|\langle -10,-8,-8 \rangle|} = \frac{\langle -5,-4,-4 \rangle}{|\langle -5,-4,-4 \rangle|} = \frac{\langle -5,-4,-4 \rangle}{\sqrt{5^2 + 4^2 + 4^2}} = \frac{1}{\sqrt{57}}\langle -5,-4,-4 \rangle.$$

The derivative of $f(x,y,z) = (x + y)\sinh(y - z)$ at $P(5,4,4)$ in the direction toward $Q(-5,-4,-4)$ is

$$\overrightarrow{\text{grad}}\ f(5,4,4)\cdot\vec{u} = \ <0,9,-9>\cdot[\frac{1}{\sqrt{57}}<-5,-4,-4>]$$

$$= \frac{1}{57}[(0)(-5) + (9)(-4) + (-9)(-4)]\ = 0.$$

(19) The tangent plane to the surface $f(x,y,z) = c$ at $(5,10,\frac{1}{5})$ has the equation

$$f_x(5,10,\tfrac{1}{5})(x - 5) + f_y(5,10,\tfrac{1}{5})(y - 10) + f_z(5,10,\tfrac{1}{5})(z - \tfrac{1}{5}) = 0$$

and the gradient

$$\vec{n} = \overrightarrow{\text{grad}}\ f(5,10,\tfrac{1}{5})\ = \ <f_x(5,10,\tfrac{1}{5}),f_y(5,10,\tfrac{1}{5}),f_z(5,10,\tfrac{1}{5})>$$

is a normal vector to that surface at that point.

In the case of $f(x,y,z) = x\ \ln(xz) = x\ \ln(x) + x\ \ln(z)$, we have

$$f_x(x,y,z) = \frac{\partial}{\partial x}[x\ \ln(x) + x\ \ln(z)] = [\frac{\partial}{\partial x}\ x]\ln(x) + x[\frac{\partial}{\partial x}\ \ln(x)] + \ln(z)$$

$$= \ \ln(x) + 1 + \ln(z)$$

$$f_y(x,y,z) = \frac{\partial}{\partial y}[x\ \ln(xz)] = 0$$

$$f_z(x,y,z) = \frac{\partial}{\partial z}[x\ \ln(x) + x\ \ln(z)] = \frac{x}{z}$$

Hence,

$$f_x(5,10,\tfrac{1}{5}) = \ \ln(5) + 1 + \ln(\tfrac{1}{5}) = \ \ln(5) + 1 - \ln(5) = 1$$

$$f_y(x,10,\tfrac{1}{5}) = 0$$

$$f_z(5,10,\tfrac{1}{5}) = \frac{5}{\frac{1}{5}}\ = 25.$$

(a) The vector $\vec{n} = <1,0,25>$ is normal to the surface $x\ \ln(xz) = 0$ at $(5,10,\frac{1}{5})$.

(b) The tangent plane to the surface $x\ \ln(xz) = 0$ at $(5,10,\frac{1}{5})$ has the equation

$$1(x - 5) + 0(y - 10) + 25(z - \tfrac{1}{5}) = 0$$

which may be rewritten in the form

$$x + 25z = 10.$$

(23) The gradient vector

$$\overrightarrow{\text{grad}}(x^2y^3z^4 + xyz) = \ <\frac{\partial}{\partial x}(x^2y^3z^4 + xyz),\frac{\partial}{\partial y}(x^2y^3z^4 + xyz),\frac{\partial}{\partial z}(x^2y^3z^4 + xyz)>$$

$$= <2xy^3z^4 + yz,3x^2y^2z^4 + xz,4x^2y^3z^3 + xy>$$

is normal to the level surface of $x^2y^3z^4 + xyz$ through (x,y,z). At $(2,1,-1)$ the gradient vector is

$$\langle 2(2)(1)^3(-1)^4 + (1)(-1), 3(2)^2(1)^2(-1)^4 + (2)(-1), 4(2)^2(1)^3(-1)^3 + (2)(1) \rangle$$

$$= \quad \langle 4 - 1, 12 - 2, -16 + 2 \rangle = \langle 3, 10, -14 \rangle.$$

The line through $(2,1,-1)$ parallel to this normal vector is the normal line and has the parametric equations

$$x = 2 + 3t, \quad y = 1 + 10t, \quad z = -1 - 14t.$$

(27)   For $V = \frac{1}{3}\pi h(R^2 + Rr + r^2)$ we have

$$V_h = \frac{1}{3}\pi (R^2 + Rr + R^2)$$

$$V_R = \frac{2}{3}\pi hR + \frac{1}{3}\pi hr$$

$$V_r = \frac{1}{3}\pi hR + \frac{2}{3}\pi hr,$$

and at $h = 3$, $R = 10$, $r = 5$, these derivatives are

$$V_h = \frac{1}{3}\pi (10^2 + 10(5) + 5^2) = \frac{175\pi}{3}$$

$$V_R = \frac{2}{3}\pi (3)(10) + \frac{1}{3}\pi (3)(5) = 25\pi$$

$$V_r = \frac{1}{3}\pi (3)(10) + \frac{2}{3}\pi (3)(5) = 20\pi ,$$

so the total differential of V at that point is $dV = V_h dh + V_R dR + V_r dr$ or

(*) $dV = \frac{175\pi}{3} dh + 25\pi dR + 20\pi dr$

For $|dh| \le 0.01$, $|dR| \le 0.03$, and $|dr| \le 0.03$, we obtain

$$|dV| \le \frac{175\pi}{3}(0.01) + 25\pi(0.03) + 20\pi(0.03)$$

$$= \frac{\pi}{300}[175 + (3)(25)(3) + (3)(20)(3)] = \frac{580}{300}\pi \approx 6.07$$

Therefore, the maximum possible error in computing the volume is approximately 6.07 cubic inches.

(43)   Since $P(t) = f(t, t^2, t^3)$ for the differentiable function $f(x,y,z)$, we have

$$P'(t) = \frac{d}{dt} f(t, t^2, t^3) = f_x(t, t^2, t^3) \frac{d}{dt}(t) + f_y(t, t^2, t^3) \frac{d}{dt}(t^2) + f_z(t, t^2, t^3) \frac{d}{dt}(t^3)$$

$$= f_x(t, t^2, t^3) + 2t f_y(t, t^2, t^3) + 3t^2 f_z(t, t^2, t^3). \text{ Consequently, } P(2) = f(2, 2^2, 2^3)$$

$$= f(2,4,8) = 3 \text{ and } P'(2) = f_x(2,4,8) + 2(2)f_y(2,4,8) + 3(2^2)f_z(2,4,8)$$

$$= (4) + 4(5) + 12(-6) = 4 + 20 - 72 = -48.$$

(49) By the product rule, $f_x = [\frac{\partial}{\partial x}(xyz)] \sin(x + y + z) + (xyz)\frac{\partial}{\partial x} \sin(x + y + z)$

$= yz \sin(x + y + z) + xyz \cos(x + y + z)\frac{\partial}{\partial x}(x + y + z) = yz \sin(x + y + z) + xyz \cos(x+y+z)$.

Similarly, $f_y = xz \sin(x + y + z) + xyz \cos(x + y + z)$ and $f_z = xy \sin(x + y + z)$

$+ xyz \cos(x + y + z)$. Therefore $df = [yz \sin(x + y + z) + xyz \cos(x + y + z)]dx$

$+ [xz \sin(x + y + z) + xyz \cos(x + y + z)]dy + [xy \sin(x + y + z) + xyz \cos(x + y + z)]dz$.

SECTION 14.1

(1)   The derivatives $\frac{\partial}{\partial x}(x^2 - xy + y) = 2x - y$ and $\frac{\partial}{\partial y}(x^2 - xy + y) = -x + 1$ are
both zero for x and y that satisfy the simultaneous equations

$$\begin{cases} 2x - y = 0 \\ -x + 1 = 0. \end{cases}$$

The second equation gives $x = 1$ and then the first gives $y = 2$. The one critical point
of $x^2 - xy + y$ is (1,2).

(6) $\frac{\partial}{\partial x}(3xy^2 + x^3 - 3x) = 3y^2 + 3x^2 - 3 = 3(y^2 + x^2 - 1)$

$\frac{\partial}{\partial y}(3xy^2 + x^3 - 3x) = 6xy$.

The critical points of $3xy^2 + x^3 - 3x$ are given by the simultaneous equations

$$\begin{cases} y^2 + x^2 - 1 = 0 \\ 6xy = 0. \end{cases}$$

The second equation shows that either x or y or both must be zero. For $x = 0$ the
first equation gives $y^2 = 1$ or $y = \pm 1$. For $y = 0$ the first equation gives $x^2 = 1$
or $x = \pm 1$. The critical points are (0,1), (0,-1), (1,0), and (-1,0).

(9) $\frac{\partial}{\partial x}(x^3 + y^4 - 36y^2 - 12x) = 3x^2 - 12 = 3(x^2 - 4)$

$\frac{\partial}{\partial y}(x^3 + y^4 - 36y^2 - 12x) = 4y^3 - 72y = 4y(y^2 - 18)$

The critical points of $x^3 + y^4 - 36y^2 - 12x$ are given by the simultaneous equations

$$\begin{cases} x^2 - 4 = 0 \\ y(y^2 - 18) = 0. \end{cases}$$

The first equation is satisfied by taking $x = 2$ or $x = -2$. The second is satisfied by taking $y = 0$, $y = 3\sqrt{2}$, or $y = -3\sqrt{2}$. There are six critical points: $(2,0)$, $(2,3\ 2)$, $(2,-3\ 2)$, $(-2,0)$, $(-2,3\ 2)$, and $(-2,-3\ 2)$.

(12) By the product rule,

$$\frac{\partial}{\partial x}(xye^{2x+3y}) = (\frac{\partial}{\partial x}x)(ye^{2x+3y}) + xy(\frac{\partial}{\partial x}e^{2x+3y}) = (y + 2xy)e^{2x+3y} = y(1 + 2x)e^{2x+3y}$$

$$\frac{\partial}{\partial y}(xy\ e^{2x+3y}) = x(\frac{\partial}{\partial y}y)(e^{2x+3y}) + xy(\frac{\partial}{\partial y}e^{2x+3y}) = (x + 3xy)e^{2x+3y} = x(1 + 3y)e^{2x+3y}$$

The exponential function e^{2x+3y} is never zero, so the critical points of xye^{2x+3y} are given by the simultaneous equations

$$\begin{cases} y(1 + 2x) = 0 \\ x(1 + 3y) = 0. \end{cases}$$

The first equation is satisfied by taking either $y = 0$ or $x = -\frac{1}{2}$. For $y = 0$, the second equation reads $x(1) = 0$ and shows that $x = 0$. For $x = -\frac{1}{2}$, the second equation reads $-\frac{1}{2}(1 + 3y) = 0$ and shows that $y = -\frac{1}{3}$. The critical points are $(0,0)$ and $(-\frac{1}{2},-\frac{1}{3})$.

(18) We find the values of x and y where the square of the distance from $(x,y,\frac{1}{xy})$ on the surface to the origin is a minimum. The square of the distance is

$$f(x,y) = (x - 0)^2 + (y - 0)^2 + (\frac{1}{xy} - 0)^2 = x^2 + y^2 + x^{-2}y^{-2}.$$

The first derivatives of $f(x,y)$ are

$$f_x(x,y) = 2x - 2x^{-3}y^{-2} = \frac{2}{x^3}(x^4 - \frac{1}{y^2})$$

$$f_y(x,y) = 2y - 2x^{-3}y^{-2} = \frac{2}{y^3}(y^4 - \frac{1}{x^2})$$

At a critical point of $f(x,y)$ we have $f_x(x,y) = 0$ and $f_y(x,y) = 0$ so that

$$x^4 = \frac{1}{y^2} \qquad \text{and} \qquad y^4 = \frac{1}{x^2} .$$

The second equation gives $x^2 = \frac{1}{y^4}$ and hence $x^4 = \frac{1}{y^8}$ and with this substitution the first equation yields $\frac{1}{y^8} = \frac{1}{y^2}$. Consequently $y^2 = y^8$ and since $y \neq 0$, we have $y^6 = 1$ which means that $y = \pm 1$. From the equation $x^2 = \frac{1}{y^4}$ we find that $x^2 = 1$, which means that $x = \pm 1$. The four critical points of f are $(1,1)$, $(1,-1)$, $(-1,1)$, and $(-1,-1)$ and at each of these points f has the value $1^2 + 1^2 + 1^2 = 3$. The corresponding points on the surface $z = 1/(xy)$ are $(1,1,1)$, $(1,-1,-1)$, $(-1,1,-1)$,   and $(-1,-1,1)$.

(30)   We solve the equation $x + 2y + z = 17$ for $z = 17 - x - 2y$ and substitute the result in the expression $2x^2 + 3y^2 + z^2$ to be minimized.   This yields a function $f(x,y) = 2x^2 + 3y^2 + (17 - x - 2y)^2$ whose minimum we want to find. The   derivatives are

$$f_x = 4x + 2(17 - x - 2y)\frac{\partial}{\partial x}(17 - x - 2y) = 4x + 2(17 - x - 2y)(-1)$$

$$= 4x - 34 + 2x + 4y = 6x + 4y - 34$$

$$f_y = 6y + 2(17 - x - 2y)\frac{\partial}{\partial y}(17 - x - 2y) = 6y + 2(17 - x - 2y)(-2)$$

$$= 6y - 68 + 4x + 8y = 4x + 14y - 68.$$

The critical points of $f(x,y)$ are given by the equations

$$\begin{cases} 6x + 4y - 34 = 0 \\ 4x + 14y - 68 = 0. \end{cases}$$

We multiply both sides of the second equation by $\frac{3}{2}$ to obtain the equivalent equations

$$\begin{cases} 6x + 4y = 34 \\ 6x + 21y = 102. \end{cases}$$

Then, subtracting the first equation from the second shows that $17y = 68$ and hence $y = 4$. With this value of y, the first equation gives $6x + 16 = 34$ to show   that $6x = 18$ and $x = 3$. The value of $f(x,y)$ at $(3,4)$ is

$$f(3,4) = 2(3)^2 + 3(4)^2 + (17 - 3 - 2(4))^2 = 18 + 48 + 36 = 102.$$

(This value of $2x^2 + 3y^2 + z^2$ occurs at the point $(3,4,6)$ on the plane $x + 2y + z = 17$.)

(32)   The horizontal cross sections of the surface $z = x^2 + xy + y^2 + 3x - 9y$ are given by the equations $x^2 + xy + y^2 + 3x - 9y = c$, $z = c$ and are ellipses because the discrimininant $B^2 - 4AC = 1^2 - 4(1)(1) = -3$ is   negative. The paraboloid opens upward, rather than downward, because for $y = 0$ the   z-coordinate $z = x^2 + 3x$ of a point on the surface tends to ∞ as x tends to $\pm\infty$.

To find the minimum value of $x^2 + xy + y^2 + 3x - 9y$ we locate its critical point:

$$\frac{\partial}{\partial x}(x^2 + xy + y^2 + 3x - 9y) = 2x + y + 3$$

$$\frac{\partial}{\partial y}(x^2 + xy + y^2 + 3x - 9y) = x + 2y - 9.$$

The critical point is given by the simultaneous equations

$$\begin{cases} 2x + y = -3 \\ x + 2y = 9. \end{cases}$$

We multiply both sides of the second equation by 2 to obtain

$$\begin{cases} 2x + y = -3 \\ 2x + 4y = 18. \end{cases}$$

Then subtracting the first equation from the second yields $3y = 21$ to show that $y = 7$. The first equation then gives $2x + 7 = -3$, which implies that $2x = -10$ and $x = -5$. The one critical point of $x^2 + xy + y^2 + 3x - 9y$ is $(-5,7)$ where the function has the value

$$(-5)^2 + (-5)(7) + (7)^2 + 3(-5) - 9(7) = 25 - 35 + 49 - 15 - 63 = -39.$$

SECTION 14.2

(1b) We set $f(x,y) = \frac{3}{2}x - \frac{1}{2}x^3 - xy^2 + \frac{1}{16}$. Then

$$f_x = \frac{\partial}{\partial x}(\frac{3}{2}x - \frac{1}{2}x^3 - xy^2 + \frac{1}{16}) = \frac{3}{2} - \frac{3}{2}x^2 - y^2$$

$$f_y = \frac{\partial}{\partial y}(\frac{3}{2}x - \frac{1}{2}x^3 - xy^2 + \frac{1}{16}) = -2xy$$

so the critical points are given by the equations

$$\begin{cases} \frac{3}{2} - \frac{3}{2}x^2 - y^2 = 0 \\ -2xy = 0. \end{cases}$$

surface $z = \frac{1}{xy}$ are $(1,1,1)$, $(1,-1,-1)$, $(-1,1,-1)$, and $(-1,-1,1)$. Each of these points are a distance of $\sqrt{3}$ from the origin, which is the minimum of that distance for all points on the surface.

(30) To find the minimum of $2x^2 + 3y^2 + z^2$ subject to the condition $x + 2y + z = 17$, we can solve for $z = 17 - x - 2y$ in the equation and make that substitution in the expression we are to minimize. This reduces the problem to that of finding the minimum of

$$f(x,y) = 2x^2 + 3y^2 + (17 - x - 2y)^2$$

for all (x,y). The first order derivatives of $f(x,y)$ are

$$f_x = 4x + 2(17 - x - 2y)\frac{\partial}{\partial x}(17 - x - 2y) = 4x + 2(17 - x - 2y)(-1)$$

To satisfy the second equation we must take $x = 0$ or $y = 0$. For $x = 0$ the first equation reads $\frac{3}{2} - y^2 = 0$ and shows that $y = \pm\sqrt{\frac{3}{2}}$. For $y = 0$ the first equation reads $\frac{3}{2} - \frac{3}{2} x^2 = 0$ and shows that $x = \pm 1$. The critical points are $(0,\sqrt{\frac{3}{2}})$, $(0,-\sqrt{\frac{3}{2}})$, $(1,0)$, and $(-1,0)$. We have

$$f_{xx} = \frac{\partial}{\partial x} f_x = \frac{\partial}{\partial x}(\frac{3}{2} - \frac{3}{2} x^2 - y^2) = -3x$$

$$f_{xy} = \frac{\partial}{\partial y} f_x = \frac{\partial}{\partial y}(\frac{3}{2} - \frac{3}{2} x^2 - y^2) = -2y$$

$$f_{yx} = \frac{\partial}{\partial x} f_y = \frac{\partial}{\partial x}(-2xy) = -2y$$

$$f_{yy} = \frac{\partial}{\partial y} f_y = \frac{\partial}{\partial y}(-2xy) = -2x.$$

(Of course, f_{xy} and f_{yx} are equal. We found them both to check our calculations.)

We make the following table to employ the second derivative test.

Critical point	$A = f_{xx} = -3x$	$B = f_{xy} = -2y$	$C = f_{yy} = -2x$	$B^2 - AC$	Type of critical point
$(0,\sqrt{\frac{3}{2}})$	0	$-2\sqrt{\frac{3}{2}}$	0	6	Saddle point
$(0,-\sqrt{\frac{3}{2}})$	0	$2\sqrt{\frac{3}{2}}$	0	6	Saddle point
$(1,0)$	-3	0	-3	-9	Local maximum
$(-1,0)$	3	0	3	-9	Local minimum

The surface which shows two saddle points, one local maximum, and one local minimum oriented as indicated in the table above is the surface in Figure 14.20 in the text.

(2b) The level curves in Figure 14.24 in the text show one saddle point on the positive y-axis and one on the negative y-axis, a local maximum or local minimum on the positive x-axis, and a local maximum or local minimum on the negative x-axis. These are level curves of $\frac{3}{2} x - \frac{1}{2} x^3 - xy^2 + \frac{1}{16}$.

(3) For $f(x,y) = x \sin y$, we have $f_x = \sin y$ and $f_y = x \cos y$. The critical points are given by the equations

$$\begin{cases} \sin y = 0 \\ x \cos y = 0. \end{cases}$$

The first equation is satisfied for $y = n\pi$ with integers n, and for these values of y, $\cos y$ is not zero, so the second equation gives $x = 0$. The critical points are $(0, n\pi)$ with integers n. The second derivatives are $f_{xx} = \frac{\partial}{\partial x} \sin y = 0$, $f_{xy} = \frac{\partial}{\partial y} \sin y = \cos y$, and $f_{yy} = \frac{\partial}{\partial y}(x \cos y) = x \sin y$. At the critical point $(0, n\pi)$, we have $f_{xx} = 0$, $f_{xy} = \cos(n\pi) = (-1)^n$, and $f_{yy} = 0$, so that $B^2 - AC = (f_{xy})^2 - f_{xx}f_{yy} = [(-1)^n]^2 - (0)(0) = 1$ and each critical point is a saddle point.

(9) For $f(x,y) = 4x^3 + y^2 - 12x^2 - 36x$ we have $f_x = 12x^2 - 24x - 36$ and $f_y = 2y$. so the critical points are given by the equations

$$\begin{cases} 12x^2 - 24x - 36 = 0 \\ \qquad\qquad 2y = 0. \end{cases}$$

The second equation gives $y = 0$ and the first gives $x^2 - 2x - 3 = 0$, which shows that

$$x = \frac{-(-2) \pm \sqrt{(-2)^2 - 4(1)(-3)}}{2(1)} = \frac{2 \pm \sqrt{16}}{2} = -1 \text{ or } 3.$$

The critical points are $(-1,0)$ and $(3,0)$.

The second derivatives are $f_{xx} = \frac{\partial}{\partial x}(12x^2 - 24x - 36) = 24x - 24$, $f_{xy} = \frac{\partial}{\partial y}(12x^2 - 24x - 36) = 0$, and $f_{yy} = \frac{\partial}{\partial y}(2y) = 2$. We make the following table.

Critical point	$A = f_{xx} = 24x - 24$	$B = f_{xy} = 0$	$C = f_{yy} = 2$	$B^2 - AC$	Type of critical point
$(-1,0)$	-48	0	2	384	Saddle point
$(3,0)$	48	0	2	-384	Local minimum

(10) For $f(x,y) = 4x^2 y + 3xy^2 - 12xy$ we have $f_x = 8xy + 3y^2 - 12y = y(8x + 3y - 12)$ and $f_y = 4x^2 + 6xy - 12x = x(4x + 6y - 12)$. Hence the critical points are given by the simultaneous equations

$$\begin{cases} y(8x + 3y - 12) = 0 \\ x(4x + 6y - 12) = 0. \end{cases}$$

To satisfy the first equation, we must take $y = 0$ or $8x + 3y - 12 = 0$. If $y = 0$, then the second equation reads $x(4x - 12) = 0$, which shows that $x = 0$ or $x = 3$. The points

(0,0) and (3,0) are critical points. If $8x + 3y - 12 = 0$, then $3y = 12 - 8x$ and consequently

(*) $y = \frac{1}{3}(12 - 8x).$

In this case the second of the simultaneous equations becomes $x[4x + 2(12 - 8x) - 12] = 0$, which simplifies to

(**) $x(12 - 12x) = 0.$

The solutions of equation (**) are $x = 0$ and $x = 1$. With $x = 0$, equation (*) gives $y = 4$ and with $x = 1$ it gives $y = \frac{4}{3}$. The points (0,4) and $(1,\frac{4}{3})$ are also critical points.

The second derivatives are

$$f_{xx} = \frac{\partial}{\partial x}(8xy + 3y^2 - 12y) = 8y$$

$$f_{xy} = \frac{\partial}{\partial y}(8xy + 3y^2 - 12y) = 6y - 12$$

$$f_{yy} = \frac{\partial}{\partial y}(4x^2 + 6xy - 12x) = 6x.$$

To classify the critical points, we make the following table.

Critical point	$A = f_{xx} = 8y$	$B = f_{xy} = 6y - 12$	$C = f_{yy} = 6x$	$B^2 - AC$	Type of critical point
(0,0)	0	-12	0	144	Saddle point
(3,0)	0	-12	18	144	Saddle point
(0,4)	32	12	0	144	Saddle point
$(1,\frac{4}{3})$	$\frac{32}{3}$	-4	6	-48	Local minimum

(11) Set $f(x,y) = (x + 1)(y + 1)(x + y + 1)$. Then

$$f_x = [\frac{\partial}{\partial x}(x + 1)](y + 1)(x + y + 1) + (x + 1)(y + 1)[\frac{\partial}{\partial x}(x + y + 1)]$$

$$= (y + 1)(x + y + 1) + (x + 1)(y + 1) = (y + 1)(x + y + 1 + x + 1)$$

$$= (y + 1)(2x + y + 2)$$

$$f_y = (x + 1)[\frac{\partial}{\partial y}(y + 1)](x + y + 1) + (x + 1)(y + 1)[\frac{\partial}{\partial y}(x + y + 1)]$$

$$= (x + 1)(x + y + 1) + (x + 1)(y + 1) = (x + 1)(x + y + 1 + y + 1)$$

$$= (x + 1)(x + 2y + 2)$$

so the critical points are given by the simultaneous equations

$$(y + 1)(2x + y + 2) = 0$$

$$(x + 1)(x + 2y + 2) = 0.$$

To satisfy the first equation, we must have $y = -1$ or $2x + y + 2 = 0$. If $y = -1$, the second equation reads $(x + 1)(x) = 0$ and has the solutions $x = -1$ and $x = 0$. The points $(0,-1)$ and $(-1,-1)$ are critical points. If $2x + y + 2 = 0$, then

(*) $$y = -2 - 2x$$

and the second of the simultaneous equations reads $(x + 1)[x + 2(-2 - 2x) + 2] = 0$, which we write as

$$(x + 1)(-3x - 2) = 0$$

to see that it has the solutions $x = -1$ and $x = -\frac{2}{3}$. For $x = -1$, equation (*) gives $y = -2 - 2(-1) = -2 + 2 = 0$, so $(-1,0)$ is a critical point. For $x = -\frac{2}{3}$, equation (*) gives $y = -2 - 2(-\frac{2}{3}) = -2 + \frac{4}{3} = -\frac{2}{3}$, so $(-\frac{2}{3}, -\frac{2}{3})$ is also a critical point.

Next, we compute the second derivatives:

$$f_{xx} = \frac{\partial}{\partial x}[(y + 1)(2x + y + 2)] = (y + 1)(2) = 2y + 2$$

$$f_{xy} = \frac{\partial}{\partial y}[(y + 1)(2x + y + 2)] = [\frac{\partial}{\partial y}(y + 1)](2x + y + 2) + (y + 1)[\frac{\partial}{\partial y}(2x + y + 2)]$$

$$= (1)(2x + y + 2) + (y + 1)(1) = 2x + 2y + 3$$

$$f_{yy} = \frac{\partial}{\partial y}[(x + 1)(x + 2y + 2)] = (x + 1)(2) = 2x + 2$$

To classify the critical points, we make the following table.

Critical point	$A = f_{xx} = 2y + 2$	$B = f_{xy} = 2x + 2y + 3$	$C = f_{yy} = 2x + 2$	$B^2 - AC$	Type of critical point
$(0,-1)$	0	1	2	1	Saddle point
$(-1,-1)$	0	-1	0	1	Saddle point
$(-1,0)$	2	1	0	1	Saddle point
$(-\frac{2}{3}, -\frac{2}{3})$	$\frac{2}{3}$	$\frac{1}{3}$	$\frac{2}{3}$	$-\frac{1}{3}$	Local minimum

(17)   We set $f = \cos x \sinh(y^2)$. Then $f_x = [\frac{\partial}{\partial x} \cos x] \sinh(y^2) = - \sin x \sinh(y^2)$ and

$f_y = \cos x \frac{\partial}{\partial y} \sinh(y^2) = \cos x \cosh(y^2) \frac{\partial}{\partial y}(y^2) = 2y \cos x \cosh(y^2)$. Because $\sinh(y^2)$ is

zero only at $y = 0$, the x-derivative is zero if $x = n\pi$ with n an integer or if

$y = 0$. Because $\cosh(y^2)$ is never zero, the y-derivative is zero if $x = (n + \frac{1}{2})\pi$ or

if $y = 0$. Hence the critical points (where f_x and f_y are both zero) consist of the

entire x-axis, $y = 0$.

The second derivatives are $f_{xx} = - \cos x \sinh(y^2)$, $f_{xy} = -2y \sin x \cosh(y^2)$, and

$f_{yy} = 2 \cos x \cosh(y^2) + 4y^2 \cos x \sinh(y^2)$. At the critical points $(y = 0)$ the second

derivatives are $f_{xx} = 0$, $f_{xy} = 0$ and $f_{yy} = 2$, so that $f_{xy}^2 - f_{xx}f_{yy} = 0^2 - (0)(2) = 0$

and the second derivative test fails.

SECTION 14.3

(2) $\overrightarrow{grad}(3x - y + 1) = \langle \frac{\partial}{\partial x}(3x - y + 1), \frac{\partial}{\partial y}(3x - y + 1) \rangle = \langle 3,-1 \rangle$

$\overrightarrow{grad}(3x^2 + y^2) = \langle \frac{\partial}{\partial x}(3x^2 + y^2), \frac{\partial}{\partial y}(3x^2 + y^2) \rangle = \langle 6x, 2y \rangle$

By Theorem 14.3 with $f(x,y) = 3x - y + 1$ and $g(x,y) = 3x^2 + y^2$ the maximum and minimum

values of $3x - y + 1$ for $3x^2 + y^2 = 16$ occur at points (x,y) such that

$\overrightarrow{grad}(3x - y + 1) = \lambda\ \overrightarrow{grad}(3x^2 + y^2)$ for some numbers λ . This gives the vector equation

$$\langle 3,-1 \rangle = \lambda \langle 6x, 2y \rangle$$

which is equivalent to the simultaneous equations

$$\begin{cases} 3 = 6\lambda x \\ -1 = 2\lambda y \end{cases}$$

which give

(*) $x = \dfrac{1}{2\lambda}$ and $y = -\dfrac{1}{2\lambda}$.

   Because the point (x,y) must lie on the constraint **curve**, x and y must satisfy

its equation $3x^2 + y^2 = 16$. With equations (*) this yields the equation

$$3(\tfrac{1}{2\lambda})^2 + (-\tfrac{1}{2\lambda})^2 = 16$$

which simplifies to $\dfrac{1}{\lambda^2} = 16$ and shows that $\lambda = \pm\tfrac{1}{4}$. With $\lambda = \tfrac{1}{4}$, equations (*) give

$x = 2, y = -2,$ and with $\lambda = -\tfrac{1}{4},$they give $x = -2, y = 2.$ The maximum and minimum of

$3x - y + 1$ for $3x^2 + y^2 = 16$ occur at $(2,-2)$ or $(-2,2)$. At $(2,-2)$the function

$3x - y + 1$ has the value $3(2) - (-2) + 1 = 9$, and at $(-2,2)$ it has the value

$3(-2) - 2 + 1 = -7$. The maximum is 9 and occurs at $(2,-2)$; the minimum is -7 and occurs

at $(-2,2)$.

(5) By Theorem 14.4 the maximum and minimum of $x + 5z$ for $2x^2 + 3y^2 + 5z^2 = 198$ occur

at points where $\overrightarrow{grad}(x + 5z) = \lambda\ \overrightarrow{grad}(2x^2 + 3y^2 + 5z^2)$ for some numbers λ . Computing

the gradients gives the **vector** equation

$$\langle 1,0,5 \rangle = \lambda \langle 4x, 6y, 10z \rangle .$$

The equivalent system of equations

(*) $\begin{cases} 1 = 4\lambda x \\ 0 = 6\lambda y \\ 5 = 10\lambda z \end{cases}$

has the solutions

(**) $x = \dfrac{1}{4\lambda}$, $y = 0$, $z = \dfrac{1}{2\lambda}$.

(We conclude that $y = 0$ because λ cannot be zero if the first and third equations in (*) are satisfied.) We make substitutions (**) in the equation $2x^2 + 3y^2 + 5z^2 = 198$ for the constraint surface to obtain

$$2(\tfrac{1}{4\lambda})^2 + 3(0)^2 + 5(\tfrac{1}{2\lambda})^2 = 198$$

which simplifies to $\dfrac{11}{8\lambda^2} = 198$ and shows that $\lambda = \pm\dfrac{1}{12}$. Equations (**) give the point $(3,0,6)$ for $\lambda = \dfrac{1}{12}$ and the point $(-3,0,-6)$ for $\lambda = -\dfrac{1}{12}$. The value of $x + 5z$ at $(3,0,6)$ is 33 and the value at $(-3,0-6)$ is -33. The maximum is 33 and occurs at $(3,0,6)$; the minimum is -33 and occurs at $(-3,0,-6)$.

(7) The maximum and minimum of xyz for $6x^2 + 5y^2 + 4z^2 = 90$ occurs at points (x,y,z) where $\overrightarrow{\text{grad}}(xyz) = \lambda\ \overrightarrow{\text{grad}}(6x^2 + 5y^2 + 4z^2)$ for some numbers λ . With the gradients computed, this equation reads

$$\langle yz, xz, xy \rangle = \lambda \langle 12x, 10y, 8z \rangle$$

and is equivalent to the simultaneous equations

$$\begin{cases} yz = 12\lambda x \\ xz = 10\lambda y \\ xy = 8\lambda z. \end{cases}$$

If λ is 0, these equations show that two of the three variables x, y, and z must be zero, and at such points the function xyz is 0.

If λ is not zero, we multiply the first equation by x, the second by y, and the third by z to obtain xyz on the left side of each equation. This leads to the two equations

$$12\lambda x^2 = 10\lambda y^2 = 8\lambda z^2.$$

Dividing all three expressions by 2λ shows that $6x^2$, $5y^2$, and $4z^2$ are all equal to the same number k. The constraint equation $6x^2 + 5y^2 + 4z^2 = 90$ shows that the number k is 30, so that $6x^2 = 30$, $5y^2 = 30$, and $4z^2 = 30$. Therefore

(*) $x = \pm\sqrt{5}$, $y = \pm\sqrt{6}$, and $z = \pm\sqrt{\dfrac{15}{2}}$.

For these values of x, y, and z, we have $xyz = \pm\ (\sqrt{5})(\sqrt{6})(\sqrt{\tfrac{15}{2}}) = \pm 15$. The maximum is 15 and occurs at $(\sqrt{5},\sqrt{6},\sqrt{\frac{15}{2}})$, $(\sqrt{5},-\sqrt{6},-\sqrt{\frac{15}{2}})$, $(-\sqrt{5},-\sqrt{6},\sqrt{\frac{15}{2}})$, and $(-\sqrt{5},\sqrt{6},-\sqrt{\frac{15}{2}})$.

The minimum is -15 and occurs at $(-\sqrt{5},-\sqrt{6},-\sqrt{\frac{15}{2}})$, $(-\sqrt{5},\sqrt{6},\sqrt{\frac{15}{2}})$, $(\sqrt{5},\sqrt{6},\sqrt{\frac{15}{2}})$, and $(\sqrt{5},-\sqrt{6},-\sqrt{\frac{15}{2}})$.

(10) The maximum and minimum of $x^2 + y^2$ for $x^2 + 2x + y^2 - 4y$ occurs at points (x,y) where $\overrightarrow{grad}(x^2 + y^2) = \lambda\,\overrightarrow{grad}(x^2 + 2x + y^2 - 4y)$ for some numbers λ. This gives

the vector equation $\langle 2x, 2y\rangle = \lambda \langle 2x + 2, 2y - 4\rangle$ which is equivalent to the simultaneous equations $2x = \lambda(2x + 2)$ and $2y = \lambda(2y - 4)$. We divide each equation by 2 to obtain

$$\begin{cases} x = \lambda x + \lambda \\ y = \lambda y - 2\lambda. \end{cases}$$

We solve the first equation for x and the second for y :

(*) $$x = \frac{\lambda}{1 - \lambda}, \qquad y = \frac{-2\lambda}{1 - \lambda}$$

To determine the possible values of λ we substitute formulas (*) into the equation $x^2 + 2x + y^2 - 4y = 0$:

$$(\frac{\lambda}{1 - \lambda})^2 + 2(\frac{\lambda}{1 - \lambda}) + (\frac{-2\lambda}{1 - \lambda})^2 - 4(\frac{-2\lambda}{1 - \lambda}) = 0.$$

Multiplying both sides of the equation by $(1 - \lambda)^2$ yields

$$\lambda^2 + 2\lambda(1 - \lambda) + 4\lambda^2 - 4(-2\lambda)(1 - \lambda) = 0$$

or

$$-5\lambda^2 + 10\lambda = 0$$

and this equation has the solutions $\lambda = 0$ and $\lambda = 2$. For $\lambda = 0$, equations (*) give $x = 0$ and $y = 0$; for $\lambda = 2$ they give $x = -2$, $y = 4$. At $(0,0)$ the function $x^2 + y^2$ has the value 0; at $(-2,4)$ its value is 20. The minimum of $x^2 + y^2$ for $x^2 + 2x + y^2 - 4y = 0$ is 0 and occurs at $(0,0)$. The maximum is 20 and occurs at $(-2,4)$.

(13) The maximum and minimum values of $x^2 + 2x + y^2$ for $x^2 + y^2 \le 4$ may occur inside the circle (where $x^2 + y^2 < 4$) or on its circumference (where $x^2 + y^2 = 4$). We apply the first derivative test to the points inside the circle and Lagrange multipliers to its circumference. Because $\frac{\partial}{\partial x}(x^2 + 2x + y^2) = 2x + 2$ and $\frac{\partial}{\partial y}(x^2 + 2x + y^2) = 2y$, the one critical point of $x^2 + 2x + y^2$ is $(-1,0)$ where the function has the value $(-1)^2 + 2(-1) + 0^2 = -1$.

To find the points on the circumference where the maximum or minimum might occur

we use the equation $\overrightarrow{grad}(x^2 + 2x + y^2) = \lambda\ \overrightarrow{grad}(x^2 + y^2)$, which reads

$\langle 2x + 2, 2y\rangle = \lambda\langle 2x, 2y\rangle$ and is equivalent to the simultaneous equations

(*)
$$2x + 2 = 2\lambda x$$
$$2y = 2\lambda y$$

The second equation shows that either $y = 0$ or $\lambda = 1$.   If $y = 0$, then the equation

$x^2 + y^2 = 4$ shows that $x = \pm\,2$. The Lagrange multiplier cannot be   1, because in this

case the first of equations (*) reads $2x + 2 = 2x$ and has no solutions. If the maximum

or minimum occurs on the circumference, it occurs at   (2,0)   or   (-2,0). The function

$x^2 + 2x + y^2$ has the value $2^2 + 2(2) + 0^2 = 8$ at   (2,0)   and the value

$(-2)^2 + 2(-2) + 0^2 = 0$ at   (-2,0). The maximum of $x^2 + 2x + y^2$ for $x^2 + y^2 \leq 4$ is

8   and occurs at the point   (2,0)   on the circumference of the circle; the minimum is

-1   and occurs at   (-1,0)   inside the circle.

SECTION 15.1

(2) The region bounded by the lines $y = x$, $y = 2x$, and $x = 1$ is the triangle shown in

Fig. 15.1.2. It extends from $x = 0$ on the left to $x = 1$ on the right and from the

line $y = x$ on the bottom to the line $y = 2x$ on the top. By Rule 15.1 the integral equals

$$\iint_R 3x^2y^2\ dx\ dy = \int_{x=0}^{x=1}\left\{\int_{y=x}^{y=2x} 3x^2y^2\ dy\right\}dx = \int_{x=0}^{x=1}[x^2y^3]_{y=x}^{y=2x}\ dx$$

$$= \int_{x=0}^{x=1}[x^2(2x)^3 - x^2(x)^3]\ dx = \int_0^1 (8x^5 - x^5)dx = \int_0^1 7x^5\ dx$$

$$= [\tfrac{7}{6}x^6]_0^1 = [\tfrac{7}{6}(1)^6] - [\tfrac{7}{6}(0)^6] = \tfrac{7}{6}$$

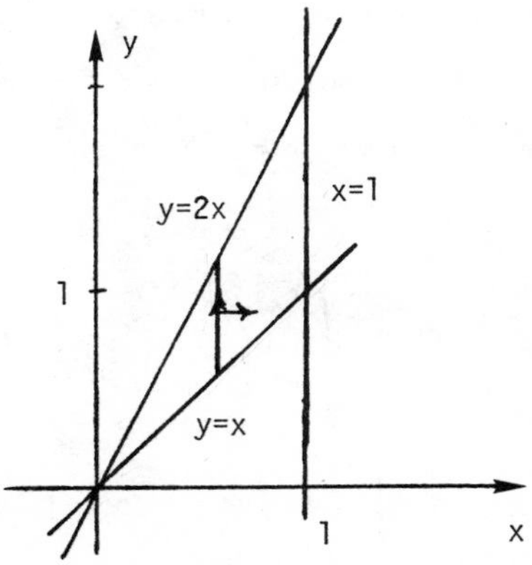

Fig. 15.1.2

(5) The parabolas $y = x^2$ and $y = -x^2$ intersect at the origin, so the region extends from $x = 0$ on the left to $x = 4$ on the right, and by Rule 15.1 the integral equals

$$\iint_R 3y^2 x^{1/2} \ dx \ dy = \int_{x=0}^{x=4} \int_{y=-x^2}^{y=x^2} 3y^2 x^{1/2} \ dy \quad dx \ = \ \int_{x=0}^{x=4} [y^3 x^{1/2}]_{y=-x^2}^{y=x^2} \quad dy$$

$$= \int_{x=0}^{x=4} [(x^2)^3 \ x^{1/2} - (-x^2)^3 \ x^{1/2}] dx = \int_0^4 2x^{13/2} \ dx \ = \ [\tfrac{2}{15/2} x^{15/2}]_0^4$$

$$= [\tfrac{4}{15} x^{15/2}]_0^4 \ = \ \tfrac{4}{15}(4)^{15/2} - \tfrac{4}{15}(0)^{15/2} \ = \ \tfrac{4}{15}(2)^{15} \ = \ \tfrac{1}{15} 2^{17},$$

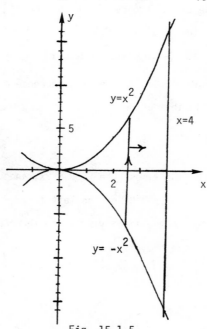

$y = x^2$

$x = 4$

5

2

$y = -x^2$

Fig. 15.1.5

(11) We integrate first with respect to y. The region extends from $y = 1$ on the bottom to $y = 4$ on the top. Solving $y = x^{-2}$ for x gives $x = \pm \ y^{-1/2}$, so the region is bounded on the left by the curve $x = - y^{-1/2}$ and on the right by $x = y^{1/2}$. By Rule 15.2 the integral equals

$$\iint_R \cos\!\sqrt{y} \ dx \ dy = \int_{y=1}^{y=4} \left\{ \int_{x=-y^{-1/2}}^{x=y^{-1/2}} \cos\!\sqrt{y} \ dx \right\} dy \ = \ \int_{y=1}^{y=4} [x \cos\!\sqrt{y} \ ]_{x=-y^{-1/2}}^{x=y^{-1/2}} dy$$

$$= \int_{y=1}^{y=4} [y^{-1/2} \cos\!\sqrt{y}] - [-y^{-1/2} \cos\!\sqrt{y}] \ dy \ = \ \int_1^4 2y^{-1/2} \cos\!\sqrt{y} \ dy.$$

To evaluate the indefinite integral, we make the substitution $u = y^{1/2}$, $du = \frac{1}{2} y^{-1/2} dy$.

$$\int 2y^{-1/2} \cos(\sqrt{y}) \, dy \;=\; 4 \int \cos(y^{1/2})(\tfrac{1}{2} y^{-1/2}) dy \;=\; 4 \int \cos u \, du = 4 \sin u \; + C$$
$$= 4 \sin(\sqrt{y}) + C$$

The double integral equals

$$\int_{1}^{4} 2y^{-1/2} \cos(\sqrt{y}) dy \;=\; \left[4 \sin(\sqrt{y}) \right]_{1}^{4} \;=\; 4 \sin(2) - 4 \sin(1)$$

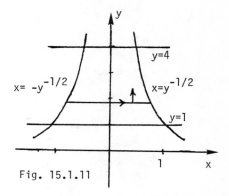

Fig. 15.1.11

(15) The region is shown in Fig. 15.1.15. To find the coordinates of the intersections of the line $x + y = 3$ with the hyperbola $y = \frac{2}{x}$ we solve the simultaneous equations

$$\begin{cases} x + y = 3 \\ \quad y = \frac{2}{x} . \end{cases}$$

We substitute the expression $y = \frac{2}{x}$ into the first equation to obtain $x + \frac{2}{x} = 3$ and then

$$x^2 - 3x + 2 = 0$$

which has the solutions

$$x = \frac{-(-3) \pm \sqrt{(-3)^2 - 4(1)(2)}}{2(1)} \;=\; \frac{3 \pm 1}{2} = 1 \text{ or } 2.$$

The line and the hyperbola intersect at $(1,2)$ and $(2,1)$. The region extends from $x = 1$ on the left to $x = 2$ on the right. The bottom is formed by the hyperbola $y = \frac{2}{x}$ and the top by the line, whose equation we write in the form $y = 3 - x$. By Rule 15.1 the integral equals

$$\iint_R x\ dx\ dy\ =\ \int_{x=1}^{x=2}\left\{\int_{y=\frac{2}{x}}^{y=3-x} x\ dy\right\}dx\ =\ \int_{x=1}^{x=2}[xy]_{y=2/x}^{y=3-x}\ dx$$

$$=\ \int_1^2\left\{[x(3-x)]-[x(\tfrac{2}{x})]\right\}dx\ =\ \int_1^2(3x-x^2-2)dx\ =\ [\tfrac{3}{2}x^2-\tfrac{1}{3}x^3-2x]_1^2$$

$$=\ [\tfrac{3}{2}(2)^2-\tfrac{1}{3}(2)^3-2(2)]-[\tfrac{3}{2}(1)^2-\tfrac{1}{3}(1)^3-2(1)]\ =\ [6-\tfrac{8}{3}-4]-[\tfrac{3}{2}-\tfrac{1}{3}-2]\ =\ \tfrac{1}{6}\ .$$

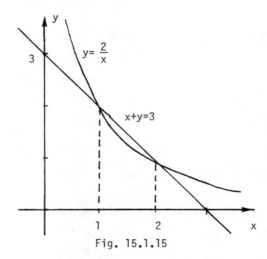

Fig. 15.1.15

(16) Because the region of integration is the rectangle $0 \le x \le 1$, $1 \le y \le 2$, the double integral may be expressed as an iterated integral in the following two ways.

$$\iint_R y^{-2}\ e^{x/\sqrt{y}}\ dx\ dy\ =\ \int_{x=0}^{x=1}\ \int_{y=1}^{y=2} y^{-2}\ e^{x/\sqrt{y}}\ dy\ dx\ =\ \int_{y=1}^{y=2}\ \int_{x=0}^{x=1} y^{-2}\ e^{x/\sqrt{y}}\ dx\ dy.$$

It is the second iterated integral that we can evaluate. It equals

$$\int_{y=1}^{y=2}\ [y^{-2}\ (\sqrt{y})e^{x/\sqrt{y}}]_{x=0}^{x=1}\ dy\ =\ \int_{y=1}^{y=2}\left\{[y^{-2}(\sqrt{y})e^{1/\sqrt{y}}]-[y^{-2}(\sqrt{y})e^0]\right\}dy$$

$$=\ \int_{y=1}^{y=2} y^{-3/2}(1-e^{1/\sqrt{y}})\ dy.$$

To evaluate the corresponding indefinite integral we make the substitution $u = \dfrac{1}{\sqrt{y}} = y^{-1/2}$, for which $du = -\tfrac{1}{2}\ y^{-3/2}\ dy$:

$$\int y^{-3/2}(1-e^{1/\sqrt{y}})dy\ =\ -2\int(1-e^{1/\sqrt{y}})(-\tfrac{1}{2}\ y^{-3/2}\ dy)\ =\ -2\int(1-e^u)du$$

$$=\ -2(u-e^u)+C\ =\ -2\ y^{-1/2}+2e^{1/\sqrt{y}}\ +\ C$$

The double integral equals

$$\int_1^2 y^{-3/2}(1 - e^{1/y})dy = [-2\, y^{-1/2} + 2e^{1/\sqrt{y}}]_1^2 = [-2(2)^{-1/2} + 2e^{1/\sqrt{2}}] - [-2(1)^{-1/2} + 2e^1]$$

$$= -\sqrt{2} + 2e^{1/\sqrt{2}} + 2 - 2e.$$

(22) In the iterated integral

(*) $$\int_{x=-1}^{x=1} \int_{y=-1}^{y=x^3} f(x,y)\ dy\ dx$$

x runs from -1 to 1 and for each x with $-1 \leq x \leq 1$, the variable y runs from
y = -1 to $y = x^3$. The region of integration is, therefore, the one shown in Fig. 15.1.22a.
To perform the x-integration first,we integrate with respect to x from $x = y^{1/3}$ to
x = 1 and then with respect to y from -1 to 1 (Fig. 15.1.22b). Accordingly, the
iterated integral (*) equals

$$\int_{y=-1}^{y=1} \int_{x= y^{1/3}}^{x=1} f(x,y)\ dx\ \ dy.$$

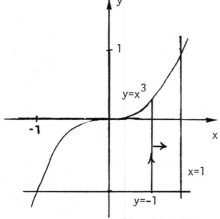

Fig. 15.1.22a

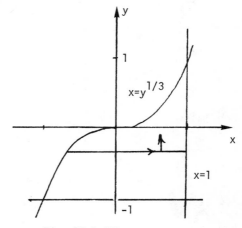

Fig. 15.1.22b

(30) In the integral

$$(*) \qquad \int_{y=0}^{y=1} \int_{x=y}^{x=2y} f(x,y) \; dx \; dy$$

the region of integration extends from $y = 0$ on the bottom to $y = 1$ on the top
and from the line $x = y$ on the left to $x = 2y$ on the right (Fig. 15.1.30a). Because
the top of the region is formed by the two lines $y = x$ and $y = 1$, we have to use two
integrals to perform the y-integration first. We integrate from $y = \frac{1}{2} x$ to $y = x$ for
$0 \le x \le 1$ and from $y = \frac{1}{2} x$ to $y = 1$ for $1 \le x \le 2$. (Fig. 15.1.30b). The integral $(*)$ equals

$$\int_{x=0}^{x=1} \int_{y=\frac{1}{2} x}^{y=x} f(x,y) \; dy \; dx \; + \; \int_{x=1}^{x=2} \int_{y=\frac{1}{2} x}^{y=1} f(x,y) \; dy \; dx.$$

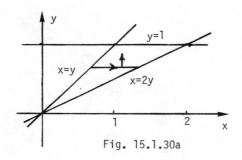

Fig. 15.1.30a

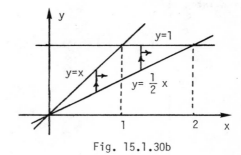

Fig. 15.1.30b

(34)
$$\iint_R (\sin x)(\sin y) \; dx \; dy = \left\{ \int_0^{\pi} \sin x \; dx \right\} \left\{ \int_0^{\pi} \sin y \; dy \right\} = \left[- \cos x \right]_0^{\pi} \; \left[-\cos y \right]_0^{\pi}$$

$$= \; [- \cos(\pi) + \cos(0)][- \cos(\pi) + \cos(0)] = [1 + 1][1 + 1] = 4$$

SECTION 15.2

(2) Because $(\sin x)(\sin y)$ lies between -1 and 1 for all x and y, the
top of the solid is formed by the surface $z = (\sin x)(\sin y)$ and the bottom by the
plane $z = -1$. By Rule 15.3 the volume is

$$\iint_R [(\sin x)(\sin y) - (-1)]\, dx\, dy = \int_{x=0}^{x=\pi} \int_{y=0}^{y=\pi} [(\sin x)(\sin y) + 1]\, dy\, dx$$

$$= \int_{x=0}^{x=\pi} [(\sin x)(-\cos y) + y]\Big|_{y=0}^{y=\pi}\, dx$$

$$= \int_0^\pi [(\sin x)(-\cos(\pi)) + \pi] - [(\sin x)(-\cos(0)) + 0]\, dx$$

$$= \int_0^\pi (2\sin x + \pi)\, dx = [-2\cos x + \pi x]\Big|_0^\pi$$

$$= [-2\cos(\pi) + \pi^2] - [-2\cos(0) + 0] = 4 + \pi^2.$$

Here   R   is the square $0 \le x \le \pi,\ 0 \le y \le \pi$.

(7)   The solid is bounded by the plane   z = 2x - y - 4   and by the coordinate planes.
The point on the plane   z = 2x - y - 4   at   x = 0, y = 0   has   z-coordinate   z = -4,
so that plane forms the bottom of the solid and the solid lies beneath the   xy-plane   which
forms its top. By Rule 15.3 the volume is

(*) $$\iint_R [0 - (2x - y - 4)]dx\, dy = \iint_R (4 + y - 2x)dx\, dy$$

where   R   is the projection of the solid on the   xy-plane (which in this case is the top
of the solid). The region   R   is a triangle formed by the   x-axis, the   y-axis, and the
intersection of the plane   z = 2x - y - 4   with the   xy-plane   (Fig. 15.2.7a). The   xy-plane
has the equation   z = 0, so the intersection is the graph of the line   0 = 2x - y - 4
in the   xy-plane. The line's equation may be written   y = 4 - 2x; the triangle   R   is
shown in Fig. 15.2.7b. The right corner of the triangle is at   x = 2   where the line
y = 4 - 2x   intersects the   x-axis. The volume (*) equals

$$\iint_R (4 + y - 2x)dx\, dy = \int_{x=0}^{x=2} \int_{y=0}^{y=4-2x} (4 + y - 2x)\, dy\, dx$$

$$= \int_{x=0}^{x=2} [4y + \tfrac{1}{2}y^2 - 2xy]\Big|_{y=0}^{y=4-2x}\, dx$$

$$= \int_0^2 \left\{ [4(4-2x) + \tfrac{1}{2}(4 - 2x)^2 - 2x(4 - 2x)] - [4(0) + \tfrac{1}{2}(0)^2 - 2x(0)] \right\} dx$$

$$= \int_0^2 (6x^2 - 24x + 24)dx = [2x^3 - 12x^2 + 24x]_0^2$$

$$= [2(2)^3 - 12(2)^2 + 24(2)] - [2(0)^3 - 12(0)^2 + 24(0)] = 16 - 48 + 48 = 16.$$

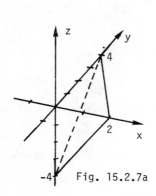

Fig. 15.2.7a

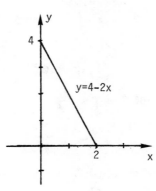

Fig. 15.2.7b

(12) By Rule 15.4 the weight of the plate is

$$\iint_R (x + y^2)dx\,dy \;=\; \int_{x=0}^{x=2} \int_{y=0}^{y=1} (x + y^2)dy\;dx \;=\; \int_{x=0}^{x=2} \left[xy + \tfrac{1}{3}y^3 \right]_{y=0}^{y=1} dx$$

$$= \int_0^2 \left\{ [x(1) + \tfrac{1}{3}(1)^3] - [x(0) + \tfrac{1}{3}(0)^3] \right\} dx \;=\; \int_0^2 (x + \tfrac{1}{3})dx$$

$$= \quad [\tfrac{1}{2}x^2 + \tfrac{1}{3}x]_0^2 = [\tfrac{1}{2}(2)^2 + \tfrac{1}{3}(2)] - [\tfrac{1}{2}(0)^2 - \tfrac{1}{3}(0)] = 2 + \tfrac{2}{3} = \tfrac{8}{3}.$$

Here R is the rectangle $0 \le x \le 2,\ 0 \le y \le 1$.

(15) By Rule 15.4 the moment of the plate about the y-axis is

$$\text{Moment about the y-axis} = \iint_R x(x + y^2)dx\,dy = \int_{x=0}^{x=2} \int_{y=0}^{y=1} (x^2 + xy^2)dy\ dx$$

$$= \int_{x=0}^{x=2} [x^2 y + \frac{1}{3} xy^3]_{y=0}^{y=1}\ dx = \int_0^2 \left\{ [x^2(1) + \frac{1}{3} x(1)^3] - [x^2(0) + \frac{1}{3} x(0)^3] \right\} dx$$

$$= \int_0^2 (x^2 + \frac{1}{3} x)dx = [\frac{1}{3} x^3 + \frac{1}{6} x^2]_0^2 = [\frac{1}{3}(2)^3 + \frac{1}{6}(2)^2] - [\frac{1}{3}(0)^3 + \frac{1}{6}(0)^2] = \frac{10}{3}.$$

The moment about the x-axis is

$$\text{Moment about the x-axis} = \iint_R y(x + y^2)dx\,dy = \int_{x=0}^{x=2} \int_{y=0}^{y=1} (xy + y^3)dy\ dx$$

$$= \int_{x=0}^{x=2} [\frac{1}{2} xy^2 + \frac{1}{4} y^4]_{y=0}^{y=1}\ dx = \int_0^2 \left\{ [\frac{1}{2} x(1)^2 + \frac{1}{4}(1)^4] - [\frac{1}{2} x(0)^2 + \frac{1}{4}(0)^4] \right\} dx$$

$$= \int_0^2 (\frac{1}{2} x + \frac{1}{4})dx = [\frac{1}{4} x^2 + \frac{1}{4} x]_0^2 = [\frac{1}{4}(2)^2 + \frac{1}{4}(2)] - [\frac{1}{4}(0)^2 + \frac{1}{4}(0)] = \frac{3}{2}.$$

The center of gravity is $(\overline{x}, \overline{y})$ where

$$\overline{x} = \frac{\text{Moment about the y-axis}}{\text{Weight}} = \frac{\frac{10}{3}}{\frac{8}{3}} = \frac{5}{4}$$

$$\overline{y} = \frac{\text{Moment about the x-axis}}{\text{Weight}} = \frac{\frac{3}{2}}{\frac{8}{3}} = \frac{9}{16}.$$

(20a) By Rule 15.5 the area is

(*)
$$\iint_D \sqrt{[z_x(x,y)]^2 + [z_y(x,y)]^2 + 1}\ dx\,dy$$

where $z = (R^2 - x^2)^{1/2}$ and D is the rectangle $-k \le x \le k,\ 0 \le y \le h$. We have

$$z_x = \frac{\partial}{\partial x}(R^2 - x^2)^{1/2} = \frac{1}{2}(R^2 - x^2)^{-1/2} \frac{\partial}{\partial x}(R^2 - x^2) = \frac{1}{2}(R^2 - x^2)^{-1/2} (-2x)$$

$$= \frac{x}{\sqrt{R^2 - x^2}} \qquad \text{and} \quad z_y = \frac{\partial}{\partial y}(R^2 - x^2)^{1/2} = 0.$$

Therefore,

$$[z_x(x,y)]^2 + [z_y(x,y)]^2 + 1 = \frac{x^2}{R^2 - x^2} + 1 = \frac{x^2 + R^2 - x^2}{R^2 - x^2} = \frac{R^2}{R^2 - x^2}$$

and the surface area (*) equals

$$\iint_D \frac{R}{\sqrt{R^2 - x^2}}\, dx\, dy = \int_{x=-k}^{x=k} \int_{y=0}^{y=h} \frac{R}{\sqrt{R^2 - x^2}}\, dy\, dx = \int_{x=-k}^{x=k} \left[\frac{Ry}{\sqrt{R^2 - x^2}}\right]_{y=0}^{y=h} dx$$

$$= \int_{-k}^{k} \frac{Rh}{\sqrt{R^2 - x^2}}\, dx = \left[Rh\, \arcsin(\tfrac{x}{R})\right]_{-k}^{k} = Rh\, \arcsin(\tfrac{k}{R}) - Rh\, \arcsin(\tfrac{-k}{R})$$

$$= 2Rh\, \arcsin(\tfrac{k}{R}).$$

(23) By Exercise 21 with $(x_0, y_0) = (1,1)$, $\rho(x,y) = 12y$, and R the triangle $0 \le x \le 1$, $0 \le y \le x$ (Fig. 15.2.23), the moment of inertia is

$$\iint_R 12y[(x - 1)^2 + (y - 1)^2]\, dx\, dy = \int_{x=0}^{x=1} \int_{y=0}^{y=x} 12y[x^2 - 2x + 1 + y^2 - 2y + 1]\, dy\, dx$$

$$= \int_{x=0}^{x=1} \int_{y=0}^{y=x} (12x^2 y - 24xy + 24y + 12y^3 - 24y^2)\, dy\, dx$$

$$= \int_{x=0}^{x=1} \left[6x^2 y^2 - 12xy^2 + 12y^2 + 3y^4 - 8y^3\right]_{y=0}^{y=x} dx$$

$$= \int_{x=0}^{x=1} \left\{ [6x^2(x)^2 - 12x(x)^2 + 12(x)^2 + 3(x)^4 - 8(x)^3] - [0] \right\} dx$$

$$= \int_0^1 (9x^4 - 20x^3 + 12x^2)\, dx = \left[\tfrac{9}{5}x^5 - 5x^4 + 4x^3\right]_0^1 = [\tfrac{9}{5} - 5 + 4] - [0] = \tfrac{4}{5}$$

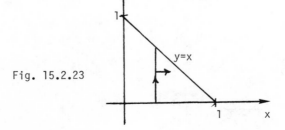

Fig. 15.2.23

SECTION 15.3

(1) The region R is the washer shaped region lying between the circles of radius $\sqrt{2}$
and radius 2 with their centers at the origin (Fig. 15.3.1). In polar coordinates the
inner circle has the equation $r = \sqrt{2}$ and the outer circle has the equation $r = 2$.

For each Θ with $0 \le \Theta \le 2\pi$ we integrate with respect to r from $\sqrt{2}$ to 2, and
then we integrate with respect to Θ from 0 to 2π. We make the substitutions
$r = (x^2 + y^2)^{1/2}$ and $dx\,dy = r\,dr\,d\Theta$ to obtain

$$\int_{\Theta=0}^{\Theta=2\pi} \int_{r=\sqrt{2}}^{r=2} r^{-4}\, r\, dr\, d\Theta = \int_{\Theta=0}^{\Theta=2\pi} \int_{r=\sqrt{2}}^{r=2} r^{-3}\, dr\, d\Theta = \int_0^{2\pi} [-\tfrac{1}{2} r^{-2}]_{r=\sqrt{2}}^{r=2}\, d\Theta$$

$$= \int_0^{2\pi} \left\{[-\tfrac{1}{2}(2)^{-2}] - [-\tfrac{1}{2}(\sqrt{2})^{-2}]\right\} d\Theta = \int_0^{2\pi} \tfrac{1}{8}\, d\Theta = [\tfrac{1}{8}\Theta]_0^{2\pi} = \tfrac{1}{8}(2\pi) = \tfrac{\pi}{4}.$$

(2) The curve $y = \sqrt{16 - x^2}$ is the upper half and the curve $y = -\sqrt{16 - x^2}$ is the lower
half of the circle $x^2 + y^2 = 16$ in which x runs from -4 to 4 (Fig. 15.3.2). The region
of integration is the disk $x^2 + y^2 \le 16$, which in polar coordinates is described by the
condition $r \le 4$. We make the substitutions $x^2 + y^2 = r^2$ and $dx\,dy = r\,dr\,d\Theta$ and
integrate with respect to r from 0 to 4 and with respect to Θ from 0 to 2π:

$$\int_{\Theta=0}^{\Theta=2\pi} \int_{r=0}^{r=4} e^{-r^2}\, r\, dr\, d\Theta = \int_{\Theta=0}^{\Theta=2\pi} [-\tfrac{1}{2} e^{-r^2}]_{r=0}^{r=4}\, d\Theta = \int_0^{2\pi} [-\tfrac{1}{2} e^{-16} + \tfrac{1}{2} e^{-0}]\, d\Theta$$

$$= \int_0^{2\pi} \tfrac{1}{2}(1 - e^{-16})\, d\Theta = [\tfrac{1}{2}(1 - e^{-16})\Theta]_0^{2\pi} = \tfrac{1}{2}(1 - e^{-16})(2\pi) = \pi(1 - e^{-16})$$

In evaluating the indefinite integral with respect to r, we made the substitution $u = -r^2$,
$du = -2r\,dr$:

$$\int e^{-r^2}\, r\, dr = -\tfrac{1}{2}\int e^{-r^2}(-2r\,dr) = -\tfrac{1}{2}\int e^u\, du = -\tfrac{1}{2} e^u + C = -\tfrac{1}{2} e^{-r^2} + C.$$

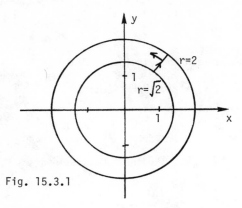

Fig. 15.3.1

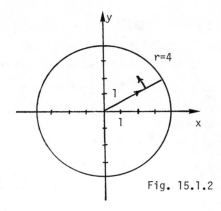

Fig. 15.1.2

(7) The intersection of the ellipsoid $x^2 + y^2 + 4z^2 \leq 4$ with the xy-plane (z = 0) is the disk R: $x^2 + y^2 \leq 4$. We find the volume of the ellipsoid as twice the volume of its upper half, which lies between the surface $z = \sqrt{1 - \frac{1}{4} x^2 - \frac{1}{4} y^2}$ and above the xy-plane:

$$\text{Volume} = 2 \iint_R \sqrt{1 - \frac{1}{4} x^2 - \frac{1}{4} y^2} \ dx \ dy$$

The disk R is described in polar coordinates by the condition $r \leq 2$. When we make the substitutions $x^2 + y^2 = r^2$ and $dx \ dy = r \ dr \ d\Theta$, we obtain

$$\text{Volume} = 2 \int_{\Theta=0}^{\Theta=2\pi} \int_{r=0}^{r=2} \sqrt{1 - \frac{1}{4} r^2} \ r \ dr \ d\theta.$$

To evaluate the indefinite integral with respect to r, we make the substitution $u = 1 - \frac{1}{4} r^2$, $du = - \frac{1}{2} r \ dr$:

$$\int \sqrt{1 - \frac{1}{4} r^2} \ r \ dr = -2 \int (1 - \frac{1}{4} r^2)^{1/2} (- \frac{1}{2} r \ dr) = -2 \int u^{1/2} du$$

$$= -2 (\frac{1}{3/2}) u^{3/2} + C = - \frac{4}{3} u^{1/2} + C = - \frac{4}{3} (1 - \frac{1}{4} r^2)^{3/2} + C$$

Hence,

$$\text{Volume} = 2 \int_{\Theta=0}^{\Theta=2\pi} [- \frac{4}{3} (1 - \frac{1}{4} r^2)^{3/2}]_{r=0}^{r=2} \ d\Theta = 2 \int_0^{2\pi} \left\{ [0] - [- \frac{4}{3}] \right\} d\Theta$$

$$= \frac{8}{3} \int_0^{2\pi} d\Theta = \frac{8}{3} (2\pi) = \frac{16\pi}{3} .$$

(10) The intersection of the cylinder $(x - 1)^2 + y^2 \leq 1$ with the xy-plane is the

disk $(x - 1)^2 + y^2 \leq 1$ of radius 1 with its center at (1,0) and lies inside the

disk $x^2 + y^2 \leq 4$ which is the intersection of the sphere $x^2 + y^2 + z^2 \leq 4$ with the

xy-plane (Fig. 15.3.10). The sphere and the cylinder are consequently tangent at x = 2

on the x-axis, the top of the solid under consideration is formed by the hemisphere

$z = \sqrt{4 - x^2 - y^2}$, its bottom is formed by the hemisphere $z = -\sqrt{4 - x^2 - y^2}$, and

its projection on the xy-plane is the disk R: $(x - 1)^2 + y^2 \leq 1.$ The

volume of the solid is

(*) $\iint_R [\sqrt{4 - x^2 - y^2} -(-\sqrt{4 - x^2 - y^2})]dx\ dy = 2 \iint_R \sqrt{4 - x^2 - y^2}\ dx\ dy.$

The boundary of the region R has the equation $(x - 1)^2 + y^2 = 1$, which in polar

coordinate becomes $r = 2 \cos \Theta.$ We integrate with respect to r from 0 to r cos Θ

for each Θ with $-\frac{\pi}{2} < \Theta < \frac{\pi}{2}$, then we integrate with respect to Θ from $-\frac{\pi}{2}$ to $\frac{\pi}{2}$

(Fig. 15.3.10). With the substitutions $x^2 + y^2 = r^2$ and $dx\ dy = r\ dr\ d\Theta$, the integral

(*) takes the form

$$2 \int_{\Theta = -\pi/2}^{\Theta = \pi/2} \int_{r=0}^{r=2\cos\Theta} \sqrt{4 - r^2}\ r\ dr\ d\Theta \quad = \int_{\Theta = -\pi/2}^{\Theta = \pi/2} [-\tfrac{2}{3}(4 - r^2)^{3/2}]_{r=0}^{r=2\cos\Theta}\ d\Theta$$

$$= \int_{-\pi/2}^{\pi/2} [-\tfrac{2}{3}(4 - 4\cos^2\Theta)^{3/2}] - [-\tfrac{2}{3}(4 - 4(0)^2)^{3/2}]\ d\Theta$$

$$= \int_{-\pi/2}^{\pi/2} [-\tfrac{16}{3}|\sin\Theta|^3 + \tfrac{16}{3}]d\Theta = 2 \int_{0}^{\pi/2} \tfrac{16}{3}(1 - \sin^3\Theta)d\Theta$$

$$= \tfrac{32}{3} \int_{0}^{\pi/2} [1 - \sin\Theta(1 - \cos^2\Theta)]d\Theta = \tfrac{32}{3} \int_{0}^{\pi/2} [1 - \sin\Theta + \cos^2\Theta \sin\Theta]d\Theta$$

$$= \tfrac{32}{3}[\Theta + \cos\Theta - \tfrac{1}{3}\cos^3\Theta]_{0}^{\pi/2}$$

$$= \tfrac{32}{3}[\tfrac{\pi}{2} + \cos(\tfrac{\pi}{2}) - \tfrac{1}{3}\cos^3(\tfrac{\pi}{2})] - \tfrac{32}{3}[0 + \cos(0) - \tfrac{1}{3}\cos^3(0)]$$

$$= \tfrac{32}{3}[\tfrac{\pi}{2} - 1 + \tfrac{1}{3}] = \tfrac{16\pi}{3} - \tfrac{64}{9} \ .$$

We used the substitution $u = 4 - r^2$, $du = -2r\ dr$ to evaluate the integral with respect

to r and the substitution $u = \cos\theta$, $du = -\sin\theta\ d\theta$ to evaluate the last term in the

integral with respect to θ .

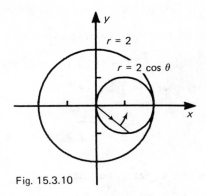

Fig. 15.3.10

(13) The curve $r = \sec\theta$ is the line $x = 1$ and the curve $r = 2\cos\theta$ is the

circle $(x - 1)^2 + y^2 = 1$ of radius 1 with its center at 1 on the x-axis (Fig. 15.3.13).

In the integral

(*) $$\int_{\theta=0}^{\theta=\pi/4}\int_{r=\sec\theta}^{r=2\cos\theta}\frac{r^2}{1 + r\sin\theta}\ dr\ d\theta$$

we integrate with respect to r from the line $r = \sec\theta$ to the circle $r = 2\cos\theta$ for

each θ between 0 and $\frac{\pi}{4}$, then we integrate with respect to θ from 0 to $\frac{\pi}{4}$. The

region of integration R is the quarter circle that is shaded in Fig. 15.3.13. The top of

that circle has the equation $y = \sqrt{1 - (x - 1)^2}$. We make the substitutions $r = \sqrt{x^2 + y^2}$,

$r\sin\theta = y$, and $r\ dr\ d\theta = dx\,dy$ to see that the integral equals

$$\iint_R \frac{\sqrt{x^2 + y^2}}{1 + y}\ dx\ dy = \int_{x=1}^{x=2}\int_{y=0}^{y = \sqrt{1 - (x - 1)^2}}\frac{\sqrt{x^2 + y^2}}{1 + y}\ dy\ dx.$$

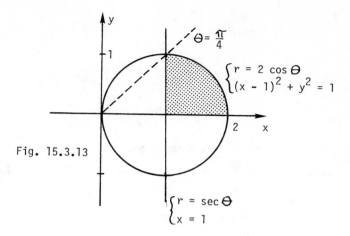

Fig. 15.3.13

SECTION 15.4

(1) The cone $z = \sqrt{x^2 + y^2}$ lies above the plane $z = 0$ (touching it at the origin), so the top of the solid V is formed by the cone and the bottom by the plane. Because the sides of the solid are formed by the vertical planes $x = 1$, $x = -1$, $y = 1$, and $y = -1$, its projection on the xy-plane is the square R: $-1 \leq x \leq 1$, $-1 \leq y \leq 1$. By Rule 15.7, we integrate with respect to z from $z = 0$ to $z = \sqrt{x^2 + y^2}$ for each (x,y) in R and then we integrate with respect to x and y over R:

$$\iiint_V z\ dx\ dy\ dz = \iint_R \int_{z=0}^{z=\sqrt{x^2+y^2}} z\ dz\ dx\ dy = \iint_R \left[\tfrac{1}{2} z^2\right]_{z=0}^{z=\sqrt{x^2+y^2}} dx\ dy$$

$$= \iint_R \left[\tfrac{1}{2}(x^2 + y^2)^2\right] - \left[\tfrac{1}{2}(0)^2\right]\ dx\ dy = \iint_R \tfrac{1}{2}(x^2 + y^2)\ dx\ dy$$

To evaluate the integral over the square R, we integrate with respect to y from -1 to 1 and then with respect to x from -1 to 1. The original integral equals

$$\iint_R \tfrac{1}{2}(x^2 + y^2)\ dx\ dy = \int_{x=-1}^{x=1} \int_{y=-1}^{y=1} (\tfrac{1}{2} x^2 + \tfrac{1}{2} y^2)\ dy\ dx = \int_{x=-1}^{x=1} \left[\tfrac{1}{2} x^2 y + \tfrac{1}{6} y^3\right]_{y=-1}^{y=1} dx$$

$$= \int_{-1}^{1} \left\{ [\frac{1}{2}x^2(1) + \frac{1}{6}(1)^3] - [\frac{1}{2}x^2(-1) + \frac{1}{6}(-1)^3] \right\} dx = \int_{-1}^{1} (x^2 + \frac{1}{3}) \, dx$$

$$= [\frac{1}{3}x^3 + \frac{1}{3}x]_{-1}^{1} = [\frac{1}{3}(1)^3 + \frac{1}{3}(1)] - [\frac{1}{3}(-1)^3 + \frac{1}{3}(-1)] = \frac{4}{3}.$$

(2) The surface $x^2 + y^2 = 1$ is a vertical circular cylinder of radius 1 with the z-axis as its axis. The surface $x^2 + z^2 = 1$ is a horizontal circular cylinder of radius 1 with the y-axis as its axis. Accordingly, the top of the solid V is formed by the half cylinder $z = \sqrt{1 - x^2}$, the bottom is formed by the half cylinder $z = -\sqrt{1 - x^2}$, and the projection of V on the xy-plane is the disk R: $x^2 + y^2 \le 1$. The triple integral equals

$$\iiint_V 15x^2z^2 \, dx \, dy \, dz = \iint_R \int_{z=-\sqrt{1-x^2}}^{z=\sqrt{1-x^2}} 15x^2z^2 \, dz \, dx \, dy = \iint_R [5x^2z^3]_{z=-\sqrt{1-x^2}}^{z=\sqrt{1-x^2}} dx \, dy$$

$$= \iint_R [5x^2(\sqrt{1-x^2})^3] - [5x^2(-\sqrt{1-x^2})^3] \, dx \, dy = \iint_R 10x^2(1-x^2)^{3/2} \, dx \, dy.$$

To evaluate the resulting double integral we integrate with respect to y from $y = -\sqrt{1-x^2}$ to $y = \sqrt{1-x^2}$ and then with respect to x from -1 to 1 (Fig. 15.4.2):

$$\iint_R 10x^2(1-x^2)^{3/2} \, dx \, dy = \int_{x=-1}^{x=1} \int_{y=-\sqrt{1-x^2}}^{y=\sqrt{1-x^2}} 10x^2(1-x^2)^{3/2} \, dy \, dx$$

$$= \int_{x=-1}^{x=1} [10x^2(1-x^2)^{3/2} y]_{y=-\sqrt{1-x^2}}^{y=\sqrt{1-x^2}} dy = \int_{x=-1}^{x=1} 20x^2(1-x^2)^{3/2}\sqrt{1-x^2} \, dx$$

$$= \int_{-1}^{1} 20x^2(1-x^2)^2 dx = \int_{-1}^{1} 20x^2(1 - 2x^2 + x^4) dx = \int_{-1}^{1} (20x^2 - 40x^4 + 20x^6) dx$$

$$= [\frac{20}{3}x^3 - 8x^5 + \frac{20}{7}x^7]_{-1}^{1} = [\frac{20}{3} - 8 + \frac{20}{7}] - [-\frac{20}{3} + 8 - \frac{20}{7}] = \frac{64}{21}.$$

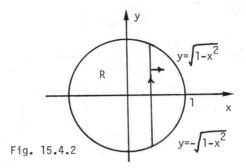

Fig. 15.4.2

(5) The top of the solid V is formed by the plane z = 6 and the bottom by the plane
z = 0, and because the sides of the solid are formed by the vertical planes y = x, y = 0,
and x = 4, its projection on the xy-plane is the triangle shown in Fig. 15.4.5.

$$\iiint_V (\sin y)e^{3z} \; dx \; dy \; dz = \iint_R \int_{z=0}^{z=6} (\sin y)e^{3z} \; dz \; dx \; dy = \iint_R [(\sin y)\tfrac{1}{3} e^{3z}]_{z=0}^{z=6} \; dx \; dy$$

$$= \iint_R \left\{ [(\sin y)\tfrac{1}{3} e^{3(6)}] - [(\sin y)\tfrac{1}{3} e^{3(0)}] \right\} dx \; dy = \iint_R \tfrac{1}{3}(\sin y)(e^{18} - 1) \; dx \; dy$$

$$= \int_{x=0}^{x=4} \int_{y=0}^{y=x} \tfrac{1}{3}(\sin y)(e^{18} - 1) dy \; dx = \int_{x=0}^{x=4} [- \tfrac{1}{3}(\cos y)(e^{18} - 1)]_{y=0}^{y=x} \; dx$$

$$= \int_0^4 \left\{ [- \tfrac{1}{3}(\cos x)(e^{18} - 1)] - [- \tfrac{1}{3}(\cos(0))(e^{18} - 1)] \right\} dx$$

$$= \tfrac{1}{3}(e^{18} - 1) \int_0^4 (1 - \cos x) dx = \tfrac{1}{3}(e^{18} - 1)[x - \sin x]_0^4$$

$$= \tfrac{1}{3}(e^{18} - 1) \left\{ [4 - \sin(4)] - [0 - \sin(0)] \right\} = \tfrac{1}{3}(e^{18} - 1)(4 - \sin(4)) \; .$$

(7) The surface $z = x^2 - y^2$ is a hyperbolic paraboloid that intersects the xy-plane
where $x^2 - y^2 = 0$, which is on the intersecting lines $y = \pm x$. Those lines divide the
xy-plane into four quarter planes. The paraboloid is above the xy-plane in the right

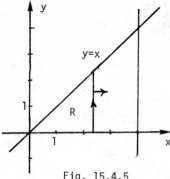

Fig. 15.4.5

and left quarter planes where $|x|$ is greater than $|y|$ and is below the xy-plane in the upper and lower quarter planes where $|y|$ is greater than $|x|$(Fig. 15.4.7a). The projection of the solid V on the xy-plane is, therefore, the triangle R bounded on the bottom by the line $y = -x$, on the top by the line $y = x$, and on the right by the line $x = 1$ (Fig. 15.4.7b). The triple integral equals

$$\iiint_V x^2y^2z \, dx \, dy \, dz = \iint_R \int_{z=0}^{z=x^2-y^2} x^2y^2z \, dz \, dx \, dy = \iint_R [\tfrac{1}{2} x^2y^2z^2]_{z=0}^{x=x^2-y^2} dx \, dy$$

$$= \iint_R \tfrac{1}{2} x^2y^2(x^2 - y^2)^2 \, dx \, dy = \iint_R \tfrac{1}{2} x^2y^2(x^4 - 2x^2y^2 + y^4) dx \, dy$$

$$= \iint_R (\tfrac{1}{2} x^6y^2 - x^4y^4 + \tfrac{1}{2} x^2y^6) dx \, dy = \int_{x=0}^{x=1} \int_{y=-x}^{y=x} (\tfrac{1}{2} x^6y^2 - x^4y^4 + \tfrac{1}{2} x^2y^6) dy \, dx$$

$$= \int_{x=0}^{x=1} [\tfrac{1}{6} x^6y^3 - \tfrac{1}{5} x^4y^5 + \tfrac{1}{17} x^2y^7]_{y=-x}^{y=x} dx = \int_{x=0}^{x=1} 2[\tfrac{1}{6} x^6x^3 - \tfrac{1}{5} x^4x^5 + \tfrac{1}{17} x^2x^7] dx$$

$$= \tfrac{8}{105} \int_0^1 x^9 \, dx = (\tfrac{8}{105})[\tfrac{1}{10} x^{10}]_0^1 = \tfrac{8}{105}(\tfrac{1}{10} - 0) = \tfrac{4}{525} \; .$$

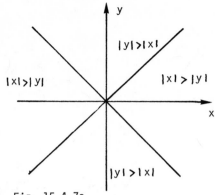

Fig. 15.4.7a

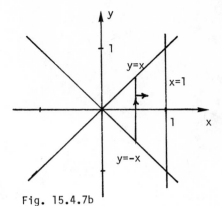

Fig. 15.4.7b

(10) $\iiint_V e^{2x + 3y - 4z}\, dx\, dy\, dz = \int_{x=-4}^{x=4} \int_{y=-3}^{y=3} \int_{z=-2}^{z=2} e^{2x}\, e^{3y}\, e^{-4z}\, dz\, dy\, dx$

$\qquad = \left\{ \int_{x=-4}^{x=4} e^{2x}\, dx \right\} \left\{ \int_{y=-3}^{y=3} e^{3y}\, dy \right\} \left\{ \int_{z=-2}^{z=2} e^{-4z}\, dz \right\}$

$\qquad = \left\{ [\tfrac{1}{2} e^{2x}]_{-4}^{4} \right\} \left\{ [\tfrac{1}{3} e^{3y}]_{-3}^{3} \right\} \left\{ [-\tfrac{1}{4} e^{-4z}]_{-2}^{2} \right\} = \tfrac{1}{2}(e^8 - e^{-8})\ \tfrac{1}{3}(e^9 - e^{-9})\ -\tfrac{1}{4}(e^{-8} - e^8)$

$\qquad = \tfrac{1}{24}(e^8 - e^{-8})^2 (e^9 - e^{-9}).$

(13) Because we integrate with respect to y from $y = 0$ to $y = 4 - x^2$ and then with respect to x from $x = 0$ to $x = 2$, the projection of the solid of integration is the half disk R: $0 \le y \le \sqrt{4 - x^2}$ shown in Fig. 15.4.13. Because we integrate with respect to z from $z = 0$ to $z = \sqrt{4 - x^2 - y^2}$, the bottom of the solid of integration is the xy-plane $(z = 0)$ and the top is the hemisphere $z = \sqrt{4 - x^2 - y^2}$ of radius 2 The region R is the base of the hemisphere, so the region of integration is the entire hemisphere.

(16) In the second integration we integrate with respect to x from $x = 0$ to $x = z + 2$ with fixed z between -2 and 0, then we integrate with respect to z from $z = -2$ to $z = 0$. Hence the projection of the solid of integration on the xz-plane is the triangle

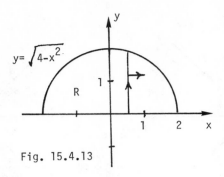

$y=\sqrt{4-x^2}$

R

Fig. 15.4.13

R bounded by the x-axis, the z-axis, and the line x = z + 2 (z = x - 2) (Fig. 15.4.16a). In the innermost integration we integrate with respect to y from y = 0 to y = 2 - x + z. The plane y = 2 - x + z   has y-intercept 2 and intersects the xz-plane (y = 0) along the line x = 2 + 2. Therefore the solid of integration is the tetrahedron formed by the coordinate planes and the plane y = 2 - x + z (Fig. 15.4.16b).

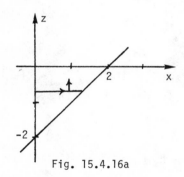

Fig. 15.4.16a

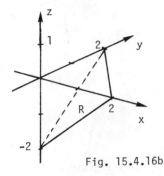

Fig. 15.4.16b

(19) Let V denote the region occupied by the solid. Then the center of gravity is $(\overline{x},\overline{y},\overline{z})$ where .

$$\overline{x} = \frac{\iiint_V x(xy)\ dx\ dy\ dz}{\iiint_V xy\ dx\ dy\ dz}\ , \qquad \overline{y} = \frac{\iiint_V y(xy)\,dx\ dy\ dz}{\iiint_V xy\ dx\ dy\ dz}\ , \qquad \overline{z} = \frac{\iiint_V z(xy)\ dx\ dy\ dz}{\iiint_V xy\ dx\ dy\ dz}\ .$$

The top of V is formed by the circular paraboloid $z = x^2 + y^2$ and its bottom by the xy-plane. The projection of V on the xy-plane is the square $0 \le x \le 1,\ 0 \le y \le 1$.

Therefore,

$$\iiint_V xy \; dx \; dy \; dz = \int_{x=0}^{x=1} \int_{y=0}^{y=1} \int_{z=0}^{z=x^2+y^2} xy \; dz \; dy \; dx = \int_{x=0}^{x=1} \int_{y=0}^{y=1} [xyz]_{z=0}^{z=x^2+y^2} dx \; dy$$

$$= \int_{x=0}^{x=1} \int_{y=0}^{y=1} xy(x^2 + y^2) \; dy \; dx = \int_{x=0}^{x=1} \int_{y=0}^{y=1} (x^3 y + xy^3) dy \; dx$$

(*)

$$= \int_{x=0}^{x=1} \left[\frac{1}{2} x^3 y^2 + \frac{1}{4} xy^4\right]_{y=0}^{y=1} dx = \int_0^1 (\frac{1}{2} x^3 + \frac{1}{4} x) dx = \left[\frac{1}{8} x^4 + \frac{1}{8} x^2\right]_0^1 = \frac{1}{4}$$

and

$$\iiint_V x(xy) \; dx \; dy \; dz = \int_{x=0}^{x=1} \int_{y=0}^{y=1} \int_{z=0}^{z=x^2+y^2} x^2 y \; dz \; dy \; dx = \int_{x=0}^{x=1} \int_{y=0}^{y=1} x^2 yz]_{z=0}^{z=x^2+y^2} dx dy$$

$$= \int_{x=0}^{x=1} \int_{y=0}^{y=1} x^2 y(x^2 + y^2) dy \; dx = \int_{x=0}^{x=1} \int_{y=0}^{y=1} (x^4 y + x^2 y^3) dy \; dx$$

(**)

$$= \int_{x=0}^{x=1} \left[\frac{1}{2} x^4 y^2 + \frac{1}{4} x^2 y^4\right]_{y=0}^{y=1} dx = \int_0^1 (\frac{1}{2} x^4 + \frac{1}{4} x) dx = \left[\frac{1}{10} x^5 + \frac{1}{12} x^3\right]_0^1$$

$$= \frac{1}{10} + \frac{1}{12} = \frac{11}{60} \; .$$

Calculations (*) and (**) show that

$$\overline{x} = \frac{\frac{11}{60}}{\frac{1}{4}} = \frac{11}{15} \; .$$

Similarly, we have

$$\iiint_V z(xy) \; dx \; dy \; dz = \int_{x=0}^{x=1} \int_{y=0}^{y=1} \int_{z=0}^{z=x^2+y^2} xyz \; dz \; dy \; dx$$

$$= \int_{x=0}^{x=1} \int_{y=0}^{y=1} [\frac{1}{2} xyz^2]_{z=0}^{z=x^2+y^2} dx \; dy = \int_{x=0}^{x=1} \int_{y=0}^{y=1} \frac{1}{2} xy(x^2 + y^2)^2 \; dx \; dy$$

$$= \int_{x=0}^{x=1} \int_{y=0}^{y=1} (\frac{1}{2} x^5 y + x^3 y^3 + \frac{1}{2} xy^5) dy \; dx = \int_{x=0}^{x=1} \left[\frac{1}{4} x^5 y^2 + \frac{1}{4} x^3 y^4 + \frac{1}{12} xy^6\right]_{y=0}^{y=1} dx$$

$$= \int_0^1 (\tfrac{1}{4} x^5 + \tfrac{1}{4} x^3 + \tfrac{1}{12} x)dx = [\tfrac{1}{24} x^6 + \tfrac{1}{16} x^4 + \tfrac{1}{24} x^2]_0^1 = \tfrac{1}{24} + \tfrac{1}{16} + \tfrac{1}{24} = \tfrac{7}{48} .$$

Consequently,

$$\bar{z} = \frac{\frac{7}{48}}{\frac{1}{4}} = 4(\tfrac{7}{48}) = \tfrac{7}{12} .$$

Because the solid and its density are symmetric about the plane $y = x$, we have $\bar{y} = \bar{x}$ and the center of gravity is $(\tfrac{11}{15}, \tfrac{11}{15}, \tfrac{7}{12})$.

SECTION 15.5

(1b) We plot the point $(-\sqrt{3},-1)$ in an xy-plane to see that its polar coordinates (with positive r) are $r = 2$, $\theta = \tfrac{7\pi}{6} + 2n\pi$ with integers n. We want only one choice of cylindrical coordinates for the point $(-\sqrt{3},-1,-5)$, so we take $[2,\tfrac{7\pi}{6},-5]$ (Fig. 15.5.1b)

(2b) If the point (x,y,z) has cylindrical coordinates $[1,\tfrac{3\pi}{2},-2]$, then $z = -2$ and the point (x,y) in an xy-plane has polar coordinates $r = 1$, $\theta = \tfrac{3\pi}{2}$. Hence, $x = 0$ and $y = -1$ (Fig. 15.5.2b), so the point is $(0,-1,-2)$.

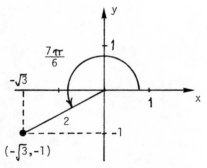

Fig. 15.5.1b

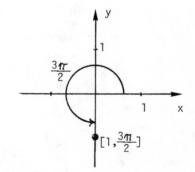

Fig. 15.5.2b

(3b) If the point has spherical coordinates $[0,5,\pi]$, then its distance ρ from the origin is 0 and the point is the origin $(0,0,0)$.

(3d) If a point has spherical coordinates $[5,1,\pi]$, then the angle Ψ between the positive z-axis and the line from the point to the origin is π radians and the point is on the **negative** z-axis. Its distance ρ to the origin is 5, so the point has rectangular coordinates (0,0,-5).

(4c) The point $(-2,-2\sqrt{3},0)$ lies in the xy-plane, so the angle Ψ in its spherical coordinates is $\frac{\pi}{2}$. Its distance to the origin is $\rho = \sqrt{(-2)^2 + (-2\ 3)^2 + 0^2} = \sqrt{16} = 4$, and one choice of the angle Θ is $\Theta = \frac{4\pi}{3}$. The point has spherical coordinates $[4,\frac{4\pi}{3}, \frac{\pi}{2}]$.

(4f) The projection of the point $(-\sqrt{3},1,-2\sqrt{3})$ on the x-y-plane is $(-\sqrt{3},1)$ and its distance to the origin is $\sqrt{(-\sqrt{3})^2 + 1^2} = \sqrt{4} = 2$. We draw the plane containing the z-axis and the line from the point $(-\sqrt{3},1,-2\sqrt{3})$ to the origin to see that the angle Ψ in the

spherical coordinates is $\frac{5\pi}{6}$ (Fig. 15.5.4fi). We plot the point $(-\sqrt{3},1)$ in the xy-plane to see that the angle Θ may be taken to be $\frac{5\pi}{6}$ (Fig. 15.5.4fii). The distance from the

point $(-\sqrt{3},1,-2\sqrt{3})$ to the origin is $\rho = \sqrt{(-\sqrt{3})^2 + 1^2 + (-2\sqrt{3})^2} = \sqrt{16} = 4$. The point has spherical coordinates $[4, \frac{5\pi}{6}, \frac{5\pi}{6}]$.

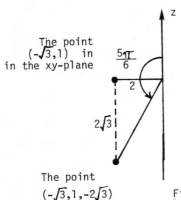

Fig. 15.5.4fi

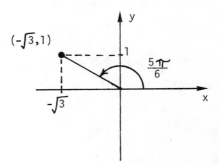

Fig. 15.5.4fii

(4h) The projection of the point $(\sqrt{\frac{3}{2}},\sqrt{\frac{3}{2}},1)$ on the xy-plane is $(\sqrt{\frac{3}{2}},\sqrt{\frac{3}{2}})$ and is a

distance $\sqrt{(\sqrt{\frac{3}{2}})^2 + (\sqrt{\frac{3}{2}})^2} = \sqrt{3}$ from the origin. A sketch of the plane containing the

z-axis and the line from the point $(\sqrt{\frac{3}{2}},\sqrt{\frac{3}{2}},1)$ to the origin shows that the angle ψ in

spherical coordinates of the point is $\frac{\pi}{3}$ (Fig. 15.5.4hi). Plotting the point $(\sqrt{\frac{3}{2}},\sqrt{\frac{3}{2}})$

in the xy-plane shows that we can take $\frac{\pi}{4}$ as the angle θ. The distance from

$(\sqrt{\frac{3}{2}},\sqrt{\frac{3}{2}},1)$ to the origin is

$$\rho = \sqrt{(\sqrt{\frac{3}{2}})^2 + (\sqrt{\frac{3}{2}})^2 + 1^2} = \sqrt{4} = 2$$

so the point has spherical coordinates $[2,\frac{\pi}{4},\frac{\pi}{3}]$.

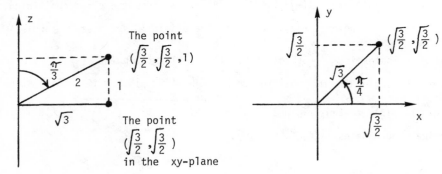

Fig. 15.5.4hi   Fig. 15.5.4hii

(9) A similar integral was evaluated in Example 1 of Section 15.5 in the text by doing
the z-integration first. We will evaluate this integral by doing the z-integration last.
The intersection of the solid V with the coordinate plane z = constant is a horizontal
disk. We integrate with respect to r and θ over the disk at z and then integrate with
respect to z from 0 to 1 (the radius of the hemisphere) (Fig. 15.5.9a). The disk at z
has radius $\sqrt{1 - z^2}$ (Fig. 15.5.9b), so we integrate with respect to r from 0 to $\sqrt{1 - z^2}$:

$$\iiint_V z^2 \, dx \, dy \, dz = \int_{z=0}^{z=1} \int_{\theta=0}^{\theta=2\pi} \int_{r=0}^{r=\sqrt{1-z^2}} z^2 \, r \, dr \, d\theta \, dz$$

$$= \int_{z=0}^{z=1} \int_{\theta=0}^{\theta=2\pi} \left[\tfrac{1}{2} z^2 r^2\right]_{r=0}^{r=\sqrt{1-z^2}} d\theta \; dz \;=\; \int_{z=0}^{z=1} \int_{\theta=0}^{\theta=2\pi} \tfrac{1}{2} z^2 (\sqrt{1-z^2})^2 \; d\theta \; dz$$

$$= \int_{z=0}^{z=1} \left[\tfrac{1}{2} z^2 - \tfrac{1}{2} z^4\right] 2\pi \; dz \;=\; \pi \int_0^1 (z^2 - z^4) dz = \pi \left[\tfrac{1}{3} z^3 - \tfrac{1}{5} z^5\right]_0^1 = \frac{2\pi}{15} \; .$$

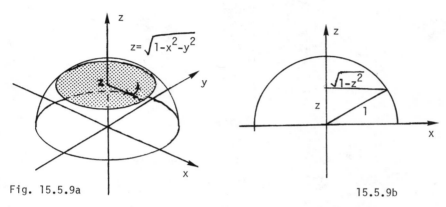

Fig. 15.5.9a   15.5.9b

(12) The top and bottom of the solid are formed by the two sheets of the hyperboloid $z^2 = 1 + x^2 + y^2$ and the sides by the circular cylinder $x^2 + y^2 = 1$. The coordinate surface r = constant intersects the solid in a cylinder that runs from $z = -\sqrt{1 + r^2}$ to $z = \sqrt{1 + r^2}$. We integrate first over that cylinder with **respect** to z and then integrate with respect to r from 0 to 1 (Fig. 15.5.12):

$$\text{Volume} = \iiint_V dx \; dy \; dz = \int_{r=0}^{r=1} \int_{\theta=0}^{\theta=2\pi} \int_{z=-\sqrt{1+r^2}}^{z=\sqrt{1+r^2}} r \; dz \; d\theta \; dr$$

$$= \int_{r=0}^{r=1} \int_{\theta=0}^{\theta=2\pi} [rz]_{z=-\sqrt{1+r^2}}^{z=\sqrt{1+r^2}} d\theta \; dz = \int_{r=0}^{r=1} 4\pi r \sqrt{1 + r^2} \; dr \; .$$

To evaluate the integral with respect to r, we make the substitution $u = 1 + r^2$, $du = 2rdr$:

$$\int 4\pi r \sqrt{1 + r^2} \; dr \;=\; 2\pi \int (1 + r^2)^{1/2} (2r \; dr) = 2\pi \int u^{1/2} \; du = \frac{2\pi}{3/2} u^{3/2} + C$$

$$= \frac{4\pi}{3} u^{3/2} + C = \frac{4\pi}{3} (1 + r^2)^{3/2} + C.$$

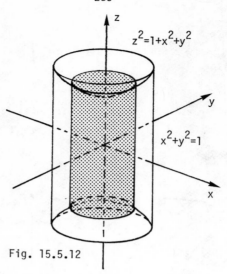

$z^2 = 1 + x^2 + y^2$

$x^2 + y^2 = 1$

Fig. 15.5.12

The volume equals

$$\int_0^1 4\pi r \sqrt{1 + r^2}\ dr = \frac{4\pi}{3}\left[(1 + r^2)^{3/2}\right]_0^1 = \frac{4\pi}{3}(2^{3/2} - 1).$$

(14) The solid V: $\quad x^2 + y^2 \leq 25,\quad x \geq 0,\quad 0 \leq z \leq 1\quad$ is half a circular cylinder of radius 5 and height 1 which is described in cylindrical coordinates by writing V: $\quad 0 \leq r \leq 5,\quad -\frac{\pi}{2} \leq \theta \leq \frac{\pi}{2},\quad 0 \leq z \leq 1$. The weight of the solid with density z^2 at (x,y,z) is

$$\iiint_V z^2\ dx\ dy\ dz = \int_{r=0}^{r=5} \int_{\theta=-\pi/2}^{\theta=\pi/2} \int_{z=0}^{z=1} z^2 r\ dz\ d\theta\ dr$$

$$= \left\{\int_0^5 r\ dr\right\} \left\{\int_{-\pi/2}^{\pi/2} d\theta\right\} \left\{\int_0^1 z^2\ dz\right\} = \left[\tfrac{1}{2} r^2\right]_0^5\ \left[\theta\right]_{-\pi/2}^{\pi/2}\ \left[\tfrac{1}{3} z^3\right]_0^1$$

$$= (\tfrac{25}{2})(\pi)(\tfrac{1}{3}) = \frac{25\pi}{6}.$$

(15) Because in the integral

$$\int_{\theta=0}^{\theta=\pi/2} \int_{r=0}^{r=2} \int_{z=-r^2}^{z=4} \frac{zr^3}{r \sin\theta + 4}\ dz\ dr\ d\theta$$

we integrate with respect to r from 0 to 2 and then with respect to θ from 0 to $\frac{\pi}{2}$,

the projection of the region of integration on the xy-plane is the quarter disk shown in
Fig. 15.5.15. Because in the innermost integral we integrate with respect to z from
$z = -r^2 = -x^2 - y^2$ to z = 4, the bottom of the region of integration is formed by the
circular paraboloid $z = - x^2 - y^2$ and the top by the plane z = 4. To use rectangular
coordinates we make the substitutions r dr dΘ dz = dx dy dz, $r^2 = x^2 + y^2$ and
r sin Θ = y, and we integrate with respect to z from $- x^2 - y^2$ to 4, with respect
to y from 0 to $\sqrt{4 - x^2}$, and then with respect to x from 0 to 2:

$$\int_{x=0}^{x=2} \int_{y=0}^{y=\sqrt{4-x^2}} \int_{z=-x^2-y^2}^{z=4} \frac{z(x^2 + y^2)}{y + 4} \, dz \, dy \, dx$$

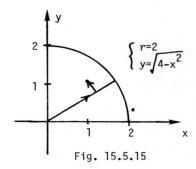

Fig. 15.5.15

(20) Suppose that the center of the sphere is at the origin. We will compute its moment
of inertia about the z-axis:

$$\text{Moment of inertia} = \iiint_V k(x^2 + y^2)\,dx\,dy\,dz = \int_{\Theta=0}^{\Theta=2\pi} \int_{\phi=0}^{\phi=\pi} \int_{\rho=0}^{\rho=R} k(\rho \sin\phi)\rho^2 \sin\phi \, d\rho \, d\phi \, d\Theta$$

$$= \int_{\Theta=0}^{\Theta=2\pi} k \, d\Theta \int_{\phi=0}^{\phi=\pi} \sin^3\phi \, d\phi \int_{\rho=0}^{\rho=R} \rho^4 \, d\rho = (2\pi k)(\frac{4}{3})(\frac{1}{5} R^5) = \frac{8k}{15}\pi \ R^5 .$$

We used the substitutions $x^2 + y^2 = (\rho \sin \phi)^2$ and dx dy dz = $\rho^2 \sin\phi \, d\rho \, d\Theta \, d\phi$
in setting up the integral in spherical coordinates and we made the calculation

$$\int_0^\pi \sin^3\phi \, d\phi = \int_0^\pi \sin\phi (1 - \cos^2\phi)\,d\phi = [- \cos\phi + \frac{1}{3} \cos^3\phi]_0^\pi$$

$$= [-(-1) + \tfrac{1}{3}(-1)^3] - [-(1) + \tfrac{1}{3}(1)^3] = \tfrac{4}{3} .$$

(21) The region of integration is described in spherical coordinates by the conditions $0 \leq \rho \leq 1, \ \tfrac{3\pi}{4} \leq \phi \leq \pi$, $0 \leq \theta \leq \pi$. The coordinate surface $\rho = 1$ is the sphere $x^2 + y^2 + z^2 = 1$; the coordinate surface $\phi = \tfrac{3\pi}{4}$ is the cone $z = -\sqrt{x^2 + y^2}$. The bottom of the solid is formed by the sphere and the top by the cone. The ranges of θ and ρ mean that the projection of the solid on the xy-plane is the half-disk $0 \leq y \leq \sqrt{1 - x^2}$.

We make the substitutions $\rho^2 \sin\phi \ d\rho \ d\theta \ d\phi = dx \ dy \ dz, \ \rho \sin\phi \ \cos\theta = x,$ and $\rho^2 = x^2 + y^2 + z^2$ in the integral to obtain

$$\int_{x=0}^{x=1} \int_{y=0}^{y=\sqrt{1-x^2}} \int_{z=-\sqrt{1-x^2-y^2}}^{z=-\sqrt{x^2+y^2}} x(x^2 + y^2 + z^2) dz \ dy \ dx \ ,$$

(32) Because the longitude of Wassau, Wisconsin is 90^0 W, its spherical coordinate θ is $- \tfrac{\pi}{2}$; because its latitude is 45^0 N, its spherical coordinate ϕ is $\tfrac{\pi}{4}$. Hence its redtangular coordinates are

$$x = 4000 \sin(\tfrac{\pi}{4}) \cos(- \tfrac{\pi}{2}) = 4000(\tfrac{1}{\sqrt 2})(0) = 0$$
$$x = 4000 \sin(\tfrac{\pi}{4}) \sin(- \tfrac{\pi}{2}) = 4000(\tfrac{1}{\sqrt 2})(-1) = - 2000\sqrt 2$$
$$z = 4000 \cos(\tfrac{\pi}{4}) = 4000(\tfrac{1}{\sqrt 2}) = 2000\sqrt 2.$$

(35) Because the longitude of Chiangchunmiao is 90^0 E, its spherical coordinate θ is $\tfrac{\pi}{2}$; because its latitude is 45^0 N, its spherical coordinate ϕ is $\tfrac{\pi}{4}$. The unit vector pointing from the origin toward it is

$$\vec{A} = \left\langle \sin(\tfrac{\pi}{4}) \cos(\tfrac{\pi}{2}), \ \sin(\tfrac{\pi}{4}) \sin(\tfrac{\pi}{2}), \ \cos(\tfrac{\pi}{4}) \right\rangle = \left\langle \tfrac{1}{\sqrt 2}(0), \tfrac{1}{\sqrt 2}(1), \tfrac{1}{\sqrt 2} \right\rangle = \left\langle 0, \tfrac{1}{\sqrt 2}, \tfrac{1}{\sqrt 2} \right\rangle.$$

Because the longitude of Esquina is 60^0 W, its spherical coordinate θ is $- \tfrac{\pi}{3}$; because its latitude is 30^0 S, its spherical coordinate ϕ is $\tfrac{2\pi}{3}$. The unit vector pointing toward it from the origin is

$$\vec{B} = \langle \sin(\tfrac{2\pi}{3})\cos(-\tfrac{\pi}{3}), \ \sin(\tfrac{2\pi}{3})\sin(-\tfrac{\pi}{3}), \cos(\tfrac{2\pi}{3}) \rangle$$

$$= \langle (\tfrac{\sqrt{3}}{2})(\tfrac{1}{2}), (\tfrac{\sqrt{3}}{2})(-\tfrac{\sqrt{3}}{2}), -\tfrac{1}{2} \rangle = \langle \tfrac{\sqrt{3}}{4}, -\tfrac{3}{4}, -\tfrac{1}{2} \rangle .$$

The angle Θ between the vectors $\vec{A}$ and $\vec{B}$ is given by

$$\cos\Theta = \vec{A}\cdot\vec{B} = (0)(\tfrac{\sqrt{3}}{4}) + (\tfrac{1}{\sqrt{2}})(-\tfrac{3}{4}) + (\tfrac{1}{\sqrt{2}})(-\tfrac{1}{2}) = -\tfrac{3}{4\sqrt{2}} - \tfrac{1}{2\sqrt{2}} \approx -0.88$$

From the table of values of cosine in the text we find that

$$-0.88 \approx -\cos(0.49) = \cos(\pi - 0.49) \approx \cos(2.65)$$

so the angle Θ is approximately 2.65 radians. This angle subtends an arc of length $2.65(4000) = 10,600$ miles on a circle of radius 4000 miles, so this is the approximate distance between the towns.

(40) Cylindrical coordinates: By examining the limits of integration with respect to x and y we see we can write

$$\int_{x=-3}^{x=0} \int_{y=0}^{y=\sqrt{9-x^2}} \int_{z=0}^{z=\sqrt{x^2+y^2}} xy \ dz \ dy \ dx = \iint_R \int_{z=0}^{z=\sqrt{x^2+y^2}} xy \ dz \ dx \ dy$$

where R is the region shown in Fig. 15.5.40a. To switch to cylindrical coordinates, we note that the region R can be expressed in polar coordinates by the inequalities $0 \le r \le 3$, $\tfrac{1}{2}\pi \le \Theta \le \pi$ (Fig. 15.5.40b) and we make the substitutions $x = r\cos\Theta$, $y = r\sin\Theta$, $\sqrt{x^2+y^2} = r$, and $dx \ dy = r \ dr \ d\Theta$. We see that the given integral equals

$$\int_{r=0}^{r=3} \int_{\Theta=\pi/2}^{\Theta=\pi} \int_{z=0}^{z=r} (r\cos\Theta)(r\sin\Theta) \ r \ dz \ d\Theta \ dr = \int_{r=0}^{r=3} \int_{\Theta=\pi/2}^{\Theta=\pi} \int_{z=0}^{z=r} r^3 \cos\Theta \sin\Theta \ dz \ d\Theta \ dr$$

$$= \int_{r=0}^{r=3} \int_{\Theta=\pi/2}^{\Theta=\pi} r^4 \cos\Theta \sin\Theta \ d\Theta \ dr = \left\{ \int_0^3 r^4 \ dr \right\} \left\{ \int_{\Theta=\pi/2}^{\Theta=\pi} \cos\Theta \sin\Theta \ d\Theta \right\}$$

$$= [\tfrac{1}{5} r^5]_0^3 \ [\tfrac{1}{2}\sin^2\Theta]_{\pi/2}^{\pi} = \tfrac{1}{5}(3^5)(-\tfrac{1}{2}) = -\tfrac{1}{10} 3^5 .$$

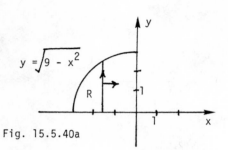

Fig. 15.5.40a

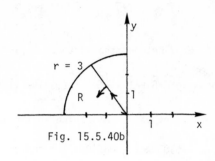

Fig. 15.5.40b

SECTION 16.1

(2) For C: $x = 2 + t$, $y = 3 - 2t$, $z = 4t$, $0 \xrightarrow{t} 2$, we have $dy = -2\, dt$ and

$$\int_C e^{x+y-z}\, dy = \int_0^2 e^{2+t+3-2t-4t}\, (-2\, dt) = -2 \int_0^2 e^5\, e^{-5t}\, dt = -2e^5[-\tfrac{1}{5}\, e^{-5t}]_0^2$$

$$= -2e^5[-\tfrac{1}{5}\, e^{-10} + \tfrac{1}{5}\, e^0] = \tfrac{2}{5}\, e^{-5} - \tfrac{2}{5}\, e^5 = -\tfrac{4}{5}\sinh(5).$$

(5a) The line segment C from $(0,0)$ to $(7,-6)$ has the parametric equations
C: $x = 7t$, $y = -6t$, $0 \xrightarrow{t} 1$, for which

$$ds = \sqrt{(\tfrac{dx}{dt})^2 + (\tfrac{dy}{dt})^2}\, dt = \sqrt{(7)^2 + (-6)^2}\, dt = \sqrt{85}\, dt$$

and, because t increases as the curve is traversed,

$$\int_C e^{x+2y}\, ds = \int_0^1 e^{7t+2(-6t)} \sqrt{85}\, dt = \sqrt{85} \int_0^1 e^{-5t}\, dt = \sqrt{85}\ [-\tfrac{1}{5}\, e^{-5t}]_0^1$$

$$= \sqrt{85}\ [-\tfrac{1}{5}\, e^{-5} + \tfrac{1}{5}\, e^0] = \tfrac{\sqrt{85}}{5}(1 - e^{-5}).$$

(5b) With the parametric equations for part (a), we have $dy = -6\, dt$ and

$$\int_C \sin x\, dy = \int_0^1 \sin(7t)(-6\, dt) = -6 \int_0^1 \sin(7t)dt = -6(-\tfrac{1}{7})[\cos(7t)]_0^1$$

$$= \tfrac{6}{7}[\cos(7) - \cos(0)] = \tfrac{6}{7}[\cos(7) - 1].$$

(11a) For C: $x = \sin t$, $y = \sin(2t)$, $z = \sin(3t)$, $\pi \xrightarrow{t} 0$, we have $dz = 3\cos(3t)\, dt$

and

$$\int_C \sin(xy)\ dz\ =\ \int_\pi^0 \sin[(\sin t)\ \sin(2t)]\ 3\ \cos(3t)\ dt.$$

(11b) For the parametric equations in part (a) we have $\frac{dx}{dt} = \cos t$, $\frac{dy}{dt} = 2\cos(2t)$, and $\frac{dz}{dt} = 3\cos(3t)$ and the curve is oriented with decreasing t. Hence,

$$\int_C e^z\ ds\ =\ \int_{-C} e^z\ ds\ =\ \int_0^\pi e^{\sin(3t)} \sqrt{[\cos t]^2 + [2\cos(2t)]^2 + [3\cos(3t)]^2}\ dt$$

$$=\ \int_0^\pi e^{\sin(3t)} \sqrt{\cos^2 t + 4\cos^2(2t) + 9\cos^2(3t)}\ dt.$$

(14a) Because $g \approx -11$ all along the curve, we have

$$\int_C g\ dx \approx -11 \int_C dx\ =\ -11 \left\{ \begin{bmatrix} x \text{ at the end} \\ \text{of the curve} \end{bmatrix} - \begin{bmatrix} x \text{ at the beginning} \\ \text{of the curve} \end{bmatrix} \right\}$$

$$\approx\ -11[(1) - (3)]\ =\ 22.$$

Of the numbers given, 20 is the closest approximation to the integral.

(14b) We have

$$\int_C g\ dy \approx -11 \int_C dy\ =\ -11 \left\{ \begin{bmatrix} y \text{ at the end} \\ \text{of the curve} \end{bmatrix} - \begin{bmatrix} y \text{ at the beginning} \\ \text{of the curve} \end{bmatrix} \right\}$$

$$\approx\ -11[(-5) - (-4)]\ =\ 11.$$

Of the numbers given, 10 is the closest approximation to this integral.

(14c) $\int_C g\ ds \approx -11 \int_C ds\ =\ -11[\text{Length of the curve}] \approx -11(38) = -418.$

Of the numbers given, -400 is the closest to this integral.

(22) For the curve $y = \frac{3}{2} x^{2/3}$, $1 \le x \le 8$, we have $\frac{dy}{dx} = x^{-1/3}$ and

$$ds\ =\ \sqrt{1 + (\tfrac{dy}{dx})^2}\ dt\ =\ \sqrt{1 + x^{-2/3}}\ dt\ =\ \sqrt{\frac{x^{2/3} + 1}{x^{2/3}}}\ dt\ =\ x^{-1/3}\sqrt{x^{2/3} + 1}\ dt$$

so that the integral of $(1 + \frac{2}{3} y)^2$ with respect to ds along the curve is

$$\int_C (1 + \tfrac{2}{3} y)^2\ ds\ =\ \int_1^8 [1 + \tfrac{2}{3}(\tfrac{3}{2} x^{2/3})]^2\ x^{-1/3}(x^{2/3} + 1)^{1/2}\ dx$$

$$=\ \int_1^8 (1 + x^{2/3})^{5/2}\ x^{-1/3}\ dx.$$

We employ the substitution $u = 1 + x^{2/3}$, $du = \frac{2}{3} x^{-1/3} dx$ to see that

$$\int (1 + x^{2/3})^{5/2} x^{-1/3} dx = \frac{3}{2} \int (1 + x^{2/3})^{5/2} (\frac{2}{3} x^{-1/3} dx)$$

$$= \frac{3}{2} \int u^{5/2} du = \frac{3}{2}(\frac{1}{7/2}) u^{7/2} = \frac{3}{7}(1 + x^{2/3})^{7/2} + C.$$

Consequently, the integral of $(1 + \frac{2}{3} y)^2$ is

$$\int_C (1 + \frac{2}{3} y)^2 ds = [\frac{3}{7}(1 + x^{2/3})^{7/2}]_1^8 = [\frac{3}{7}(1 + 8^{2/3})^{7/2}] - [\frac{3}{7}(1 + 1^{2/3})^{7/2}]$$

(*)
$$= \frac{3}{7}(5^{7/2} - 2^{7/2}).$$

On the other hand, the length of the curve is

$$\int_C ds = \int_1^8 (x^{2/3} + 1)^{1/2} x^{-1/3} dx = \frac{3}{2} \int_1^8 (x^{2/3} + 1)^{1/2} (\frac{2}{3} x^{-1/3} dx)$$

(**)
$$= \frac{3}{2}(\frac{1}{3/2})[(x^{2/3} + 1)^{3/2}]_1^8 = (8^{2/3} + 1)^{3/2} - (1^{2/3} + 1)^{3/2} = 5^{3/2} - 2^{3/2}.$$

The average value of $(1 + \frac{2}{3} y)^2$ along the curve is the integral (*) divided by the length of the curve (**):

$$\text{Average value} = \frac{\frac{3}{7}(5^{7/2} - 2^{7/2})}{(5^{3/2} - 2^{3/2})} = \frac{3}{7}(5^{7/2} - 2^{7/2})/(5^{3/2} - 2^{3/2})$$

SECTION 16.2

(10) Because

$$\frac{\partial}{\partial y}[\sin(3y) + x] = 3\cos(3y) \quad \text{and} \quad \frac{\partial}{\partial x}[3x \cos(3y) - y] = 3\cos(3y)$$

are equal or all (x,y), the vector field $\langle \sin(3y) + x, 3x \cos(3y) - y \rangle$ is the gradient field of a function $U(x,y)$. Such functions U satisfy the equations

(i) $U_x(x,y) = \sin(3y) + x$

(ii) $U_y(x,y) = 3x \cos(3y) - y.$

We integrate (anti-differentiate) both sides of equation (i) with respect to x with y constant:

(iii) $U(x,y) = \int U_x(x,y) \, dx = \int [\sin(3y) + x] \, dx = x \sin(3y) + \frac{1}{2} x^2 + \phi(y)$

We next differentiate the expressions on the left and right of (iii) with respect to y

to obtain

(iv) $U_y(x,y) = 3x \cos(3y) + \phi'(y).$

Comparing equations (ii) and (iv) shows that we must take $\phi'(y) = -y$ and hence
$\phi(y) = -\frac{1}{2}y^2 + C.$ Then equation (iii) gives the final form of the suitable functions U:

$$U(x,y) = x \sin(3y) + \frac{1}{2}x^2 - \frac{1}{2}y^2 + C.$$

(18) With $p = yz + 2xy^2$, $q = xz + 2x^2y$, and $r = 2x^2y^2$, the derivatives

$$p_y = \frac{\partial}{\partial y}(yz + 2xy^2) = z + 4xy \quad \text{and} \quad q_x = \frac{\partial}{\partial x}(xz + 2x^2y) = z + 4xy$$

are equal; but the derivatives

$$p_z = \frac{\partial}{\partial z}(yz + 2xy^2) = y \quad \text{and} \quad r_x = \frac{\partial}{\partial x}(2x^2y^2) = 4xy^2$$

are not equal (except for $y = 0$ or $y = 1/4x$). Hence $\langle p,q,r \rangle$ is not the gradient

field of a function $U(x,y,z)$ in any box.

(20) The derivatives

$$\frac{\partial}{\partial y}(2xy^3 - 3x^2) = 6xy^2 \quad \text{and} \quad \frac{\partial}{\partial x}(3xy^2 + 2y) = 3y^2$$

are not equal, so the integral is not path independent.

(22) With $p = 2x \sin z$, $q = z^3 - e^y$, and $r = x^2 \cos z + 3yz^2$, the derivatives
$p_y = 0$ and $q_x = 0$ are equal; the derivatives $p_z = 2x \cos z$ and $r_x = 2x \cos z$ are
equal; and the derivatives $q_z = 3z^2$ and $r_y = 3z^2$ are equal **for all x, y, and z.**
Therefore, the line integral

(*) $\int_C [p\ dx + q\ dy + r\ dz]$

is path independent for all curves C. We want a function $U(x,y,z)$ such that

    (i) $U_x(x,y,z) = 2x \sin z$

    (ii) $U_y(x,y,z) = z^3 - e^y$

    (iii) $U_z(x,y,z) = x^2 \cos z + 3yz^2.$

Equation (i) implies that

(iii) $U(x,y,z) = \int U_x(x,y,z)\ dx = \int 2x \sin z\ dx = x^2 \sin z + \phi(y,z).$

Differentiating (iii) with respect to y yields

$$U_y(x,y,z) = \phi_y(y,z)$$

which with equation (ii) shows that $\phi_y(y,z) = z^3 - e^y$ and hence

(iv) $\phi(y,z) = \int \phi_y(y,z)\ dy = \int (z^3 - e^y)dy = z^3 y - e^y + \psi(z).$

We substitute expression (iv) for ϕ into (iii) to see that

(v) $U(x,y,z) = x^2 \sin z + z^3 y - e^y + \psi(z).$

Then we differentiate (v) with respect to z to obtain

$$U_z(x,y,z) = x^2 \cos z + 3yz^2 + \psi'(z)$$

and compare with (iii) to shows that $\psi'(z) = 0$ and hence $\psi(z) = C.$ Finally equation (v) gives the formula $U = x^2 \sin z + z^3 y - e^y + C$ for the functions U.

Because the curve C runs from $(0,0,0)$ to $(1,2,3)$, the integral (*) equals

$$U(1,2,3) - U(0,0,0) = [1^2 \sin(3) + 3^3(2) - e^2 + C] - [0^2 \sin(0) + 0^3(0) - e^0 + C]$$

$$= \sin(3) + 54 - e^2 + 1 = \sin(3) - e^2 + 55.$$

(26) Let C_1 denote the first, horizontal portion of the curve and C_2 the second, oblique portion (Fig. 16.2.26). Along C_1 the vectors $\vec{F}(x,y)$ are vertical and $\vec{F} \cdot \vec{T} = 0.$ Along C_2, $\vec{F} \cdot \vec{T}$ is approximately $-\frac{7}{4}$ (Fig. 16.2.26), and C_2 is approximately 13 units long. Hence,

$$\int_C \vec{F} \cdot \vec{T}\ ds = \int_{C_1} \vec{F} \cdot \vec{T}\ ds + \int_{C_2} \vec{F} \cdot \vec{T}\ ds \approx \int_{C_1} 0\ ds + \int_{C_2} (-\tfrac{7}{4})ds$$

$$= 0 - \tfrac{7}{4}[\text{Length of } C_2] \approx -\tfrac{7}{4}(13) = -22\tfrac{3}{4}.$$

Of the numbers given, -25 is the closest approximation of the integral.

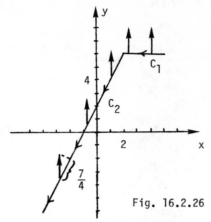

Fig. 16.2.26

(28) We set $p = yz \cos(xyz)$, $q = xz \cos(xyz)$, and $r = xy \cos(xyz)$. The derivatives $p_y = z \cos(xyz) - (yz)^2 \sin(xyz)$ and $q_x = z \cos(xyz) - (xz)^2 \sin(xyz)$ are equal; the

derivatives $p_z = y \cos(xyz) - xy^2z \sin(xyz)$ and $r_x = y \cos(xyz) - xy^2z \sin(xyz)$ are equal;

and the derivatives $q_z = x \cos(xyz) - x^2yz \sin(xyz)$ and $r_y = x \cos(xyz) - x^2yz \sin(xyz)$

are equal. Therefore, the force field $pi + qj + rk$ is conservative. A potential function

for the field is a function $U(x,y,z)$ such that grad $U = pi + qj + rk$, i.e., such that

   (i) $U_x(x,y,z) = yz \cos(xyz)$

   (ii) $U_y(x,y,z) = xz \cos(xyz)$

   (iii) $U_z(x,y,z) = xy \cos(xyz)$.

Equation (i) gives

(iv) $U(x,y,z) = \int U_x(x,y,z)\, dx = \int yz \cos(xyz)\, dx = \sin(xyz) + \phi(y,z)$

We differentiate (iv) with respect to y to see that $U_y = xz \cos(xyz) + \phi_y(y,z)$, and

then equation (ii) shows that $\phi_y(y,z) = 0$ so that $\phi(y,z) = \Psi(z)$. Differentiating (iv)

with respect to z then gives $U_z = xy \cos(xyz) + \Psi'(z)$ and (iii) implies that $\Psi'(z) = 0$.

Thus, $\Psi(z) = C$ and the potential functions are $U(x,y,z) = \sin(xyz) + C$.

   The work done on an object that traverses a curve C from $(0,0,0)$ to $(2,3,4)$ is

$$\int_C F \cdot T\, ds = U(2,3,4) - U(0,0,0) = \sin((2)(3)(4)) - \sin((0)(0)(0)) = \sin(24).$$

Here we have used the potential function $U(x,y,z) = \sin(xyz)$.

(29) With $p = 3x^2y^2z$, $q = 2x^2y^2z$, $q = x^3y^2 + x$, the derivatives $p_y = 6x^2yz$ and

$q_x = 4xy^2z$ are not equal (except on the planes $x = 0$, $y = 0$, $z = 0$ and $y = \frac{3}{2}x$), so

the force field is not conservative.

(31a) The work done by the force field $< x^2y, xy^2 >$ on an object that traverses the curve

C: $y = x^2$, $0 \xrightarrow{x} 1$ is

$$\int_C (x^2y \; dx + xy^2 \; dy) = \int_0^1 [x^2(x^2) + x(x^2)^2(2x)]dx = \int_0^1 (x^4 + 2x^6)dx$$

$$= [\tfrac{1}{5} x^5 + \tfrac{2}{7} x^7]_0^1 = [\tfrac{1}{5}(1)^5 + \tfrac{2}{7}(1)^7] - [\tfrac{1}{5}(0)^5 + \tfrac{2}{7}(0)^7] = \tfrac{1}{5} + \tfrac{2}{7} = \tfrac{17}{35} \; .$$

(31b) The work done on an object that traverses the curve C: $y = x$, $0 \xrightarrow{x} 1$ is

$$\int_C (x^2y \; dx + xy^2 \; dy) = \int_0^1 [x^2(x) + x(x)^2]dx = \int_0^1 2x^3 \; dx = [\tfrac{1}{2} x^4]_0^1 = \tfrac{1}{4} \; .$$

(31c) The line segment from (0,0) to (1,0) is the curve C_1: $y = 0$, $0 \xrightarrow{x} 1$; the
line segment from (1,0) to (1,1) is the curve C_2: $x = 1$, $0 \xrightarrow{y} 1$. The work done by the
force field $< x^2y, xy^2 >$ on an object that traverses C_1 is

$$\int_{C_1} (x^2y \; dx + xy^2 \; dy) = \int_0^1 0 \; dx = 0.$$

The work done on an object that traverses C_2 is

$$\int_{C_2} (x^2y \; dx + xy^2 \; dy) = \int_0^1 y^2 \; dy = [\tfrac{1}{3} x^3]_0^1 = \tfrac{1}{3} \; .$$

SECTION 16.3

(3) $\displaystyle \int_C [\sin(xy) \; dx + \cos(xy) \; dy] = \int_R [- \tfrac{\partial}{\partial y} \sin(xy) + \tfrac{\partial}{\partial x} \cos(xy)] \; dx \; dy$

$$= \iint_R [- x \cos(xy) - y \sin(xy)] \; dx \; dy$$

(7) The origin is on the curve C: $x = \cos(t)$, $y = \sin(t)\cos(t)$, $-\pi \xrightarrow{t} \pi$ at

$t = \pm \tfrac{\pi}{2}$. The right loop of the curve (see Figure 16.40 in the text) may be described as

C_1: $x = \cos(t)$, $y = \sin(t)\cos(t)$, $-\tfrac{\pi}{2} \xrightarrow{t} \tfrac{\pi}{2}$. The area inside the entire curve is twice

the area inside C_1 or

$$-2 \int_{C_1} y \; dx = -2 \int_{-\pi/2}^{\pi/2} \sin(t) \cos(t)[- \sin(t) \; dt] = 2 \int_{-\pi/2}^{\pi/2} \sin^2 t \cos t \; dt$$

$$= 2[\tfrac{1}{3} \sin^3 t]_{-\pi/2}^{\pi/2} = \tfrac{2}{3}[(1)^3 - (-1)^3] = \tfrac{4}{3} \; .$$

(If you compute $\displaystyle\int_C y\,dx$ for the original curve C, you obtain 0 because one loop of the curve is oriented counterclockwise and the other clockwise.)

(12a) $\text{div}[\sin(xy)\vec{i} + \cos(x - y)\vec{j}] = \dfrac{\partial}{\partial x}[\sin(xy)] + \dfrac{\partial}{\partial y}[\cos(x - y)]$

$\qquad\qquad = \cos(xy)\dfrac{\partial}{\partial x}(xy) - \sin(x - y)\dfrac{\partial}{\partial y}(x - y) = y\cos(xy) + \sin(x - y)$

(12b) $\text{curl}[\sin(xy)\vec{i} + \cos(x - y)\vec{j}] = -\dfrac{\partial}{\partial y}[\sin(xy)] + \dfrac{\partial}{\partial x}[\cos(x - y)]$

$\qquad\qquad = -\cos(xy)\dfrac{\partial}{\partial y}(xy) - \sin(x - y)\dfrac{\partial}{\partial x}(x - y) = -x\cos(xy) - \sin(x - y)$

(16) Let C_1 denote the first, vertical portion of the curve and C_2 the second, horizontal portion (Fig. 16.3.16). Along C_1, $\vec{v}\cdot\vec{n}$ is approximately -4 and long C_2, $\vec{v}\cdot\vec{n}$ is approximately -2. C_1 is approximately 4 units long and C_2 is approximately 14 units long. Therefore,

$$\int_C \vec{v}\cdot\vec{n}\,ds = \int_{C_1}\vec{v}\cdot\vec{n}\,ds + \int_{C_2}\vec{v}\cdot\vec{n}\,ds \approx \int_{C_1}(-4)ds + \int_{C_2}(-2)\,ds$$

$$= -4[\text{Length of } C_1] - 2[\text{Length of } C_2] \approx -4(4) - 2(14) = -44.$$

Of the numbers given, the closest approximation of the integral is -50.

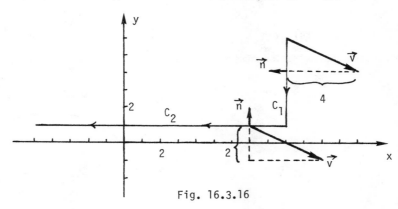

Fig. 16.3.16

(19) Let R denote the region bounded by the curves C_1 and C_2 in Figure 16.43 of the text and let C denote its boundary oriented counterclockwise. By Stokes' Theorem,

$$\int_C \vec{F}\cdot\vec{T}\,ds = \iint_R \text{curl } \vec{F}\,dx\,dy.$$

Because $C = C_1 - C_2$ and $\text{curl }\vec{F} = \dfrac{1}{2}$, this equation gives

$$\int_{C_1} \vec{F} \cdot \vec{T} \, ds \; - \; \int_{C_2} \vec{F} \cdot \vec{T} \, ds \; = \; \frac{1}{2} \iint_R dx \, dy \; = \frac{1}{2}[\text{Area of } R].$$

The integral over C_1 is 10 and the area of R is approximately 58 , so we have

$$10 \; - \; \int_{C_2} \vec{F} \cdot \vec{T} \, ds \; \approx \; 29$$

which shows that the integral over C_2 is approximately -19. Of the numbers given, - 20 is the closest approximation of the integral.

(21) Let R denote the region bounded by the curves C_3 and C_4 in Figure 16.44 of the test and let C denote its boundary oriented positively. Then $C = C_4 - C_3$, and because div $\vec{A} = -2$, the Divergence Theorem

$$\int_C \vec{A} \cdot \vec{n} \, ds \; = \; \iint_R \text{div } \vec{A} \; dx \, dy$$

gives

$$\int_{C_4} \vec{A} \cdot \vec{n} \, ds \; - \; \int_{C_3} \vec{A} \cdot \vec{n} \, ds = \quad -2[\text{Area of } R].$$

Because the integral over C_3 is 35 and the area of R is approximately 42, we obtain

$$\int_{C_4} \vec{A} \cdot \vec{n} \, ds - 35 \; \approx \; -2(42)$$

which shows that the integral over C_4 is approximately -49 and of the numbers given, - 50 is the closest approximation of the integral.

SECTION 17.1

(3) The third degree Taylor polynomial of $f(x)$ centered at 0 is

(*) $\qquad P_3(x) = f(0) + f'(0)x + \frac{1}{2} f''(0)x^2 + \frac{1}{3!} f^{(3)}(0)x^3.$

For $f(x) = (1 - x)^{-1}$, we have $f'(x) = (1 - x)^{-2}$, $f''(x) = 2(1 - x)^{-3}$, and

$f^{(3)}(x) = 2(3)(1 - x)^{-4}$, so that $f(0) = 1$, $f'(0) = 1$, $f''(0) = 2$, and $f^{(3)}(0) = 6$. The

Taylor polynomial (*) is $P_3(x) = 1 + x + x^2 + x^3.$

(5) The second degree Taylor polynomial of $f(x)$ centered at 9 is

(*) $\qquad P_2(x) = f(9) + f'(9)(x - 9) + \frac{1}{2} f''(9)(x - 9)^2.$

With $f(x) = x^{1/2}$, we have $f'(x) = \frac{1}{2} x^{-1/2}$ and $f''(x) = \frac{1}{2}(-\frac{1}{2})x^{-3/2} = -\frac{1}{4} x^{-3/2}$, and

$f(9) = 3$, $f'(9) = \frac{1}{6}$, $f''(9) = -\frac{1}{108}$. The Taylor polynomial (*) is

$\qquad P_2(x) = 3 + \frac{1}{6}(x - 9) - \frac{1}{216}(x - 9)^2.$

(15) The fourth degree Taylor polynomial of $f(x)$ centered at 1 is

(*) $\qquad P_4(x) = f(1) + f'(1)(x - 1) + \frac{1}{2} f''(1)(x - 1)^2 + \frac{1}{3!} f^{(3)}(1)(x - 1)^3 + \frac{1}{4!} f^{(4)}(1)(x - 1)^4.$

For $f(x) = \cos(6x)$, we have $f'(x) = -6 \sin(6x)$, $f''(x) = -36 \cos(6x)$, $f^{(3)}(x) = 216 \sin(6x)$,

and $f^{(4)}(x) = 1296 \cos(6x)$. The Taylor polynomial (*) is

$\qquad P_4(x) = \cos(6) - 6 \sin(6)(x - 1) - 18 \cos(6)(x - 1)^2 + 36 \sin(6)(x - 1)^3$

$\qquad\qquad + 54 \cos(6)(x - 1)^4.$

(19) For $f(x) = x^5 - x^4$, we have $f'(x) = 5x^4 - 4x^3$, $f''(x) = 20x^3 - 12x^2$, and

$f^{(3)}(x) = 60x^2 - 24x$, so that $f(1) = 0$, $f'(1) = 1$, $f''(1) = 8$, and $f^{(3)}(1) = 36$. The Taylor

polynomial approximation centered at 1 is

$\qquad P_3(x) = f(1) + f'(1)(x - 1) + \frac{1}{2} f''(1)(x - 1)^2 + \frac{1}{3!} f^{(3)}(1)(x - 1)^3$

$\qquad\qquad = (x - 1) + 4(x - 1)^2 + 6(x - 1)^3.$

(22a) For $f(x) = \sin x$, we have $f'(x) = \cos x$, $f''(x) = -\sin x$, $f^{(3)}(x) = -\cos x$,

$f^{(4)}(x) = \sin x$, and $f^{(5)}(x) = \cos x$, so that $f(0) = 0$, $f'(0) = 1$, $f''(0) = 0$, $f^{(3)}(0) = -1$,

$f^{(4)}(0) = 0$, and $f^{(5)}(0) = 1$ and the Taylor polynomial centered at 0 is

$$P_5(x) = 0 + (1)x + \frac{1}{2}(0)x^2 + \frac{1}{3!}(-1)x^3 + \frac{1}{4!}(0)x^4 + \frac{1}{5!}(1)x^5 = x - \frac{1}{3!}x^3 + \frac{1}{5!}x^5.$$

(22b) $\sin(\frac{\pi}{10}) \approx P_5(\frac{\pi}{10}) = \frac{\pi}{10} - \frac{1}{3!}(\frac{\pi}{10})^3 + \frac{1}{5!}(\frac{\pi}{10})^5 = 0.3090170\ldots$

(22c) Taylor's Theorem with $a = 0$ and $n = 5$ states that if $f(x)$ has six derivatives
for all x in an open interval containing 0, then for each x in that interval there is
a number c between 0 and x such that

(*) $f(x) = P_5(x) + R_5(x)$

with $P_5(x)$ the Taylor polynomial of degree 5 centered at 0 and with

(**) $R_5(x) = \frac{1}{6!}f^{(6)}(c)x^6.$

In the case of $f(x) = \sin x$, $f^{(6)}(x)$ is $-\sin x$. We set $x = \frac{\pi}{10}$ in (*) and (**) to obtain

(**) $\sin(\frac{\pi}{10}) = P_5(\frac{\pi}{10}) + \frac{1}{6!}[-\sin(c)](\frac{\pi}{10})^6.$

Because c is between 0 and $\frac{\pi}{10}$, $\sin(c)$ is positive and the remiander term is negative.
Therefore, the approximation $P_5(\frac{\pi}{10})$ is greater than the exact value of $\sin(\frac{\pi}{10})$.

(27a) The first degree Taylor polynomial centered at 1 is the function

$$P_1(x) = f(1) + f'(1)(x - 1)$$

whose graph is the tangent line to $y = f(x)$ at $x = 1$. For $f(x) = \arctan x$, we have

$f'(x) = \dfrac{1}{x^2 + 1}$, $f(1) = \arctan(1) = \frac{\pi}{4}$, and $f'(1) = \dfrac{1}{1^2 + 1} = \frac{1}{2}$. Hence

$$P_1(x) = \frac{\pi}{4} + \frac{1}{2}(x - 1).$$

(27b) Setting $x = 0.9$ gives the approximation

$$\arcsin(0.9) \approx P_1(0.9) = \frac{\pi}{4} + \frac{1}{2}(0.9 - 1) = 0.735398\ldots$$

(27c) By Taylor's Theorem with $n = 1$ and $a = 1$, there is for each x a number c between x and 1 such that

(*) $\arctan x = P_1(x) + R_1(x)$

where

(**) $R_1(x) = \frac{1}{2} f''(c)(x - 1)^2 = - \frac{c}{(c^2 + 1)^2} (x - 1)^2 .$

Here we use the fact that the second derivative of $\arctan x$ is

$$f''(x) = \frac{d}{dx}(x^2 + 1)^{-1} = -(x^2 + 1)^{-2} \frac{d}{dx}(x^2 + 1) = \frac{-2x}{(x^2 + 1)^2} .$$

For $x = 0.9$, c is positive and $R_1(c)$ is negative, so the approximation $P_1(0.9)$ is greater than the exact value of $\arctan(0.9)$.

(30a) For $f(x) = \tan x$, we have $f'(x) = \sec^2 x$, $f''(x) = 2 \sec x \frac{d}{x} \sec x = 2 \sec^2 x \tan x$,

$f(\frac{\pi}{3}) = \tan(\frac{\pi}{3}) = \sqrt{3}$, $f'(\frac{\pi}{3}) = \sec^2(\frac{\pi}{3}) = 2^2 = 4$, and $f''(\frac{\pi}{3}) = 2 \sec^2(\frac{\pi}{3}) \tan(\frac{\pi}{3}) = 2(2)^2\sqrt{3} = 8\sqrt{3}$,

so the **second** degree Taylor polynomial approximation of $\tan x$ centered at $\frac{\pi}{3}$ is

$$P_2(x) = f(\frac{\pi}{3}) + f'(\frac{\pi}{3})(x - \frac{\pi}{3}) + \frac{1}{2} f''(\frac{\pi}{3})(x - \frac{\pi}{3})^2$$

$$= \sqrt{3} + 4(x - \frac{\pi}{3}) + 4\sqrt{3}(x - \frac{\pi}{3})^2 .$$

(30b). Setting $x = \frac{4\pi}{15}$, we obtain the approximation

$$\tan(\frac{4\pi}{15}) \approx P_2(\frac{4\pi}{15}) = \sqrt{3} + 4(\frac{4\pi}{15} - \frac{\pi}{3}) + 4\sqrt{3}(\frac{4\pi}{15} - \frac{\pi}{3})^2$$

$$= \sqrt{3} + 4(- \frac{\pi}{15}) + 4\sqrt{3}(- \frac{\pi}{15})^2 = \sqrt{3} - \frac{4\pi}{15} + \frac{4}{225}\sqrt{3}\pi^2 \quad = 1.198...$$

(30c) The third derivative of $\tan x$ is

$$f^{(3)}(x) = \frac{d}{dx}[2 \sec^2 x \tan x] = 4 \sec x[\frac{d}{dx} \sec x] \tan x + 2 \sec^2 x \frac{d}{dx} \tan x$$

$$= 4 \sec^2 x \tan^2 x + 2 \sec^4 x .$$

Taylor's Theorem gives $\tan x = P_2(x) + R_2(x)$ where

$$R_2(x) = \frac{1}{3!} f^{(3)}(c)(x - \frac{\pi}{3})^3 = \frac{1}{3!}[4 \sec^2 c \tan^2 c + 2 \sec^4 c](x - \frac{\pi}{3})^3$$

with c a number between 1 and x $(- \frac{\pi}{2} < x < \frac{\pi}{2})$. For $x = \frac{4\pi}{15}$, c is a positive acute angle, $\sec(c)$ and $\tan(c)$ are positive, and $x - \frac{\pi}{3} = -\frac{4\pi}{15}$ is negative. Hence $R_2(\frac{4\pi}{15})$ is negative and the approximation $P_2(\frac{4\pi}{15})$ is greater than the exact value of $\tan(\frac{4\pi}{15})$.

(32a) For $f(x) = \cos x$, we have $f'(x) = -\sin x$, $f''(x) = -\cos x$, and $f^{(3)}(x) = \sin x$, so that $f(\frac{\pi}{4}) = \frac{1}{\sqrt{2}}$, $f'(\frac{\pi}{4}) = -\frac{1}{\sqrt{2}}$, $f''(\frac{\pi}{4}) = -\frac{1}{\sqrt{2}}$, and $f^{(3)}(\frac{\pi}{4}) = \frac{1}{\sqrt{2}}$ and the third degree Taylor polynomial approximation centered at $\frac{\pi}{4}$ is

$$P_3(x) = f(\tfrac{\pi}{4}) + f'(\tfrac{\pi}{4})(x - \tfrac{\pi}{4}) + \tfrac{1}{2} f''(\tfrac{\pi}{4})(x - \tfrac{\pi}{4})^2 + \tfrac{1}{3!} f^{(3)}(\tfrac{\pi}{4})(x - \tfrac{\pi}{4})^3$$

$$= \frac{1}{\sqrt{2}}[1 - (x - \tfrac{\pi}{4}) - \tfrac{1}{2}(x - \tfrac{\pi}{4})^2 + \tfrac{1}{3!}(x - \tfrac{\pi}{4})^3].$$

(32b) At $x = \frac{7\pi}{20}$, we obtain the approximation

$$\cos(\tfrac{7\pi}{20}) \approx P_3(\tfrac{7\pi}{20}) = \frac{1}{\sqrt{2}}[1 - (\tfrac{7\pi}{20} - \tfrac{\pi}{4}) - \tfrac{1}{2}(\tfrac{7\pi}{20} - \tfrac{\pi}{4})^2 + \tfrac{1}{6}(\tfrac{7\pi}{20} - \tfrac{\pi}{4})^3]$$

$$= \frac{1}{\sqrt{2}}[1 - \tfrac{\pi}{10} - \tfrac{1}{2}(\tfrac{\pi}{10})^2 + \tfrac{1}{6}(\tfrac{\pi}{10})^3] = 0.45372\ldots$$

(32c) The fourth derivative of $\cos x$ is $f^{(4)}(x) = \cos x$, so for each x there is a c between $\frac{\pi}{4}$ and x such that

$$\cos x = P_3(x) + R_3(x)$$

where

$$R_3(x) = \tfrac{1}{4!} f^{(4)}(c)(x - \tfrac{\pi}{4})^4 = \tfrac{1}{24} \cos(c)(x - \tfrac{\pi}{4})^4.$$

For $x = \frac{7\pi}{20}$, the number c is between $\frac{\pi}{4}$ and $\frac{7\pi}{20}$ and hence between $\frac{\pi}{4}$ and $\frac{\pi}{2}$. Therefore, we have

$$0 < \cos(c) < \frac{1}{\sqrt{2}}$$

and

$$0 < R_3(\tfrac{7}{20}) < \tfrac{1}{24}(\tfrac{1}{\sqrt{2}})(\tfrac{1}{10})^4 = 0.000286\ldots$$

(35a) With $f(x) = (1 + x)^{-1}$, we have $f'(x) = -(1 + x)^{-2}$, $f''(x) = 2(1 + x)^{-3}$, $f^{(3)}(x) = -6(1 + x)^{-4}$, $f(0) = 0$, $f'(0) = -1$, $f''(0) = 2$, $f^{(3)}(0) = -6$ and the third degree

Taylor polynomial approximation centered at 0 is

$$P_3(x) = f(0) + f'(0)x + \frac{1}{2} f''(0)x^2 + \frac{1}{3!} f^{(3)}(0)x^3$$

$$= 1 - x + x^2 - x^3.$$

(35b) At $x = 0.01$ we have the approximation

$$\frac{1}{1.01} = \frac{1}{1 + 0.01} \quad P_3(0.01) = 1 - (0.01) + (0.01)^2 - (0.01)^3 = 0.990099.$$

(35c) The fourth derivative of $(1 + x)^{-1}$ is $24(1 + x)^{-5}$, so for each $x > -1$ there is a number c between x and 0 such that

$$\frac{1}{1 + x} = P_3(x) + R_3(x)$$

where

$$R_3(x) = \frac{1}{4!} f^{(4)}(c) x^4 = \frac{1}{(1 + c)^5} x^5.$$

For $x = 0.01$ the number c lies between 0 and 0.01, so we have $0 < c < 1$ and

$$3.125 \quad 10^{-10} < R_3(0.01) < 10^{-8}.$$

(40a) Set $f(x) = x^{60}$. Then $f'(x) = 60x^{59}$, $f''(x) = 3540x^{58}$, $f(1) = 1$, $f'(1) = 60$, $f''(1) = 3540$, and the second degree Taylor polynomial approximation centered at 1 is

$$P_2(x) = f(1) + f'(1)(x - 1) + \frac{1}{2} f''(1)(x - 1)^2$$

$$= 1 + 60(x - 1) + 1770(x - 1)^2.$$

(40b) At $x = 0.99$, we have the approximation

$$(0.99)^{60} \approx P_2(0.99) = 1 + 60(0.99 - 1) + 1770(0.99 - 1)^2$$

$$= 1 - 60(0.01) + 1770(0.0001) = 0.577.$$

(40c) The third derivative of x^{60} is $205,320x^{57}$, so that

$$(0.99)^{60} = P_2(0.99) + R_2(0.99)$$

where

$$R_2(0.99) = \frac{1}{3!}(205,320)c^{57}(0.99 - 1)^3 = - 0.03422c^{57}$$

with some number c between 0.99 and 1. We have $0 < c < 1$ and hence

$$-0.03422 < R_2(0.99) < 0.$$

SECTION 17.2

(1) Because $\sin(3x)$ and $\sin(2x)$ both tend to 0 as x tends to 0, we can apply l'Hopital's rule:

$$\lim_{x \to 0} \frac{\sin(3x)}{\sin(2x)} = \lim_{x \to 0} \frac{\frac{d}{dx}\sin(3x)}{\frac{d}{dx}\sin(2x)} = \lim_{x \to 0} \frac{3\cos(3x)}{2\cos(2x)} = \frac{3}{2}$$

(3) Because $\tan(4 - 2x)$ and $x^3 - 8$ both tend to 0 as x tends to 2, we can apply l'Hopital's rule:

$$\lim_{x \to 2} \frac{\tan(4 - 2x)}{x^3 - 8} = \lim_{x \to 2} \frac{\frac{d}{dx}\tan(4 - 2x)}{\frac{d}{dx}(x^3 - 8)} = \lim_{x \to 2} \frac{-2\sec^2(4 - 2x)}{3x^2} = -\frac{1}{6}$$

(5) Because $1 - 6x^2$ and $5x^2 + 4x$ and their first derivatives all tend to ∞ as x tends to ∞ , we apply l'Hopital's rule twice:

$$\lim_{x \to \infty} \frac{1 - 6x^2}{5x^2 + 4x} = \lim_{x \to \infty} \frac{\frac{d}{dx}(1 - 6x^2)}{\frac{d}{dx}(5x^2 + 4x)} = \lim_{x \to \infty} \frac{-12x}{10x + 4}$$

$$= \lim_{x \to \infty} \frac{\frac{d}{dx}(-12x)}{\frac{d}{dx}(10x + 4)} = \lim_{x \to \infty} \frac{-12}{10} = -\frac{6}{5}$$

(8) The expression $x^2 e^{-x}$ is an indeterminate form of type $\infty 0$ as x tends to ∞. We write it as x^2/e^x so that it becomes an indeterminate form of type ∞/∞ to which we make two applications of l'Hopital's rule:

$$\lim_{x \to \infty} \frac{x^2}{e^x} = \lim_{x \to \infty} \frac{\frac{d}{dx} x^2}{\frac{d}{dx} e^x} = \lim_{x \to \infty} \frac{2x}{e^x} = \lim_{x \to \infty} \frac{\frac{d}{dx}(2x)}{\frac{d}{dx} e^x} = \lim_{x \to \infty} \frac{2}{e^x} = 0$$

(12) Because x^2 and $1 - e^x$ both tend to 0 as x tends to 0, we can use l'Hopital's rule:

$$\lim_{x \to 0} \frac{x^2}{1 - e^x} = \lim_{x \to 0} \frac{\frac{d}{dx} x^2}{\frac{d}{dx}(1 - e^x)} = \lim_{x \to 0} \frac{2x}{e^x} = 0$$

We do not need to (and, in fact, cannot) apply l'Hopital's rule a second time in this exercise even though 2x tends to 0 as x tends to 0. This is because e^x does not tend to 0.

(20) We write

$$\frac{1}{x} - \frac{1}{\sin x} = \frac{\sin x - x}{x \sin x}$$

We can apply l'Hopital's rule twice to this expression because sin x - x, x sin x, and their first derivatives all tend to 0 as x tends to 0:

$$\lim_{x \to 0} \frac{\sin x - x}{x \sin x} = \lim_{x \to 0} \frac{\frac{d}{dx}[\sin x - x]}{\frac{d}{dx}[x \sin x]} = \lim_{x \to 0} \frac{\cos x - 1}{x \cos x + \sin x}$$

$$= \lim_{x \to 0} \frac{\frac{d}{dx}[\cos x - 1]}{\frac{d}{dx}[x \cos x + \sin x]} = \lim_{x \to 0} \frac{- \sin x}{2 \cos x - x \sin x} = 0 .$$

(23) The expression $x(\frac{\pi}{2} - \arctan x)$ is an indeterminate form of type $\infty \cdot 0$ as x tends to ∞ . We write it as $(\frac{\pi}{2} - \arctan x)/x^{-1}$ to make it of type 0/0   and apply l'Hopital's rule to find its limit:

$$\lim_{x \to \infty} \frac{\frac{\pi}{2} - \arctan x}{x^{-1}} = \lim_{x \to \infty} \frac{\frac{d}{dx}[\frac{\pi}{2} - \arctan x]}{\frac{d}{dx} x^{-1}}$$

$$= \lim_{x \to \infty} \frac{\frac{-1}{1 + x^2}}{\frac{-1}{x^2}} = \lim_{x \to \infty} \frac{x^2}{1 + x^2} = 1.$$

We can see that the limit of the last expression is 1 either by applying l'Hopital's rule two more times or by writing

$$\frac{x^2}{1 + x^2} = \frac{1}{(\frac{1}{x})^2 + 1} .$$

(29) Because $\cos(6y)$ and $\cos(5y)$ do not tend to 0 as x tends to 0, we do not need to (and cannot) apply l'Hopital's rule. We have

$$\lim_{y \to 0} \frac{\cos(6y)}{\cos(5y)} = \frac{1}{1} = 1.$$

SECTION 17.3

(1) Because e^{-10x} is continuous for all x, the integral is improper only because of the infinite upper limit:

$$\int_1^\infty e^{-10x}\, dx = \lim_{X \to \infty} \int_1^X e^{-10x}\, dx = \lim_{X \to \infty} [-\frac{1}{10} e^{-10x}]_1^X$$

$$= \lim_{X \to \infty} [-\frac{1}{10} e^{-X} + \frac{1}{10} e^{-10}] = \frac{1}{10} e^{-10}$$

(3) The integrand $\frac{x}{1 + x^2}$ is continuous for all x, so the integral is improper only because of the infinite upper limit:

$$\int_0^\infty \frac{x}{1 + x^2}\, dx = \lim_{X \to \infty} \int_0^X \frac{x}{1 + x^2}\, dx = \lim_{X \to \infty} [\frac{1}{2} \ln(1 + x^2)]_0^X$$

$$= \lim_{X \to \infty} [\frac{1}{2} \ln(1 + X^2) - \frac{1}{2} \ln(1)] = \infty$$

(7) The integrand $x^{-1/3}$ tends to ∞ as $x \longrightarrow 0^+$, so the integral is improper at the lower limit of integration:

$$\int_0^{27} x^{-1/3}\, dx = \lim_{X \to 0^+} \int_X^{27} x^{-1/3}\, dx = \lim_{X \to 0^+} \left[\tfrac{3}{2} x^{2/3}\right]_X^{27}$$

$$= \lim_{X \to 0^+} \left[\tfrac{3}{2}(27)^{2/3} - \tfrac{3}{2} x^{2/3}\right] = \tfrac{3}{2}(9) - 0 = \tfrac{27}{2}$$

(9) This integral is improper because both limits of integration are infinite. We look at the integrals from $-\infty$ to 0 and from 0 to ∞ separately:

$$\int_0^{\infty} x^3\, dx = \lim_{X \to \infty} \int_0^X x^3\, dx = \lim_{X \to \infty} \left[\tfrac{1}{4} x^4 - \tfrac{1}{4} 0^4\right] = \infty$$

$$\int_{-\infty}^0 x^3\, dx = \lim_{X \to -\infty} \int_X^0 x^3\, dx = \lim_{X \to -\infty} \left[\tfrac{1}{4} 0^4 - \tfrac{1}{4} x^4\right] = -\infty$$

Because one of these is ∞ and the other is $-\infty$, the original integral (which would be their sum) is not defined.

(11) This integral is improper because $x^{-4/5}$ tends to ∞ as $x \longrightarrow 0^-$:

$$\int_{-32}^0 x^{-4/5}\, dx = \lim_{X \to 0^-} \int_{-32}^X x^{-4/5}\, dx = \lim_{X \to 0^-} \left[5 x^{1/5}\right]_{-32}^X$$

$$= \lim_{X \to 0^-} \left[5 X^{1/5} - 5(-32)^{1/5}\right] = -5(-2) = 10$$

(15) This integral is improper because $\dfrac{1}{\sqrt{16 - x^2}}$ tends to ∞ as $x \longrightarrow 4^-$:

$$\int_0^4 \frac{1}{\sqrt{16 - x^2}}\, dx = \lim_{X \to 4^-} \int_0^X \frac{1}{\sqrt{16 - x^2}}\, dx = \lim_{X \to 4^-} \left[\arcsin(\tfrac{X}{4})\right]_0^X$$

$$= \lim_{X \to 4^-} \left[\arcsin(\tfrac{X}{4}) - \arcsin(0)\right] = \arcsin(1) = \tfrac{\pi}{2}$$

(20) The integral is improper because of the infinite lower limit of integration. We use the substitution $u = 1 + e^x$, $du = e^x dx$ in evaluating the integral:

$$\int_{-\infty}^{0} \frac{e^x}{1 + e^x} dx = \lim_{X \to -\infty} \int_{X}^{0} \frac{e^x}{1 + e^x} dx = \lim_{X \to -\infty} [\ln(1 + e^x)]_{X}^{0}$$

$$= \lim_{X \to -\infty} [\ln(1 + 1) - \ln(1 + e^x)] = \ln(2) - \ln(1) = \ln(2)$$

(23) The integrand is continuous for $x \geq 10$, so the integral is improper only because of the infinite upper limit of integration. To evaluate the indefinite integral, we use the partial fraction decomposition

$$\frac{2}{x^2 - 1} = \frac{1}{x - 1} - \frac{1}{x + 1} :$$

$$\int_{10}^{\infty} \frac{2}{x^2 - 1} dx = \lim_{X \to \infty} \int_{10}^{X} \frac{2}{x^2 - 1} dx = \lim_{X \to \infty} [\ln|x - 1| - \ln|x + 1|]_{10}^{X}$$

$$= \lim_{X \to \infty} [\ln\left|\frac{x - 1}{x + 1}\right|]_{10}^{X} = \lim_{X \to \infty} [\ln\left|\frac{X - 1}{X + 1}\right| - \ln(\frac{9}{11})]$$

$$= \ln(1) - \ln(\frac{9}{11}) = \ln(\frac{11}{9})$$

(26) Area $= \lim_{X \to \infty} \int_{2}^{X} x^{-3} dx = \lim_{X \to \infty} [-\frac{1}{2} x^{-2}]_{2}^{X} = \lim_{X \to \infty} [-\frac{1}{2} X^{-2} + \frac{1}{2} 2^{-2}] = \frac{1}{8}$

(27) Area $= \lim_{X \to 0^+} \int_{X}^{2} x^{-3} dx = \lim_{X \to 0^+} [-\frac{1}{2} x^{-2}]_{X}^{2} = \lim_{X \to 0^+} [-\frac{1}{2} 2^{-2} + \frac{1}{2} X^{-2}] = \infty$

SECTION 18.1

(7) $\dfrac{(n + 1)(n + 2)(n + 3)}{n + 2n^2 + 3n^3} = \dfrac{(1 + \frac{1}{n})(1 + \frac{2}{n})(1 + \frac{3}{n})}{\frac{1}{n^2} + \frac{2}{n} + 3} \rightarrow \dfrac{1}{3}$ as $n \rightarrow \infty$

(11) $(-n)^n$ is a large positive number if n is a large positive even integer and is a large negative number if n is a large positive odd integer. Consequently, the sequence does not have a limit.

(14) Set $x = \dfrac{1}{n}$. Then because $\cos(1 + x) - \cos(1)$ and x tend to 0 as x tends to 0^+, l'Hopital's rule gives

$$\lim_{n \rightarrow \infty} \left\{ n[\cos(1 + \tfrac{1}{n}) - \cos(1)] \right\} = \lim_{x \rightarrow 0^+} \dfrac{\cos(1 + x) - \cos(1)}{x}$$

$$= \lim_{x \rightarrow 0^+} \dfrac{\frac{d}{dx}[\cos(1 + x) - \cos(1)]}{\frac{d}{dx}(x)} = \lim_{x \rightarrow 0^+} [- \sin(1 + x)] = - \sin(1).$$

(We could also obtain this result by applying the definition of the derivative of $\cos(1 + x)$ at $x = 0$.)

(15) Set $x = \dfrac{1}{n}$. The functions x^2 and $\sin x$ tend to 0 as x tends to 0^+, so by l'Hopital's rule

$$\lim_{n \rightarrow \infty} n^2 \sin(\tfrac{1}{n}) = \lim_{x \rightarrow 0^+} \dfrac{\sin x}{x^2} = \lim_{x \rightarrow 0^+} \dfrac{\frac{d}{dx} \sin x}{\frac{d}{dx} x^2} = \lim_{x \rightarrow 0^+} \dfrac{\cos x}{2x} = \infty.$$

The sequence has the limit ∞ ; it diverges to ∞ .

(23) The expression

$$\dfrac{1}{n}[\sin(\tfrac{1}{n}) + \sin(\tfrac{2}{n}) + \ldots + \sin(\tfrac{4n - 1}{n}) + \sin(4)]$$

is a Riemann sum for the integral

$$\int_0^4 \sin x \, dx = \left[- \cos x \right]_0^4 = - \cos(4) + \cos(0) = 1 - \cos(4)$$

corresponding to the partition $0 < \frac{1}{n} < \frac{2}{n} < \cdots < \frac{4n-1}{n} < 4$ of the interval $0 \leq x \leq 4$. The limit of the sequence is the integral, which equals $1 - \cos(4)$.

(32) We study first the logarithms of the sequence:

$$\lim_{n \to \infty} \ln[(1 - \frac{2}{n})^n] = \lim_{n \to \infty} [n \ln(1 - \frac{2}{n})] = \lim_{x \to 0^+} \frac{\ln(1 - 2x)}{x}$$

$$= \lim_{x \to 0^+} \frac{\frac{d}{dx} \ln(1 - 2x)}{\frac{d}{dx} x} = \lim_{x \to 0^+} \frac{-2}{1 - 2x} = -2$$

We can apply l'Hopital's rule here because $\ln(1 - 2x)$ and x both tend to 0 as x tends to 0^+. Because the logarithms of the terms of the sequence tend to -2, the sequence converges to e^{-2}.

(34) $\ln(1 + x)$ and x both tend to ∞ as x tends to ∞, so by l'Hopital's rule

$$\lim_{x \to \infty} \ln[(1 + x)^{1/x}] = \lim_{x \to \infty} \frac{\ln(1 + x)}{x} = \lim_{x \to \infty} \frac{\frac{d}{dx} \ln(1 + x)}{\frac{d}{dx} x}$$

$$= \lim_{x \to \infty} \frac{1}{1 + x} = 0.$$

Hence the limit of $\ln[(1 + n)^{1/n}]$ as n tends to ∞ is 0 and the limit of $(1 + n)^{1/n}$ is 1. The sequence converges to 1.

(37) For $n > 2$

$$\frac{(n!)^2}{(n^2)!} = \frac{1 \cdot 2 \cdot 3 \cdots n}{1 \cdot 2 \cdot 3 \cdots n} \frac{1 \cdot 2 \cdot 3 \cdots n}{(n+1)(n+2)(n+3) \cdots (2n)} \frac{1}{(2n+1)(2n+2)(2n+3) \cdots (n^2)}$$

$$< \frac{1}{(2n+1)(2n+2)(2n+3) \cdots (n^2)}$$

so the sequence tends to 0 as n tends to ∞.

SECTION 18.2

(3) We multiply and divide the difference $\sqrt{9} - \sqrt{9 - \frac{5}{n}}$ of square roots by the

sum $\sqrt{9} + \sqrt{9 - \frac{5}{n}}$ of square roots (rationalization): For $n \geq 1$

(*) $\left| 3 - \sqrt{9 - \frac{5}{n}} \right| = \left| \frac{[\sqrt{9} - \sqrt{9 - \frac{5}{n}}][\sqrt{9} + \sqrt{9 - \frac{5}{n}}]}{\sqrt{9} + \sqrt{9 - \frac{5}{n}}} \right| = \left| \frac{9 - (9 - \frac{5}{n})}{3 + \sqrt{9 - \frac{5}{n}}} \right| = \frac{5}{n} \left| \frac{1}{3 + \sqrt{9 - \frac{5}{n}}} \right| < \frac{5}{3n}$

We want to make expression (*) be less than ϵ , so we solve the inequality $\frac{5}{3n} < \epsilon$ for n:

(**) $\frac{5}{3n} < \epsilon \iff \frac{5}{3\epsilon} < n.$

Given $\epsilon > 0$ we set $N = \frac{5}{3\epsilon}$. Then statements (*) and (**) show that $\left| 3 - \sqrt{9 - \frac{5}{n}} \right| < \epsilon$

for all $n > N$.

(5) For $n \geq 1$, we have

(*) $\left| \frac{n^2}{n^2 + 4} - 1 \right| = \left| \frac{n^2 - (n^2 + 4)}{n^2 + 4} \right| = \frac{4}{n^2 + 4} < \frac{4}{n^2}$

We want to make (*) less than ϵ , so we solve the inequality $\frac{4}{n^2} < \epsilon$ for n:

(**) $\frac{4}{n^2} < \epsilon \iff \frac{4}{\epsilon} < n^2 \iff \frac{2}{\sqrt{\epsilon}} < n$ (since $n > 0$)

Given $\epsilon > 0$, we set $N = \frac{2}{\sqrt{\epsilon}}$. Then statements (*) and (**) show that for $n > N$

(**) $\left| \frac{n^2}{n^2 + 4} - 1 \right| < \epsilon$.

Alternate solution. We deal directly with inequality (**) without making the simplifications

in (*): Because $n^2/(n^2 + 4)$ is less than 1, we have

$$\left| \frac{n^2}{n^2 + 4} - 1 \right| = 1 - \frac{n^2}{n^2 + 4} = \frac{4}{n^2 + 4} .$$

Accordingly, we have

$$\left| \frac{n^2}{n^2 + 4} - 1 \right| < \epsilon \iff \frac{4}{n^2 + 4} < \epsilon \iff \frac{4}{\epsilon} < n^2 + 4$$

$$\iff n^2 > \frac{4}{\epsilon} - 4 \iff \begin{cases} n > 0 & \text{if} \quad \epsilon \geq 1 \\ n > \sqrt{\frac{4}{\epsilon} - 4} & \text{if} \quad 0 < \epsilon < 1, \end{cases}$$

and we set N equal to 0 if $\epsilon \geq 1$ and equal to $\sqrt{\frac{4}{\epsilon} - 4}$ if $0 < \epsilon < 1$.

(7) By the Mean Value Theorem for derivatives there is, for each $x > 0$, a number c with $0 < c < x$ such that

$$e^x - 1 = e^c(x).$$

Here we use the fact that $\frac{d}{dx} e^x = e^x$. For $x = \frac{1}{n}$ with n a positive integer, we have $0 < x < 1$, so that $0 < c < 1$ and

$$\left| e^{1/n} - 1 \right| = e^c\left(\frac{1}{n}\right) < \frac{e}{n}.$$

Given $\epsilon > 0$, we set $N = \frac{e}{\epsilon}$. Then for $n > N$, we have $\left| e^{1/n} - 1 \right| < \frac{e}{N} = \epsilon$.

(25) The derivative

$$\frac{d}{dx}\left(x - \frac{1}{x}\right) = 1 + \frac{1}{x^2}$$

is positive for all $x > 0$, so the sequence $\left\{ n - \frac{1}{n} \right\}_{n=1}^{\infty}$ is increasing. It is bounded below and its greatest lower bound is its first term $1 - \frac{1}{1} = 0$. It is not bounded above because $n - \frac{1}{n}$ tends to ∞ as n tends to ∞.

(27) The expression $(-1)^n + 1$ is 2 if n is an even positive integer and is 0 if n is an odd positive integer. The sequence is not monotone, but is bounded above and below. Its greatest lower bound is 0 and its least upper bound is 2.

(33) The derivative

$$\frac{d}{dx}[xe^{-x}] = \left[\frac{d}{dx} x\right]e^{-x} + x\left[\frac{d}{dx} e^{-x}\right] = xe^{-x} - e^{-x} = e^{-x}(x - 1)$$

is positive for $x < 1$ and negative for $x > 1$. Therefore the sequence $\{ne^{-n}\}$ increases from 0 to e^{-1} as n changes from 0 to 1 and decreases for $n > 1$. The sequence is not monotone. It is bounded above and below. Because ne^{-n} is positive

for all $n > 0$ and its maximum value is e^{-1}, the greatest lower bound of the sequence is 0 and the least upper bound is e^{-1}.

SECTION 18.3

(1) By the finite geometric series formula (Equation (2) in Section 18.3 of the text) with $r = \frac{1}{2}$ and $n = 12$,

$$1 + \frac{1}{2} + \left(\frac{1}{2}\right)^2 + \left(\frac{1}{2}\right)^3 + \dots + \left(\frac{1}{2}\right)^{12} = \frac{1 - \left(\frac{1}{2}\right)^{13}}{1 - \frac{1}{2}} \approx \frac{1 - 0.000122}{\frac{1}{2}} = 1.999756 .$$

(5) By the finite geometric series formula with $r = \frac{1}{10}$ and $n = 5$,

$$6 + 0.6 + 0.06 + 0.006 + 0.0006 + 0.00006 = 6\left[\frac{1}{10} + \left(\frac{1}{10}\right)^2 + \left(\frac{1}{10}\right)^3 + \left(\frac{1}{10}\right)^4 + \left(\frac{1}{10}\right)^5\right]$$

$$= 6\left[\frac{1 - \left(\frac{1}{10}\right)^6}{1 - \frac{1}{10}}\right] = 6\left[\frac{0.999999}{\frac{9}{10}}\right] = 60(0.111111) = 6.66666 .$$

(8) By the finite geometric series formula with $r = -0.99$ and $n = 1023$

$$\sum_{j=0}^{1023} (-1)^j (0.99)^j = \sum_{j=0}^{1023} (-0.99)^j = \frac{1 - (-0.99)^{1024}}{1 - (-0.99)} = \frac{1 - (0.99)^{1024}}{1.99}$$

$$\approx \frac{1 - 0.0000339}{1.99} \approx 0.502495528.$$

(9) Every term in the sum equals 1 and there are 101 terms, so the sum equals 101.

(10) $\displaystyle\sum_{j=3}^{34} (1.1)^j = \sum_{j=0}^{34} (1.1) - (1.1)^0 - (1.1)^1 - (1.1)^2 = \frac{1 - (1.1)^{35}}{1 - 1.1} - 3.31$

$\approx \dfrac{1 - 28.10}{-0.1} - 3.31 = 271.0 - 3.31 = 267.69$

SECTION 18.4

(1) This geometric series with $r = \frac{1}{7}$ converges because r is less than 1. Its value

is $\qquad \dfrac{1}{1 - \frac{1}{7}} = \dfrac{1}{\frac{6}{7}} = \dfrac{7}{6}$.

(7) This series is obtained from the geometric series with $r = \frac{9}{8}$ by deleting the first 10 terms and dividing it by 100. This series diverges to ∞ because the geometric series does.

(10) $5.8999\ldots = \frac{1}{10}(58 + 0.999\ldots) = \frac{1}{10}[58 + 9(0.111\ldots)] = \frac{1}{10}[58 + 9\displaystyle\sum_{j=1}^{\infty} (\frac{1}{10})^j]$

$= \frac{1}{10}[58 + 9(\frac{1}{9})] = \dfrac{59}{10}$

(16) The series diverges because $(1 + \frac{1}{j})^j$ tends to e as $j \to \infty$ and the terms do not tend to 0.

(18) $\qquad \dfrac{\frac{2n - 5}{10 + n^2}}{\frac{1}{n}} = \dfrac{n(2n - 5)}{10 + n^2} = \dfrac{2 - \frac{5}{n}}{\frac{10}{n^2} + 1} \to 2$ as $n \to \infty$. Therefore,

the series diverges by the Limit Comparison Test with the divergent harmonic series

$\displaystyle\sum_{n=1}^{\infty} \frac{1}{n}$.

(20) $\lim\limits_{j\to\infty} \dfrac{\dfrac{1}{3^j + 1}}{\dfrac{1}{3^j}} = \lim\limits_{j\to\infty} \dfrac{3^j}{3^j + 1} = \lim\limits_{j\to\infty} \dfrac{1}{1 + (\frac{1}{3})^j} = 1$

The series converges by the Limit Comparison Test with the geometric series $\sum\limits_{j=0}^{\infty} (\frac{1}{3})^j$.

(26) For $j \geq 1$ we have $\sqrt{j} \leq j$ so that $\dfrac{1}{\sqrt{j}} \geq \dfrac{1}{j}$ and the series diverges

by the Comparison Test with the divergent harmonic series $\sum\limits_{j=1}^{\infty} \dfrac{1}{j}$.

(32) The partial fraction decomposition has the form

(*) $\dfrac{2j + 1}{j^2(j + 1)^2} = \dfrac{A}{j} + \dfrac{B}{j^2} + \dfrac{C}{j + 1} + \dfrac{D}{(j + 1)^2} = \dfrac{Aj(j + 1)^2 + B(j + 1)^2 + Cj^2(j + 1) + Dj^2}{j^2(j + 1)^2}$.

We obtain the fraction on the right by taking the _least_ common denominator, which is the
denominator of the original fraction on the left. This equation gives

$$2j + 1 = Aj(j + 1)^2 + B(j + 1)^2 + Cj^2(j + 1) + Dj^2.$$

Setting $j = 0$ yields $1 = B$ and setting $j = -1$ gives $-1 = D$, so we have

$$2j + 1 = Aj(j^2 + 2j + 1) + (j^2 + 2j + 1) + Cj^2(j + 1) - j^2$$

$$= Aj^3 + 2Aj^2 + Aj + j^2 + 2j + 1 + Cj^3 + Cj^2 - j^2$$

$$= (A + C)j^3 + (2A + 1 + C - 1)j^2 + (A + 2)j + 1.$$

Equating coefficients of powers of j on the two sides of this equation gives the four
equations

$$A + C = 0, \ 2A + C = 0, \ A + 2 = 2, \text{ and } \ 1 = 1$$

which show that A and C are both zero. We set $A = 0, B = 1, C = 0,$ and $D = -1$
in (*) to obtain

$$\dfrac{2j + 1}{j^2(j + 1)^2} = \dfrac{1}{j^2} - \dfrac{1}{(j + 1)^2}$$

so that

$$\sum\limits_{j=2}^{J} \dfrac{2j + 1}{j^2(j + 1)^2} = [\dfrac{1}{2^2} - \dfrac{1}{3^2}] + [\dfrac{1}{3^2} - \dfrac{1}{4^2}] + [\dfrac{1}{4^2} - \dfrac{1}{5^2}] + \cdots + [\dfrac{1}{J^2} - \dfrac{1}{(J + 1)^2}]$$

$$= \dfrac{1}{2^2} - \dfrac{1}{(J + 1)^2} .$$

Since this tends to $\dfrac{1}{4}$ as J tends to ∞ , the sum of the infinite series is $\dfrac{1}{4}$.

SECTION 18.5

(1) x and $\ln x$ are increasing functions of x, so $\dfrac{1}{x(\ln x)^2}$ is a decreasing function

of x for $x \geq 2$. Furthermore, with the substitution $u = \ln x$, $du = \dfrac{1}{x} dx$ in the integral,

we have

$$\int \frac{1}{x(\ln x)^2} dx = \int u^{-2} du = -u^{-1} + C = -\frac{1}{\ln x} + C$$

and

$$\int_2^\infty \frac{1}{x(\ln x)^2} dx = \lim_{X \to \infty} \int_2^X \frac{1}{x(\ln x)^2} dx = \lim_{X \to \infty} \left[-\frac{1}{\ln x} \right]_2^X$$

$$= \lim_{X \to \infty} \left[-\frac{1}{\ln(X)} + \frac{1}{\ln(2)} \right] = \frac{1}{\ln(2)} .$$

The series converges by the Integral Test.

(5) $\displaystyle \lim_{n \to \infty} \frac{\dfrac{3n}{n^2 + 4}}{\dfrac{1}{n}} = \lim_{n \to \infty} \frac{3n^2}{n^2 + 4} = \lim_{n \to \infty} \frac{3}{1 + \dfrac{4}{n^2}} = 3$

The series diverges by the Limit Comparison Test with the harmonic series $\displaystyle \sum_{n=1}^{\infty} \frac{1}{n}$

<u>Alternate solution</u> The derivative

$$\frac{d}{dx} \left[\frac{3x}{x^2 + 4} \right] = \frac{(x^2 + 4) \frac{d}{dx}(3x) - 3x \frac{d}{dx}(x^2 + 4)}{(x^2 + 4)^2} = \frac{12 - 3x^2}{(x^2 + 4)^2}$$

is negative for $x > 2$, so the function

$$\frac{3x}{x^2 + 4}$$

is decreasing for $n \geq 2$. The substitution $u = x^2 + 4$, $du = 3x$ in the integral shows that

$$\int_2^\infty \frac{3x}{x^2 + 4} dx = \lim_{X \to \infty} \frac{3}{2} \int_2^X \frac{1}{x^2 + 4} (2x\, dx) = \lim_{X \to \infty} \left[\frac{3}{2} \ln(x^2 + 4) \right]_2^X$$

$$= \lim_{X \to \infty} \left[\frac{3}{2} \ln(X^2 + 4) - \frac{3}{2} \ln(8) \right] = \infty.$$

The series diverges by the Integral Test.

(7) With $a_j = j(\frac{1}{2})^j$, we have

$$\frac{|a_{j+1}|}{|a_j|} = \frac{(j+1)(\frac{1}{2})^{j+1}}{j(\frac{1}{2})^j} = (\frac{1}{2})\frac{j+1}{j} = \frac{1}{2}(1+\frac{1}{j}) \longrightarrow \frac{1}{2} \text{ as } j \to \infty.$$

The series converges by the Ratio Test with $\rho = \frac{1}{2}$.

(9) We set $a_k = \frac{2^k}{(2k)!}$. Then

$$\frac{|a_{k+1}|}{|a_k|} = \frac{\frac{2^{k+1}}{[2(k+1)]!}}{\frac{2^k}{(2k)!}} = 2\left[\frac{(2k)!}{(2k+2)!}\right] = \frac{2}{(2k+1)(2k+2)} \longrightarrow 0 \text{ as } k \to \infty.$$

The series converges by the Ratio Test with $\rho = 0$.

(11) We set $a_k = (-1)^k \frac{k!}{k^k}$. Then

$$\frac{|a_{k+1}|}{|a_k|} = \frac{\frac{(k+1)!}{(k+1)^{k+1}}}{\frac{k!}{k^k}} = \frac{k^k}{k!}\frac{(k+1)!}{(k+1)^{k+1}} = (\frac{k}{k+1})^k(\frac{k+1}{k+1}) = \frac{1}{(1+\frac{1}{k})^k}$$

and this ratio tends to $\frac{1}{e}$ as $k \to \infty$. Because $\rho = \frac{1}{e}$ is less than 1, the series converges by the Ratio Test.

(17)   Because the highest degree term in the denominator of $\dfrac{j^{1/3}}{1 + j^{1/2} + j + j^{3/2}}$ is

$j^{3/2}$, we compare with the series with terms $\dfrac{j^{1/3}}{j^{3/2}} = j^{-7/6}$. Because

$$\frac{\frac{j^{1/3}}{1 + j^{1/2} + j + j^{3/2}}}{\frac{1}{j^{7/6}}} = \frac{j^{7/6} j^{1/3}}{1 + j^{1/2} + j + j^{3/2}} = \frac{j^{3/2}}{1 + j^{1/2} + j + j^{3/2}} =$$

$$= \frac{1}{j^{-2/3} + j^{-1} + j^{-1/2} + 1}$$

tends to 1 as j tends to ∞ and the series

$$\sum_{j=1}^{\infty} \frac{1}{j^{7/6}}$$

converges, the given series converges by the Limit Comparison Test.

(19) For $a_j = \dfrac{(100)^j}{j!}$ we have

$$\frac{|a_{j+1}|}{|a_j|} = \frac{1}{|a_j|}\,|a_{j+1}| = \frac{j!}{(100)^j}\;\frac{(100)^{j+1}}{(j+1)!} = \frac{100}{j+1} \to 0 \text{ as } j \to \infty .$$

The series converges by the Ratio Test with $\rho = 0$.

(25) Because $|\sin(j)|$ is no greater than 1, we have

$$\left|\frac{1}{j^3}\,e^{\sin(j)}\right| \le e\!\left(\frac{1}{j^3}\right).$$

The series converges by the Comparison Test with the convergent series $\displaystyle\sum_{j=1}^{\infty} \frac{1}{j^3}$.

(31) For $n \ge 0$, we have $0 \le \arctan(n) < \dfrac{\pi}{2}$. Therefore

$$\left|\frac{\arctan(n)}{n^2 + 1}\right| < \frac{\pi}{2n^2} \quad \text{for } n \ge 1.$$

The series converges by the Comparison Test with the convergent series $\displaystyle\sum_{n=1}^{\infty} \frac{1}{n^2}$.

<u>Alternate solution</u> The derivative

$$\frac{d}{dx}\left[\frac{\arctan x}{x^2 + 1}\right] = \frac{(x^2 + 1)\frac{d}{dx}\arctan x - \arctan x \frac{d}{dx}(x^2 + 1)}{(x^2 + 1)^2}$$

$$= \frac{1 - 2x\arctan x}{(x^2 + 1)^2}$$

is negative for $x \ge 1$ because $\arctan(1) = \dfrac{\pi}{4}$ and $1 - \dfrac{\pi}{2}$ is negative. Hence the sequence

is negative for $x > 1$ because $\arctan x$ is greater than $\dfrac{\pi}{4}$ for $x > 1$ and $1 - \dfrac{\pi}{2}$ is

negative. Hence, the function $\dfrac{\arctan x}{x^2 + 1}$ is decreasing for $x \ge 1$. The substitution

$u = \arctan x, \quad du = \dfrac{1}{x^2 + 1}\,dx$ in the integral

$$\int_1^{\infty} \frac{\arctan x}{x^2 + 1}\,dx = \lim_{X \to \infty} \int_1^{X} \frac{\arctan x}{x^2 + 1}\,dx = \lim_{X \to \infty} [\ln(\arctan x)]\Big|_1^{X}$$

$$= = \lim_{X \to \infty} [\ln(\arctan X) - \ln(\arctan(1)] = \ln\!\left(\frac{\pi}{2}\right) - \ln\left(\frac{\pi}{4}\right) = \ln(2)$$

shows that the improper integral is finite, and the series converges by the Integral Test.

SECTION 18.6

(1)   For $j \geq 1$, we have $\left| \dfrac{\sin j}{j^3 + 1} \right| < \dfrac{1}{j^3}$, so the series converges absolutely

by the Comparison Test with the convergent series $\sum\limits_{j=1}^{\infty} \dfrac{1}{j^3}$.

(7) Set $a_j = \dfrac{(-j)^j}{(2j)!}$. Then

$$\frac{|a_{j+1}|}{|a_j|} = \frac{1}{|a_j|} |a_{j+1}| = \frac{(2j)!}{j^j} \frac{(j + 1)^{j+1}}{(2j + 2)!} = [\frac{j + 1}{j}]^j \frac{(j + 1)}{(2j + 1)(2j + 2)}$$

$$= [1 + \tfrac{1}{j}]^j \frac{1}{2(2j + 1)} \longrightarrow (e)(0) = 0 \quad \text{as} \quad j \to \infty .$$

The series converges absolutely by the Ratio Test with $\rho = 0$.

(9) $\text{Cos}(n\pi)$ equals $(-1)^n$; the sequence $\dfrac{1}{\sqrt{n\pi}}$ is a decreasing function of $n \geq 1$

and tends to 0 as $n \to \infty$. Hence the series $\sum\limits_{n=1} \dfrac{\cos(n\pi)}{\sqrt{n\pi}}$ converges

The series $\sum\limits_{n=1} \left| \dfrac{\cos(n\pi)}{\sqrt{n\pi}} \right|$ is the series $\dfrac{1}{\sqrt{\pi}} \sum\limits_{n=1} \dfrac{1}{n^{1/2}}$, which diverges. The

original series converges conditionally.

(11) For $a_n = \dfrac{(-n)^n}{n!}$ we have

$$\frac{|a_{n+1}|}{|a_n|} = \frac{1}{|a_n|} |a_{n+1}| = \frac{n!}{n^n} \frac{(n + 1)^{n+1}}{(n + 1)!} = (\frac{n + 1}{n})(\frac{n + 1}{n + 1}) = (1 + \frac{1}{n})^n$$

This ratio tends to e, which is greater than 1, as n   tends to ∞ , so th series

diverges by the Ratio Test.

(13) The series diverges because $\arctan(k)$ tends to $\dfrac{\pi}{2}$ as k tends to ∞ and the

terms in the series do not tend to zero.

(19) Because $\sin x$ is an increasing function for $0 < x < 1$, the sequence $\{\sin(\tfrac{1}{n})\}$

is decreasing for $n \geq 1$. The sequence $\sin(\tfrac{1}{n})$ tends to $\sin(0) = 0$ as n tends to ∞.

Therefore the series converges.

    Because $\sin(\tfrac{1}{n})$ is positive for $n \geq 1$ and the limit

$$\lim_{n \to \infty} \frac{\sin(\frac{1}{n})}{\frac{1}{n}} = \lim_{x \to 0^+} \frac{\sin x}{x} = 1$$

is a nonzero number, the series $\displaystyle\sum_{n=2} \sin(\frac{1}{n})$ diverges by the Limit Comparison Test with the harmonic series. The original series converges conditionally.

(25) We set $a_n = \dfrac{x^n}{\sqrt{n}}$ to have

$$\frac{|a_{n+1}|}{|a_n|} = \frac{1}{|a_n|}|a_{n+1}| = \frac{\sqrt{n}}{|x^n|}\frac{|x^{n+1}|}{\sqrt{n+1}} = |x|\sqrt{\frac{n}{n+1}} = \frac{|x|}{\sqrt{1+\frac{1}{n}}} \quad .$$

This ratio tends to $|x|$ as n tends to ∞. By the Ratio Test with $\rho = |x|$ the series converges absolutely for $|x| < 1$ and diverges for $|x| > 1$.

For $x = 1$ the series is $\displaystyle\sum_{n=1} \frac{1}{\sqrt{n}}$, which diverges. For $x = -1$ the series is $\displaystyle\sum_{n=1} \frac{(-1)^n}{\sqrt{n}}$, which converges conditionally.

SECTION 18.7

(2) With $a_j = \sqrt{j}\, x^j$, we have

$$\frac{|a_{j+1}|}{|a_j|} = \frac{\sqrt{j+1}\,|x|^{j+1}}{\sqrt{j}\,|x|^j} = |x|\sqrt{1+\frac{1}{j}} \longrightarrow |x| \quad \text{as} \quad j \to \infty.$$

The series converges absolutely for $|x| < 1$ and diverges for $|x| > 1$ by the Ratio Test. It diverges for $x = \pm 1$ because in these cases its terms $j(-1)^j$ do not tend to zero.

(5) Set $a_j = (jx)^j$. Then

$$\frac{|a_{j+1}|}{|a_j|} = \frac{(j+1)^{j+1}\ |x|^{j+1}}{j^j\ |x|^j} = (j+1)(\frac{j+1}{j})^j\ |x| = (j+1)(1+\frac{1}{j})^j\ |x|$$

and this ratio tends to ∞ as j tends to ∞ for any $x \neq 0$. By the Ratio Test the series diverges for all $x \neq 0$. For $x = 0$ it converges because all the terms in it are 0.

(11) Set $a_j = \frac{1}{2j} x^{2j}$. Then

$$\frac{|a_{j+1}|}{|a_j|} = \frac{1}{|a_j|}\ |a_{j+1}| = \frac{2j}{|x|^{2j}}\ \frac{|x|^{2j+2}}{2j+2} = |x|^2\ \frac{2j}{2j+2} = |x|^2\ \frac{1}{1+\frac{1}{j}}$$

and this ratio tends to $|x|^2$ as j tends to ∞. By the Ratio Test the series converges absolutely for $|x| < 1$ and diverges for $|x| > 1$. It diverges for $x = \pm 1$ because then it is the series

$$\sum_{j=1}^{\infty} \frac{1}{2j}(\pm 1)^2 = \sum_{j=1}^{\infty} \frac{1}{2j} = \frac{1}{2} \sum_{j=1}^{\infty} \frac{1}{j} = \infty$$

(17) For $f(x) = \sin x$, we have for each nonnegative integer k

$$f^{(4k)}(x) = \sin x, \quad f^{(4k+1)}(x) = \cos x, \quad f^{(4k+2)}(x) = -\sin x, \quad f^{(4k+3)}(x) = -\cos x,$$

so that if $P_n(x)$ is the nth degree Taylor polynomial approximation of $\sin x$ centered at 0, then

(*) $\sin x = P_n(x) + R_n(x)$

where

$$R_n(x) = \frac{1}{(n+1)!}\ [\pm \sin(c)]\ x^{n+1} \quad or \quad = \frac{1}{(n+1)!}\ [\pm \cos(c)]\ x^{n+1}.$$

In any case

$$|R_n(x)| \leq \frac{|x|^{n+1}}{(n+1)!}$$

which tends to zero as n tends to ∞ for any x (see Exercise 31). Hence, by equation (*)

$$\sin x = \lim_{n \to} P_n(x);$$

the Maclaurin series for $\sin x$ converges for all x; and its value is $\sin x$.

For each nonnegative integer k, we have $f^{(4k)}(0) = \sin(0) = 0$, $f^{(4k+1)}(0) = \cos(0) = 1$, $f^{(4k+2)}(0) = -\sin(0) = 0$, and $f^{(4k+3)}(0) = -\cos(0) = -1$. Therefore the Maclaurin series is

$$x - \frac{1}{3!} x^3 + \frac{1}{5!} x^5 - \frac{1}{7!} + \cdots = \sum_{j=0}^{\infty} \frac{(-1)^j}{(2j+1)!} x^{2j+1}$$

(19) For $f(x) = \sinh x$, we have for every nonnegative integer k,

$$f^{(2k)}(x) = \sinh x \qquad \text{and} \quad f^{(2k+1)}(x) = \cosh x$$

Accordingly,

(*) $\sinh x = P_n(x) + R_n(x)$

where

$$R_n(x) = \frac{1}{(n+1)!} \sinh(c) \, x^{n+1} \quad \text{or} \quad = \frac{1}{(n+1)!} \cosh(c) \, x^{n+1}$$

and c is a number between x and 0. We have

$$|\sinh c| = \left| \tfrac{1}{2}(e^c - e^{-c}) \right| \leq \tfrac{1}{2}(e^{|x|} + e^{|x|}) = e^{|x|}$$

$$|\cosh c| = \left| \tfrac{1}{2}(e^c + e^{-c}) \right| \leq \tfrac{1}{2}(e^{|x|} + e^{|x|}) = e^{|x|}$$

so that

$$|R_n(x)| \leq e^{|x|} \frac{|x|^{n+1}}{(n+1)!} \longrightarrow 0 \quad \text{as} \quad n \longrightarrow \infty$$

and equation (*) shows that the Maclaurin series for $\sinh x$ converges for each x and equals $\sinh x$. Because $f^{(2k)}(0) = \sinh(0) = 0$ and $f^{(2k+1)}(0) = \cosh(0) = 1$, the Maclaurin series is

$$x + \frac{1}{3!} x^3 + \frac{1}{5!} x^5 + \frac{1}{7!} + \cdots = \sum_{j=0}^{\infty} \frac{1}{(2j+1)!} x^{2j+1} \quad .$$

(21) The first five derivatives of $f(x) = (1+x)^5$ are $f'(x) = 5(1+x)^4$, $f''(x) = 5(4)(1+x)^3$, $f^{(3)}(x) = 5(4)(3)(1+x)^2$, $f^{(4)}(x) = 5(4)(3)(2)(1+x)$, and $f^{(5)}(x) = 5(4)(3)(2)(1)$. All higher order derivatives are zero. Hence $R_n(x) = 0$ for $n > 5$ and because $f(0) = 1$, $f'(0) = 5$, $f''(0) = 5(4)$, $f^{(3)}(0) = 5(4)(3)$,

$f^{(4)}(0) = 5(4)(3)(2)$ and $f^{(5)}(0) = 5(4)(3)(2)(1)$

$$(1 + x)^5 = P_5(x) = 1 + 5x + \frac{1}{2}(5)(4)x^2 + \frac{1}{3!}(5)(4)(3)x^3 + \frac{1}{4!}(5)(4)(3)(2)x^4 + \frac{1}{5!}(5!)x^5$$

$$= 1 + 5x + 10x^2 + 10x^3 + 5x^5 + x^5$$

The Maclaurin series converges because it is a sum of a finite number of numbers.

(25) For $f(x) = (2 - x)^{-1}$, we have $f'(x) = -(2 - x)^{-2}\frac{d}{dx}(2 - x) = (2 - x)^{-2}$,

$f''(x) = 2(2 - x)^{-3}$, $f^{(3)}(x) = 2(3)(2 - x)^{-4}$ and in general $f^{(n)}(x) = (n!)(2 - x)^{-n+1}$.

Hence $f^{(n)}(0) = (n!)(2^{n+1})$ and the Maclaurin series is

$$\sum_{n=0} \frac{1}{n!} f^{(n)}(0) x^n = \sum_{n=0} 2^{n+1} x^n .$$

With $a_n = 2^{n+1} x^n$ the ratio

$$\frac{|a_{n+1}|}{|a_n|} = \frac{2^{n+2}|x|^{n+1}}{2^n |x|^n} = 2|x|$$

has the limit $2|x|$. By the Ratio Test the series converges absolutely for $|x| < \frac{1}{2}$
and diverges for $|x| > \frac{1}{2}$. The series diverges for $x = \pm\frac{1}{2}$ because in this case its
terms are

$$2^{n+1}(\pm\frac{1}{2})^n = \pm 2$$

and do not tend to 0 as n tends to ∞.

(27a) Replacing x by $-x^2$ in the Maclaurin series

$$e^x = \sum_{n=0} \frac{1}{n!} x^n$$

gives the Maclaurin series

$$e^{-x^2} = \sum_{n=0} \frac{1}{n!} (-x^2)^n = \sum_{n=0} \frac{1}{n!} (-1)^n x^{2n}.$$

SECTION 18.8

(1) Because $\sin x$ has the Maclaurin series $\sin x = \sum_{j=0}^{\infty} \frac{(-1)^j}{(2j+1)!} x^{2j+1}$

$$= x - \frac{1}{6} x^3 + \sum_{j=2}^{\infty} \frac{(-1)^j}{(2j+1)!} x^{2j+1} \text{, we have}$$

$$\sin x + 5x^4 + 3 = 3 + x - \frac{1}{6} x^3 + 5x^4 + \sum_{j=2}^{\infty} \frac{(-1)^j}{(2j+1)!} x^{2j+1}$$

$$= 3 + x - \frac{1}{6} x^3 + 5x^4 + \frac{1}{5!} x^5 - \frac{1}{7!} x^7 + \frac{1}{9!} x^9 - \cdots$$

(4) We write

$$\ln\left(\frac{1+x}{1-x}\right) = \ln(1+x) - \ln(1-x) = \sum_{j=1}^{\infty} \frac{(-1)^{j+1}}{j} x^j - \sum_{j=1}^{\infty} \frac{(-1)^{j+1}}{j} (-x)^j$$

$$= \sum_{j=1}^{\infty} \frac{1}{j} [(-1)^{j+1} + 1] x^j.$$

Since $(-1)^{j+1} + 1$ equals 0 when j is even and equals 2 when j is odd, we need only the terms for odd j in the last sum. We set $j = 2n + 1$ and obtain

$$\ln\left(\frac{1+x}{1-x}\right) = \sum_{n=0}^{\infty} \frac{2}{2n+1} x^{2n+1}.$$

This sum begins with $n = 0$ since that corresponds to $j = 2(0) + 1 = 1$.

(9) We can obtain $(1-x)^{-3}$ from the second derivative of $(1-x)^{-1}$. We have

$$\frac{d}{dx}(1-x)^{-1} = (-1)(1-x)^{-2} \frac{d}{dx}(1-x) = -(1-x)^{-2}(-1) = (1-x)^{-2}$$

and

$$\frac{d^2}{dx^2}(1-x)^{-1} = \frac{d}{dx}(1-x)^{-2} = (-2)(1-x)^{-3} \frac{d}{dx}(1-x) = 2(1-x)^{-3}$$

so that

$$(1-x)^{-3} = \frac{1}{2} \frac{d^2}{dx^2}(1-x)^{-1} = \frac{1}{2} \frac{d^2}{dx^2} \sum_{j=0}^{\infty} x^j = \sum_{j=0}^{\infty} \frac{1}{2} \frac{d^2}{dx^2} x^j$$

$$= \sum_{j=2}^{\infty} \frac{j(j-1)}{2} x^{j-2}.$$

We start the sum at $j = 2$ because the terms for $j = 0$ and $j = 1$ are zero.

(13) $e^x \sin x = (1 + x + \frac{1}{2} x^2 + \frac{1}{3!} x^3 + \frac{1}{4!} x^4 + \cdots)(x - \frac{1}{3!} x^3 + \frac{1}{5!} x^5 - \cdots)$

$\qquad\quad = (1 + x + \frac{1}{2} x^2 + \frac{1}{6} x^3 + \frac{1}{24} x^4 + \cdots)(x - \frac{1}{6} x^3 + \frac{1}{120} x^5 - \cdots)$

Our first attempt to solve this exercise failed because we kept track only of the terms up to degree 4 and the term of degree 4 turned out to be zero. Accordingly, to obtain four nonzero terms we also compute the term of degree 5 as follows:

$e^x \sin x = (1)(x - \frac{1}{6} x^3 + \frac{1}{120} x^5 - \cdots) + x(x - \frac{1}{6} x^3 + \frac{1}{120} x^5 - \cdots)$

$\qquad\quad + \frac{1}{2} x^2(x - \frac{1}{6} x^3 + \cdots) + \frac{1}{6} x^3(x - \frac{1}{6} x^3 + \cdots) + \frac{1}{24} x^4(x - \cdots) + \cdots$

$\qquad = x - \frac{1}{6} x^3 + \frac{1}{120} x^5 + x^2 - \frac{1}{6} x^4 + \frac{1}{2} x^3 - \frac{1}{12} x^5 + \frac{1}{6} x^4 + \frac{1}{24} x^5 + \cdots$

$\qquad = x + x^2 + (- \frac{1}{6} + \frac{1}{2})x^3 + (- \frac{1}{6} + \frac{1}{6})x^4 + (\frac{1}{120} - \frac{1}{12} + \frac{1}{24})x^5 + \cdots$

$\qquad = x + x^2 + \frac{1}{3} x^3 - \frac{1}{30} x^5 + \cdots$

(23)   We need to make the substitution $u = \sin x = x - \frac{1}{6} x^3 + \frac{1}{120} x^5 - \cdots$ in the Maclaurin series $e^u = 1 + u + \frac{1}{2} u^2 + \frac{1}{6} u^3 + \frac{1}{24} u^4 + \cdots$. We first find the series for the powers of $\sin x$, after learning by trial and error that we need the terms up to degree 4 to obtain four nonzero terms in the result. We have

$\sin x = x - \frac{1}{6} x^3 + \cdots$

$\sin^2 x = (x - \frac{1}{6} x^3 + \cdots)(x - \frac{1}{6} x^3 + \cdots) = x(x - \frac{1}{6} x^3 + \cdots) - \frac{1}{6} x^3(x - \frac{1}{6} x^3 + \cdots) + \cdots$

$\qquad = x^2 - \frac{1}{6} x^4 - \frac{1}{6} x^4 + \cdots = x^2 - \frac{1}{3} x^4 + \cdots$

$\sin^3 x = (\sin x)(\sin^2 x) = (x - \frac{1}{6} x^3 + \cdots)(x^2 - \frac{1}{3} x^4 + \cdots)$

$\qquad = x(x^2 - \frac{1}{3} x^4 + \cdots) - \frac{1}{6} x^4(x^2 - \frac{1}{3} x^4 + \cdots) = x^3 - \cdots$

and

$\sin^4 x = (\sin x)(\sin^3 x) = (x - \frac{1}{6} x^3 + \cdots)(x^3 - \cdots) = x^4 + \cdots$

so that

$$e^{\sin x} = 1 + \sin x + \frac{1}{2} \sin^2 x + \frac{1}{6} \sin^3 x + \frac{1}{24} \sin^4 x + \cdots$$

$$= 1 + (x - \frac{1}{6} x^3 + \cdots) + \frac{1}{2}(x^2 - \frac{1}{3} x^4 + \cdots) + \frac{1}{6}(x^3 - \cdots) + \frac{1}{24}(x^4 + \cdots) + \cdots$$

$$= 1 + x + \frac{1}{2} x^2 + (-\frac{1}{6} + \frac{1}{6})x^3 + (-\frac{1}{6} + \frac{1}{24})x^4 + \cdots$$

$$= 1 + x + \frac{1}{2} x^2 - \frac{1}{8} x^4 + \cdots .$$

(28) We recognize $j(j - 1)x^{j-2}$ as the second derivative of x^j, so that $j(j - 1)x^j$

equals $x^2 \dfrac{d^2}{dx^2} x^j$ and

$$\sum_{j=1}^{\infty} j(j - 1)x^j = \sum_{j=1}^{\infty} x^2 \frac{d^2}{dx^2} x^j = \sum_{j=0}^{\infty} x^2 \frac{d^2}{dx^2} x^j = x^2 \frac{d^2}{dx^2} \sum_{j=0}^{\infty} x^j .$$

Because the last series is the geometric series, we have

$$\sum_{j=1}^{\infty} j(j - 1)x^j = x^2 \frac{d^2}{dx^2}(1 - x)^{-1} = x^2(2)(1 - x)^{-3} = \frac{2x^2}{(1 - x)^3}$$

(32)   For $x \neq 0$ we have

$$\frac{\sin x}{x} = \frac{1}{x} \sum_{j=0}^{\infty} \frac{(-1)^j}{(2j + 1)!} x^{2j+1} = \sum_{j=0}^{\infty} \frac{(-1)^j}{(2j + 1)!} x^{2j}$$

$$= 1 - \frac{1}{3!} x^2 + \frac{1}{5!} x^4 - \frac{1}{7!} x^6 + \cdots .$$

Therefore, if we define $f(x)$ to equal 1 for $x = 0$ and to equal $\dfrac{\sin x}{x}$ for $x \neq 0$,

then for all x, $f(x)$ has the convergent Maclaurin series

$$f(x) = \sum_{j=0}^{\infty} \frac{(-1)^j}{(2j + 1)!} x^{2j} = 1 - \frac{1}{3!} x^2 + \frac{1}{5!} x^4 - \frac{1}{7!} x^6 + \cdots .$$

SECTION 19.1

(1) Here $P(x) = \sin x$, so $\int P(x) \, dx = \int \sin x \, dx = -\cos x + C$. Taking $C = 0$

we obtain the integrating factor $I = e^{\int P \, dx} = e^{-\cos x}$. We multiply both sides of the

equation by I:

$$e^{-\cos x} \frac{dy}{dx} + (\sin x) \, e^{-\cos x} \, y = -(\sin x) e^{-\cos x}$$

As should be the case, the left side of the new equation is the derivative of Iy:

$$\frac{d}{dx} [y \, e^{-\cos x}] = e^{-\cos x} \frac{dy}{dx} + y \, e^{-\cos x} \sin x$$

The equation reads

$$\frac{d}{dx} [y \, e^{-\cos x}] = -(\sin x) \, e^{-\cos x}.$$

Integrating both sides yields

$$y \, e^{-\cos x} = -\int (\sin x) e^{-\cos x} \, dx$$

We evaluate the integral by making the substitution $u = -\cos x$, $du = \sin x \, dx$ and obtain

the equation $y \, e^{-\cos x} = -e^{-\cos x} + C$, which gives the solutions

$$y = -1 + C e^{\cos x}$$

with C an arbitrary constant.

(8) Here $P(x) = \frac{10}{2x + 1}$ and $\int P(x) \, dx = 5 \int \frac{1}{2x + 1} (2 \, dx) = 5 \ln|2x + 1| + C$, so

as an integrating factor we obtain $e^{\int P \, dx} = e^{5 \ln|2x+1|} = e^{\ln|2x+1|^5} = |2x + 1|^5$. Replacing

$|2x + 1|^5$ by $(2x + 1)^5$ leaves the integrating factor unchanged or multiplies it by -1,

and in either case leaves us with an integrating factor. Hence, we take $I = (2x + 1)^5$.

Multiplying both sides of the differential equation by I gives

$$(2x + 1)^5 \frac{dy}{dx} + 10(2x + 1)^4 y = (2x + 1)^5$$

and we note that this can be written

$$\frac{d}{dx} [y(2x + 1)^5] = (2x + 1)^5$$

We integrate both sides with respect to x:

$$y(2x + 1)^5 = \int (2x + 1)^5 \, dx = \frac{1}{2} \int (2x + 1)^5 (2 \, dx)$$

$$= \frac{1}{2}(\frac{1}{6})(2x + 1)^6 + C = \frac{1}{12}(2x + 1)^6 + C.$$

Solving for y gives the general solution of the differential equation

(*)　　　　　　　　　$y = \frac{1}{12}(2x + 1) + C(2x + 1)^{-5}.$

　　We choose the constant C to have y satisfy the initial condition $y(0) = 1$. Setting $x = 0$ and $y = 1$ in (*) yields

$$1 = \frac{1}{12}(1) + C$$

to show that $C = \frac{11}{12}$ and that the solution of the initial value problem is

$$y = \frac{1}{12}(2x + 1) + \frac{11}{12}(2x + 1)^{-5}.$$

(12) For $P(x) = \dfrac{2 \cos x}{\sin x}$, we have

$$\int P(x) \, dx = 2 \int \frac{\cos x}{\sin x} \, dx = 2 \ln|\sin x| + C = \ln[\sin^2 x] + C$$

and for an integrating factor we can take

$$I(x) = e^{\ln[\sin^2 x]} = \sin^2 x.$$

We multiply both sides of the integrating factor by I to obtain

$$\sin^2 x \, \frac{dy}{dx} + (2 \sin x \cos x)y = \sin^3 x$$

which we write as

$$\frac{d}{dx}[y \, \sin^2 x] = \sin^3 x.$$

We integrate both sides with respect to x (with the substitution $u = \cos x$, $du = - \sin x \, dx$):

$$y \sin^2 x = \int \sin^3 x \, dx$$

$$= \int \sin x(1 - \cos^2 x) \, dx$$

$$= -\int (1 - u^2) du \quad = \quad - u + \frac{1}{3} u^3 + C$$

$$= - \cos x + \frac{1}{3} \cos^3 x + C$$

When we solve for y , we obtain

(*) $$y = \frac{-\cos x + \frac{1}{3} \cos^3 x + C}{\sin^2 x} .$$

To satisfy the initial condition $y(\frac{\pi}{2}) = 4$, we set $x = \frac{\pi}{2}$ and $y = 4$ in equation (*). We conclude that C = 4 and obtain the solution

$$y = \frac{-\cos x + \frac{1}{3} \cos^3 x + 4}{\sin^2 x} .$$

(15a) Because the solution is flowing in 4 gallons per minute and out 1 gallon per minute, and because the volume in the tank is 8 gallons at t = o, the volume at t > 0 is 8 + 3t gallons. Let y(t) be the pounds of salt in the tank at time t. We obtain

$$\frac{dy}{dt} = [\frac{1}{2} \frac{pound}{gallon}][4 \frac{gallon}{minute}] - [\frac{y}{8 + 3t} \frac{pounds}{gallon}][1 \frac{gallon}{minute}] = 2 - \frac{y}{8 + 3t} \quad \frac{pounds}{minute}$$

or

$$\frac{dy}{dt} + \frac{y}{8 + 3t} = 2.$$

For $P = \frac{1}{8 + 3t}$, we obtain   (since $8 + 3t$ is positive)

$$\int P(x)\ dx = \int \frac{1}{8 + 3t}\ dt = \frac{1}{3} \int \frac{1}{8 + 3t}\ (3\ dt) = \frac{1}{3}\ \ln(8 + 3t) + C$$

$$= \ln(8 + 3t)^{1/3} + C.$$

Taking $C = 0$ gives the integrating factor $e^{\ln(8+3t)^{1/3}} = (8 + 3t)^{1/3}$. We multiply both sides of the differential equation by it:

$$(8 + 3t)^{1/3}\ \frac{dy}{dt} + (8 + 3t)^{-2/3}\ y = 2(8 + 3t)^{1/3}$$

This may be written

$$\frac{d}{dt}[y(8 + 3t)^{1/3}] = 2(8 + 3t)^{1/3}$$

which gives

$$y(8 + 3t)^{1/3} = \int 2(8 + 3t)^{1/3}\ dt\ = \frac{2}{3} \int (8 + 3t)^{1/3}(3\ dt)\ = \frac{2}{3} \int u^{1/3}\ du$$

$$= \frac{2}{3}(\frac{3}{4})\ u^{4/3} + C = \frac{1}{2}(8 + 3t)^{4/3} + C.$$

Here we used the substitution $u = 8 + 3t$, $du = 3\ dt$. Solving for y gives

(*) $y = \frac{1}{2}(8 + 3t) + C(8 + 3t)^{-1/3}.$

We are told that $y = 5$ at $t = 0$. Setting $t = 0$ and $y = 5$ in (*) shows that $C = 2$ and that $y = \frac{1}{2}(8 + 3t) + 2(8 + 3t)^{-1/3}$ pounds.

(15b) Because the volume at time $t > 0$ is $8 + 3t$ gallons, the concentration is

$$\frac{y\ \text{pounds}}{8 + 3t\ \text{gallons}} = \frac{\frac{1}{2}(8 + 3t) + 2(8 + 3t)^{-1/3}}{8 + 3t} = \frac{1}{2} + 2(8 + 3t)^{-4/3}\quad \frac{\text{pounds}}{\text{gallon}}\ .$$

(Notice that the concentration approaches the concentration of the incoming solution as $t \rightarrow \infty$.)

(19) Because the slope at a point (x,y) on the curve is $x - y$, we have the differential equation $\frac{dy}{dx} = x - y$, which we write in the form

$$\frac{dy}{dx} + y = x.$$

Here $P = 1$, so $\int P\ dx = x + C$ and $I = e^x$ is an integrating factor. When we multiply the differential equation by it, we obtain

$$e^x \frac{dy}{dx} + e^x y = xe^x$$

or

$$\frac{d}{dx}[ye^x] = xe^x.$$

Integrating yields

$$ye^x = \int xe^x\ dx = xe^x - e^x + C$$

We solve for $y = x - 1 + Ce^{-x}$. The graph is to pass through the origin, so we set $x = 0$ and $y = 0$ to find that $C = 1$ and the function is $y = x - 1 + e^{-x}$.

SECTION 19.2

(3)   In the differential equation $(5x^3y^4 - 2y)dx + (3x^2y^5 + x)dy = 0$, we have $p = 5x^3y^4 - 2y$ and $q = 3x^2y^5 + x$. The derivatives

$$p_y = \frac{\partial}{\partial y}(5x^3y^4 - 2y) = 20x^3y^3 - 2 \quad \text{and} \quad q_x = \frac{\partial}{\partial x}(3x^2y^5 + x) = 6xy^5 + 1$$

are not equal (except along the curve $20x^3y^3 - 2 = 6xy^5 + 1$) so the differential equation is not exact.

(5)   Here $p = y\cos(xy) + y\sin x$ and $q = x\cos(xy) - \cos x$ and the derivatives

$$p_y = \frac{\partial}{\partial y}[y\cos(xy) + y\sin x] = \cos(xy) - xy\sin(xy) + \sin x$$

$$q_x = \frac{\partial}{\partial x}[x\cos(xy) - \cos x] = \cos(xy) - xy\sin(xy) + \sin x$$

are equal, so the differential equation is exact. We need to find a function $U(x,y)$ such that

(i) $U_x = y\cos(xy) + y\sin x$

(ii) $U_y = x\cos(xy) - \cos x.$

Integrating equation (i) with   respect to x with y constant gives

$$U(x,y) = \int U_x(x,y)\ dx = \int (y\cos(xy) + y\sin x)\ dx$$

or

(iii) $U(x,y) = \sin(xy) - y \cos x + \phi(y)$

with $\phi(y)$ an arbitrary function of y.

When we differentiate equation (iii) with respect to y, we obtain

$U_y = x \cos(xy) - \cos x + \phi'(y)$, and comparing this with equation (ii) shows that $\phi'(y) = 0$

and $\phi(y)$ is a constant. The functions $U(x,y)$ satisfying conditions (i) and (ii) are

$U(x,y) = \sin(xy) - y \cos x + C$, and their level curves

$$\sin(xy) - y \cos x = c$$

are the solutions of the differential equation.

(8) For $p = 3x^2y^2 + 2x$ and $q = 2x^3y - 3y^2$ the derivatives

$$p_y = \frac{\partial}{\partial y}(3x^2y^2 + 2x) = 6x^2y \quad \text{and} \quad q_x = \frac{\partial}{\partial x}(2x^3y - 3y^2) = 6x^2y$$

are equal, so the differential equation is exact. We want a function $U(x,y)$ such that

(i) $U_x = 3x^2y^2 + 2x$

(ii) $U_y = 2x^3y - 3y^2.$

For variety, we will integrate with respect to y first. Equation (ii) gives

(iii) $U(x,y) = \displaystyle\int U_y(x,y)\, dy = \int (2x^3y - 3y^2)dy = x^3y^2 - y^3 + \phi(x)$

with $\phi(x)$ an arbitrary function of x. We differentiate (iii) with respect to x to see that $U_x(x,y) = 3x^2y^2 + \phi'(x)$, and then equation (i) implies that $\phi'(x) = 2x$ and $\phi(x) = x^2 + C$. The functions satisfying (i) and (ii) are $U(x,y) = x^3y^2 - y^3 + x^2 + C$. Their level curves

$$x^3y^2 - y^3 + x^2 = c$$

are the solutions of the differential equation.

(11) With $p = 2xy - 2x$ and $q = x^2 + 1$, the derivatives

$$p_y = \frac{\partial}{\partial y}(2xy - 2x) = 2x \quad \text{and} \quad q_x = \frac{\partial}{\partial x}(x^2 + 1) = 2x$$

are equal, so the differential equation is exact. We need a function $U(x,y)$ such that ·

(i) $U_x = 2xy - 2x$

(ii) $U_y = x^2 + 1.$

Integrating (i) with respect to x   yields

(iii) $U(x,y) = \int U_x(x,y)\ dx = \int (2xy - 2x)dx = x^2y - x^2 + \phi(y)$

with $\phi(y)$ an arbitrary function of y. We differentiate (iii) with respect to y to see

that $U_y = x^2 + \phi'(y)$, and then (ii) shows that $\phi'(y) = 1$ and $\phi(y) = y + C$. The

suitable functions U are $U(x,y) = x^2y - x^2 + y + C$. Their level curves

(*) $x^2y - x^2 + y = c$

are the solutions of the differential equation. To satisfy the initial condition $y(0) = 2$,

we set $x = 0$ and $y = 2$ in (*). This shows that $c = 2$ and $(x^2 + 1)y = x^2 + 2$. The

solution of the initial-value problem is

$$y = \frac{x^2 + 2}{x^2 + 1}.$$

(14) Here $p = x^2y - xy^2$ and $q = xy^3 - x^3y$ and the derivatives

$$p_y = \frac{\partial}{\partial y}(x^2y - xy^2) = x^2 - 2xy \quad \text{and} \quad q_x = \frac{\partial}{\partial x}(xy^3 - x^3y) = y^3 - x^3$$

are not equal (except on the curve $x^2 - 2xy = y^3 - x^3$), so the differential equation is

not exact.

SECTION 19.3

(2) The differential equation $y'' - y' - 6y = 0$ has the characteristic equation

$r^2 - r - 6 = 0$, which has the solutions

$$r = \frac{-(-1) \pm \sqrt{(-1)^2 - 4(1)(-6)}}{2(1)} = \frac{1 \pm \sqrt{25}}{2} = 3 \text{ or } -2.$$

Accordingly, the general solution of the differential equation is

(*) $y = Ae^{3x} + Be^{-2x}$

for which

(**)
$$\frac{dy}{dx} = 3Ae^{3x} - 2Be^{-2x}.$$

Equations (*) and (**) show that $y(0) = A + B$ and $y'(0) = 3A - 2B$. To satisfy the initial conditions $y(0) = 1$, $y'(0) = 8$, we must choose A and B to satisfy the simultaneous equations

$$\begin{cases} A + B = 1 \\ 3A - 2B = 8 \end{cases}$$

Multiplying the first of these equations by 2 and adding it to the second gives $5A = 10$ to show that $A = 2$. Then either equation gives $B = -1$. The solution is $y = 2e^{3x} - e^{-2x}$.

(4) The differential equation $y'' - 4y' + 4y = 0$ has the characteristic equation $r^2 - 4r + 4 = 0$, which may be written $(r - 2)^2 = 0$ and has the one solution $r = 2$. The general solution of the differential equation is

(*)
$$y = (A + Bx)e^{2x}$$

for which

(**)
$$\frac{dy}{dx} = (2A + 2Bx + B)e^{2x}.$$

Thus, $y(1)=(A + B)e^2$ and $y'(1) = (2A + 3B)e^2$ and to satisfy the initial conditions we must have

$$\begin{cases} (A + B)e^2 = 3 \\ (2A + 3B)e^2 = -5. \end{cases}$$

We multiply the first of these equations by 2 and subtract it from the second to obtain $Be^2 = -11$. Multiplying the first equation by 3 and subtracting it from the second gives $-Ae^2 = -14$. Hence $B = -11e^{-2}$, $A = 14e^{-2}$, and the solution is $y = (14 - 11x)e^{2x-2}$.

(7) The differential equation $y'' + 4y' + 5y = 0$ has the characteristic equation $r^2 + 4r + 5 = 0$, which has the solutions

$$r = \frac{-4 \pm \sqrt{(4)^2 - 4(1)(5)}}{2(1)} = \frac{-4 \pm \sqrt{-4}}{2} = -2 \pm i.$$

The general solution of the differential equation is

$$y = e^{-2x}[A \cos x + B \sin x]$$

and has the derivative

$$\frac{dy}{dx} = e^{-2x}[-2A \cos x - 2B \sin x - A \sin x + B \cos x]$$

$$= e^{-2x}[(B - 2A) \cos x + (-2B - A) \sin x].$$

Hence $y(0) = A$ and $y'(0) = B - 2A$, and to satisfy the initial conditions $y(0) = -1$,
$y'(0) = 0$, we must have

$$\begin{cases} A = -1 \\ B - 2A = 0. \end{cases}$$

We find that $A = -1$, $B = -2$ and the solution is $y = e^{-2x}[- \cos x - 2 \sin x]$.

(10) The homogeneous equation $y'' + 4y = 0$ has the characteristic equation $r^2 + 4 = 0$,
which has the solutions $r = \pm 2i$. The general solution of the homogeneous equation is

(*) $y_h = A \cos(2x) + B \sin(2x).$

The term on the right side of the differential equation $y'' + 4y = 5e^x$ is $5e^x$. It
and all of its derivatives can be expressed in the form ce^x with constants c. The
function e^x is not a solution of the homogeneous equation, so   the one function e^x
forms a U.C. set for the differential equation. There is a particular solution in the form

(**) $y_p = ce^x.$

When we substitute $y = y_p = ce^x$ in the differential equation $y'' + 4y = 5e^x$, we obtain

$$ce^x + 4ce^x = 5e^x$$

which shows that we should take $c = 1$. The function $y = e^x$ is a particular solution of
the inhomogeneous equation. The general solution of the inhomogeneous equation is

(***) $y = y_p + y_h = e^x + A \cos(2x) + B\sin(2x)$

and has the derivative

(****) $\frac{dy}{dx} = e^x - 2A \sin(2x) + 2B \cos(2x).$

Hence $y(0) = 1 + A$, $y'(0) = 1 + 2B$, and to satisfy the initial conditions $y(0) = 0$, $y'(0) = 3$, we must choose A and B to satisfy

$$\begin{cases} 1 + A = 0 \\ 1 + 2B = 3. \end{cases}$$

We find that $A = -1$ $B = 1$, and the solution is $y = e^x - \cos(2x) + \sin(2x)$.

(13) The homogeneous equation $y'' - y = 0$ has the characteristic equation $r^2 - 1 = 0$. The solutions of the characteristic equation are $r = \pm 1$ and the general solution of the homogeneous differential equation is

$$(*) \qquad\qquad y_h = Ae^x + Be^{-x}.$$

The derivatives of $2e^x$ are all $2e^x$, so they can all be expressed in the form ce^x. The function e^x is a solution of the homogeneous differential equation, but xe^x is not, Hence the one function xe^x forms a U.C. set for the differential equation. There is a particular solution of the form $y_p = cxe^x$. This function has derivatives

$$y_p' = (c + cx)e^x \quad \text{and} \quad y_p'' = (2c + cx)e^x,$$

and for it to satisfy the differential equation $y'' - y = 2e^x$, we must have

$$(2c + cx)e^x - cxe^x = 2e^x$$

which shows that $c = 1$. The particular solution is $y_p = xe^x$ and the general solution of the inhomogeneous differential equation is

$$y = y_p + y_h = xe^x + Ae^x + Be^{-x}.$$

Its first derivative is

$$\frac{dy}{dx} = (x + 1)e^x + Ae^x - Be^{-x}.$$

We have $y(0) = A + B$ and $y'(0) = 1 + A - B$, so to satisfy the initial conditions $y(0) = -1$ and $y'(0) = 0$ we must have

$$\begin{cases} A + B = -1 \\ 1 + A - B = 0. \end{cases}$$

Adding these equations gives $1 + 2A = -1$ to show that $A = -1$. Either equation then shows that $B = 0$ and that the solution of the initial value problem is $y = xe^x - e^x$.

(15) The characteristic equation of the homogeneous differential equation is $r^2 + 4r + 4 = 0$, which may be written $(r + 2)^2 = 0$ and has the one solution $r = -2$. The general solution of the homogeneous equation is

$$y_h = (A + Bx)e^{-2x}.$$

The function $2e^{-2x}$ and each of its derivatives can be expressed in the form ce^{-2x}.

The functions e^{-2x} and xe^{-2x} are solutions of the homogeneous equation, but x^2e^{-2x} is not, so the one function x^2e^{-2x} forms a U.C. set for the differential equation. There is a particular solution of the inhomogeneous differential equation of the form $y_p = cx^2e^{-2x}$. Its derivatives are

$$y_p' = (2cx - 2cx^2)e^{-2x} \quad \text{and} \quad y_p'' = (2c - 8cx + 4cx^2)e^{-2x}$$

and for it to satisfy the equation $y'' + 4y' + 4y = 2e^{-2x}$ we must have

$$(2c - 8cx + 4cx^2)e^{-2x} + 4(2cx - 2cx^2)e^{-2x} + 4cx^2e^{-2x} = 2e^{-2x}.$$

This equation simplifies to the equation

$$2ce^{-2x} = 2e^{-2x}$$

and shows that $c = 1$. The particular solution is $y_p = x^2e^{-2x}$ and the general solution of the inhomogeneous equation is

$$y = y_p + y_h = x^2e^{-2x} + (A + Bx)e^{-2x}.$$

Its derivative is

$$\frac{dy}{dx} = (2x - 2x^2)e^{-2x} + (B - 2A - 2Bx)e^{-2x}.$$

Therefore, $y(0) = A$, $y'(0) = B - 2A$ and to satisfy $y(0) = 0$, $y'(0) = 1$, we must have

$$\begin{cases} A = 0 \\ B - 2A = 1 \end{cases}$$

so that $A = 0$, $B = 1$, and the solution is $y = x^2e^{-2x} + xe^{-2x}$.

SECTION 19.4

(4a) Because f is 0, the motion is free. Because $R^2 - 4Mk = 6^2 - 4(2)(4) = 4$ is positive, the motion is overdamped.

(4b) Of all the curves in Figures 19.11 through 19.25 in the text, only the curve in Figure 19.24 passes through (0,-1) and has slope 4 there; it is the graph of the only function that satisfies the initial conditions y(0) = -1, y'(0) = 4. This must be the graph of the solution. Also, notice that the graph in Figure 19.24 does not oscillate so it is either critically damped or over damped (or its oscillations occur for t > 4. where we cannot see them).

(4c) The differential equation is   2y" + 6y' + 4y = 0. Dividing it by 2 gives y" + 3y' + 2y = 0, which has the characteristic equation $r^2 + 3r + 2 = 0$. We can factor this equation as (r + 2)(r + 1) = 0 or we can use the quadratic formula to see that its solutions are r = -1 and r = -2. The general solution of the differential equation is

$$y = Ae^{-t} + Be^{-2t}$$

and its first derivative is

$$\frac{dy}{dt} = -Ae^{-t} - 2Be^{-2t}.$$

Because y(0) = A + B   and y'(0) = -A - 2B, we must have

$$\begin{cases} A + B = -1 \\ -A - 2B = 4 \end{cases}$$

to satisfy the initial conditions. Adding these equations shows that -B = 3 and B = -3. Then either equation gives A = 2. The solution is $y = 2e^{-t} - 3e^{-2t}$.

(6a) Because f is 0, the motion is free. Because $R^2 - 4Mk = 4^2 - 4(4)(1) = 0$ is zero, the motion is critically damped.

(6b) Figures 19.11, 19.12, and 19.15 show the graphs of functions that appear to satisfy the initial conditions y(0) = 2, y'(0) = -2. Because the graphs in Figures 19.11 and oscillate, the graph of the critically_damped motion of this exercise must be in Figure 19.15.

(6c) The differential equation is $4y'' + 4y' + y = 0$ and it has the characteristic

equation $4r^2 + 4r + 1 = 0$. The characteristic equation has only the one solution

$$r = \frac{-4 \pm \sqrt{4^2 - 4}}{2(4)} = -\frac{1}{2}$$

so the general solution of the differential equation is

$$y = (A + Bt)e^{-t/2}.$$

Its derivative is

$$\frac{dy}{dt} = (-\frac{1}{2} A - \frac{1}{2} Bt + B)e^{-t/2}$$

and we have $y(0) = A$, $y'(0) = -\frac{1}{2} A + B$. To satisfy $y(0) = 2$, $y'(0) = -2$, we must have

$$\begin{cases} A = 2 \\ -\frac{1}{2} A + B = -2. \end{cases}$$

and, therefore, $A = 2$, $B = -1$. The solution is $y = (2 - t)e^{-t/2}.$

(9a) The motion is free because f is 0. It is underdamped because $R^2 - 4Mk = 10^2 - 4(5)(10)$

is negative and R is not zero.

(9b) Figure 19.19 is the only one of the collection that shows the graph of a function

satisfying the initial conditions $y(0) = -1$, $y'(0) = 0$. (The oscillations of this underdamped

motion are barely visible in the drawing.)

(9c) The differential equation is $5y'' + 10y' + 10y = 0$. We divide it by 5 to obtain the

equation $y'' + 2y' + 2y$ which has the characteristic equation $r^2 + 2r + 2 = 0$. The

solutions are

$$r = \frac{-2 \pm \sqrt{2^2 - 4(1)(2)}}{2(1)} = -1 \pm i$$

and the general solution of the differential equation is

$$y = e^{-t}[A \cos t + B \sin t]$$

The first derivative is

$$y' = e^{-t}[-A \cos t - B \sin t - A \sin t + B \cos t],$$

so we have $y(0) = A$ and $y'(0) = -A + B$. The initial conditions $y(0) = -1$, $y'(0) = 0$ give the equations

$$A = -1$$
$$-A + B = 0.$$

Hence $A = -1$, $B = -1$ and the solution is $y = - e^{-t}(\cos t + \sin t)$.

(12a) The motion is forced because f is not zero. It is critically damped because $R^2 - 4Mk = 2^2 - 4(1)(1)$ is zero.

(12b) Figures 19.16, 19.18, 19.21, and 19.22 show graphs of functions that appear to satisfy the initial conditions $y(0) = 0$, $y'(0) = 1$. The motion oscillates about the

rest position of the spring without dying down because the forcing term is $4 \sin t$, which oscillates between -4 and 4. Figure 19.18 shows the graph of the solution.

(12c) The differential equation is $y'' + 2y' + y = 4 \sin t$. The homogeneous equation $y'' + 2y' + y = 0$ has the characteristic equation $r^2 + 2r + 1 = 0$, which has the one solution $r = -1$. The general solution of the homogeneous differential equation is

$$y_h = (A + Bt)e^{-t}.$$

The function $4 \sin t$ and each of its derivatives can be expressed in the form $c_1 \sin t + c_2 \cos t$. Neither $\sin t$ nor $\cos t$ is a solution of the homogeneous equation. Hence the functions $\sin t$ and $\cos t$ form a U.C. set for the differential equation and there is a particular solution of the form $y_p = c_1 \sin t + c_2 \cos t$. The derivatives of y_p are

$$y_p' = c_1 \cos t - c_2 \sin t \quad \text{and} \quad y_p'' = - c_1 \sin t - c_2 \cos t.$$

We need to find constants c_1 and c_2 such that

$$(-c_1 \sin t - c_2 \cos t) + 2(c_1 \cos t - c_2 \sin t) + (c_1 \sin t + c_2 \cos t) = 4 \sin t.$$

This equation simplifies to

$$-2c_2 \sin t + 2c_1 \cos t = 4 \sin t$$

and shows that $c_1 = 0$, $c_2 = -2$. The particular solution is $y_p = - 2 \cos t$ and the general solution of the inhomogeneous equation is

$$y = y_p + y_h = -2 \cos t + (A + Bt)e^{-t}$$

The first derivative is

$$\frac{dy}{dt} = 2 \sin t + (-A - Bt + B)e^{-t}$$

so we have $y(0) = -2 + A$, $y'(0) = B - A$, and the initial conditions $y(0) = 0$, $y'(0) = 1$ require

$$\begin{cases} -2 + A = 0 \\ B - A = 1 \end{cases}$$

Consequently, $A = 2$, $B = 3$, and the solution is $-2 \cos t + (2 + 3t)e^{-t}$.

(21) The differential equation is $Lq'' + Rq' + \frac{1}{C} q = f$ with $L = 2$, $R = 4$, $C = \frac{1}{10}$, and $f = 0$: $2q'' + 4q' + 10q = 0$. Dividing by 2 gives $q'' + 2q' + 5q$, which has the characteristic equation $r^2 + 2r + 5 = 0$. The solutions are

$$r = \frac{-2 \pm \sqrt{2^2 - 4(1)(5)}}{2(1)} = -1 \pm 2i$$

and the general solution of the differential equation is

$$q = e^{-t}[A \cos(2t) + B \sin(2t)].$$

Its first derivative is

$$\frac{dq}{dt} = e^{-t}[-A \cos(2t) - B \sin(2t) - 2A \sin(2t) + 2B \cos(2t)].$$

We have $q(0) = A$, $q'(0) = -A + 2B$. At $t = 0$ the charge on the capacitor is 5 and there is no current. Hence, $q(0) = 5$ and $q'(0) = 0$. These conditions require

$$\begin{cases} A = 5 \\ -A + 2B = 0. \end{cases}$$

We find that $A = 5$, $B = \frac{5}{2}$, and the solution is $q = e^{-t}[5 \cos(2t) + \frac{5}{2} \sin(2t)]$.

SECTION 19.5

(5) Set

$$y = \sum_{j=0}^{\infty} a_j x^j$$

Then

(*)

$$xy = \sum_{j=0}^{\infty} a_j x^{j+1} = \sum_{j=1}^{\infty} a_{j-1} x^j$$

and

(**)

$$y' = \sum_{j=1}^{\infty} j a_j x^{j-1} = \sum_{j=0}^{\infty} (j + 1) a_{j+1} x^j$$

We obtained the second sum in (*) by replacing j with $j - 1$ and the second sum in (**) by replacing j with $j + 1$.

The equation $y' - 2xy = 0$ gives

$$\sum_{j=0}^{\infty} (j + 1) a_{j+1} x^j - 2 \sum_{j=1}^{\infty} a_{j-1} x^j = 0$$

We separate out the term for $j = 0$ in the first sum to obtain

$$a_1 + \sum_{j=1}^{\infty} [(j + 1) a_{j+1} - 2a_{j-1}] x^j = 0$$

which gives the equations

$$a_1 = 0 \quad \text{and} \quad (j + 1) a_{j+1} - 2a_{j-1} = 0 \quad \text{for} \quad j = 1, 2, 3, \ldots$$

We write the last equation as

(***)

$$a_{j+1} = \frac{2}{j + 1} a_{j-1}$$

and note that the initial condition $y(0) = 1$ implies that $a_0 = 1$. Applying (***) repeatedly shows that $a_j = 0$ for all odd j. We also have

$$a_2 = \frac{2}{2} a_0 = 1$$

$$a_4 = \frac{2}{4} a_2 = \frac{1}{2}$$

$$a_6 = \frac{2}{6} a_4 = \frac{1}{3!}$$

and in general $a_{2k} = \frac{1}{k!}$ for $k = 0, 1, 2, 3, \ldots$ The solution is

$$y = \sum_{k=0}^{\infty} \frac{1}{k!} x^{2k} = e^{x^2}.$$

(14) We need to find $y''(0)$, $y^{(3)}(0)$, and $y^{(4)}(0)$. We have $y'' = y^2$, so

$y''(0) = [y(0)]^2 = 1^2 = 1$. Differentiating the equation $y'' = y^2$ yields $y^{(3)} = 2yy'$

so that $y^{(3)}(0) = 2y(0)y'(0) = 2(1)(2) = 4$. Differentiating again, we obtain

$y^{(4)} = 2yy'' + 2[y']^2$, so that $y^{(4)}(0) = 2(1)(1) + 2(2)^2 = 10$. The Maclaurin series for

y begins

$$y = y(0) + y'(0)x + \frac{1}{2} y''(0) x^2 + \frac{1}{3!} y^{(3)}(0)x^3 + \frac{1}{4!} y^{(4)}(0) x^4 + \ldots$$

$$= 1 + 2x + \frac{1}{2}(1)x^2 + \frac{1}{6}(4)x^3 + \frac{1}{24}(10)x^4 + \ldots$$

$$= 1 + 2x + \frac{1}{2} x^2 + \frac{2}{3} x^3 + \frac{5}{12} x^4 + \ldots$$

(17)   We write $y = \sum_{j=0}^{\infty} a_j x^j$ so that $y' = \sum_{j=1}^{\infty} j a_j x^{j-1}$,

$xy' = \sum_{j=1}^{\infty} j a_j x^j$, and $y'' = \sum_{j=2}^{\infty} j(j-1)a_j x^{j-2}$. To express y'' as a sum

involving the expression x^j, we first set $k = j - 2$, so that $j - 1 = k + 1$ and

$j = k + 2$. Then k runs from 0 to ∞, and we obtain

$$y'' = \sum_{k=0}^{\infty} (k + 2)(k + 1)a_{k+2} x^k.$$

Now we replace k by j to have $y'' = \sum_{j=0}^{\infty} (j + 2)(j + 1)a_{j+2} x^j.$

With these expressions for y'', xy', and y, the differential equation

$y'' - 2xy' - 2y = 0$ reads

$$\sum_{j=0}^{\infty} (j + 2)(j + 1)a_{j+2}\, x^j \quad -2 \sum_{j=1}^{\infty} ja_j\, x^j \quad -2 \sum_{j=0}^{\infty} a_j x^j = 0$$

or

$$2a_2 - 2a_0 + \sum_{j=1}^{\infty} [(j + 2)(j + 1)a_{j+2} - 2(j + 1)a_j]x^j = 0.$$

Here we have separated out the terms from the first and last sums for $j = 0$. For this equation to be satisfied, we must have $2a_2 - 2a_0 = 0$ and $(j + 2)(j + 1)a_{j+2} - 2(j + 1)a_j = 0$ for $j = 1, 2, 3, \ldots$ The first of these equations simplifies to $a_2 = a_0$ and the second to

$$(*) \qquad\qquad\qquad a_{j+2} = \frac{2}{j + 2}\, a_j \qquad (j = 1, 2, 3, \ldots).$$

The condition $y(0) = 1$ implies that $a_0 = 1$ and the condition $y'(0) = 0$ implies that $a_1 = 0$. The equation $a_2 = a_0$ shows that $a_2 = 1$. Equation $(*)$ shows that a_j is zero for all odd j and for even $j = 2n$ that

$$a_{2n+2} = \frac{2}{2n + 2}\, a_{2n} \qquad \text{or} \qquad a_{2n+2} = \frac{1}{n + 1}\, a_{2n}.$$

Since $a_0 = a_2 = 1$, we obtain $a_4 = \frac{1}{2} a_2 = \frac{1}{2}$, $a_6 = \frac{1}{3} a_4 = \frac{1}{3!}$ and in general $a_{2n} = \frac{1}{n!}$.

Thus

$$y = \sum_{n=0}^{\infty} \frac{1}{n!}\, x^{2n} = \sum_{n=0}^{\infty} \frac{1}{n!}\, (x^2)^n = e^{x^2}.$$